# RACIAL THEMES IN SOUTHERN RHODESIA:

## THE ATTITUDES AND BEHAVIOR OF THE WHITE POPULATION

# RACIAL THEMES IN SOUTHERN RHODESIA:
## THE ATTITUDES AND BEHAVIOR OF THE WHITE POPULATION

## BY CYRIL A. ROGERS AND C. FRANTZ
### WITH A FOREWORD BY SIR ROBERT C. TREDGOLD
#### FORMER CHIEF JUSTICE OF THE FEDERATION OF RHODESIA AND NYASALAND

KENNIKAT PRESS
Port Washington, N. Y./London

RACIAL THEMES IN SOUTHERN RHODESIA

Copyright © 1962 by Yale University
Reissued in 1973 by Kennikat Press by arrangement
Library of Congress Catalog Card No.: 72-85295
ISBN 0-8046-1724-4

Manufactured by Taylor Publishing Company     Dallas, Texas

# ACKNOWLEDGMENTS

This study was conceived during the early months of 1957. On March 27th, a plan of intended research was submitted for approval to the Social Sciences Research Committee of the University College of Rhodesia and Nyasaland. To Professor B. A. Fletcher, Chairman of the Committee, who encouraged the research in its initial stages, a large measure of credit is due; similarly, my colleagues in the social sciences gave the benefit of their personal interest and advice. When the study was under way, Professor H. J. Rousseau generously contributed many of the resources of the Education Department toward the development of the project; this contribution is greatly appreciated. Nor is it inappropriate to mention the attitude of the Principal of the University College, Dr. W. Adams; when the study ran into criticism (as it did during the 1959 State of Emergency in Southern Rhodesia), he firmly supported the traditional right of a University man to proceed with research of his own choosing.

During 1957, and the early part of 1958, various laws, customs, and practices were examined for inclusion in the questionnaire. In this task, assistance was obtained from a considerable number of persons, including the following graduates: E. Andersen, Angeline S. Dube, N. W. Schafer, L. S. Tachuana, and Prudence D. Wheeldon. The last named continued working with the project in 1959 when she was awarded a Gilchrist Research Assistantship. The Assistantship was but a part of the generous financial support furnished by the University College of Rhodesia and Nyasaland.

In September, 1958, Dr. C. Frantz, of Portland State College, arrived in Salisbury and plunged into the research. He remained until May 1960, and the fact that he and I are joint authors of the book speaks for itself. Our collaboration, which stretched ruthlessly over evenings and vacations, was possible through a fundamental unity of purpose and a desire to see an important task accomplished. Dr. Frantz's period in Central Africa was underwritten by the African Universities Program of the University of Chicago. To Dr. E. S. Munger, a Director of the A.U.P., special thanks are due; without his support and encouragement the study would have been considerably less extensive and thorough. Similarly, Professor S. Tax,

Chairman of the Department of Anthropology at Chicago, lent strategic help when the research plan was put to him. It is also fitting to mention the unflagging assistance of Mrs. Charlotte Frantz, her skill in interviewing, and her patient work on the manuscript.

Special reference must be made to the historical sections of the book. For over a year, during 1958 and 1959, Dr. P. J. Duignan, a Ford Foundation Fellow from the History Department, Stanford University, read at the Central African Archives, Salisbury, collating material on the early history of the Colony. In the final months of his stay in Southern Rhodesia, he worked in close collaboration with the present research, and later, after returning to Stanford, he generously supplied a wealth of information from which were extracted many illustrations of past European * attitudes and behavior. A number of the historical judgments and inferences in this study, therefore, find more substantial documentation in Dr. Duignan's "Native Policy in Southern Rhodesia, 1890–1923" (Doctoral dissertation, Stanford University, 1961) to which readers are referred.

More than 500 Rhodesians, who gave much time and hospitality to the fieldworkers, also deserve to be considered joint authors of this study.

Many other productive minds and hands made significant contributions. J. R. H. Shaul, sometime Director of the Central African Statistical Office, advised on the sampling model, checked the statistical and mathematical rationale, and suggested important changes in the interpretation of data. K. D. Leaver, Chief Information Officer of the Native Affairs Department, Southern Rhodesia, corrected many of the statements in the first drafts of the questionnaire. Much appreciation also goes to Dr. C. A. L. Myburgh and his colleagues of the Central African Statistical Office; they kindly supplied a great deal of the data on which the sampling model was based. The staff of International Computers and Tabulators (Central Africa), through the good offices of Sir Thomas Chegwidden, Chairman, and C. F. Hackett, Manager, were exceedingly helpful in making available their Hollerith machines; without this equipment the numerous computations would not have been possible. P. A. C. Laundy, Librarian of the Southern Rhodesian Legislative Assembly, has been unselfish in locating historical and other documents, while, for the section on legal justice, much benefit was derived from discussions with H. H. C. Holderness, Attorney at Law, and Advocate H. T. Wheeldon. To my wife, Bette, who faced with me the task of extracting the common factors from a 50 x 50 matrix, I owe much.

The following individuals, from their various disciplinary backgrounds, undertook the invaluable task of reading and commenting on the manuscript in whole or in part: Advocate H. W. Chitepo of

* "European" is synonymous with "white" throughout southern Africa.

Salisbury; Professor L. W. Doob, Department of Psychology, Yale University; L. H. Gann, Historian, Central African Archives; Professor M. J. Herskovits, Program of African Studies, Northwestern University; H. R. G. Howman, Under-Secretary of Native Affairs, Southern Rhodesia; S. H. Irvine, Department of Education, University College of Rhodesia and Nyasaland; Professor V. McKay, Faculty of African Studies, Johns Hopkins University; Professor J. C. Mitchell, Department of African Studies, University College of Rhodesia and Nyasaland; W. J. Sampson, Director of Sigma Statistics and Economic Research, Salisbury; and Professor P. E. Vernon, Department of Psychology, Institute of Education, University of London. In particular, L. H. Gann, H. R. G. Howman, and Professor J. C. Mitchell, with their very extensive knowledge of Southern Rhodesia, suggested a number of valuable emendations and improvements.

A separate note of recognition is due to Sir Robert C. Tredgold, Chief Justice of the Federation of Rhodesia and Nyasaland.* Over a span of half a century, and more, he has witnessed much of the social change we attempt to describe. It is no exaggeration to say that he has rendered insights and illuminations that would not have been available from the formal deposits of history. Equally significant, his sensitive and constructive criticisms have fallen without hesitation on the partiality in our thinking. To Sir Robert, and all the others who collaborated, it is appropriate to express unreserved gratitude and appreciation. Although they have endeavored to dispel mistakes and correct interpretations, it is understood that, for such errors of omission and commission that remain, sole responsibility rests with the authors.

Finally, acknowledgment is made to the Yale University Press for accepting the work for publication, and for seeing it into print. The Secretary to the Publications Committee, B. F. Houston, the editor of the book, Marian Neal Ash, and the staff of the Press have been unstinting in their cooperation and encouragement.

Naturally, it is hoped that the vibrant activities of this enterprising young society, Southern Rhodesia, emerge with the print.

Cyril A. Rogers

*University College of Rhodesia and Nyasaland*
*Salisbury*
*October 14, 1960*

* Sir Robert resigned from the Bench on November 1, 1960, in protest against the Law and Order (Maintenance) Bill, then before the Southern Rhodesian Parliament.

# CONTENTS

# FOREWORD

BY SIR ROBERT C. TREDGOLD, P.C., K.C., M.G.

*Chief Justice of the Federation of Rhodesia and Nyasaland* *

This is a remarkable and valuable book. In it are to be found the answers to a large number of questions that hitherto have been unanswerable.

In our approach to the many problems that confront the country, there is room enough for differences of opinion, even where the opinions are based upon agreed facts. Where the basic facts have to be assumed or inferred from inadequate premises, the possibilities of disagreement are multiplied almost infinitely, particularly when account is taken of the very human tendency to allow preconceived ideas to influence the interpretation of evidence that is itself uncertain.

The main purpose of the authors has been to make what is in effect a survey of European public opinion, in so far as it relates to racial matters. They give their techniques in some detail, and anyone who takes the trouble to study this aspect of the work will be compelled to admit that every effort has been made to ensure that the investigation proceeded upon strictly scientific lines, with all reasonable cross-checks upon possible sources of error. Every student of human affairs must, at a certain point, encounter imponderable elements. Allowing for this, the material here collected and analyzed appears as accurate as careful research can make it. The least imaginative must be impressed by the immense labor and thought that have gone into the making of the book.

The presentation of the material collected, and the conclusions based upon it, are linked by a fair and objective relation to the general background. Some of the views expressed may prove unpalatable upon first impression but, on mature consideration, the reader will find them difficult to refute.

It is an obvious criticism, anticipated by the authors, that the picture is incomplete, in that it deals only with the attitudes of Europeans.

* See note, p. vii.

xi

A complete investigation of the whole population was impracticable at this stage and, whilst so much economic and political power is in the hands of Europeans, an examination even of the limited field is of first importance. It may further be suggested that events and opinions are moving so rapidly that the conclusions in the book may be out of date even as they are published. The answer to this is that an accurate presentation of the situation, at a given point of time, must be a profitable starting point for further investigation. This is especially true when the point of time occurs in a crucial period.

If the spate of publications on this country is to continue, it is to be hoped that future authors will rely upon the information here made available and not upon assumptions of doubtful validity. Leaders in public affairs may move more confidently for knowing, with some assurance, what the rank and file are thinking. All good Rhodesians, who are prepared to face up squarely to the facts upon which our future depends, will be the better equipped for having read and reflected upon this detached and impartial study of our mental processes. To know ourselves is a condition precedent to the readjustment and reorientation without which we can never successfully tread the labyrinth path that lies between us and the ideal of a society in which our thoughts and actions are no longer influenced by considerations of race or color.

*Salisbury*
*October 14, 1960*

# PREFACE

Southern Rhodesia is a British Colony in south central Africa where Europeans have resided for less than a century, if a few earlier pioneers, traders, and missionaries are excluded. The year 1890 marked the real beginning of European immigration into the territory between the Limpopo and Zambesi rivers.

Some kind of accommodation or integration was inevitable among the diverse cultural and ethnic groups which gradually became absorbed in the emergent social systems. Cooperation had to prevail over naked conflict if the Colony were to remain viable. Historians and others have provided much information about the struggles and development of the new society during the past seventy years. We seek to understand these opposing kinds of behavior partly through documentary evidence, but we focus mainly upon the attitudes expressed by Europeans now in Southern Rhodesia. We are primarily concerned with the nature of *European* (i.e., White) attitudes about Africans, the largest group in the Colony maintaining a distinctive way of life.

Attitudes are inextricably related to the social situations in which they occur. They may be separated *logically* for the purpose of analysis, but their significance cannot be determined if they are divorced from the past and present courses of society. It is dangerous to assume that a knowledge of the attitudes and behavior of a single group in a culturally heterogeneous or "plural" society can be magically transmuted into a complete description of the whole. A plural society is obviously composed of several interacting groups, whether their bases of identity be "race," language, culture, or other features. To ignore this fundamental fact results in an incomplete analysis.[1] Therefore, the larger context is constantly kept in mind when describing and analyzing European attitudes in Southern Rhodesia.

## PLAN OF THE BOOK

The inquiry begins with a description of the historical and sociological contexts from which Southern Rhodesia will be viewed. We also examine some of the past social relations of Africans and Europeans. Two recent studies, however, have made it unnecessary to do this as fully as was originally planned. Philip Mason's *The Birth of a Dilemma* (1958) deals broadly with "race relations" until Southern Rhodesian Europeans attained Self-Government in 1923. Colin Leys' *European Politics in Southern Rhodesia* (1959) provides an illuminating, though controversial, analysis of the Colony's central political organization in relation to other aspects of society and culture. Leys' perspective lies primarily in the period from 1923 onward.

In Chapter 3, the general relations between attitudes, society, and culture are explored. Next, we describe the techniques used in investigating contemporary European attitudes about Africans, and discuss the procedures and problems of sampling. The general results of our questionnaire are first presented in Chapter 7. In the following chapter, we test for common factors in European race attitudes by the use of established statistical techniques. Then, attitudes are related to the structure of European society in order to understand the variation between feelings and beliefs, on the one hand, and personal and social characteristics, on the other. Questions are asked about the relations between race attitudes and the age, religious affiliation, country of birth, political party preference, and other characteristics of individuals.

In addition, an analysis is made of European attitudes about legal justice, educational and training opportunities, political activities, the use of various public services and facilities, sexual relations, personal courtesies and etiquette, and the continuation of segregated or reserved lands that have been apportioned to the two major culture groups. Sociological and historical discussions of race relations and attitudes in these areas introduce Chapters 10 to 17. Attention is also given to the type and range of reasons expressed by the sample for wanting to maintain or discontinue the laws and customs that differentiate between Africans and Europeans in Southern Rhodesia. The variations of attitudes about these practices are analyzed next in terms of different subgroupings of the population. We conclude these substantive chapters by educing various themes from the reasons given by Europeans for wanting to change contemporary laws and customs, or to maintain the status quo.

In Chapters 18 and 19, we summarize the data obtained in our research, and make some cross-cultural comparisons. We conclude with a discussion of the theoretical importance of our findings for the general understanding of race attitudes and race relations. These should be applicable to such culturally or racially heterogeneous societies as the Union of South Africa, Kenya, the (ex-Belgian) Congo, the West Indian Federation, Malaya, New Zealand, and the United States of America. Our historical and contemporary data should also permit a better understanding of some of the processes of political and economic organization, and other mechanisms of social, cultural, and attitudinal change.

## PROCEDURES

Our primary data were obtained in 1959 through the use of questionnaires and interviews. Since Southern Rhodesia has a relatively small European population, we were able to undertake a nation-wide sample. As far as we know, this is the first systematic attempt to investigate attitudes on race throughout an entire country. Other social scientists have made inferences about attitudes on race from selected and unrepresentative populations: college students, the residents of a single neighborhood, town, or city, or the members of unions, churches, clubs, or other associations. The results of these studies are valuable and often extremely accurate, but they lack the cross-sectional reliability that is desirable in characterizing a whole society. Various statistical devices will be employed in analyzing our data, but we shall proceed beyond statistical significance to discuss further the sociological importance of our findings.

Ideally, perhaps, our study should include parallel data on the attitudes of Africans about Europeans. There are also strong reasons why the attitudes held by and about Asians and Coloreds, or Eurafricans, should be examined if we are to get a complete picture of group interaction in Southern Rhodesia. The exclusion of non-Europeans from our study derives from limitations of time, money, and other factors rather than from a dismissal of their importance. There would have been other difficulties to overcome in studying the attitudes of Africans, especially (1) the finding of a sufficiently large population literate in English, and (2) the widespread uneasiness among Africans at the time when the study could have been undertaken.* A study of African attitudes about Europeans would be invaluable in the near future.

## UTILITY OF THE STUDY

The study is aimed particularly at social scientists, but an attempt is made to keep in mind the general public who are also interested in Southern Rhodesia. Because of this multiple approach, some of the explanations of concepts, and the statistical rationale, may appear unnecessary to the specialist, while they may still seem unduly

* An official State of Emergency existed in Southern Rhodesia from Feb. 26 to May 20, 1959. One European man, two African women, and 507 African men were detained because of their membership—usually they were officers —in one of four African National Congresses. With the gazetting of the Proclamation of the State of Emergency on Feb. 26, membership in these organizations became illegal (see Ch. 15 for further details). The psychological atmosphere during this period made it improbable that an adequately representative study of African attitudes could be undertaken.

complex to the general reader. We recognize that it is difficult to encompass such diverse approaches in a single work.

The findings may prove useful in several ways. Firstly, they should lead to an increased understanding of current European attitudes about Africans, and, to a lesser degree, attitudes during past decades. Since this is the first such empirical investigation undertaken in the country, one may also speak about European attitudes with greater precision than has been possible before.

The study may also have significance for the review of the Federal Constitution. Since Southern Rhodesia is viewed as the senior partner in the Federation of Rhodesia and Nyasaland, the attitudes held by Europeans about African participation in the wider society may be of special importance. Federation in 1953 radically changed the number of Africans with whom Europeans in Southern Rhodesia were politically associated. In 1956, there were twelve times as many Africans as Europeans in Southern Rhodesia. But in the Federation as a whole, the ratio was 26:1, or more than double that which existed in Southern Rhodesia itself. Our data thus allow a measure of prediction as to the possible receptivity and agreement among Europeans respecting the maintenance or change of the present political and social systems.

It cannot be assumed, however, that this scientific cross-section of European attitudes will permit completely accurate predictions, or that attitudes should be the sole or prime basis for determining public policy. Obviously politicians and officials work within a framework of public opinions and attitudes, but their policies need not be fully accountable to or commensurate with the wishes of the public. Organized social pressures and the power structure of the society may be more important than a cross-section of public opinion.[2] Many internal and external factors influence the continuity and change of European attitudes and governmental policies toward Africans. We must confine our attention to a selected number of these.

## The Problem of Values

Africa, and especially Southern Rhodesia, is intimately enmeshed in the rapid social and cultural changes attending the industrialization, urbanization, and "modernization" of the whole world. In large measure the future of different societies depends upon the receptivity of individuals to the idea and fact of change. Individual behavior is related in turn to values, motivations, and the structure of society.

Many social scientists have approached the study of society and culture with the assumption that they are well integrated, while others have emphasized conflicting values and relations in virtually all groups. Gluckman (1955) has lately revived the idea that conflict and change are not necessarily disruptive to society; on the contrary, they may further its cohesion and continuance. We suggest that it is theoretically preferable to assume that competition and conflict are normal and perhaps necessary aspects of both continuity and change. Societies and cultures are, therefore, only relatively, not completely or absolutely integrated.

We cannot avoid being aware of the conflicting value systems existing within Southern Rhodesia. Our study, in fact, has made us more cognizant of their existence and importance. Neither do we deny the presence of salient differences in the cultural, social, and biological characteristics of the inhabitants. The ignorant and foolish may ignore these differences, but social scientists should not.

As human beings we have acquired preferences for particular institutions and types of social relations; our experiences in other societies have reinforced many of our ideas and values. Both of us endorse social policies that rely primarily upon rationality and little upon magical thinking. Although we think it impossible to find any society or personality completely void of tensions or strains, we endorse efforts to reduce intergroup tensions as speedily and fairly as possible. These may be more intense in culturally or racially heterogeneous societies (Rex, 1959); but they also seem to be related to rapid rates of change in industry, commerce, and agriculture, in familial and political structures, and in ideologies and value systems. Hence, the problem we study in Southern Rhodesia is one repeated in societies where there are few or no European conquerors and settlers, such as Uganda, Burma, and Malaya.

The philosophy of natural law so prevalent in the Age of Enlightenment tended to identify what *is* with what *should be*. Much of current social science terminology can be divorced from this philosophy only with great difficulty (Myrdal, 1958). We have tried, however, to exclude or minimize the frequency with which we use such words as "minority," [3] "progress," "civilized," "democracy," "integration," and the like. To preclude further and unnecessary complications, we have eschewed the terms "backward," "Kaffir," "native," "police state," "primitive," and others of similar genre. To adopt such a vocabulary would imply looking at intergroup relations and attitudes in Southern Rhodesia as social rather than sociological problems.

We are interested in the broader perspective, in analyzing rather than "improving" the rights and status of any particular group in Southern Rhodesia. The latter may be worthy goals in other contexts, but they are tangential to our study. However, the findings of social scientists increasingly affect social legislation and, once published, our study may have implications beyond our control. "Science is criticism," argues Myrdal (1958:41), "and social sciences imply criticism of society." Criticism befalls scientists because they seek for precise knowledge of relations between events, an activity in which most of the public have only a marginal involvement.

Much research on race relations in the Western world has been initiated because it is widely assumed that "non-democratic" relations are "improper" (Blumer, 1958:405). We must plead *nolo contendere* on the validity of this assumption. We cannot answer unequivocally, for example, whether British parliamentary traditions ultimately will succeed in Southern Rhodesia. There have been increasing discussions on whether certain societies or nations "really are ready for a political party structure." It is unknown, however, whether "good" government and "stable" society require either racial or cultural homogeneity or a system of competing political parties. It would be erroneous to assume that "the only basis for social, political, and economic equality is the lack of differences between the groups concerned." [4] At the moment, the question of introducing universal adult franchise in Southern Rhodesia is analogous to whether or not the control of Oxford University should or could be transferred to the groundskeepers and typists. We cannot infer, in Myrdal's words, that the contemporary political situation provides a complete guide to what it *should be* today or tomorrow. We can only suggest that inasmuch as some Western institutions, such as Christianity, have had limited success in much of Africa and Asia, so may other institutions be only partially borrowed or adopted. Such selective borrowings by one society from another are fundamental data for social scientists.

We approach our study with the skills and ideas we learned in the fields of psychology, anthropology, and sociology. We have done research separately in a number of societies other than our own and have traveled or studied in various countries. One of us grew up in a mixed Maori-Pakeha (Polynesian-White) community in New Zealand and the other was reared among Americans of European, Mexican, Japanese, and African descent. Most of our training and studies have been in the English-speaking world, however.

We seek to avoid a narrow or partisan point of view in this study, and not to write as Englishmen, New Zealanders, Americans, or Southern Rhodesians of one persuasion or another. While we try not to pass judgment on Southern Rhodesia, it is impossible to observe without certain criteria or to analyze without a conceptual apparatus. It is naive empiricism to assume that a "purely factual" analysis, independent of valuations, can be carried out.[5] Thus we rely as best we can upon the common assumptions and valuations of social science to organize our observations into categories and systems.

Cyril A. Rogers
C. Frantz

# RACIAL THEMES IN SOUTHERN RHODESIA:
## THE ATTITUDES AND BEHAVIOR OF THE WHITE POPULATION

# 1

# A WORLD OF PLURAL SOCIETIES

The intriguing variety of peoples and cultures throughout the world is the product of many millennia. Archaeologists, anthropologists, human biologists, historians, and others have described and analyzed man's past and present accomplishments and his incessant mobility.[1] There are no pure races known to scientists, and human behavior is seldom determined by racial differences. What is called "race" is only a population which shares a given frequency of peculiar genetic and constitutional characteristics at a particular time and place. Races, societies, and cultures frequently are discrete entities because they are so designated; that is, they are hypothetical constructs. No race, society, or culture is totally unlike another. Were this true, then any attempt to classify and analyze them would be futile. Westermann (1949:7) has pointed out, "No culture is autonomous and autochthonous. All have been fertilized from without." The same heterogeneity is characteristic of every race and every society.

Southern Rhodesia provides an excellent opportunity for studying the structure and operation of a culturally plural and multiracial society. Although Southern Rhodesia is not unique in time or space, since cultural and racial pluralism are found on every continent and on islands throughout both hemispheres, the ingredients of its future society are, so to speak, in the early stages of distillation.

3

A quick examination of books by Linton (1945, 1952), Maunier (1949), or Frazier (1957) will reveal that, while the particular pattern of Southern Rhodesia's society and culture may be distinctive, many of its aspects are found in other situations. Like the emigrants to Australia, Canada, and elsewhere, the majority of Europeans in Southern Rhodesia are of British descent. They carried with them much of British and Western European culture, political organization, and individual outlook. Remarkable similarities in the social structure of many colonies also arose from the interaction of the immigrant and indigenous societies irrespective of cultural differences. These similarities are of particular importance to anthropologists and sociologists who wish to generalize from what may appear to the layman to be discrete and unconnected phenomena. In Southern Rhodesia, for example, it is frequently believed that the Colony is unlike all others; that no generalizations about human society or culture "really" apply to local circumstances. The social scientist suggests that Southern Rhodesia is one of a class of phenomena: it is but an example of the building of a culture, a society, and a nation from smaller units which possess different ways of life. Southern Rhodesia, therefore, needs to be analyzed in both historical and sociological or cultural contexts.[2]

The necessity for evolving a workable political system is not confined to culturally or biologically mixed societies, yet such heterogeneity may complicate the process. The experience of Ireland, Canada, Mexico, Algeria, the Union of South Africa, Malaya, and numerous other countries tends to sustain this observation. In each country, wide social and cultural differences have impeded the growth of a common loyalty, a consensus of values, and a shared set of attitudes about authority. But various types of accommodation have frequently resolved these differences, and common values and sentiments have arisen.

As in many other new societies in the making, the social relationships between the constituent cultural or racial groups in Southern Rhodesia are changing continually. The new social system that is developing leaves no subgroup within the country free from modification.

## COLONIALISM AND THE PLURAL SOCIETY

Western Europe's Age of Exploration, and the revolutions in agriculture, commerce, and industry, accelerated the old and universal process of dispersing peoples into strange lands. Colonial expansion, in all its kaleidoscopic manifestations, was but one aspect of the larger process of rapid social and cultural change (Fortes, 1945:215). It was not confined to Europeans, of course, contrary to much popular thinking and propaganda. The spread of all civilizations brought

an intermingling of peoples who diverged in culture, social organization, and biological characteristics. In some cases expansion occurred
gradually through the occupation of contiguous territories. Frequently
intentional settlements were established by voluntary emigrants. But
in other cases, population mixing resulted from the forced removal of
Africans, Indians, Malays, Chinese, or criminals and others as slaves
or bonded property.

Colonial expansion only hastened the creation of multiracial and
multicultural societies.[3] History provides few examples of an immigrant population that has maintained complete or permanent control
over, or independence from, an indigenous population. That the two
segments of the new society differed in their biological characteristics
had no importance in itself. Differences in color or physique became
relevant only if so defined. The importance placed upon physical
differences was, of course, an important determinant of the social
system that developed in the new society.

The interdependence of immigrant and indigenous peoples in colonial situations was undeniable, and it has ramified increasingly with
industrial and commercial development. In the process both groups
were modified, but change occurred unevenly in land use and agricultural technology; in religion, magic, and mythology; in trade, foreign relations, and sovereignty; and in attitudes, values, motivations,
and goals.

Colonization generally involved more than mere territorial expansion. The movements of people had many consequences, frequently
unforeseen, upon the values, subsistence patterns, and the distribution of power of both immigrant and indigenous societies. The newcomers transferred many of their institutions and attitudes from a
"mother" country, but these were modified in various degrees in foreign lands (Frankel, 1953:6). Despite differences in culture, similar
structural relationships of dominance and subordination frequently
developed between immigrant and indigenous populations, and the
extent of dominance was significantly influenced by the attitudes of
one group toward the other.

The kinds of colonization and the motivations behind the process
had different consequences. The nature of the new colonial society
varied according to whether European immigrants intended to control commerce, to spread Christianity, to exploit minerals and other
resources, to restrict slavery, to establish permanent settlements, or to
escape from discomforts in the home country. The governments of
European countries were sometimes reluctant to assume control over
their citizens abroad, as was often the case with Britain. Royal trade
charters were commonly issued and various imperial claims made
upon foreign lands. Thus, history shows that the idea of empire was
seldom monolithic and inflexible.[4]

The destiny of colonial settlement and development was further affected by the size and density of population, climate, nutrition and disease, the methods used to establish political control, and the period in history when the contact or settlement occurred. The relative freedom of past centuries, when European nations could exert unilateral power and control over indigenous peoples, contrasts strongly with the twentieth century. Southern Rhodesia's European occupation took place so recently that many of the factors influencing the settlement and future of the Americas, Australia, and New Zealand were no longer of equal magnitude.

The imperial activities of Britain were but one variety of colonialism, yet they sired divergent offspring in time and place. The number of British emigrants who permanently settled in Southern Rhodesia, the Union of South Africa, Kenya, the United States of America, Canada, Australia, and New Zealand was far greater than in Nyasaland, Singapore, Burma, Fiji, the Caribbean, West Africa, Egypt, or Cyprus.

British motives for extending political control likewise varied. The Crown was often more interested in the suppression of the slave trade and the expansion of commerce than in territorial aggrandizement.[5] Although there were few significant anti-imperialistic restraints upon Britain until the present century (Evans, 1950:10), Parliament was reluctant to grant funds to colonies or to permit an official increase in the size of territorial holdings. As a result, large numbers of private, usually mercantile, charters were granted (Mitchell, 1955:10).

Africa became a potential market for surplus industrial goods particularly during the last quarter of the nineteenth century, at a time when Europe was experiencing an economic crisis. The European powers partitioned Africa among themselves when there was a lull in the struggle for political supremacy in Europe (Rudin, 1955). But of all the territories acquired by Britain, significant numbers of immigrants settled only in the Union of South Africa, Kenya, and the Rhodesias.

The British were late arrivals on the African scene. For many millennia, Africa had been a continent where diverse peoples and cultures had spread and intermingled. It is known that the Phoenicians, Greeks, Romans, Arabs, Indians, Chinese, and possibly the Melanesians had important influences upon the history of the sub-Sahara.[6] Later arrivals included the Portuguese, Spanish, and other Europeans. In eastern Africa, the Arabs had developed a brisk trade in search of ivory, gold, and slaves, spreading the word of Islam as their trade pushed further into the interior.

## THE LAND OF RHODES

The Portuguese, arriving in the sixteenth century, were the first known Europeans to establish contact in what is now Southern Rhodesia. Disease, climate, and a shortage of manpower and resources confined them chiefly to the coast and a few outposts along the Zambezi River. Interior explorations were made only by an adventuresome or courageous few like Antonio Fernandez, Father Silveira, and later Doctor de Lacerda.[7]

The next and most important penetration of Southern Rhodesia came from the south. Both Africans and Europeans crossed the Limpopo River, the former as tribes or segments of tribes and the latter as hunters, traders, prospectors, and missionaries who prepared the way for the subsequent conquest of the indigenous peoples. The Matabele were the most important group coming into Southern Rhodesia during the first half of the nineteenth century to rule over the Makaranga and the Mashona peoples. One of Chaka's commanders, Mziligazi, moved out of Zululand following a quarrel, fought unsuccessfully to maintain a new home in the Transvaal, and finally crossed the Limpopo about the year 1839.[8]

South African hunters and traders initiated the European penetration of Southern Rhodesia during the 1830's, and contributed to the eventual settlement of the high veld. Missionary zeal and the desire for trade combined in 1854 when Sam Edwards, a trader, and Robert Moffatt, of the London Missionary Society, obtained permission from Mziligazi to remain in Matabeleland. In 1859, they founded the first mission station in Southern Rhodesia.

An increasing number of European traders, hunters, prospectors, and explorers began circulating in Matabeleland. Extravagant accounts of gold prospecting swelled the trickle of immigrants from the south. Meanwhile, various European nations were extending their control southward from regions further north in Africa. The Rhodesias, as a "power vacuum," became a meeting ground of various imperial claims. From this time, Southern Rhodesia's history was affected by two different sets of interacting forces: first, the European-African context of internal relations; and second, the political and economic pressures from South Africa, Germany, Portugal, and Great Britain. More recently, other nations and international organizations have exerted influence upon the internal affairs of Southern Rhodesia.

It was mentioned earlier that the British Treasury and Parliament opposed large expenditures on its African colonies during the nineteenth century. This known reluctance has contributed to the belief that, without Cecil Rhodes, south central Africa would have been lost to the British Empire. It is unlikely, however, that Britain would have permitted the alienation of such a strategic area to the Boers, Portuguese, or Germans. It happened to be cheaper to let Rhodes acquire it on her behalf.

Rhodes eventually secured the Rudd Concession of mineral rights from Lobengula, Mziligazi's successor, and then succeeded in obtaining an imperial charter for his British South Africa Company in 1889. The following year, Frank Johnson organized a "Pioneer Column" which peacefully occupied Mashonaland, the eastern half of Southern Rhodesia. "Rhodesia began," says McGregor (1940:16), "as an experiment in modern imperialism, with a predominantly commercial motive, directed by a monopolistic company."

The beginnings of a plural society had now been laid, although it was to be shaped by disparate systems of economics, labor, political organization, belief, and family life during the following century.[9] The European wage economy clashed with the Matabele raiding system, for example. European farmers and miners disliked the attacks on their Mashona laborers and viewed the Matabele as an ever-present threat to their rule. These difficulties encouraged the Europeans in Mashonaland to look westward to the land of Lobengula, which was rich in cattle, and where, it was believed, the main extensions of the Witwatersrand gold reef lay.

At first Europeans tried to modify the Africans' way of life through religious conversion and incorporation into a wage economy but the Matabele, as the missionaries had learned, rejected Christianity and refused to modify their raiding system.[10] As the immigrants discovered, to their cost, Lobengula's raids interfered with labor supplies in Mashonaland. He declined to cooperate with the missions, opposed conversion to their religion, and was not interested in his men acquiring skills and arts useful for peaceful occupations. He apparently saw clearly that Christianity and the Matabele system were incompatible. Matabele and European attitudes, culture, and social structure were too dissimilar for easy fusion to occur, and hostilities broke out.

War seemed inevitable if the British South Africa Company was to remain and establish its control in Southern Rhodesia. If Rhodes had not moved in, the British Government would probably have had to establish a protectorate. The same kind of pacification as in Nyasaland might have been necessary, and this could have brought more rather than less bloodshed.

In 1893, many of the European immigrants awaited an excuse to deal with Lobengula and his Matabele raiders. Although opinions have differed on the matter,[11] it now appears that the Company's officer, Jameson, at first tried to avoid trouble but later favored offensive action. It soon came, but hostilities flared only briefly. The real issue was a clash of two groups with antagonistic values and social structures. It was a question of which group would control and exploit Rhodesia's land and labor. The immediate reason given for the war was the need to shoulder the white man's burden, to advance Christianity and civilization among the Africans. Christianity and civilization followed, it is true, but the men who defeated the Matabele were primarily interested in land, cattle, and gold rather than in the Queen and civilization.

The Matabele were to try their strength against the immigrants once more, in 1896, but even with the assistance of the Mashona, the effort was futile. The Martin Committee, appointed to investigate the troubles, cited the loss of African cattle and land to the Europeans, forced labor, and the behavior of some Native Commissioners and African messengers among the major reasons for the rebellion.[12] That Africans were abused by the settlers is undeniable, but the rebellion probably can be understood more fully by considering it as a "nativistic movement," a resistance among Africans to the loss of their sovereignty. It was a desire to return to the old ways and to reject the new influences—a desperate effort to avoid the tensions and dislocations that frequently accompany the contact of societies with vastly different cultures. Reactions of this nature have been widespread in the world, and, as sociological phenomena, they have been the object of considerable research and discussion.[13]

Peace was restored in Southern Rhodesia in 1897, and new kinds of relationships began to develop between Europeans and Africans. The B. S. A. Company, unlike other royal chartered firms, did not engage directly in trade. Rather, it encouraged the immigration of farmers, miners, missionaries, and capital into Rhodesia, "a policy which relegated Native development to a secondary place" (Evans, 1934:114). It provided the necessary economic framework for future development —roads, railways, and capital funds. By 1899, a railway spanned the territory and allowed for the development of European mining and farming. Southern Rhodesia never proved to be a second Rand; although gold was for many years the chief export, it was usually mined in relatively small operations.

The skeleton B. S. A. Administration, founded in 1889, was formalized in 1897. A separate Native Affairs Department assumed responsibility for the Africans, while civil commissioners and magistrates dealt with the European population. Certain of the chiefs' powers were reduced to prevent the threat of new rebellions. In 1898, an Order-in-Council defined the Company's responsibilities toward Africans and laid the basis for administrative and judicial affairs in the plural society.

In the following chapter, we will provide a panoramic view of the interplay of groups, persons, goals, and values in Southern Rhodesia since it became a "state" in 1898. In later chapters, more specific details will be given where they are relevant to various social institutions, practices, and attitudes. The serious reader may wish to consult other sources for a more traditional account of Southern Rhodesia's history.[14] Our focus will be upon the two major subdivisions of the population, the Europeans and Africans, and the relations between them.

# 2

## THE PLURAL SOCIETY OF SOUTHERN RHODESIA

There seem to be five significant factors that both affect and reflect intergroup relations and attitudes—demography, ecology, personality, social structure, and culture—and our discussion will be organized around them. These factors are interrelated; no single one has determined what Europeans traditionally have thought about Africans or how they have behaved toward them. The causes of behavior, whether verbal or nonverbal, are always complex and multiple.

### CHARACTERISTICS OF THE POPULATION

The attitudes and behavior of one cultural or social group toward another are often related to their respective sizes.[1] When the first European immigrants arrived in Southern Rhodesia, an estimated 500,000 Africans were living in the country, and the Europeans had little alternative but to compromise with the situation. No widespread decimation of the population occurred as it had in such colonial situations as Australia and the Americas. As the result of the limited warfare in the 1890's, however, the Europeans were able to assume political control over the territory. European settlement not only stopped the predatory raiding of the Matabele upon the Mashona, but it occurred late enough in history for advances in medical knowledge

11

actually to increase the health and size of the indigenous population.

Table 1 shows the comparative growth of the Southern Rhodesian population and gives the ratio of Africans to Europeans in the total population. When the first census was taken in 1901, there were 11,032 Europeans in the Colony in addition to the estimated half million Africans and a handful of Coloreds and Asians. The very small proportion of Coloreds and Asians is noteworthy, for the presence of only two large subgroups within Southern Rhodesia means that fewer varieties of distinctive attitudes and relationships would develop than, say, in the Union of South Africa. Although the table includes the 1959 population estimates, the last official census in 1956 enumerated

TABLE 1. *Population Growth and Distribution*

| Census | Total population * | Percentage of total | | | | Ratio of Africans to Europeans * |
|--------|--------|--------|--------|--------|--------|--------|
| | | *European* | *African* * | *Colored* | *Asian* | |
| 1901 | 513,000 | 2.2 | 97.5 | 0.1 | 0.2 | 44:1 |
| 1904 | 606,000 | 2.1 | 97.6 | .2 * | .1 * | 46:1 |
| 1911 | 772,000 | 3.1 | 96.5 | .3 | .1 | 31:1 |
| 1921 | 899,000 | 3.8 | 95.9 | .2 | .1 | 25:1 |
| 1926 | 977,000 | 4.0 | 95.6 | .2 | .2 | 24:1 |
| 1931 | 1,130,000 | 4.4 | 95.2 | .2 | .2 | 22:1 |
| 1936 | 1,320,000 | 4.2 | 95.4 | .2 | .2 | 23:1 |
| 1941 | 1,480,000 | 4.7 | 94.9 | .2 | .2 | 20:1 |
| 1946 | 1,794,000 | 4.6 | 95.0 | .2 | .2 | 21:1 |
| 1951 | 2,146,000 | 6.3 | 93.2 | .3 | .2 | 15:1 |
| 1956 | 2,610,000 | 6.8 | 92.7 | .3 | .2 | 14:1 |
| 1959 * | 2,860,000 | 7.5 | 92.0 | .3 * | .2 | 12:1 |

* Estimated. No complete census of the African population has been taken.
Sources: Censuses of Southern Rhodesia and (for 1959 estimate) *Monthly Digest of Statistics,* Vol. 6, No. 5.

177,124 Europeans and an estimated 2,420,000 Africans. Thus, in the fifty-five years between the first and last censuses, the European population expanded in size sixteen times, the Coloreds had become eight times more numerous, while the African and Asian increases were approximately fivefold. It is known, however, that the estimates for the Colored population have been affected considerably by changes in census definitions; accordingly, they must be accepted with caution.

The amount and per cent of population increase for each census group during the intervals between the censuses are shown in Table 2. The rate of growth for all census groups has been quite variable. The most important factor affecting the rate of growth has been immigration, not the birth rate.

It has been assumed, perhaps erroneously, that the growth of the African population was the result of a natural increase, that is, the excess number of births over deaths. However, large numbers of non-indigenous Africans have resided temporarily or quasi-permanently in Southern Rhodesia. There are no reliable estimates of the number that have entered illegally and established residence in the country. It is also known that large numbers still enter unofficially, while many others remain beyond the legally permitted period of residence.

TABLE 2. *Population Increase in Intercensal Periods*

| Intercensal period | Europeans | | Africans | | Coloreds | | Asians | | Total increase | |
|---|---|---|---|---|---|---|---|---|---|---|
| | No. | % | No. | % | No. | % | No. | % | No. | % |
| –1901 | 11,032 | — | 500,000 | — | NA | NA | 1,093 | — | 513,000 | — |
| 1901–1904 | 1,564 | 14 | 91,000 | 18 | NA | NA | 851 * | 78 * | 93,000 | 18 |
| 1904–1911 | 11,010 | 87 | 154,000 | 26 | NA | NA | 968 * | 50 * | 166,000 | 27 |
| 1911–1921 | 10,014 | 42 | 117,000 | 16 | –44 | –2 | 380 | 44 | 127,000 | 16 |
| 1921–1926 | 5,554 | 17 | 72,000 | 8 | 160 | 8 | 204 | 16 | 78,000 | 9 |
| 1926–1931 | 10,736 | 27 | 142,000 | 15 | 244 | 11 | 246 | 17 | 153,000 | 16 |
| 1931–1936 | 5,498 | 11 | 183,000 | 17 | 785 | 33 | 480 | 28 | 190,000 | 17 |
| 1936–1941 | 13,546 | 24 | 145,000 | 12 | 787 | 25 | 367 | 17 | 160,000 | 12 |
| 1941–1946 | 13,432 | 19 | 300,000 | 21 | 585 | 15 | 364 | 14 | 314,000 | 21 |
| 1946–1951 | 53,210 | 65 | 296,000 | 17 | 1,432 | 31 | 1,381 | 48 | 352,000 | 20 |
| 1951–1956 | 41,528 | 31 | 420,000 | 21 | 2,088 | 35 | 835 | 19 | 464,000 | 22 |
| Totals | 177,124 | | 2,420,000 | | | | | | 2,610,000 | |

* Includes Coloreds.
Sources: Censuses of Southern Rhodesia.

TABLE 3. *Sources of European Population Growth*

| Intercensal period | Total increase | Net immigration | | Natural increase | |
|---|---|---|---|---|---|
| | | No. | % | No. | % |
| 1901–1904 | 1,564 | NA | NA | NA | NA |
| 1904–1911 | 11,010 | 9,928 * | 90 | 1,082 * | 10 |
| 1911–1921 | 10,014 | 5,835 | 58 | 4,179 | 42 |
| 1921–1926 | 5,554 | 2,724 | 49 | 2,830 | 51 |
| 1926–1931 | 10,736 | 7,421 | 69 | 3,315 | 31 |
| 1931–1936 | 5,498 | 2,032 | 37 | 3,466 | 63 |
| 1936–1941 | 13,546 | 5,700 * | 56 | 4,553 | 44 |
| 1941–1946 | 13,432 | 2,050 * | 25 | 6,124 | 75 |
| 1946–1951 | 53,210 | 42,758 | 80 | 10,452 | 20 |
| 1951–1956 | 41,528 | 25,190 | 61 | 16,338 | 39 |
| 1956–1959 | 37,876 ** | — | — | — | — |

* Approximate. Net immigration figures in 1936–41 and 1941–46 obtained after excluding war movement of armed forces, internees, and refugees. Percentages obtained by assuming total increases were 10,253 in 1936–41 and 8,174 in 1941–46.
** Estimated.
Sources: Censuses of Southern Rhodesia.

The sources of the population increase among Europeans since 1904 are well-known. The greater proportion of the growth has generally been due to immigration rather than natural increase. Following the Second World War, the number of immigrants jumped. The greatest intercensal gain was between 1946 and 1951; since then a steady decrease in immigration has occurred. Immigration quotas were first imposed, in fact, in 1952. In 1958 there were 12,100 immigrants and 4,900 emigrants; hence the net figure was only 7,200 immigrants. Table 3 shows the comparative importance of natural increase and immigration as sources of European population growth.

European attitudes and behavior toward Africans have undoubtedly been affected by the increased proportion of recent immigrants in the population. But another factor, country of origin, is perhaps of even more importance. In view of the dissimilar cultural and racial compositions of the Union of South Africa and the United Kingdom, the significant increase since World War II in the proportion of the population born in the United Kingdom should be noted. It is perhaps not coincidental that many of the basic differentiating customs of Southern Rhodesia were solidified by legislation in the period 1921–31, when people born in South Africa constituted the largest nationality group among the Europeans. Table 4 gives data on the country of birth of the European population since 1904.

TABLE 4. *European Population by Country of Birth*

| Census | Total population | Percentage of total | | | |
|---|---|---|---|---|---|
| | | S. Rhodesia | Union of S.A. | U.K. and Eire | Other countries |
| 1901 | 11,032 | NA | NA | NA | NA |
| 1904 | 12,596 | 10.1 | 27.3 | 44.4 | 18.2 |
| 1911 | 23,606 | 13.6 | 30.7 | 40.9 | 14.8 |
| 1921 | 33,620 | 24.7 | 34.6 | 31.4 | 9.3 |
| 1926 | 39,174 | 29.1 | 32.6 | 29.2 | 9.1 |
| 1931 | 49,910 | 29.2 | 34.5 | 27.1 | 9.2 |
| 1936 | 55,408 | 34.1 | 32.8 | 23.8 | 9.3 |
| 1941 | 68,954 | 34.1 | 27.9 | 26.4 | 11.6 |
| 1946 | 82,386 | 37.7 | 26.4 | 18.3 | 17.6 |
| 1951 | 135,596 | 31.4 | 30.4 | 28.8 | 9.4 |
| 1956 | 177,124 | 32.5 | 28.9 | 28.1 | 10.5 |

Sources: Censuses of Southern Rhodesia.

Another factor affecting intergroup attitudes and relations is the proportion of women in the population. Where there have been unbalanced sex ratios, as in Brazil, Mexico, French Canada, and the Union of South Africa in the early periods of European settlement, large hybrid populations often resulted. In the early years of European penetration into Southern Rhodesia, there also was a far larger number of males than females; Table 5 indicates that there were almost three times as many males at the beginning of the century. Through the years, however, this imbalance was rectified. The relatively quick attainment of a normal sex ratio among Europeans probably discouraged sexual liaisons and marriages with Africans.

TABLE 5. *European Sex Ratio* *

| Census | Sex ratio | Census | Sex ratio |
|--------|-----------|--------|-----------|
| 1901 | 278 | 1936 | 116 |
| 1904 | 246 | 1941 | 113 |
| 1911 | 194 | 1946 | 116 |
| 1921 | 130 | 1951 | 111 |
| 1926 | 126 | 1956 | 107 |
| 1931 | 120 | | |

* Sex Ratio equals $\dfrac{Males}{Females} \times 100.$

Sources: Censuses of Southern Rhodesia.

TABLE 6. *Age and Sex Distribution of Europeans in Southern Rhodesia, 1956, and Africans in Salisbury, 1958*

| Age category | Europeans * in S. Rhodesia, 1956 | | | | Africans * in Salisbury, 1958 | | | |
|---|---|---|---|---|---|---|---|---|
| | Male | | Female | | Male | | Female | |
| | No. | % | No. | % | No. | % | No. | % |
| 0– 4 | 10,627 | 6.0 | 10,265 | 5.8 | 10,250 | 6.4 | 10,910 | 6.9 |
| 5– 9 | 10,110 | 5.7 | 9,614 | 5.4 | 7,030 | 4.4 | 7,030 | 4.4 |
| 10–14 | 7,567 | 4.3 | 7,138 | 4.1 | 6,490 | 4.1 | 4,720 | 3.0 |
| 15–19 | 5,827 | 3.3 | 5,289 | 3.0 | 12,240 | 7.7 | 4,520 | 2.8 |
| 20–24 | 6,409 | 3.6 | 5,433 | 3.1 | 19,680 | 12.4 | 6,180 | 3.9 |
| 25–29 | 8,068 | 4.6 | 7,317 | 4.1 | 21,400 | 13.5 | 5,860 | 3.7 |
| 30–34 | 8,401 | 4.8 | 7,618 | 4.3 | 13,840 | 8.7 | 3,950 | 2.5 |
| 35–39 | 8,018 | 4.5 | 7,083 | 4.0 | 9,760 | 6.1 | 2,510 | 1.6 |
| 40–44 | 7,248 | 4.1 | 6,697 | 3.8 | 4,690 | 3.0 | 870 | .5 |
| 45–49 | 6,255 | 3.5 | 5,457 | 3.1 | 3,080 | 1.9 | 400 | .2 |
| 50–54 | 4,491 | 2.5 | 3,883 | 2.2 | 1,470 | .9 | 220 | .1 |
| 55–59 | 2,803 | 1.6 | 2,878 | 1.6 | 1,300 | .8 | 180 | .1 |
| 60+ | 5,558 | 3.2 | 6,790 | 3.8 | 420 | .3 | 130 | .1 |
| Totals | 91,382 | 51.7 | 85,462 | 48.3 | 111,650 | 70.2 | 47,480 | 29.8 |

* Excluding 280 Europeans and 5,500 Africans of unspecified ages. African figures based on 10% sample.
Sources: Censuses of Southern Rhodesia.

In the absence of accurate data, it has been assumed that African men and women were almost equal in number. But because of the extensive employment of immigrant African laborers, especially in urban areas and during the earlier decades, it is probable that some male predominance was characteristic. Although the number of African women living in towns has steadily increased, in 1958 the African population of Salisbury still contained 116,870 males compared to 47,760 females. This was a ratio of 245 males to every 100 females, and was almost identical with the European sex ratio in Salisbury back in 1904. The European sex ratio in Salisbury in 1956, in contrast, was 103 males to every 100 females.

Finally, the age structures of the European and African populations probably are quite different. Since no complete census of the African population has been taken, however, it is impossible to make exact comparisons at any period in history. We can assume from a general knowledge of other "undeveloped" countries that the African population is heavily biased toward the younger ages. Among Europeans, the census of 1904 revealed a major concentration in the 20-50-year age range. The age structure of the European population has been gradually modified through the years, but it still displays a bulge that is due to immigration rather than to natural increase.

FIGURE 1. *Age and Sex Distribution of Europeans in Southern Rhodesia, 1956, and Africans in Salisbury, 1958*

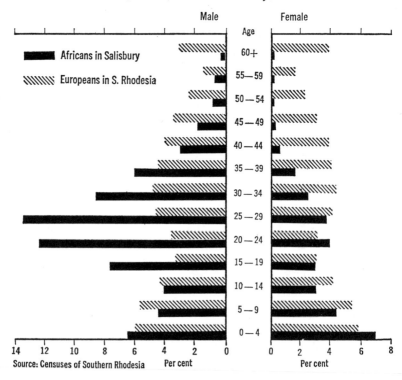

The best possible comparison of the European and African age structures can be made with the 1956 and 1958 census data. Table 6 and Figure 1 indicate the significant differences between the age (and sex) structures of Africans in Salisbury and of all Europeans in Southern Rhodesia.

Africans who live in Salisbury, as in other urban centers, are concentrated in the middle or working years. Very few Africans age sixty or above reside there. The disproportionate numbers in the middle and other age categories among the African population would probably be reduced if sufficient housing were available for married couples in urban areas. Nevertheless, the trend is clearly toward an age distribution among urban Africans which approximates that of the Europeans. But at the moment, it can be assumed that the attitudes of many urban Europeans are not based on contact with, or knowledge of, a representative sample of Africans of all ages.

SPATIAL ARRANGEMENTS

A second influence upon intergroup behavior derives from men's relationships with the physical environment and with other men. Studies have shown that attitudes about members of a different cultural, racial, or religious group are related to degree of proximity.[2] Hence the ecological or spatial arrangement of the European and African populations in Southern Rhodesia must be appreciated if attitudes are to be understood.

Much of the land sought and taken by European immigrants had few or no African inhabitants upon it in 1890 when the Pioneer Column arrived.* Europeans settled primarily upon the higher veld lands where minerals were found and where greater agricultural productivity seemed probable. They generally occupied the lands of dark and clayey texture, leaving the lighter and sandier soils to the Africans.

The first relations between Europeans and Africans were usually peaceful, and only later did competition for land arise. An early decision made by Europeans to impose a hut tax upon African males —forcing them to work for wages—brought widespread changes in the distribution of the African population, and in its relations with Europeans. As in other colonial situations, the indigenous people lost their sovereignty and some of their land. Lands were demarcated for European or African occupation, and gradually a policy of territorial segregation arose. Segregation was most clearly sanctioned by the

---

* In the Western hemisphere, European penetration also was less successful in areas of high aboriginal population density. These areas generally were characterized by permanent villages based on intensive agriculture, and had specialized developments in trade, craftsmanship, fairly large political units, and other features (Steward, 1945).

Land Apportionment Act of 1930, but some lands had been reserved exclusively for Africans since 1898.

Africans recruited to work on farms and in the towns had little opportunity (or desire) to own their land or houses. Africans who worked for European farmers, however, were often given the use of sufficient land to grow their own maize (mealies) and vegetables. Other Africans were either slowly or never removed from areas legally reserved for European occupation, and, as a result, constituted a class of squatters. Relocation is still incomplete in some sections of the country.

Most Africans today still live in Native Reserves, Native Purchase Areas, or Special Native Areas. In general, these apportioned areas are parts of the Africans' traditional homelands, and a modified version of their precontact culture and social organization persists there. In the Reserves, Africans have little direct contact with Europeans other than traders, missionaries, and government officials. Almost all of their personal and social activities are carried on within the designated areas. The extensive implementation of land apportionment has been accompanied by the creation of numerous facilities and services on a bifurcated basis. The location of homes, businesses, schools, churches, hospitals, and cemeteries all reflect the basic territorial segregation of Europeans and Africans. Separate farmers' associations, conservation programs, local governments, and transport facilities have been developed; and the responsibilities of the central government toward the inhabitants of Southern Rhodesia have been served through dual administrative structures.

The economic development and population growth of the country resulted in increasing urbanization. Industry was relatively unimportant in the early decades, but its expansion influenced the subsequent spatial distribution of the population. Table 7 shows the number and per cent of Europeans, and of Africans employed in the wage economy, who have resided in centers containing one hundred or more Europeans since 1904.

It should be noted that more than half the European population has resided in such centers almost from the beginning of settlement—a striking contrast to many colonies in their early years. There are no comparable figures for the total African population, however, since no complete census of them has been taken. But the figures show a similar increase in the urban concentration of Africans in employment.

Sample surveys of the total African population—not just those in employment—have recently been undertaken in the larger towns and cities of Southern Rhodesia. The figures indicate, for example, that in 1959 Salisbury had a population of 84,000 Europeans and 185,000 Africans. In Bulawayo the respective figures are 50,000 and 140,000.

The proportions in the five other municipalities of the country are approximately one European to four Africans.[3]

In the early days, Africans were not prohibited from living in towns if they wished. But during the first decade of this century, segregated areas were established for the residences of those who worked in the towns. Europeans believed Africans to be transient in urban centers, however, and provided no opportunities for them to acquire freehold title to the land on which they lived. Then, in 1946, the Government made it *compulsory* for municipalities to establish African locations or townships.

TABLE 7. *Distribution of Europeans and Employed Africans in Centers Containing 100 or More Europeans*

| | Europeans | | Africans in employment | |
|---|---|---|---|---|
| Census | Total | % in centers | Total | % in centers |
| 1901 | 11,032 | 64.1 | NA | NA |
| 1904 | 12,596 | 57.4 | 27,151 | NA |
| 1911 | 23,606 | 51.6 | 84,860 | NA |
| 1921 | 33,620 | 55.7 | 140,304 | NA |
| 1926 | 39,174 | 58.1 | 173,598 | NA |
| 1931 | 49,910 | 59.5 | 180,158 | 34.7 |
| 1936 | 55,408 | 59.0 | 254,297 | 27.6 |
| 1941 | 68,954 | 66.2 | 303,279 | 33.0 |
| 1946 | 82,386 | 64.5 | 376,868 | 35.6 |
| 1951 | 135,596 | 69.7 | 530,203 | 39.5 |
| 1956 | 177,124 | 76.9 | 609,953 | 42.6 |

Sources: Censuses of Southern Rhodesia.

Unless they live in European residential areas as domestic servants, urban Africans are required to live in one of several types of residential areas: Native Village Settlements, Native Townships, Native Village Locations, Native Urban Areas, the locations of statutory bodies, or the licensed premises of private businesses and industries. The policy has clearly been to maintain the residential and commercial segregation of Africans. Thus, the spatial distribution of the country's population has been greatly influenced by organized social controls, as in the United States and elsewhere,[4] and cultural differences within the Colony. Residential segregation has been reinforced by parliamentary legislation, but there have also been real estate, financial, and commercial interests to support the legal barriers.

Urban residential segregation is far from complete, however. The widespread European desire to employ African domestic servants, and to license private locations for other workmen, has brought a dispersal of Africans throughout the designated European areas. Almost as many Africans (57,600 in 1958) as Europeans (61,930 in 1956) lived in the "European" residential areas of Salisbury.[5] In Salisbury there were 19,170 Africans who lived in family units—man, wife, and children—and the size of African families varied from 2.58 in the Salisbury municipality to 3.85 in some of the suburbs.[6]

Except for economic activities, and excluding domestic servants who reside in kias * behind their masters' homes, most of the life of urban Africans is carried on within the African residential areas. Sports facilities, clubs, auditoria, hospitals, churches, cemeteries, schools, cinemas, and cafes are centered there. In the European areas, Africans have traditionally been excluded from hotels, restaurants, and other social and recreational facilities. They have been required to ride in separate buses and train compartments, to be served at hatches in commercial shops, to sit on assigned park benches, to use separate entrances to banks, post offices, and booking offices, and to buy clothing in many shops without the opportunity of trying it on.

A few African beerhalls and recreational grounds have been established in European urban areas by local authorities. These facilities, or plans for the establishment of new ones, have aroused frequent protests among the Europeans who live in those areas. Similar problems have arisen over the location of new African residential areas. In Salisbury, in particular, African townships have virtually been surrounded by industrial or commercial districts, or European and Colored residential areas, leaving little room for expansion to meet the need for urban African housing.

Since rural lands reserved for Africans are estimated, under "peasant" cultivation, to have a carrying capacity of only 1,025,000,[7] it is assumed that the surplus population will need to be absorbed in urban centers. Pressures have recently developed against the traditional exclusion of urban Africans from the right to acquire title to land. For example, the Report of the Southern Rhodesian Urban African Affairs Commission (1958) recommended the introduction of expanded home ownership schemes, as well as an increased proportion of quarters for married rather than single or unattached Africans.

The ecological structure of a human community or society is always the product of both the existing natural resources and man's knowledge and initiative. The policy of "possessory segregation," † which Europeans introduced into Southern Rhodesia, was designed primarily to enable them to acquire a secure land base upon which they could

---

* Kia is a Sindebele word designating a hut or home. It is now used to refer to small residences for African servants that are erected behind European homes.

† The term "possessory segregation" has been used by Sir Godfrey Huggins (1941) and others to denote, broadly, the territorial separation of races.

transplant Western society and culture. The spatial distribution of the European population was the outcome of free choices and the competitive economic processes that exist in most European and American cities and countries.[8] Unlike Africans, they were virtually free to live where they wished, near to or far from their places of business.

The size, characteristics, and distribution of African communities also reflected European needs, values, and attitudes, although the earlier symbiotic relationships Africans had established with the physical environment should not be overlooked. The European demand for, and the increasing African acceptance of, labor on European farms, and in mines, businesses, and industries, initiated a continually pervasive process that drew Africans away from their villages. This movement, confined at first mainly to men, also multiplied the opportunities for cross-cultural contacts.

Since social and cultural changes generally occur more rapidly in urban than in rural areas, the city is the scene of actual and potential conflict between different groups (Munger, 1955). Time will provide a test of Brown's (1955:202) expectation that conflict between Africans and Europeans in Southern Rhodesia will be intensified over the next few years. Certainly the changing densities and location of the African and European populations will have implications for European behavior and attitudes toward Africans.

## PERSONALITY

Another influence upon intergroup behavior and attitudes is the human personality. Some writers, such as Nietzsche and Carlyle, have eloquently expressed the "great man" theory of historical interpretation. White (1949) and others have challenged this theory as an easy explanation that leads to facile overgeneralizations. The latter argue that particular individuals are relatively unimportant in the historical process, that almost the same broad social and cultural changes would have occurred in history irrespective of the personalities of Napoleon, Churchill, or Mao Tse-tung. In their view, the individual reflects the wishes of a group more than he directs them. Social scientists generally have shown that leadership is more a product of particular situations than personality "traits" (Gibb, 1954). We also know that much of the content of personality is determined by culture (Kluckhohn, 1954). Actually, the importance of personality in the history of any society probably lies somewhere between these rather exclusive systems of explanation.

Since Southern Rhodesia's history, for example, is a matter of changing conditions over time, these theories can never be scientifically tested. We would need to know whether historical events in the long run would have been substantially different if someone other than

Cecil Rhodes had played the leading role in the invasion and conquest of the peoples north of the Limpopo River.

A provocative hypothesis has been offered by Mannoni that certain types of personalities are attracted to, and remain in, colonial situations.[9] A selective and limited range of personality types find the new situation satisfying to their psychological needs. Colonies provide an opportunity for immigrants to establish dominance over indigenous peoples. Not only are economic profits sought by "the colonials," but so also are psychological rewards. Being able to gather the dependent local people around him, the privileged immigrant receives the security, satisfaction, and personal deference he needs. In colonial societies, Mannoni's argument runs, membership in the dominant "race" offers compensation for the basic "inferiority complex" which exists, if only in germinal form, among almost all Europeans.

The idea is suggestive, and it may be supported by the knowledge we have of some, but by no means all, colonial situations. Whether it relates to personality differences is another matter, however. What is needed to test this hypothesis is a scientifically controlled study of immigrants into a colonial territory. Information would first have to be obtained on the range of personality types in the mother country. Then the personalities of emigrants would need to be tested and, finally, data would have to be obtained in the colony about changes in personality and patterns of behavior over a period of time. These data are fundamental if the question posed by Mannoni is to be answered.

In lieu of such information, only speculations can be made about the influence of personality (or personality types) in colonial societies. This is especially true regarding intergroup relations and attitudes in Southern Rhodesia. Unfortunately, our study will provide no enlightenment on the importance of personality variables. Thus, the question of the sociological importance of Cecil Rhodes, as an individual with a unique personality, must remain unanswered.

SOCIAL STRUCTURE

The characteristics and spatial distribution of the African and European populations were influenced by the nature of the society that developed in Southern Rhodesia after European occupation began. They were, in a sense, some of the more visible aspects of the social structure of the country. The terms "social structure" and "social organization" are given to the social relationships that may be inferred from the behavior of individuals and groups.[10] Clans, families, clubs, and parliament are parts of the social structure. Each of these groups is built upon particular relationships, and they describe certain kinds of behavior which generally, but not always, can be observed.

When the first European immigrants arrived in Southern Rhodesia, there was no all-inclusive social structure among the inhabitants of the territory. In time, accommodation between the divergent African and European societies occurred, and the new social structure has progressively embraced more and more of the country's inhabitants.

As we have noted, the early European immigrants were predominantly unmarried males (more than two-thirds even in 1904) whose interests theoretically involved little disruption of African life. But with increasing European family settlement, new tensions were created. Given the aims of the later immigrants, together with their systems of government, economy, religion, and family, conflict between Europeans and Africans was virtually inevitable. Hostilities broke out because there was no other way at the time to resolve or eradicate the social and cultural incompatibilities. Thereafter, the Africans' participation in the total social structure was profoundly influenced by the greater ability of Europeans to exploit natural resources, to organize human labor, and to govern with consistent success.[11] From these differences, there easily and naturally developed a set of relations in which Europeans were superordinate and Africans were subordinate.

If the immigrants' first struggle was against the Africans, their second was against the British South Africa Company. From the days of the Pioneer Column, the settlers sought to win control of the Southern Rhodesian Government by whittling down the privileges of the Company. A Legislative Council was established in 1898, but it was dominated by Company nominees. In 1903, the immigrants gained equal representation, and in 1907 a majority, although this was not ratified until 1911. The next significant political development came in 1922 when the electorate voted for Responsible Government rather than an amalgamation with South Africa. In 1923, the administration of the B. S. A. Company terminated and Self-Government began. Southern Rhodesia had achieved virtual independence from the Imperial Government, and this position remained unchanged until the country federated with its two northern neighbors in 1953. The Federation of Rhodesia and Nyasaland was the culmination of attempts made from 1916 on to bring about a closer union between British territories in south central Africa.[12]

Through the *indabas* (talks) between chiefs and administrators, Africans were consulted about government legislation, but the process of political decision-making rested largely in other hands.[13] Africans were in the State, so to speak, but not a part of it; they were excluded almost entirely from the political structure of the Colony. On the other hand, freedom of negotiation and action for the Europeans of Southern Rhodesia was not unlimited; continuing political and economic pressures during the early decades of government were applied by both South Africa and Great Britain. The 1889 B. S. A. Company Charter, the 1898 Order-in-Council, the 1924 Constitution of Southern Rhodesia, and the 1953 Federal Constitution all contained provisions which reserved for the Crown certain powers over African affairs.

The absence of rapprochement in the political system of the territory was not paralleled as fully in economic relations. On the contrary, the composite nature of Southern Rhodesian society was most evident in the economic activities started by the European immigrants: mining, large-scale farming, and the construction of roads, railways, and buildings. Superficially, African laborers appeared to be plentiful, but repeated difficulties were encountered in engaging and retaining them. In 1901, such a scarcity of African labor existed in the gold mines that agitation began for importing Chinese workmen. This idea was soon forgotten, though later an abortive attempt was made to import Arabs through Aden.[14]

In an attempt to alleviate the shortage of African labor, a hut tax of ten shillings per year was established. This, it was assumed, would oblige Africans to offer their labor for cash. A poll tax was substituted in 1901; three years later, the rate was fixed at £1 for each adult African male, and ten shillings for each wife other than the first. The Legislative Council, in which Company officials and elected members were now equally represented, had proposed a tax of £2, but the British Government disallowed it.[15] Sociologically, the tax was an effective mechanism by which African and European interdependence was born and a new economic structure nurtured.

Southern Rhodesia's social structure was also greatly affected by the occupational distribution within the country. Following the conquest of the Africans, Europeans began a variety of enterprises in which they alone were qualified to be managers, directors, and owners. Until World War II, few opportunities existed for Africans to fill highly skilled positions. Yet historically they have played a necessary and valuable role in the wage economy. Table 8 illustrates the numbers and percentages of the European and African populations active in the money economy. African farmers, although they have increasingly participated in the larger economic system, have been excluded from the data. Still it is striking to observe that eight to nine times as many Africans as Europeans have been in wage employment during most of Southern Rhodesia's history. The highest ratio, 13 to 1, occurred at the end of the abnormal period of the Second World War.

Although industry served to mix Europeans and Africans, European dominance and African subordination remained the characteristic social relationship. The division of labor was, so to speak, complementary to the structure of political control and responsibility.

In religious activities, Africans who were converted to Christianity became a part of the new religious structures. A common organization was not completely realized, however, as cultural differences frequently resulted in the growth of separatist African sects, denominations, and cults. Leading positions in the Christian organizations of the country were primarily filled and controlled by Europeans. Separate seating in churches was common even where joint services were held.

TABLE 8. *Economically Active \* Europeans and Africans*

| | Europeans | | Africans | | Ratio of Africans to Europeans |
|---|---|---|---|---|---|
| Census | No. | % of European population | No. | % of African population | |
| 1901 | NA | NA | NA | NA | NA |
| 1904 | 8,287 | 65.8 | 27,151 | 4.6 | 3:1 |
| 1911 | 13,549 | 57.4 | 84,860 | 11.4 | 6:1 |
| 1921 | 14,776 | 44.0 | 140,304 | 16.3 | 9:1 |
| 1926 | 17,449 | 44.5 | 173,598 | 18.6 | 10:1 |
| 1931 | 22,283 | 44.6 | 180,158 | 16.7 | 8:1 |
| 1936 | 24,557 | 44.3 | 254,297 | 20.2 | 10:1 |
| 1941 | 27,302 | 39.6 | 303,279 | 21.6 | 11:1 |
| 1946 | 33,245 | 40.4 | 376,868 | 22.1 | 11:1 |
| 1951 | 60,494 | 44.6 | 530,203 | 26.5 | 9:1 |
| 1956 | 78,940 | 44.6 | 609,953 | 25.2 | 8:1 |

\* Gainfully employed or employers in money/wage economy. Excludes Africans working on their own account, Africans who are employers, and in general the employees of Africans.
Sources: Censuses of Southern Rhodesia.

The separate family and kinship structures remained distinctive. The relatively few offspring who resulted from illicit sexual relations between Africans and Europeans were generally assimilated into the small Colored population which had entered Southern Rhodesia in the late nineteenth century, or else were reared by their mothers who, in general, were African. Although mixed marriages were legal—in contrast to the Union of South Africa—few took place. In broader terms, the real modification of the European family system came with the "incorporation" of African servants or nursemaids who exercised varying though usually limited degrees of influence in European family relationships, especially between mother and child.

We have mentioned earlier the separate recreational and social relations that persisted among Europeans and Africans—and in fact were encouraged through governmental policy. Yet the total separation of the two cultural groups was impossible even if it had been desired. In the unavoidable contact situations, then, Africans were generally expected to use deferential terms of address, to remove their hats, to give way to Europeans on streets or in entering elevators or shops, and to be served in shops only after European customers had been waited upon.

Southern Rhodesia in many ways appeared to be structured rigidly into a dominant caste of Europeans and a subordinate caste of Africans. Yet there was incomplete consensus among Europeans on the advisability of maintaining the system. The religious teachings of missionaries, together with humanitarian and legal pressures emanating primarily from Britain, discouraged the institutionalization of a rigid caste system. That Southern Rhodesia was and is not merely a "white protection society" is suggested by the comparative or total absence of lynchings, a Ku Klux Klan, or a Society of the White Rose. There have been several less radical and pro-European groups that have attracted relatively small memberships: the White Rhodesian Council, the Voice of the People, the Segregation Society, the European National Congress, the Southern Rhodesian Association, and the Separate Constitutional Development Party. But none of these has relied upon violence or extensive intimidation to maintain the dominant status Europeans have traditionally enjoyed.

In general, the emergent social structure was characterized by differential status, rights, and responsibilities for Europeans and Africans. The typical relations were those of master and servant, employer and employee, teacher and student, leader and follower. Africans were usually thought to be qualified to fill only a "place" which was at the bottom of the social structure. Given the conquest situation, the attitudes of Europeans toward Africans, and African attitudes toward authority, this was probably inevitable. But unlike the situation in some countries, the status superiority of the Europeans was given legal and moral sanction.

The principal goal of the European immigrants was to establish and maintain a way of life generally familiar to them but quite foreign to the indigenous peoples. The dominant group thus felt it necessary to protect its own safety and way of life, and this demanded the control of the African population. When it was necessary or convenient, statutory recognition was given to *de facto* African customs and social structure. This was clearest in the segregated reserves, where there was less possibility that Africans would threaten the position and stability of the European society. Africans were restricted otherwise in the ownership and transfer of land, in local government and criminal jurisdiction, residence, voting in territorial elections, liquor consumption, and the ownership of firearms, ammunition, and *assagais* (spears).

Today, Southern Rhodesia is undergoing rapid change. There has been a real reduction in the independence of the separate social structures existing at the time of initial European and African contact.

Some of this has resulted from increased education, industrialization, and urbanization. But administrators, missionaries, teachers, and others have contributed intentionally and unintentionally to the growth of a new social structure. The values they held and the roles they played have frequently introduced and fostered both foreseen and unforeseen consequences. In addition, the Europeans' general desire to safeguard their economic and political independence from the Union of South Africa, the continuing interest of the Crown, and the increasing focus of British and other public opinion upon the internal affairs of Southern Rhodesia have undoubtedly contributed to the growth of a common social structure for the entire country.

## CULTURE

The last, but perhaps most important, influence upon intergroup relations and attitudes is what social scientists call "culture." The culture or way of life of any group consists of the ideas, meanings, and values it puts upon behavior or the products of behavior. Although a culture changes in time, it is the basic system by which human groups develop consensus and solidarity and thereby are able to live together with a minimum of conflict and friction. As with many other terms in current usage—personality, social structure, attitude, love, justice—culture cannot be fully observed, although it exists in actuality. Rather, from behavior, which alone is open to observation, it is necessary to infer the patterned complex of a society's values, beliefs, ideas, and feelings.

We have spoken of two distinctive culture groups in Southern Rhodesia, but actually there were several distinctive African cultures in the country when the European immigrants arrived. Likewise, the Europeans were culturally diverse, especially the British and the South Africans. With time, however, the differences among the discrete African societies and among the European groups have diminished. Similarly, some of the cultural differences between Europeans and Africans have been changing, a process termed "acculturation" by the anthropologists. To understand the reasons for the establishment of territorial segregation and for the Africans' limited participation in the new social structure of the country, it is necessary to examine some of the values, beliefs, and norms of behavior which the European immigrants brought with them into the new situation.

The African and European societies on the whole possessed different systems of land use, property ownership, government, language, religion, status or prestige, and likes and dislikes. There also were biological or physical differences between them which the Europeans thought were especially important. As a part of their cultural traditions, the Europeans conceived themselves to be unique, superior, and engaged in a quasi-divine mission to extend "civilization" to Africa.[16] Europeans selected and used a few of their cultural differences from Africans to "prove" the correctness and reasonableness of their own beliefs, values, and practices.[17] As with Europeans elsewhere, the immigrants of Southern Rhodesia perceived race as a symbol of cultural differences. Intergroup relations were simplified by the idea that cultural differences were racially or biologically determined rather than the product of invention, learning, and creative contact between individuals of different cultural backgrounds.

To the Africans were attributed personal and social characteristics believed to be the obverse of the Europeans'. Africans served as a "contrast conception" by which Europeans assured themselves of their own "superiority" (Copeland, 1939). Africans were disliked not only because of their black skin color, but also because of some of their marriage customs, sexual practices, ideas of justice, land ownership, religion, and so on.

Europeans believed that certain desirable kinds of relationships ought to exist between them and Africans. Since the two groups had independent and dissimilar sets of values, codes, and moral standards, or what have been called "moral orders," there was little basis for sympathy and cooperation between them.[18] Even though missionaries generally viewed Africans as individuals and made attempts to understand them, their mission to convert Africans implied a belief that much of the Africans' moral order should be changed. The missionaries' ambivalent feelings about Africans were illustrated on occasions such as the Matabele Rebellions. Many of them supported those immigrants who wanted a show-down with the Africans, whereas others joined with the B. S. A. Company and the Imperial Government in a vain attempt to prevent the outbreak of hostilities.

As outposts of an expanding capitalist and industrial civilization, the immigrants desired to exploit the natural resources of Southern Rhodesia. They believed in "progress," and thought economic development and the expansion of "civilization"—especially if it were British—to be eminently desirable objectives. Africans would slowly, but necessarily, benefit from European activities; in the meantime their paganism and lack of "civilization" were not to be forgotten. Although Africans might eventually become "civilized," it was essential to protect European standards of health, morality, and "racial purity." These European values and beliefs, as we have seen, were manifested in the segregation of Africans, the introduction of Western schooling and Christian missionary activity, and in the provision of dual governmental structures, public services, and social and recreational facilities.

The Europeans in Southern Rhodesia differed among themselves, however, in their beliefs about Africans. Not all Europeans sanctioned the superordinate status of the Europeans, for example. The Victorian and pro-Empire attitudes of nineteenth-century England clearly contained elements of sacredness or holiness. Yet the idea of empire, of commercial and political expansion, was not entirely compatible with British legal and parliamentary traditions or with Christian standards, which for many asserted the primacy of cooperation and brotherhood. Europeans also differed among themselves in social status, and their attitudes about Africans probably varied with their social class identification (Park, 1950:234). Missionaries often had different values from miners, Catholics from members of the Dutch Reformed Church, and Englishmen from Afrikaners. As is universally true, each group or subgroup had a hierarchy of values that no other group completely shared.

One aspect of Southern Rhodesia's policy toward Africans may illustrate the importance of different values and ideas within "British culture." The policy of the Colonial Office has sometimes been termed an "upper-class" policy, partly a result of its continuing interest in legal obligations to "protect" Africans from the European immigrants. Colonial policy also has derived in some measure from the upper-class backgrounds of the officials, the theoretical impermanence of British control in many colonies, and the limited occurrence of European settlement. But with the European colonists of Southern Rhodesia, their interests vis-à-vis the Africans were more classless, and were dictated by their small size, superior technology, and the desire to establish a permanent European society. The situation "dictated" the paramountcy of their own interests if the country were to be developed economically, and if "civilization" were to be extended to the Africans. Thus, the Crown and the Colony had different beliefs and expectations about the question of self-determination, the future of the country, and the desirability and tempo of civilizing and assimilating Africans into European society. As a result, many conflicts over African policy occurred among Europeans within Southern Rhodesia, and between them and the Imperial Government, both before and after Self-Government was attained in 1923.

In other British colonies, indigenous peoples have often been taught to value their connection with the Crown even though they were eventually to gain independence. In Southern Rhodesia, on the other hand, the loyalties to British traditions were transmitted largely by an immigrant European group which intended to maintain local control. There were further complications that also affected the Europeans' success in building a local loyalty. For example, almost all missionary organizations have their headquarters outside the territory, and the Christian doctrine of brotherhood is one that theoretically deemphasizes national or cultural boundaries. In addition, the international ties and affiliations that many mining and manufacturing

companies have in Great Britain, the Union of South Africa, and the United States have influenced the Southern Rhodesian Government's policy toward Africans.

Let us summarize the influence European culture has had upon intergroup relations and attitudes in the history of Southern Rhodesia. In the demographic sphere, European ideas and values provided rough criteria for defining the optimal size and density of the population. Europeans did not believe it possible or necessary to decimate the indigenous peoples, but thought extensive European settlement essential if "civilization" were to be established and maintained. Medical services were necessary to extend the life expectancy of those who immigrated. It was desirable that the ratio of males to females should be approximately the same in order to minimize the temptation of sexual liaisons between Africans and Europeans. A preference existed for relatively young newcomers because of their greater energy and the financial savings that would accrue from not having to provide large-scale insurance and pension schemes. British and South African immigrants were preferred, and extraterritorial Africans, Asians, or Coloreds were best admitted only as temporary residents.

The ecological relationships that developed in Southern Rhodesia similarly followed from European values and goals. The spatial distribution of the population was greatly influenced by the Europeans' search for minerals and a healthy climate, as well as the Company's desire to displace Africans as little as necessary. Their felt superiority over Africans led to the apportionment of land in rural and urban areas. That the segregation could not be complete was evidenced by the establishment of accommodation for African servants or laborers ranging in size from the *kia* to the compound and location. The urban concentration of both the European and African populations which accompanied industrial and commercial expansion was met with policies and practices that reflected the Europeans' desire to maintain dominance, control, and self-protection. Africans were looked on as transients in urban centers; and the housing provided, the laws enacted, and the limited interpersonal contacts reflected what Europeans thought was right and proper.

The effect of European culture upon the social structure of the new country was largely shown in the corollaries of territorial segregation. Separate facilities, services, and administrative structures were established, and laws and regulations were passed to maintain the Europeans' dominant status. European ideas and values affected the frequency and character of their personal relations with Africans. While Europeans often disagreed among themselves about how extensively Afrikaners, British, Jews, or Italians should participate in the social structure of the country, they broadly shared the same ideas about Africans. Only minimal social contact with Africans was envisaged in churches, clubs, schools, recreation, and sexual relations. The total effect was that in virtually all "national" affairs, and in relationships that brought Europeans and Africans together, the status of the Europeans was secure.

Southern Rhodesian history began with competitive and perhaps incompatible cultures and separate social structures. The European immigrants were able to implement most of their wishes more as a result of a developed or adaptive culture than as a result of their numbers. Their culture contained a body of knowledge, motivations, and institutions that allowed them to establish control quickly in the new environment. With the passage of time, some of the cultural and social differences between Africans and Europeans have disappeared. Internal changes, especially industrialization, have created a social system in which Africans are participating in increasing measure. External pressures, which likewise reflected the values and ideas in different cultures, have been of expanding importance in the evolution of the new society. In a sense, then, Southern Rhodesia's autonomy is no longer as unfettered as half a century ago. The goals of nationalism, justice, democratic government, Christian brotherhood, and economic efficiency—none of which are solely Rhodesian, British, or European—have increasingly restricted the degree to which the future of Southern Rhodesia can be determined principally by its European population.

# 3

## INFLUENCES ON ATTITUDES AND BEHAVIOR

### The Nature of Attitudes

An "attitude" is a component of human personality that can be isolated, arbitrarily, for measurement and description. Other factors contributing to the development of personality—intelligence, neuroticism, physique, and so on—stand outside the major focus of this study, as do attitudes that are not concerned with the general orientation of Europeans toward Africans in Southern Rhodesia.

At the outset, it is proper to examine what is to be measured and described. The concept of "attitude," like many terms in the social sciences, is not defined uniformly. Vernon (1953) emphasizes the lack of agreement among definitions and so does McNemar (1946). For this study we will employ the definition of Newcomb (1952): "Attitudes represent persistent, general orientations of the individual toward his environment." In our context, then, an attitude is a personality disposition or drive which influences European behavior— verbal and nonverbal—in those situations that directly or indirectly involve Africans.

Attitudes that are predominantly unfavorable or negative are often termed "prejudicial," and Park (1950:233) has illustrated how resistant to change they are in both individuals and groups. It is also of value to note that attitudes are learned, rather than transmitted biologically; hence they have a "history" just as the groups and society into which an individual is born and lives also have histories.

An attitude cannot be observed directly and it refers to no single act or response. Rather, one looks for consistency in the responses and acts of an individual or group and, through inference, defines this consistency as an attitude.[1] As so defined, the concept of an attitude is a hypothetical construct as are other psychological and sociological concepts such as "intelligence," "drive," "habit," "cooperation," and "segregation" (Eysenck, 1954). Thus, the "race attitudes" of the Europeans in our study are inferred from their responses to a series of statements included in a questionnaire and from interview data.

Just as it is possible to extract attitudes from human personality so that they can be measured more rigorously, so it is possible to fragment attitudes into more limited components. The traditional components of cognition, affect, and conation have been clearly defined by Harding and others (1954). Classified as cognitive are the beliefs, perceptions, and expectations—including stereotypes—that individuals hold toward various social groups. The feelings associated with beliefs furnish the affective component. Such feelings may also be favorable or unfavorable, or positive and negative, and it has been demonstrated by Eysenck (1947) that they are continuously distributed. The conative side of an attitude concerns policy orientation. By this, Harding means the ideas that are held about the proper treatment of members of a given group in specific social situations. It is appreciated that these components are not separated in reality, but the division is useful for purposes of further analysis. As we see it, it is equally important to know the beliefs that Europeans hold about Africans, the feelings that accompany the beliefs, and the policies that are advocated for maintaining or changing the status quo. The methods and test instruments we employ furnish data on all three components, although our definitive analyses are concerned primarily with degrees or intensity of feeling and with policy orientation.

It has been implied in the foregoing that we regard measures of attitude as measures of a type of behavior. Because others do not make this interpretation, some explanation is necessary. Walter (1951), for example, believes that discrepancies between measured attitudes and overt behavior are caused by the failure to obtain a complete measurement. A similar observation comes from Hyman (1949) and Segerstedt (1951) who show that verbal behavior is not always followed by other behavior which ought to be a logical consequence. As one explanation of this inconsistency, Hyman suggests that many tests attempt to measure attitudes out of their social context. With this explanation we agree, and an attempt has been made to avoid such a fault by rooting our study firmly in the social context of Southern Rhodesia.

But the real problem lies in the interpretation of an attitude, whether it is regarded as a predictor of behavior or as one form of behavior. It does not take much inspection of the literature to see that there is no one-to-one relation between verbally expressed attitudes and physical action. Sometimes one follows the other, at other times not. But, Eysenck (1954) argues, "Neither words nor actions are invariably accurate reflections of underlying attitudes." Just as a person's words may mislead the unwary investigator, so may his actions. Thus while some individuals aver that their attitudes about Africans are favorable, their actions point to the contrary. Again, when it is demanded at a public protest meeting that all persons who oppose the location of African recreational centers in European areas should raise their hands, an individual may do so to avoid criticism and ostracism, even though he privately believes the reverse. Our interpretation, then, is that attitudes can be expressed verbally or nonverbally, through words or through actions. With equal validity, both can be regarded as samples of behavior from which attitudes can be inferred, even though the inferences are never complete.

No description of attitudes would be complete without mention of the concept "stereotype." The term has been used to identify the mental models that individuals have of other groups of people. Examples of stereotypes, or "pictures in the head" as Lippman calls them, are easy to come by.[2] A clear illustration of their working is seen in MacCrone's (1937) study of race attitudes in South Africa.[3] Some of his European subjects were prepared to classify Africans as intellectually inferior, oversexed, treacherous, and lazy; all were fitted into the same Procrustean straight jacket. Such generalizations—or overgeneralizations—are built into human thinking largely by the molding influences in their society, and they are noted for their inclusiveness and rigidity. Lippitt and Radke (1946) show that stereotypes, once formed, are largely independent of contrary personal experiences; they become "functionally autonomous" and operate with consistency even when contrasts and other evidence suggest that modifications would be in order. It is anticipated that stereotypes—both cognitive and conative—will be of influence in our study of attitudes about Africans.

Because of the foregoing argument, it appears necessary to draw a distinction between a stereotype and a statistical generalization. The former is derived largely from intuition. The latter is obtained from a known distribution of syndromes or traits and the intercorrelation of these at the "type" level. Thus, to arrive at a statistical generalization, one must employ the traditional methods of science: from inductive observation to hypothesis, and then to deduction and verification.

Finally, attitudes, like culture, tend to be organized; some will be more important than others (Kluckhohn, 1954). In this study, a number of techniques will be employed to organize into distinctive categories the attitudes expressed about different aspects of Southern Rhodesian society. Then, some idea of the importance of these categories will be gained by ranking them on the basis of their mean attitude scores. A different type of organization is reserved for the factorial analysis of attitudes. We have made a prior assumption that the dimensions underlying the expression of attitudes are organized hierarchically. This form of taxonomy is illustrated later, and at this point it is only necessary to mention why it has been adopted. Other taxonomic systems are available, but the theory of hierarchical organization we have followed seems to fit best the evidence of so much biological and social research.[4] Its adoption permits the factors described in our study to be related more completely to other findings that have been integrated into such a theoretical framework.

## THE CONTEXT OF ATTITUDES

Much past research has been a genuine loss to the social sciences because of the failure to provide an adequate context for the understanding of intergroup attitudes or behavior. In part, the difficulty has derived from an assumption that research in race relations should be focused on the individual or single personality. This approach conceived of behavior in atomistic or idiographic terms. Attitudes toward a plethora of racial groups and social institutions were generalized from an aggregation of individual measurements, yet little account was taken of the social and cultural milieu in which these attitudes were generated and the effect of these attitudes on behavior. Such an approach frequently resulted in a partial understanding of behavior.

A contrasting emphasis can be found in much of the work in sociology and in some of the developments in social psychology. From this different emphasis, behavior becomes meaningful as the interrelations of the individual and his environment are understood.[5] One of the better interpretations of the approach is found in the work of Kurt Lewin (1951). His most fundamental construct is the "field." All forms of behavior—including attitudes by our definition—are related to a field in a given period of time. In observing the behavior of an individual, the field that must be observed is the "life space" of the individual. This life space consists of the individual and the social and psychological environments as they exist for him. When dealing with groups, a similar formulation is advanced. The life space of a group, to Lewin, consists of the group and the environment as it exists for the group. In terms of our study, if European attitudes about Africans are to be meaningful, they must be understood in relation to the "life space" of Southern Rhodesia. This context we attempt to provide in our analyses.

But the social environment of today has developed from the past. Accordingly, it is necessary to draw on historical data for an understanding of attitudes at a given point in time. The general orientation of an individual toward other cultural or racial groups arises more from traditional group experiences and values than from unique experiences. As Frazier (1953:302) says, "The measurement of the racial attitudes of individuals and the social distances between members of different races as if they lived in a social vacuum will not provide an understanding of race and culture contacts."

### Some Influences on Attitudes

A search for the causes of an attitude involves one in treacherous logical problems. We seem on safe ground if we postulate that the causes of an attitude are seldom single and simple, but are nearly always manifold and complex. Rather than become embroiled in problems of causation, we prefer to describe the principle factors that influence the development and expression of attitudes. These may be causally related to attitudes, and some seem obviously more fundamental than others. But we will not go beyond a description of the influences and some estimation of their importance in the environment of Southern Rhodesia.

#### CULTURE

The historically derived and selected ideas, beliefs, and values of a society are principal influences upon the development and expression of the attitudes of its members. As Duijker (1955) emphasizes, attitudes are evaluations of persons and groups, and such evaluations are generally provided by a culture. Since intergroup attitudes are shared, they are social phenomena, and must be understood in relation to the social and cultural context in which they occur.[6] Religion, science, philosophy, and ideas on "civilization" will guide the way men feel, the way they behave toward each other, and their ideas of what should be done in the future.

In Chapter 2, we sketched some of the salient features of European culture in Southern Rhodesia, and tried to indicate how they shaped attitudes about and contact with Africans. These features involved the "proper" ideas and feelings about the size and characteristics of the spatial location of Europeans and Africans, the desired types of association, and African participation in the general activities of the wider society. To attempt to measure contemporary European attitudes without an appreciation of cultural differences would be to assume that people live in a vacuum.

## SOCIAL STRUCTURE

It is necessary to emphasize the interrelation of social structure and culture, concepts that can be separated more readily for analysis than in actuality. As we present the evidence, the mutual influence of the social structure and culture upon individual attitudes will be observable.

Attitudes vary with the membership and position of individuals in various groups and in Southern Rhodesian society as a whole. Because they meet different peoples, assume different responsibilities, and have different prerogatives, European civil servants and members of Parliament are likely to have different attitudes from those of ordinary citizens. Parents may also be expected to have different beliefs and feelings from unmarried and newly-wed people.[7] Priests and ministers similarly possess a body of knowledge and fill roles which may require attitudes different from those of laymen. Persons with low and high social status and prestige likewise may vary in attitudes because of their positions in the social class structure.

However, our methods of sampling do not allow an exact assessment of the relation between attitudes and the positions of a person in the social structure of the country. Europeans may be classified according to occupation, and their attitudes about Africans analyzed, but this represents a logical rather than a functional classification. Yet persons with similar occupations, or those who are employed in like businesses and industries, associate together in organized interest groups such as the Associated Chambers of Commerce, the Rhodesia National Farmers' Union, the Association of Rhodesia and Nyasaland Industries, the Rhodesian Mining Federation, and various employees' unions.[8] In terms of status and authority, the members of these groups are related to Africans in roughly equivalent ways. The same is true, as suggested earlier, with such groups as teachers, physicians, clerks, social workers, and housewives.

## PERSONALITY

An attitude has been defined as a component of personality, and a considerable number of experimental studies have demonstrated that attitudes are related to other isolable traits and dimensions of personality.[9] While we have undertaken no research on these other dimensions, it is important to stress their possible potency in the formation and growth of attitudes held about Africans. From the experimental evidence, it seems clear that attitudes are molded not only by the environment but also by the kind of constitution the individual possesses. We will do no more than look briefly at a minute portion of the evidence inasmuch as it is suggestive of further investigations that might be undertaken in Southern Rhodesia.

Allport (1935) advances arguments that attitudes may have their genesis in two nonspecific tendencies possessed by all infants, those of *approaching* and *avoiding*. From these nonspecific reactions, it is possible that others develop and give direction to the adaptive behavior of the infant and individual. Although the tendency is common to all children, the situations and objects they *should* approach or avoid are learned from their parents and others through imitation.

A great deal of seminal research has been done on the interrelation of attitudes and personality. It is neither apposite nor possible to make much reference to the findings in this study, except to reinforce the thesis that both attitudes and personality should be studied in their cultural and social contexts.

In their Californian study called *The Authoritarian Personality,* Adorno and others (1950) trace personality differences between subjects with high and low scores on tests of racial and religious prejudice. Briefly, Adorno and his fellow-workers find a strong relation between anti-Negro, anti-Jew, and anti-Catholic attitudes on the one hand, and emotional instability on the other. A similar type of study has been reported by MacCrone and Starfield (1949), a factorial study of race attitudes and neurotic tendency based on English and Afrikaans-speaking South Africans. But of the four major factors extracted from the test data, only one—named hypersensitiveness—was related to race attitude. Furthermore, although the relation was significant, it was slight. Unlike Adorno, MacCrone and Starfield found no relation between emotional and conative instability and attitude about Africans.

To us, the clue to these differing findings lies in the differing cultures and social structures of South Africa and the United States. In the former, the molding pressures of history, state, the dominant church, and the education system all contribute to conformity in thinking, feeling, and policy orientation about Africans. This conformity is relative, not absolute, but it seems clear that the differential influence of personality on attitudes is largely overlaid by the more powerful components that are external to the individual. In California, where society is more mobile and cultural norms more permissive, factors of personality come more fully into play. Support for this hypothesis comes from Pettigrew's (1958, 1960) recent investigations, which suggest that historical and sociocultural factors in South Africa have influenced European attitudes about Africans more than have the constitutional components of personality. Thus, to iterate, the context of attitudes and personality should not be divorced from their measurement.[10]

ECOLOGY

The location, proximity, and density of the European and African populations in Southern Rhodesia have an important influence on social relations and attitudes. Some of these have been described for both the early and more recent periods of history. It will be recalled that the places where people reside, work, and play reflect the cultural norms of society. Thus, the separation of ecology and social structure is a useful one that has been traditional in the analysis of attitudes and interaction patterns. Yet they are complementary frames of reference since they are, in the main, interested in the same observable data.

The literature indicates that the nearness of members of two different cultural or racial groups may increase the frequency of contact, especially at the beginning of such propinquity. This in turn may lead to changes in attitude or behavior, but it often does not because of the importance of other variables in the situation, e.g., common interests and affiliations in sacred and secular groups, and personality factors. In other circumstances, there may be high rates of interaction in economic activities, but low ones in recreational or neighborhood relations.[11] Spatial segregation may thus exist in intergroup relations outside of work. Restrictive housing covenants, racially defined rental practices, and legal enactments may all have considerable influence upon intergroup attitudes and contact. The degree of concentration or dispersion of a particular racial group—whether it be in their places of employment, residence, or recreation—are essential features of the milieu in which attitudes are developed, transmitted, and changed. This is as true in Southern Rhodesia as it is in other societies.

DEMOGRAPHY

The size and characteristics of a population may in themselves have little bearing upon race attitudes. But invariably these features are given meanings or valuations which then help to structure behavior in contact situations. The last chapter discussed the importance of such variables as age, sex, population size, and the rates and sources of population growth. A few more examples will indicate the interrelations between demographic and other factors.

There are no European groups in Southern Rhodesia that embrace all the females or all the males. Yet the sex of a person helps to define the frequency and character of contacts with Africans. By virtue of the institutionalized practice of having domestic servants, European women are in greater contact with African males than with African females. Correspondingly, the contacts of European men are more frequent with African men than women, but these occur in business and industry as well as in the home. Another factor that affects race relations is age. Young newly-wed Europeans are less likely to have African domestic servants than are older couples. Further, the ages of servants are not representative of the entire African population. Thus, the other characteristics of servants—e.g., their income, standards of health, amount of schooling, and interest in African nationalism— may also be atypical and in turn have a significant influence upon European attitudes.

Europeans who have obtained less than seven years of schooling do not form an interacting group or collectivity. Yet the amount of education is probably related to an individual's income, occupation, political party preference, and so on. These characteristics also may influence their affiliation and participation in various social groups. The length of residence in Southern Rhodesia is an additional factor that can affect attitudes and behavior. It is unlikely that attitudes about Africans that developed in Great Britain or Holland, for example, will remain unchanged after immigration. Participation in a society unlike that of the home country cannot fail to affect the individual. Further- more, as the proportion of recent immigrants in the population changes, so the attitudinal norms are likely to shift.

As a final example, MacCrone's (1937) research suggests that attitudes about Africans may be related to ethnic or national origin. This background is relevant in so far as it serves as the basis for sharing common values and for structuring relations in situations where contact with Africans occurs. Examples of groups in which na- tionality and ethnicity are important include religious denominations, private schools, debating societies, missions, youth and adult social clubs, and many informal social gatherings. Such groups may, through a combination of historically-developed attitudes and a given status in Southern Rhodesian society, be weighty influences upon the ac- tivities of their members.

From the examples offered, it can be inferred that demographic and ecological factors are usually interrelated with those of culture, social structure, and personality. All these are conceptually distinguishable, but they are integral parts of the total Southern Rhodesian context in which European attitudes about Africans develop. For this reason, among others, it is safer logic to postulate and unravel influences than to determine causes.

Cattell (1950) has picturesquely described personality as being "concerned with *all* the behavior of the individual, both overt and under the skin. It is concerned with a range of behavior extending from the individual's political and religious views to the way he digests his food." Our study comes closer to behavior of the former type, although without doubt race attitudes affect digestion on occasion. Within this broad setting, attitudes have been singled out for measurement and analysis. While it is true that the wording of definitions varies within the social sciences, there is reasonable agreement on the nature of attitudes, the areas of personality they straddle, and the need to study them in their sociocultural context. We have taken Newcomb's (1952) definition to be sufficiently catholic to accommodate the major emphases of other writers.

The historical data and our review of some of the literature illustrate the complex interrelation of variables that affect the development, expression, and context of attitudes. Even though others have suggested it (e.g., Cattell and Miller, 1952), we would hesitate to express these subtle and complex interrelations as a mathematical equation. Rather, our aims will be to trace the influences of culture, social structure, personality, ecology, and demography on race attitudes; to describe those influences; and, in the later analyses, to see how they are related to behavior—verbal and nonverbal—among Europeans in Southern Rhodesia.

# 4

## THE MEASUREMENT OF ATTITUDES

### METHODS OF MEASUREMENT

Over the years, various instruments for measuring attitudes have been developed. They differ, in part, because of the academic background of the investigator and the nature of the area being explored. In the planning stages of this study, some attention was paid to the major methods of attitudinal measurement—objective, projective, questionnaire and inventory, interview, and observational—to determine which might be best employed for the gathering of data. A brief and selective account of why some methods were selected and others rejected is necessary.

Cattell (1949, 1950a, 1956) and others have endeavored to measure attitudes "objectively" through tests of psychogalvanic response, immediate memory, expenditure of time on an activity, and so on. Some of these tests have yielded high reliabilities but validities in the much lower order of .30 to .50. Apart from the uncertain validities, there is no satisfactory way of linking the affective aspects of attitudes to the policy orientations of individuals and groupings, and such objective tests were therefore rejected. Also rejected were the various projective tests, such as the Rosenzweig Picture-Frustration, the Thematic Apperception Test, and the Rorschach. Preliminary investigation revealed the inadequacy of the different methods of quantifying projective data.[1]

At the end of the exploratory work, it seemed that a combination of the questionnaire and the interview (assisted by observation) would be the most valuable for eliciting the cognitive, affective, and conative data required for the investigation. Both the questionnaire and the interview have been subjected to critical scrutiny in a number of psychological and sociological researches, and we are aware of their imperfections.[2] However, by drawing on the more firmly established of the techniques, it was felt that acceptable reliability and validity could be achieved. These two concepts as they relate to the questionnaire will be discussed in detail in Chapter 6.

## THE QUESTIONNAIRE

A device for measuring attitudes should contain statements or items that are both practical and realistic, and they should be relevant to the respondents as well as to the attitudes to be discovered (Green, 1954:341). The verbal expressions of attitudes obtained should be those which, so far as can be determined ahead of time, relate to nonverbal "action attitudes." Earlier, it was stated that attitudes are inferred from behavior. Inasmuch as only a limited number of items can be included in a questionnaire, they should be representative of an "attitude universe," i.e., the whole area of experience to which particular attitudes are related.

### THE ATTITUDE UNIVERSE

No previous systematic work had been done in Southern Rhodesia on attitudes toward Africans. The closest approximation was MacCrone's (1937) experimental study done in the Union of South Africa. Four factors precluded the adoption of his attitude scale: (1) social and cultural changes that have occurred since the date of MacCrone's testing; (2) differences in the social structure and culture of South Africa and Southern Rhodesia; (3) criticisms of the approach utilized in his study (e.g., Merton, 1940); and (4) advances in theory since 1937. Other studies in the United Kingdom, India, the United States, and elsewhere seemed even less applicable to the circumstances of Southern Rhodesia, although not irrelevant theoretically.

Thus, we undertook the construction of a new instrument that would have greater utility for our purposes. The plan to measure European attitudes about Africans demanded that a selection of items be chosen from the attitude universe. Items for inclusion in the questionnaire were solicited from both Africans and Europeans; from advocates, teachers, housewives, farmers, students, and government officials. Other statements were suggested by Bank's (1950) study of an analogous situation in the United States, and some were formulated after an examination of Southern Rhodesian statutes, regulations, and by-laws.

## VALIDATION OF ITEMS

Thirty-six of the sixty-six statements that composed the final questionnaire were checked for validity by reference to the Statute Laws of Southern Rhodesia and the Federation. They are cited in Appendix B. A few of these laws changed during the course of administering the questionnaire. Other practices, in which Africans receive different treatment or access to the use of public and private facilities, were validated (1) by reference to officials, ministers, employers, and other residents of the Colony, (2) by descriptions, discussions, and generalizations in the press, and (3) by direct personal observation. Some of the statements, such as those on sentences for the crimes of rape and violence, could hardly be substantiated by any of these methods, but they were included to give a more complete sampling of attitudes.

## A PRIORI CLASSIFICATION

The next step was to classify the sixty-six items into a priori categories on the hypothesis that distinctive differences in attitudes would emerge between them. Following the suggestions of Myrdal's (1944) monumental American study, seven a priori categories were established: economics, politics, law, social etiquette, public services, sex, and social contact. In this classification, the number of statements in a category ranged from a minimum of eight to a maximum of twelve. The sixty-six items were then arranged randomly in the questionnaire to preclude the probability that all or most of those in any one category would appear together.

## PILOT STUDY

It was then necessary to conduct a pilot study to "pre-test" our questionnaire. This procedure is essential when no prior investigations have been made with a given test instrument, and where analogous situations are not adequate guides for the Southern Rhodesian experience (Hyman, 1955:151). The purpose of the pre-test is to eliminate ambiguity in statements or questions, to assure that they are comprehensible, and to improve the possibility that the responses will be meaningful and relevant to the situation.

Various modifications were made in the questionnaire as a result of the pilot study. The most substantial change that was necessary was in the alternative response-choices provided for each statement. In the trial draft, respondents were asked to endorse statements through a procedure we adapted from Banks (1950). The four classes offered for endorsement ranged from "Very Important and should be maintained" to "Unimportant and could be eliminated." The responses and suggestions of the twenty-seven persons who cooperated in the pilot study showed clearly that neither Banks' procedure nor a modification of it were adequate for our purposes. Choices according to his method permitted an estimation of intensity of feeling for those in favor of *maintaining* a practice, but not for those who wished to *discontinue* it. Accordingly, the response-choices were reformulated so that both intensity of feeling and direction of attitude could be accommodated.

## THE FINAL QUESTIONNAIRE

The final questionnaire (Appendix A) contained the randomly ordered sixty-six statements of the trial draft, but with minor revisions in the wording of the statements and the general directions. The sponsorship (director and academic institution) and reasons for the study were given. Instructions were provided for the respondent to indicate the direction and the intensity of his opinions about matters in which Africans and Europeans were differentiated. The four possible responses to each statement in the final version were: "Very Important—Maintain," "Important—*probably* should be Maintained," "Important—*probably* should be Discontinued," and "Very Important—Discontinue."

It can be seen that no options were provided for answers such as "neutral," "don't know," or "undecided." In this, we took heed of a considerable body of evidence—summarized by Duijker (1955)—that, by definition, attitudes are either "pro" or "anti," or "favorable" or "unfavorable." Thus, the respondents were forced to commit themselves one way or the other. There is a considerable volume of evidence to suggest that the "forced-choice" technique—of which ours is a variety—is easier than others to score, and results in higher reliability and validity coefficients and a reduction in "response sets." [3]

Finally, so that the testing could be related to a theoretical sampling model and further information gained about the structure of European society, fourteen items of personal and other data were requested on the answer sheet to the questionnaire. These data were age, sex, community of residence, district of residence, length of residence in Southern Rhodesia, country of birth, national origin, income, occupation or profession, type of business or industry in which employed, years of schooling, religious affiliation or preference, political party preference, and a self-rating of attitude about Africans.

The choices made to the sixty-six items were arbitrarily assigned values of 0, 2, 4, and 6. This procedure follows Likert (1932), who first demonstrated that arbitrarily assigned values correlated almost perfectly (.99) with a more complex sigma-scoring method. It is not assumed, however, that the assigned values are equidistant; to do so would be to imply knowledge, which we do not possess, of an underlying attitudinal metric.[4]

For the personal and other data, the coding frame of the Central African Statistical Office was adopted where applicable. In the cases where it was not applicable, *ad hoc* criteria were evolved. The number of codes varied for the fourteen items of data. For "sex," only two were necessary, whereas for "age" eleven different codes were utilized. This latter number may seem to be more than sufficient, but the decision followed from the point that Moser (1958) has made: "By and large, it is advisable to retain more rather than less detail in coding, since it is easier to amalgamate groups [classes or categories] than to split one group [class, category] into several when these have been coded alike."

## The Interview

In addition to the questionnaire, further attitudinal data were obtained by means of unstructured interviews. The interviewers sought to establish rapport and to secure a spontaneous expression of beliefs, feelings, and policy orientations about Africans in Southern Rhodesia. Through interviews, it is often held, the deeper areas of personality can be explored—i.e., the intensity of feelings and beliefs, as well as an indication of the interrelated nature of attitudes. As Moser (1958:204–5) argues, "When the survey subject is complex or emotional, it may be that the greater flexibility of an informal approach succeeds better than set questions in getting to the heart of the respondent's opinions."

The interview also enabled us, in many cases, to gather knowledge of experiences and reactions that may have influenced the respondent's attitudes toward Africans, testimony about former or different attitudes, the time involved in attitudinal change, and the other places and periods of residence in Africa or colonial situations that may have been instrumental in the development of attitudes.[5] Further valuable data were gained on the European and Southern Rhodesian social structures. The interview data were not coded.

However, material related directly to particular items in the questionnaire was transferred to the answer sheets alongside the comments, if any, which the respondents had written.

## VALIDITY

Unlike the questionnaire, the validity of the interview data is less easy to establish.[6] However, it can be assessed by the degree of similarity between an individual's "spontaneous verbal attitudes" in the interview and the "elicited verbal attitudes" to the questionnaire (Green, 1954). Upon inspection and comparison,. only two respondents were found to have given questionnaire responses significantly different * from attitudes expressed during the interview.

The problems encountered in the measurement of personality are also met in any attempt to quantify attitudinal behavior. While in theory it is possible to use a great variety of psychological and sociological instruments, research has demonstrated that some are more reliable and valid than others. From the array available, we have chosen the questionnaire and the interview as our principal instruments for assessing attitudes in the contemporary setting of Southern Rhodesia.

Some considerable time was spent in compiling, retooling, and selecting items to ensure that the responses to them would represent the universe of attitudes held by Europeans about Africans. As far as possible, these items reflected the laws of the land and social customs and practices in the Colony. The response-choices for each statement were cast so that both intensity and direction of attitude could be estimated, both necessary for proceeding to an analysis of the policy orientations commonly held by Europeans. These orientations—the manner of treating and behaving toward Africans—were gathered, in part, through the use of unstructured interviews. We are aware of the limitations in questionnaire and interview techniques and the difficulty of quantifying and evaluating data derived from them. The extent to which the limitations have been overcome will be revealed in the analyses to follow.

* "Significant" in this context cannot be given a precise statistical definition. But we estimate that (except for these two persons) less than 10% difference or variation was given.

# 5

## THE SAMPLING MODEL

In a study such as this, where the individuals tested should reflect the attitudes of the population as a whole, some attention must be focused on the problem of sampling. There are a number of ways in which samples can be drawn from a population, and the effectiveness of each is partly determined by the purpose and design of the investigation. As the present study utilized a number of interlocking methods, it is appropriate to examine them in some detail. The aim throughout was to make the sample as representative of the total population as possible.

### SIMPLE RANDOM SAMPLING

The underlying assumption in simple random sampling is that every individual in the population has an equal chance of being included in the sample. Most statistical techniques rest on the assumption of randomness, but many psychological and sociological studies do not fulfill this criterion. Not infrequently a group of university students is investigated in the hope that, on a given characteristic, it is a representative sample of a larger, more complete population. Occasionally this is so, as Miller (1941) found when studying the morale of American college students, but in general it is not. Two principles were used by us for sampling, the primary one of randomization and the secondary one of stratification, to maximize the representativeness of the sample.

## Stratified Random Sampling

By definition, a stratified random sample consists of two or more random samples drawn from two or more subdivisions (or strata) of the population. In application, the method consists of predetermining the strata of the population to be studied so that the persons drawn in the sample will be in the same proportion as they are in the total population. The end result, therefore, is a summation of a series of random samples. Peatman (1947) has shown that the method is valuable provided "(1) that there is a significant correlation between the control factor, or factors, and the trait or behavior to be studied, and (2) that the necessary information about the universe is available so that the stratification can be based on facts and not merely on guesswork."

There is a wealth of evidence from the literature describing the strata that are often related to race attitudes and behavior. It hardly seems necessary at this point to enumerate the studies that describe these areas and their relation to different facets of race attitudes and behavior; they will be examined mainly in Chapter 18. Although other researchers have indicated the strata that may be valuable for sampling purposes, their work does not prejudge the evidence gathered in Southern Rhodesia. The whole purpose of adopting a complex stratified random sampling design has been to eliminate the possibility of bias. The more variables that can be held constant and proportional to the total population, the greater the opportunity of reducing (although not eliminating) the effect of chance errors in sampling.

The thirteen control areas we selected for stratification included sex, age, community of residence, census district, country of birth, length of residence in Southern Rhodesia, income, occupation, type of industry or business, and religious affiliation or preference; the proportions of people in these ten areas were furnished by the Central African Statistical Office. In addition, the proportions of people voting for a particular political party in Southern Rhodesia were obtained from the returns of the Federal election held in 1958.

There were other factors that seemed worthy of study, but for which no reliable data existed. One of these was national origin, the ethnic group to which an individual felt he belonged. The criterion we used was different from that of the census, which classified people according to the nation to which they legally belonged. Thus, an individual may legally have been a citizen of the Union of South Africa but because of his parentage, background, and language, he may have regarded himself as an Englishman or an Afrikaner. Another factor, length of schooling, may be related to race attitudes, but there were no statistics available under this heading. However, because it can be shown that our sample approximates closely a considerable number of categories that *are* known about the population, it seems reasonable that the distributions obtained for national origin and years of schooling may also be close approximations. If one is prepared to accept this hypothesis, our figures can provide a basis for stratification in future studies.

We have eschewed basing the study on simple random sampling because it introduces chance errors that may distort one or several of the strata unless the number of cases involved is very large. Although one can calculate the standard errors of statistics based on random selection, there is no guarantee that a single sample does not draw long odds on some of the strata which are known for the population. For example, a single sample by chance may give an excess of Roman Catholics, urban dwellers, or persons born in South Africa, and an insufficient number of professional people, Jews, or supporters of the Dominion party. The effect of this can be demonstrated readily. We know from the returns of the Federal election that 37.8% of the voters in Southern Rhodesia preferred the Dominion party and 58.7% opted for the United Federal party. In a large number of random samples, it is assumed that a close approximation to these two percentages would be drawn. But the samples themselves would show fluctuations on either side of 37.8% and 58.7%, so that in an odd, exceptional sample the percentages for each party could be reversed. But as Guilford (1956) has stressed, if the restriction of stratification is imposed on random sampling, chance errors are reduced and the attitude of the general population is reflected more accurately.

Another theoretical point should be examined. It was stated previously that our stratification had been based on variables, such as country of birth, length of residence, and religious affiliation, that may be correlated with race attitudes. But what if, in fact, the study ultimately demonstrates that some of these assumptions are not justified for the population of Southern Rhodesia? Peatman (1947) has been given an unequivocal answer on the matter. In this case the stratification yields a result that has the precision of random sampling, without the expected reduction in chance errors. Accordingly, we are on safe ground in making these assumptions, for in either case they do not preclude the use of statistics based on the principle of randomization.

## SUBPOPULATIONS IN STRATIFIED RANDOM SAMPLING

As more controls are added to the sampling, the task becomes more complex. Most public opinion studies involve stratification under a small number of headings, and where this is carefully done the results can be very accurate. Cantril and others (1944), for example, have shown how the Office of Public Opinion Research at Princeton University was able to predict the outcome of the New York gubernatorial election in 1942 from a small sample of 200 voters carefully stratified by color, economic status, and age.

Thirteen major controls were applied in our study, and this increased the complexity of sampling beyond the point of most public opinion investigations. With this number of controls, the task of locating the subpopulations in which to sample randomly became difficult because such criteria as age, country of birth, and political party preference are intermingled in real life and do not designate distinctive, interacting subpopulations.

Yet this description still does not reveal the complexity of the sampling because within each of the major controls it was necessary to apply what Peatman has called "internal controls." Let us take an example. The census returns for Southern Rhodesia gave figures from which could be calculated the proportions of people who had lived in the territory for periods ranging from less than a year to over fifty years. This range was divided into twelve class intervals so that the data could be coded and punched into Hollerith cards. A total of 108 internal controls of this type were applied to the major controls or strata for which figures were available. Without doubt, some of the controls would be correlated, and it is known that correlated controls diminish the chance errors of sampling less than do the same number of uncorrelated controls. But in the absence of experimental data on the matter, it seemed best to apply all the major and internal controls from the beginning, even if the law of diminishing returns operated because of the correlation of some of them.

## THE POPULATION

At the outset, it was decided that the investigation should be carried out in Southern Rhodesia, where the majority of Europeans in the Federation of Rhodesia and Nyasaland lived. The last census (1956) enumerated 177,124 European residents within the Colony. This figure included, however, children and adolescents, whose attitudes we did not intend to measure in this investigation. We were concerned with adults who were in a position to exercise some control over the life of the country through the various political, economic, social, and educational associations. For this reason, the sample involved all those twenty years or older at the time of the investigation. It should be noted that the model embraced more people than were qualified to vote. If this had not been done, we could not have obtained an accurate picture of the total population, because the number qualified to vote at any given time is considerably smaller than the number who meet the age requirement. This fact is discussed further in the section on political party preference.

When the under-twenty-year-olds had been excluded, a population of 110,687 remained from which to draw a sample. Because of the method of sampling employed, and because of the close fit obtained between our model of the population and the sample, we hope to demonstrate that this study is representative of Europeans in Southern Rhodesia in 1959.

## THE SAMPLE

The optimal size of a sample depends on the purpose of the investigation and the method of drawing it from the population. Studies that use random methods of sampling generally involve the testing of greater numbers than those employing stratified methods. As an example, Rogers (1953) found that a stratified sample of 100 children thirteen and fourteen years of age was sufficient to identify clearly two distinct abilities in verbal fluency: "oral facility" and "facility in writing." The same observation on sampling is usually true of opinion polling, as Cantril and others (1944) have illustrated. Of course, there are examples in the literature of large and small samples that have resulted in both accurate and inaccurate predictions, the latter often being a product of faulty sampling design and unforeseen shifts in opinion. The evidence suggests that the character of a sample can be more important than its size. Such has been demonstrated clearly by Cornell (1947) in his survey of enrollments in American institutions of higher learning.

Having stressed the importance of the character of the sample, we must also be concerned with its size if we wish to test the significance of any differences that emerge between the subpopulations of the sample, for example, the differences between persons expressing a preference for each of the major political parties. Peatman (1947), Remmers (1954), and others have shown that, as a rule, the smaller the differences between groups, the larger the sample needs to be in order to establish significance. Thus, we may find a small difference that is not significant in the sample, although in the total population it may be genuine and significant. On the other hand, given that our sample represents the population, any proven differences within the sample will also be proven for the population.

Of the variables chosen for the stratification of the sample, we assumed that one of the most important was political party preference. There is some justification for this assumption, since Rogers (1959) found significant differences between the supporters of the two major political parties in their attitudes about Africans at the time of the 1958 territorial elections in Southern Rhodesia. Because race attitudes and politics are related in Africa, it seemed apposite to use the differences in voting strength of the parties to fix the minimal size of the sample.

At the Federal election of 1958, the Dominion party received 37.8% of the votes cast in Southern Rhodesia, the United Federal party received 58.7%, and the remaining 3.5% were distributed among the Constitution party, the Confederate party, and independents. If we had wished to test differences among the minor parties, and still keep the sample correctly proportioned among the two major parties, the total number necessary would have been beyond our resources. Therefore, we decided to define the size of the sample with reference to the Dominion party and the United Federal party, and to ignore the rest. Thus, between these two parties alone, the voting was split in the proportions .392 Dominion and .608 United Federal.

Guilford (1956) has described in detail the rationale of the method we employed to fix the minimal size of the sample, and only a few details need to be mentioned here. The first step was to propose the null hypothesis ($H_o$) that the parties were equally divided, and that any obtained deviation from the proportions of .500 was due to chance fluctuations in random sampling. But we had evidence from the Federal election returns that the vote for the Dominion party and the United Federal party was split in the proportions .392 and .608. Our exercise was to determine the size of sample needed to give confidence that the obtained proportions did not occur by random sampling from an equally divided voting population. By subtraction, it can be seen that each obtained proportion deviated by .108 from the null hypothesis of .500. If this deviation were to be significant at the 1.0% level of confidence, then it must have deviated $2.576\sigma$ from the mean of the normal distribution. Therefore, $\sigma_p = .108/2.576$ or .0419. To obtain the size of the sample we applied the formula,

$N = \dfrac{pq}{\sigma^2_p}$, in which p and q were the two proportions of the null hypothesis and $\sigma_p$ was already known. Substituting in the equation, $N = 142$. By definition, then, in a sample of 142 persons, the odds were 99 to 1 that the population was not divided evenly in its political preferences.

But because there may have been other differences between subpopulations that were not as marked as political party preference, we did not consider 142 cases to be sufficient. Consequently, it was decided to base the study on a sample of 500 persons in the hope that smaller but still significant differences in attitude could be ascertained and measured.

One point remains to be noted. The size of N was determined as if completely random sampling were to be employed. However, stratified random sampling has been used throughout. Inasmuch as this method should fit the population more closely than simple random sampling, the N that has been adopted is on the generous side. This is not a disadvantage.

The next step was to determine the size of the subpopulations to be studied and the weights that each would carry in a sample of 500. It was possible to do this with data from the Central African Statistical Office. From twenty years of age upward, there were 110,687 Europeans in Southern Rhodesia at the time of the census, as we have already noted. To have extracted the required information on subpopulations from this number of Hollerith cards would have been a task of some burden. To lighten it, the Statistical Office worked from an approximate 10% of the Southern Rhodesian population (11,697 persons), and the proportions for the total census are assumed to be the same as for the 10% population. Thus there will be a few minor differences in the data based upon the 10% and full populations, but they have been discounted as insignificant.

## Obtaining the Sample

The sampling was tackled first on the basis of the census districts of Southern Rhodesia. For example, within the census districts, streets or roads were drawn at random, and then, within these, householders were approached systematically. To keep track of the sampling, a flow chart was prepared and cumulative entries were made against the 108 internal controls as the data were gathered. When the numbers against any of the internal controls became greater than those needed for a matching of sample and population model, an attempt was made to eliminate the excess by means of random selection. However, because of the complexity of the model, complete matching was not expected nor was it achieved. Even so, it was necessary to test considerably more than the 500 cases needed for the sample.

In addition, many other individuals were approached to take part in the study, but when it became clear from first questioning that their entries on the flow chart would result in the overfilling of some controls, they were pursued no further. It can be said that as the sample became larger, the task of random selection became progressively more complex.

## THE PROPORTIONS IN THE SUBPOPULATIONS

Before describing the subpopulations in detail, two notes are necessary. Firstly, although 108 internal controls were employed for the sampling, this number was not retained for the analyses. Where the numbers in the subpopulations were very small, it was sometimes necessary to telescope adjacent intervals, or logically related subpopulations, before proceeding to the computations.

Secondly, for each of the subpopulations, we needed to test the significance of the differences between the number of cases expected on the basis of the 10% census returns, and the number actually obtained in the sample. The various parametric tests of significance, such as Z and *t,* were not applicable because they assume an underlying normal distribution of measurements. It might have been possible to assume that a variable such as length of schooling is distributed almost normally, but we were not prepared to make that assumption. And for the other subpopulations based upon sex, religious affiliation, and so on, there is clearly no underlying metric that can be conceived as normal. Consequently, it was necessary to adopt one of the nonparametric statistics, the chi-square test.

The chi-square possesses certain important additive qualities that allow the testing for significance of a hypothesis involving more than one set of data; for example, seven obtained age categories against an expected seven. The general formula $\chi^2 = \Sigma \left[ \dfrac{(f_o - f_e)^2}{f_e} \right]$ was used in which $f_o$ represents the frequencies obtained in the sample, and $f_e$ the frequencies expected on the basis of the 10% census returns. For each subpopulation, the null hypothesis was assumed (i.e. any differences between the obtained and expected frequencies would be due to chance factors in the sampling). The chi-square test showed whether the null hypothesis could be supported, and at what level of confidence, or whether it had to be rejected. Where the null hypothesis was rejected, an attempt has been made to discover the reasons why the test sample differs from the census returns. Let us now inspect each of the subpopulations in turn.

SEX

The subpopulations of males and females were not difficult to control. In the age range of our study, there was a 5% excess of males over females. Table 9 illustrates the comparison between population and test sample.

Chi-square equals .289 in this table. Before we calculate whether the differences would be obtained by chance, it is necessary to know the number of degrees of freedom for the table. The general rule that can be applied to the tables of this chapter is that the degrees of freedom equal the product of the number of rows (r) minus one, and the number of columns (k) minus one. In terms of a formula, $df = (r - 1)(k - 1)$, and for the table, $df = 1$. With chi-square and df known, we can now read from Fisher's (1950) tables for $\chi^2$. The obtained chi-square falls above the 50% level of confidence, meaning that by chance alone the differences we obtained can occur over fifty times in one hundred samples. Consequently, the null hypothesis is strongly supported.

TABLE 9. *Sex—a Chi-square Test of the Differences between the Southern Rhodesian Population and the Test Sample*

|  | Census | Sample | Sample | |
| --- | --- | --- | --- | --- |
| Sex | % obtained | % obtained | No. expected | No. obtained |
| Male | 52.5 | 53.8 | 263 | 269 |
| Female | 47.5 | 46.2 | 237 | 231 |
| Totals | 100.0 | 100.0 | 500 | 500 |

$\chi^2 = .289$   $df = 1$   1 of c $= >50\%$   $H_o$ = supported

Some statisticians would not reject the null hypothesis even if the level of confidence fell to 1.0%, but we have adopted the austere position that any confidence level of 5% or less has resulted from some unforeseen disturbance to the sampling. Such an outcome is possible when based on stratified random sampling with the number of known variables we have.

AGE

Among the subpopulations, it seemed important that the age distribution in Southern Rhodesia should be paralleled within the test sample. A point that can be tested is whether, within broad categories, race attitudes vary with the age of respondents. It is not uncommon in other societies to find the more conservative attitudes among the older people. At the outset, we had no way of telling whether this were true for the total population, but we took the precaution of testing at all age levels. Table 10 shows the closeness of fit of the population and the test sample.

It is noteworthy that the frequency expected (122) for the age range 20–29 years is smaller than for the next interval above this. The evidence suggests that this was due to changes in the pattern of immigration. We took particular care to sample the older members of the population, and the fit seems to be particularly close, with good matching even at seventy years and above.

TABLE 10. *Age—a Chi-square Test of the Differences between the Southern Rhodesian Population and the Test Sample*

| Age in years | Census % obtained | Sample % obtained | Sample No. expected | Sample No. obtained |
|---|---|---|---|---|
| 20–29 | 24.4 | 25.8 | 122 | 129 |
| 30–39 | 28.2 | 29.2 | 141 | 146 |
| 40–49 | 23.4 | 23.0 | 117 | 115 |
| 50–59 | 13.0 | 12.6 | 65 | 63 |
| 60–69 | 6.8 | 6.0 | 34 | 30 |
| 70–79 | 3.2 | 3.0 | 16 | 15 |
| 80 and above | 1.0 | .4 | 5 | 2 |
| Totals | 100.0 | 100.0 | 500 | 500 |

$\chi^2 = 3.009$   df $= 6$   1 of c $= {>}80\%$   $H_o =$ supported

On the age distributions, chi-square equals 3.009. With six degrees of freedom, such a chi-square can be obtained by chance over eighty times in one hundred samples. Thus, the null hypothesis is strongly supported and we can assume that the test sample reflects the age distribution of the total population. If there are variations in attitude at different ages, these have been accommodated in the sample.

COMMUNITY OF RESIDENCE

In the sampling, each respondent was asked to designate the village, town, or city in which he resided, or if he did not live in an urban area to record "rural" as his community of residence. A large number gave a nongeographical meaning to the term "community," however, and indicated instead their national, ethnic, or religious "community." Others cited the names of sections or neighborhoods within the limits of a particular municipality. Because of this confused response pattern, it was not possible to stratify the sample on the basis of community of residence.

CENSUS DISTRICT

It seemed necessary that we should secure a proper geographical distribution in the sample. A number of possibilities were available, but the most logical approach, it seemed, was to follow the divisions adopted by the Central African Statistical Office in 1956. For the census, Southern Rhodesia had been divided into districts, and these were the divisions within which the sampling was done.

It was necessary to decide next on a method of classifying census districts. A number of alternatives were considered such as agricultural versus industrial, mining versus nonmining, and the size of the population in the districts; but all of these presented some difficulty. In the end, we classified each district according to the population of its largest urban nucleus. Table 11 shows the classification in detail.

TABLE 11. *Census District—a Chi-square Test of the Differences between the Southern Rhodesian Population and the Test Sample*

| Census district by population of largest nucleus | Census % obtained | Sample % obtained | Sample No. expected | Sample No. obtained |
|---|---|---|---|---|
| Railway travelers | .2 | .0 | 1 | 0 |
| Rural: under 1,000 | 18.1 | 18.4 | 90 | 92 |
| Marandellas, Urungwe, Makoni, Selukwe, Lomagundi, Chipinga, Gwanda, Bulalima-Mangwe, Mazoe, Charter, Goromonzi, Insiza, Bubi, Chilimanzi, Matobo, Mrewa, Darwin, Mtoko, Nyamandhlovu, Sipolilo, Ndanga, Nuanetsi, Lupani, Sebungwe, Buhera, Nkai, Gutu, Chibi, Inyanga, Melsetter, Wedza, Bikita | | | | |
| Semiurban: 1,000 to 10,000 | 19.9 | 19.8 | 100 | 99 |
| Umtali, Gwelo, Belingwe, Hartley, Victoria, Wankie | | | | |
| Urban: 10,000 to 50,000 | 23.9 | 23.8 | 119 | 119 |
| Bulawayo-Umzingwane | | | | |
| Urban: over 50,000 | 37.9 | 38.0 | 190 | 190 |
| Salisbury | | | | |
| Totals | 100.0 | 100.0 | 500 | 500 |

$$\chi^2 = .021 \quad df = 3 \quad 1 \text{ of } c = >99\% \quad H_o = \text{supported}$$

Thirty-two of the forty census districts had no town or center with a population of more than 1,000 Europeans, and they were designated as rural. Districts with towns having European populations between 1,000 and 10,000 were classed as semiurban. Two districts were identified as urban, but they have been distinguished by the size of the population in Greater Bulawayo and Greater Salisbury. No railway travelers were included in the sample. As has been said, there were other ways in which the districts could have been grouped, but this one followed a principle that seemed consistent. Naturally, sampling was not confined to the urban nuclei of the districts; we were careful to ensure that testing was spread throughout in order to reduce the possibility of bias through an excess of any one socioeconomic grouping. The fact that we obtained the needed quota of farmers illustrates this point.

There is little need to discuss the statistical test of the sampling.

An almost complete fit with the population model was obtained, and the null hypothesis highly supported.

COUNTRY OF BIRTH

A breakdown of the census by country of birth was also used to stratify the sample. One or two points of explanation are necessary to interpret Table 12. Persons born in Southern Rhodesia were classified separately in case their attitudes about Africans were distinctive. Those born in Northern Rhodesia and Nyasaland and now living in Southern Rhodesia (1.8%) were grouped with individuals born in other countries of the Commonwealth. This seemed reasonable inasmuch as until 1953 the former were not politically integrated into the Federation, and also because the numbers involved were too small for separate statistical treatment. To complete the expected side of the table, we also telescoped visitors (0.9%) and those born at sea (none) into the "Other Commonwealth" classification.

TABLE 12. *Country of Birth—a Chi-square Test of the Differences between the Southern Rhodesian Population and the Test Sample*

| | Census | Sample | Sample | |
| --- | --- | --- | --- | --- |
| | % | % | No. | No. |
| *Country of birth* | *obtained* | *obtained* | *expected* | *obtained* |
| Non-Commonwealth | 9.2 | 6.2 | 46 | 31 |
| United Kingdom and Eire, incl. Channel Islands and Malta | 35.6 | 38.0 | 178 | 190 |
| Other Commonwealth, incl. Northern Rhodesia, Nyasaland, visitors, born at sea | 5.5 | 4.8 | 27 | 24 |
| Southern Rhodesia | 14.5 | 15.6 | 73 | 78 |
| Union of South Africa | 35.2 | 35.4 | 176 | 177 |
| Totals | 100.0 | 100.0 | 500 | 500 |

$$\chi^2 = 6.381 \quad df = 4 \quad 1 \text{ of } c = >17\% \quad H_o = \text{supported}$$

If the census had been followed, we should have obtained a number of visitors in the sample, but we attempted to avoid this since we were not interested in the attitudes of nonresidents. Table 12 makes the comparison between the population and the test sample.

Chi-square for Table 12 checks out at 6.381, and with four degrees of freedom the level of confidence is a little in excess of 17%. This means that by chance the obtained differences can occur about seventeen times in one hundred samples. At the 17% level of confidence we can still accept the null hypothesis, although the differences here are greater than on other criteria. The disturbing element is the non-Commonwealth group of residents, some of whom are citizens and some not. We needed another fifteen persons born outside the Commonwealth to fill the category correctly.

NATIONAL OR ETHNIC ORIGIN

Our figures on national or ethnic origin cannot be compared with the census data. As we mentioned above, the Central African Statistical Office has classified people according to their legal nationality, whereas we classified them according to the ethnic group to which they felt they belonged. Table 13 shows the national or ethnic

TABLE 13. *National or Ethnic Origin of the Test Sample*

| | Sample | |
|---|---|---|
| *Origin* | *% obtained* | *No. obtained* |
| Rhodesian | 1.4 | 7 |
| British, Welsh, and Irish | | |
| British | 2.0 | 10 |
| Welsh | 2.2 | 11 |
| Irish | 2.8 | 14 |
| Others | 7.0 | 35 |
| English | 60.4 | 302 |
| Scottish | 7.8 | 39 |
| South African | 2.4 | 12 |
| Afrikaner | 14.0 | 70 |
| Totals | 100.0 | 500 |

groups with whom individuals in the sample identified. The largest single grouping, those who regarded themselves as English, accounted for 60.4% of the sample; the Afrikaners were next with 14.0%.

LENGTH OF RESIDENCE

It is a common belief that the length of residence in Southern Rhodesia is related to race attitude. It has often been maintained that an immigrant's attitudes become more conservative the longer he lives in the Colony. The data allow us to test this hypothesis. Tables 14 and 15 show the length of residence of persons born inside Southern Rhodesia and those born elsewhere, as determined by the census, and the duration of residence of the persons included in the test sample.

Two points about these tables may be noted. In the census tabulation, a person who was born in Southern Rhodesia but had spent some years away from the country was classified as if he had been resident the whole time. Thus, in Table 14, because all persons under the age of twenty had been excluded from the census figures, there were no individuals born in Southern Rhodesia who had lived there less than twenty years. But in the test sample, four such persons were obtained, and they were tabulated accordingly. Secondly, although we sought to avoid testing visitors, a small number (under 1.0%) had been obtained in the census. To complete the *expected* side of Table 15, these were combined in the 0–4 years grouping on the assumption that visitors would be unlikely to stay longer than this. Table 16 makes the comparison between the length of residence of the total population and the test sample.

TABLE 14. *Length of Residence of Persons Born in Southern Rhodesia*

| Years of residence | Census % obtained | Sample % obtained | Sample No. expected | No. obtained |
|---|---|---|---|---|
| 0– 4 | .0 | .2 | 0 | 1 |
| 5– 9 | .0 | .2 | 0 | 1 |
| 10–19 | .0 | .4 | 0 | 2 |
| 20–29 | 6.4 | 6.6 | 32 | 33 |
| 30–39 | 4.5 | 4.0 | 23 | 20 |
| 40 and above | 3.6 | 4.2 | 18 | 21 |
| Totals | 14.5 | 15.6 | 73 | 78 |

TABLE 15. *Length of Residence of Persons Born outside Southern Rhodesia*

| Years of residence | Census % obtained | Sample % obtained | Sample No. expected | No. obtained |
|---|---|---|---|---|
| 0– 4 (incl. visitors) | 29.5 | 22.2 | 147 | 111 |
| 5– 9 | 24.0 | 20.4 | 120 | 102 |
| 10–19 | 10.5 | 16.4 | 53 | 82 |
| 20–29 | 9.5 | 11.8 | 47 | 59 |
| 30–39 | 6.2 | 6.8 | 31 | 34 |
| 40 and above | 5.8 | 6.8 | 29 | 34 |
| Totals | 85.5 | 84.4 | 427 | 422 |

By reference to the statistics, it can be seen that the test sample differs significantly from the population, and the null hypothesis must be rejected. The mean length of residence of the population over the age of twenty years is 15.8 years, whereas the mean for the test sample is 17.3 years. Thus the sample, on the average, has lived one and a half years longer in Southern Rhodesia than the mean length of residence for the whole population. It can be argued that it is best to err in this direction.

It will be remembered that our model is based on the 1956 census. Although the European population has increased since then, the proportions within the various strata used for the model do not seem to have altered significantly. On the criterion of length of residence, however, there seems to have been a significant alteration. An examination of the census data suggests the reasons. The year of the census also happened to be one of peak immigration, when 17,000 Europeans entered Southern Rhodesia. The number of newcomers has declined steadily since then, and in the first five months of 1959, when the field work was being done, the number of immigrants was about half that in 1956.[1] This means that the reservoir of recent arrivals has become smaller each year, and it is in this category that we obtained our most serious divergence. Another contributing factor was the attempt to exclude from the sample, as visitors, people who had arrived recently and had not decided whether they intended to stay.

TABLE 16. *Length of Residence—a Chi-square Test of the Differences between the Southern Rhodesian Population and the Test Sample*

| Years of residence | Census % obtained | Sample % obtained | Sample No. expected | No. obtained |
|---|---|---|---|---|
| 0– 4 (incl. visitors) | 29.5 | 22.4 | 147 | 112 |
| 5– 9 | 24.0 | 20.6 | 120 | 103 |
| 10–19 | 10.5 | 16.8 | 53 | 84 |
| 20–29 | 15.9 | 18.4 | 79 | 92 |
| 30–39 | 10.7 | 10.8 | 54 | 54 |
| 40 and above | 9.4 | 11.0 | 47 | 55 |
| Totals | 100.0 | 100.0 | 500 | 500 |

$$\chi^2 = 32.374 \quad df = 5 \quad 1 \text{ of } c = <0.1\% \quad H_o = \text{rejected}$$

Data were not available that would have allowed us to construct a fresh sampling model for 1959; but if this had been possible, it seems reasonable to suppose that the fit between the new model and our test sample would have been closer.

OCCUPATION

Like the census, the test sample can be divided into two broad occupational groupings, the economically active and the economically inactive. In the sample, the economically active grouping comprises persons over the age of twenty who are normally in wage employment. Individuals temporarily out of work because of unemployment or illness have been counted as economically active. The economically inactive are the remainder and consist of persons engaged in home duties, retired persons, invalids, and so on.

Apart from the broad categories, the list of occupations used for coding the 1956 census is too long to be reproduced here, and it is sufficient to say that we followed it exactly. A clear distinction was made between the occupation of a person and the industry in which he worked. The occupational classification was determined by the nature of the work, e.g., carpentry, bricklaying, typing, and so on, irrespective of the industry in which one worked. But in the industrial classification, a single type of industry contains people of many occupations. For example, in the mining industry there are carpenters, typists, lorry drivers, and others in addition to miners. Following the census procedure, we classified by both occupation and industry. Tables 17 and 18 show the occupations of the sample analyzed by sex, and Table 19 combines them for a test of goodness of fit with the total population.

TABLE 17. *Male Occupations*

| Occupation | Census % obtained | Sample % obtained | Sample No. expected | No. obtained |
|---|---|---|---|---|
| Professional and technical | 6.7 | 8.6 | 33 | 43 |
| Managerial, admin., and clerical | 13.9 | 15.0 | 70 | 75 |
| Farmers, hunters, and lumbermen | 6.2 | 6.6 | 31 | 33 |
| Economically inactive and unstated | 3.6 | 3.4 | 18 | 17 |
| Others | | | | |
| Sales workers | 2.4 | 3.4 | 12 | 17 |
| Operating transport workers | 1.3 | 1.6 | 7 | 8 |
| Foremen and skilled | 7.6 | 6.2 | 38 | 31 |
| Service workers | 2.1 | 1.4 | 11 | 7 |
| Mine and quarry workers | 1.1 | .8 | 5 | 4 |
| Craftsmen | 7.6 | 6.8 | 38 | 34 |
| Totals | 52.5 | 53.8 | 263 | 269 |

TABLE 18. *Female Occupations*

| Occupation | Census % obtained | Sample % obtained | Sample No. expected | No. obtained |
|---|---|---|---|---|
| Professional and technical | 3.7 | 5.0 | 19 | 25 |
| Managerial, admin., and clerical | 9.9 | 8.4 | 50 | 42 |
| Farmers, hunters, and lumbermen | .3 | .4 | 1 | 2 |
| Economically inactive and unstated | 29.9 | 30.6 | 150 | 153 |
| Others | | | | |
| Sales workers | 2.1 | .6 | 10 | 3 |
| Operating transport workers | 0.0 | 0.0 | 0 | 0 |
| Foremen and skilled | .3 | .2 | 1 | 1 |
| Service workers | 1.1 | .6 | 5 | 3 |
| Mine and quarry workers | 0.0 | 0.0 | 0 | 0 |
| Craftsmen | .2 | .4 | 1 | 2 |
| Totals | 47.5 | 46.2 | 237 | 231 |

TABLE 19. *Occupation—a Chi-square Test of the Differences between the Southern Rhodesian Population and the Test Sample*

| Occupation | Census % obtained | Sample % obtained | Sample No. expected | No. obtained |
|---|---|---|---|---|
| Professional and technical | 10.4 | 13.6 | 52 | 68 |
| Managerial, admin., and clerical | 23.8 | 23.4 | 120 | 117 |
| Farmers, hunters, and lumbermen | 6.5 | 7.0 | 32 | 35 |
| Economically inactive and unstated | 33.5 | 34.0 | 168 | 170 |
| Others | | | | |
|   Sales workers | 4.5 | 4.0 | 22 | 20 |
|   Operating transport workers | 1.3 | 1.6 | 7 | 8 |
|   Foremen and skilled | 7.9 | 6.4 | 39 | 32 |
|   Service workers | 3.2 | 2.0 | 16 | 10 |
|   Mine and quarry workers | 1.1 | .8 | 5 | 4 |
| Craftsmen | 7.8 | 7.2 | 39 | 36 |
| Totals | 100.0 | 100.0 | 500 | 500 |

$$\chi^2 = 9.565 \quad df = 9 \quad 1 \text{ of } c = >30\% \quad H_o = \text{supported}$$

The tables need little discussion. Chi-square is small and the differences between population and test sample can arise by chance over thirty times in one hundred samplings. Accordingly the null hypothesis that the population and the sample are not significantly different can be retained.

TYPE OF INDUSTRY

One or two rules for the classification of industries may be noted. Establishments were classified by the character of the industry and not by the kind of ownership; thus no account was taken of the fact that similar establishments were operated by a government authority or by private enterprise. Mixed units were classified by the principal product made or handled, or the service rendered.

Economically inactive persons were allocated to the industry on which they were dependent. Thus a farmer and his wife, the latter being engaged solely in home duties, were both classified under the heading of agriculture. Where both husband and wife were working, each was coded separately in terms of industry. Table 20 collates the data from census and sample, and shows that the differences between them are not significant. The null hypothesis is supported at a high level of confidence, and it is safe to infer that the sample adequately represents the industrial distribution of the population.

TABLE 20. *Type of Industry or Business—a Chi-square Test of the Differences between the Southern Rhodesian Population and the Test Sample*

| Industry or business | Census % obtained | Sample % obtained | Sample No. expected | No. obtained |
|---|---|---|---|---|
| Govt. and business services | 20.0 | 19.0 | 100 | 95 |
| Industry unstated and economically inactive | 9.8 | 8.6 | 49 | 43 |
| Transport and communications | 9.0 | 10.2 | 45 | 51 |
| Mining and quarrying | 4.4 | 5.6 | 22 | 28 |
| Commerce | 20.0 | 19.8 | 100 | 99 |
| Construction | 10.4 | 10.0 | 52 | 50 |
| Agriculture, forestry, and fishing | 11.0 | 11.8 | 55 | 59 |
| Manufact. and repair; elect., water, and sanitary services | 15.4 | 15.0 | 77 | 75 |
| Totals | 100.0 | 100.0 | 500 | 500 |

$\chi^2 = 3.851$   df $= 7$   1 of c $= >70\%$   $H_o =$ supported

INCOME

The sample and census figures on incomes are not exactly comparable. The census has reported data for the year 1955, whereas the respondents in the sample were asked to indicate their incomes for 1958. During the three intervening years, the average annual earning for Europeans employed in Southern Rhodesia rose from £903 to £1016, an increase of £113.[2] Since these figures concern *all* economically active people, however, it is necessary to shift attention to those twenty years or older.

Data provided by the Central African Statistical Office indicate that workers twenty years old and above in 1955 had an average income of £1048. Assuming they had the same increase of £113 during the three-year interval, their mean earnings in 1958 would be £1161. In our sample, however, the mean figure obtained was £1313, an excess of £152 over what was expected.

It is possible that the post-census rise in the average income has been greater among persons above than below the age of twenty. In June 1956, a monthly quota of 2,400 was placed upon European immigration—into the entire Federation—and entry was made more selective. This was done partly to admit only those Europeans who would be unlikely to gravitate into occupations increasingly being filled by Africans. It is difficult to determine whether the new policy of selective immigration has had much effect thus far. But if it has, fewer Europeans would be taking jobs at the lower end of the salary range.

Table 21 shows the influence of these points on incomes in 1955 and 1958. It can be seen that the number of persons earning under £600 in 1958 is less than expected, whereas above £600 the proportion obtained is greater than in 1955. The trend, therefore, is in the expected direction, but it exceeds what can be assumed to be the average mean income for 1958. Unfortunately, there is no readily available method that would allow us to gauge the accuracy of the obtained data. But inasmuch as income is related to occupation, and the sample fits well on this latter criterion, we have assumed that our data on income are not too wide of the mark.

TABLE 21. *Distribution of Income in 1955 and 1958*

| Income in £ | Census % obtained | Sample % obtained | Sample No. expected | No. obtained |
|---|---|---|---|---|
| Nil | 30.4 | 29.6 | 152 | 148 |
| 1– 299 | 8.8 | 2.8 | 44 | 14 |
| 300– 599 | 13.2 | 6.6 | 66 | 33 |
| 600– 899 | 14.2 | 14.8 | 71 | 74 |
| 900–1199 | 15.2 | 17.2 | 76 | 86 |
| 1200–1499 | 7.4 | 13.8 | 37 | 69 |
| 1500–1799 | 2.4 | 6.4 | 12 | 32 |
| 1800 and above | 6.6 | 8.8 | 33 | 44 |
| Not stated | 1.8 | .0 | 9 | 0 |
| Totals | 100.0 | 100.0 | 500 | 500 |

EDUCATION

There are no available figures to show the length of schooling of the European population of Southern Rhodesia. Children in the Colony commence primary school in the year when they become six and must continue until they reach fifteen, a total of at least ten years. It is noteworthy that something in excess of 11.2% in the past have received less schooling than the present statutory requirement. Our findings are gathered together in Table 22.

TABLE 22. *Length of Schooling of the Test Sample*

| Years | Sample % obtained | No. obtained |
|---|---|---|
| 0– 8 | 11.2 | 56 |
| 9–10 | 30.0 | 150 |
| 11–12 | 33.0 | 165 |
| 13–14 | 12.0 | 60 |
| 15–16 | 8.0 | 40 |
| 17 and above | 5.8 | 29 |
| Totals | 100.0 | 500 |

If our figures are representative of the population, then 58.8% have received an education in excess of that now required by law. Reports from the Ministry of Education show that there is a growing tendency for European children to continue their schooling after the age of fifteen years.[3]

RELIGIOUS AFFILIATION OR PREFERENCE

The religous affilations or preferences of the test sample have been grouped according to the census classification. Under the Anglican, Presbyterian, Dutch Reformed, and Methodist churches are a number of subvarieties that have not been analyzed separately. For example, included under the Dutch Reformed church are the Nederuits Gereformeerde Kerk, the Gereformeerde Kerk van Zuid Afrika, and the Hervormde Kerk. A large number of persons in other denominations of small numerical strength have also been grouped together. The one common element they share is that they are non-Roman Catholic. The expected and obtained numbers for each religious grouping are shown in Table 23.

TABLE 23. *Religious Affiliation or Preference—a Chi-square Test of the Differences between the Southern Rhodesian Population and the Test Sample*

| Affiliation or preference | Census % obtained | Sample % obtained | Sample No. expected | No. obtained |
|---|---|---|---|---|
| No affiliation | 4.8 | 5.2 | 24 | 26 |
| Roman Catholic | 11.8 | 11.6 | 59 | 58 |
| Other Christian | 7.2 | 6.6 | 36 | 33 |
| Anglican | 40.8 | 38.8 | 204 | 194 |
| Jewish | 3.2 | 3.4 | 16 | 17 |
| Presbyterian | 12.4 | 14.4 | 62 | 72 |
| Methodist | 8.8 | 10.6 | 44 | 53 |
| Dutch Reformed | 11.0 | 9.4 | 55 | 47 |
| Totals | 100.0 | 100.0 | 500 | 500 |

$\chi^2 = 5.605$  df $= 7$  1 of c $= >50\%$  $H_o =$ supported

The figures need little comment. The differences between the population and the test sample are not statistically significant. In terms of religious affiliation or preference, then, the sample is a reliable cross-section of the whole population.

POLITICAL PARTY PREFERENCE

As part of the questionnaire, each respondent was asked to state the political party for which he voted at the Federal election in 1958, or the party he preferred if he did not vote or was ineligible to vote. It will be remembered that the sample included persons of twenty years of age, who were under the minimal voting age. But in addition to the age qualification, to become registered as a voter a person must be a British subject who has resided in the territory for a minimum of two years. Furthermore, many otherwise eligible individuals do not take out citizenship in the Federation. Persons from a number of the Commonwealth nations do not lose their original citizenship if they become citizens of the Federation. For example, a British subject from Britain still remains a British subject, and a New Zealand citizen is not obliged to forfeit his New Zealand citizenship. But a citizen of the Union of South Africa must give up his South African citizenship. To the 35% of the sample born in South Africa, this fact was of some significance. Many of them expressed a reluctance to relinquish their Union citizenship in case they wished to return at some later time.

Thus the population twenty years of age and over contained a small proportion who had not reached the voting age, a number who had not resided in Southern Rhodesia long enough to qualify, some who had the necessary residential qualifications but had not taken out citizenship, a small percentage of foreigners, and under 1.0% who were visitors.

TABLE 24. *Political Party Preferences at the Federal Elections, 1958—a Chi-square Test of the Differences between the Southern Rhodesian Population and the Test Sample*

| Preference | Election returns % obtained | Sample % obtained | Sample No. expected | No. obtained |
|---|---|---|---|---|
| Constitution | 1.1 | 1.0 | 5 | 5 |
| United Federal | 58.7 | 60.8 | 281 | 290 |
| Dominion | 37.8 | 36.7 | 181 | 177 |
| Other | 2.4 | 1.5 | 12 | 7 |
|   Confederate | (0.1) | (1.5) | (1) | (7) |
|   Independent | (2.3) | (0.0) | (11) | (0) |
| Totals | 100.0 | 100.0 | 479 | 479 |
| Persons with unspecified preferences | | | | 21 |

$$\chi^2 = 2.459 \quad df = 3 \quad 1 \text{ of } c = >40\% \quad H_o = \text{supported}$$

In a previous study of political attitudes, Rogers (1959) has demonstrated that the supporters of the different political parties of Southern Rhodesia display, on the average, significantly different attitudes about the Africans. Thus it was necessary, if we wished to gain an accurate picture of the European attitudes of the Colony, to ensure that the test sample represented the political preferences of the population. Of course, an assumption was involved that the nonvoting population would be distributed by party preference in the same proportions as the voting population. Although this assumption has not been checked, it was necessary to make it. The election returns shown in Table 24 were those of the voting population of Southern Rhodesia in the Federal elections of 1958.

Twenty-one persons in the sample did not specify their party preference, so they have not been included in the chi-square test of significance. Statistically, the fit between expected and obtained frequencies is a good one, with the null hypothesis supported at over the 40% level of confidence. For the sample, another four preferences were needed to fill the Dominion party category exactly, but these were compensated by the inclusion of seven Confederate party preferences instead of the one that was expected on the basis of the election. It has been postulated frequently that the Confederate party is more conservative than the other parties on matters affecting the Africans. Eleven preferences for independent candidates should have been included in the sample, but none were found in the course of fieldwork.

A sampling model has been constructed from the 1956 census, and stratified random sampling has been used to equate the test sample with the model. Within eight of the stratification areas, differences between model and sample are not statistically significant; within four others there are no comparable data; and within one—length of residence—the test sample differs significantly from the population. All of this evidence is pulled together in Table 25 for quick reference.

TABLE 25. *Summary of the Chi-square Tests within Each of the Stratification Areas*

| Area of stratification | $\chi^2$ | Degrees of freedom | Level of confidence | Null hypothesis |
|---|---|---|---|---|
| 1. Sex | .289 | 1 | >50% | supported |
| 2. Age | 3.009 | 6 | >80% | supported |
| 3. Community of residence | *No comparable data* | | | |
| 4. Census district | .021 | 3 | >99% | supported |
| 5. Country of birth | 6.381 | 4 | >17% | supported |
| 6. National or ethnic origin | *No comparable data* | | | |
| 7. Length of residence | 32.374 | 5 | <0.1% | rejected |
| 8. Occupation | 9.565 | 9 | >30% | supported |
| 9. Type of industry or business | 3.851 | 7 | >70% | supported |
| 10. Income | *No comparable data* | | | |
| 11. Length of schooling | *No comparable data* | | | |
| 12. Religious affiliation | 5.605 | 7 | >50% | supported |
| 13. Political party preference | 2.459 | 3 | >40% | supported |

Although the European population of Southern Rhodesia rose from 177,124 in June of 1956 to an estimated 215,000 in mid-1959, it seems that the proportions within most of our subpopulations have not changed significantly, or at least significant differences were not reflected in the sampling. The exception occurs with length of residence, the reason being the reduced rate of immigration since 1956. The average length of residence of the test sample is one and a half years longer than expected on the basis of the census returns.

Summing up, the evidence lends support to the hypothesis that the test sample is a microcosm of the European population of Southern Rhodesia, and that the race attitudes measured in the one are an expression of those to be found in the other.

# 6

## THE SAMPLING TASK

With a questionnaire constructed, the interview techniques decided upon, and a model of the Southern Rhodesian population designed, the next task was to undertake the sampling against which the hypotheses could be tested. This was carried out between February and May of 1959 and took us into the high veld and low veld, town and village, farm and factory throughout the Colony.

### THE FIELDWORKERS

Throughout the months of testing and interviewing, there were always at least two fieldworkers continuously on the job, and at times there were four persons working full-time. In addition to the full-time personnel, twenty graduates who had studied at the University College of Rhodesia and Nyasaland gave some assistance in locating cases. All of them had previously taken part in the construction of attitude scales and assisted in sampling for their standardization, so they were familiar with this type of work.

### THE CONTROL OF TESTING CONDITIONS

It is hardly possible to describe all of the testing conditions we attempted to standardize and control, but the major ones are outlined below. These points were made both orally and in a written "Note to persons answering the Questionnaire," reproduced in Appendix A.

THE PURPOSE OF THE STUDY

When a person had been contacted, a first step was to give the reason for the visit and the purpose of the study. In our "Note" it was stated: "The *purpose* of this study is to secure a valid cross-section of European attitudes towards the different treatment of Africans, and the use of public and private facilities in Southern Rhodesia. There has never previously been a serious, scientific attempt to discover what these attitudes are. The results should be of value to all Rhodesians; to help us to understand our country better, the social attitudes that we hold, and the reasons for them. . . . This study, the first ever made in Southern Rhodesia as a whole, should help to dispel inaccurate assessments of opinion which Rhodesians and foreign visitors have made. It will provide statistically reliable information, where none has existed before." These purposes were illustrated more fully orally, and questions were answered.

SPONSORSHIP

It was stressed that the study was part of a research program conceived at—not by—the University College of Rhodesia and Nyasaland, and was being carried out within the traditional freedom of the University. It was made as clear as possible that the study had its genesis in Southern Rhodesia, and that it was supported with funds from the University.

THE SAMPLING MODEL

A few examples of the sampling model were given to illustrate why we were testing in the more remote areas of the Colony, and why a considerable amount of personal information was necessary if we were to avoid biases in sampling.

CONFIDENCE OF THE RECORD

Each respondent was assured, both orally and in writing, that his questionnaire responses, the personal data, and the interview material would be held in the strictest confidence, although collectively the results would be published. A space was provided on the questionnaire for the respondent to give his name if he wished, but it was stressed that this was not necessary.

There is some evidence to show that anonymity makes no difference in the responses to an attitude test. For example, in a study done with college students, Ash and Abramson (1952) have demonstrated that verbally expressed attitudes, as recorded on scales measuring ethnocentrism, political-economic conservatism, and anti-Negro prejudice, were not biased in either a more "pro" or more "anti" direction as a result of the subjects being required to sign their names.

### AVOIDING INTERVIEWER BIAS

All interviewers were carefully briefed to make no value judgments on the statements in the questionnaire or the responses of the individuals tested. Throughout the construction of the questionnaire we avoided any commitment on moral standards, and the importance of this in testing was appreciated. Naturally, our subjects were not discouraged from making value judgments, but care was taken to ensure that the valuations were theirs and not ours. We sought only to establish what Maccoby and Maccoby (1954) call an atmosphere of "friendly permissiveness." The effects of interviewer bias are well known. For example, Katz (1942) found that white-collar and working-class interviewers obtained different results when gathering data among lower-income groups. They picked up different degrees of conservative attitudes from samples of the working class, even though the samples were similar in composition. Cantril's (1944) finding is not dissimilar, although he observes that under certain conditions the biases of interviewers tend to cancel out. Being aware of the possible effects of interviewer bias, we endeavored to keep it at a minimum.

The effect of bias against the interviewer, a rather different matter, is discussed later in this chapter.

## METHODS OF COLLECTING THE DATA

### THE QUESTIONNAIRE

All the questionnaires were distributed personally, and no contacts were made by mail. In a large number of cases, the interviewers followed the "deliberative technique" (Hyman, 1955) of collecting the questionnaires a day or two after they had been distributed. This technique assumes that there is an increase in validity and in the rate of cooperation when respondents are granted sufficient time to reflect upon the items in the questionnaire before answering.

### STATEMENTS WRITTEN ON THE QUESTIONNAIRE

Besides scoring the questionnaire, each individual was invited to state the reasons for his responses and to indicate what proposals, modifications, or qualifications he would like to make about certain laws or customs. These comments were generally written alongside the statements to which they referred, or on the back of the answer sheet.

### SEPARATE STATEMENTS OF ATTITUDE

In addition to the comments given on specific items, individuals of all attitudinal persuasions volunteered to write separate statements showing, as far as possible, how their convictions had been molded, and how these might have been affected by the "Emergency" (described later in this chapter). A considerable number expressed opinions on the relations that might exist between Africans and Europeans in the future.

### THE INTERVIEW

Wherever it was possible, the questionnaire was supplemented by an informal, unstructured interview. This occurred when delivering or collecting the schedule, and the data were recorded immediately afterward by the interviewer. The value of the interview for verifying the findings of the test situation has been sketched in Chapter 4

## INFLUENCES WITHIN THE TESTING SITUATION

Within the social sciences, one has to aim at minimizing the influences which may affect the quality of a response, and to keep the conditions of measurement as rigorously controlled as possible. But even when this is done, experiments in the social sciences usually do not have the precision of those conducted in the physical sciences Hypotheses are seldom as parsimonious, deductions are seldom as secure, and the elements disturbing the variables under observation are generally less measurable. However, it is essential that the disturbing elements be recognized and some weight given to them if we are to assess the over-all validity and reliability of the investigation Both these latter terms are to some extent statistical, and before examining them in more detail it is best to mention the influences we observed, and appraise the extent to which they might, collectively, have affected the investigation.

### IMPERFECTIONS IN THE SAMPLE

*Refusals.* This type of imperfection, one that can introduce systematic error into a sample, is examined carefully in a number of studies of which a few will be reviewed. Stanton (1939), in a straightforward inquiry into the possession and use of classroom radio facilities, found that the information gained from those who mailed back his questionnaire was different from that of the nonreturning group and, therefore, not representative. Another questionnaire study, by Shuttleworth (1941), on the incidence of unemployment among college alumni, reveals different statistics for early and later returns. These differences could have resulted from chance factors in sampling, but Shuttleworth concludes that the final validation would have to be against complete returns. Similar conclusions are reported by Deming (1945) and Reuss (1943). It should be noted that the investigations just cited refer to the bias created through failing to respond to a questionnaire rather than refusing to respond. People fail to respond for many reasons that do not constitute refusal.

A method of minimizing bias is suggested by Clausen and Ford (1947). They suggest that an investigator should take particular care to reduce to a minimum the size of the nonresponding group in a study. A reason for this is furnished by Hilgard and Payne (1944) when reporting on consumer research surveys. They show that "people easily found at home on the first call differ significantly from those found at home only after repeated calls."

Turning to the present study, we kept a check on refusals as distinct from nonresponses, and they amounted to under 5% of the total number contacted. The reasons for refusal were varied. Some individuals said they were civil servants and not permitted to express opinions on matters that might appear to be political; others, from the politically conservative groups, declined because they believed the questionnaire to have "liberal" bias; a third lot—identifiable as "liberal"—refused on the ground that differential treatment could best be eliminated by keeping it out of the spotlight of research. Our small percentage of refusals compares favorably with other studies, and is much more satisfactory than many. Keeping in mind the point made by Hilgard and Payne, we revisited many households several times to deliver questionnaires, and even more times to collect them. It is arguable that the refusals, as a group, might have given responses different from those who did not refuse; but it is our assumption that their significance would have been diminished if they could have been rolled into the larger, obtained sample. But it has not been possible to test this assumption.

*Health.* Because of ill-health and general feebleness through old age, eight persons were unable to manage the questionnaire.

*Failure to Return the Questionnaire.* A number of people had not completed the questionnaire when the fieldworker returned to collect it. They were given stamped and addressed envelopes and asked to return it directly to the College. In most cases this was done, but a few failed to do so for reasons we cannot determine. However, inasmuch as we had had partial interviews with all of them, something was known of their social characteristics and race attitudes. It was only in terms of political conservatism that the individuals of this category appeared to be different from the others interviewed and tested.

*Incomplete Personal Data.* Three completed forms had to be rejected because the personal data requested on the answer sheet had not been furnished.

*Language Difficulties.* Two old pioneers in a rural district could not read English and were therefore unable to complete the questionnaire unaided. The interviewer read it to them and marked their responses in the appropriate places.

*The Omission of a Single Statement.* From time to time, a questionnaire was returned in which one or more of the statements had not been answered. A variety of reasons were given for this. On some statements individuals could not make up their minds; on others, a response was not given because the statement was no longer true; on still others, individuals did not care whether the practice was continued or discontinued. The first step was to encourage individuals to make a choice, but where this was not achieved, the omissions were later filled by us. To facilitate the calculation of tetrachoric correlations, on which the factor analysis in Chapter 8 is based, it was essential that all items be scored.

If, for example, the omitted item had been classified as belonging to the category of public facilities, the scores on all other items in that category were averaged and the blank was assigned the score nearest to this average. A number of *t* tests were made of the differences between the scores on the items originally answered and the total number of items, including those scored by the method just described. In no cases were the differences significant, and it seemed justifiable to assume that no systematic biases had been built in in this way. Of the total number of items in the study (500 x 66), just over 1% had to be handled in this manner.

*Dual Responses.* Occasionally an item embraced a dual response. This occurred when an individual made a distinction between different classes of Africans, stating that he would act differently toward them, or where an individual qualified a statement by saying that time could reduce the cultural gap between Africans and Europeans, thus bringing about a change in behavior. The response that indicated the individual's current attitude, or his attitude about most Africans, was the one used. Where this decision could not be made, the item was scored as if the response had been omitted.

*Bias toward the Interviewer.* At the beginning of the survey, before it was widely known that the study had its genesis in Southern Rhodesia, the fact that two of the interviewers had come from the United States occasioned some anti-American comment in the press. These comments, and a press editorial related to them, are reproduced, without comment by us, in Appendix C. Not all of the press comment was unfavorable, as other extracts show. It can be stated firmly, however, that the great majority of persons cooperated as soon as the reasons for the study, and its sponsorship, were made clear.

*Attitude toward the College.* The fact that the study was being undertaken by staff from the University College excited some suspicion. As a nonracial institution, the College was felt by some to constitute a threat to other institutions which were segregated, and to customs and behavior based on racial separation. Again, to others, research into attitudes toward Africans was interpreted as an attack on the status of Europeans in the Colony, and on the intentions of the Southern Rhodesian Government. Interestingly, for the latter reason, we obtained much cooperation from the Afrikaans-speaking section of the population. At all times we listened to the apprehensions of the people and stressed that our task was to measure facts, to gain more insight than hitherto possible into their problems, and to see how far these problems were shared by other nations or were unique to Southern Rhodesia.

*The "Emergency" in Southern Rhodesia.* Testing for the study commenced in February of 1959 and proceeded until February 26th when, as a result of the activities of the African National Congresses, the Governor of Southern Rhodesia proclaimed a State of Emergency. This was unfortunate from the viewpoint of the survey. Attitudes that had been stable appeared, in some cases, to have gone into a state of flux. The uncertainty was confirmed from other sources too, such as letters to the newspapers, statements in the Southern Rhodesian Legislative Assembly, and the reactions of the many civic and local bodies. On February 26th, the Prime Minister of Southern Rhodesia appealed to all people to carry on as normal, and conditions gradually appeared to become stabilized again. We continued to interview people in an endeavor to determine when attitudes had returned to "normal," and after a lapse of five weeks testing recommenced. Our decision, while taken carefully and not without evidence, is hardly capable of experimental verification. It is possible to compare results obtained in one district before the Emergency with those obtained from another during the Emergency, but this does not constitute objective proof as the attitudes may have been different in any case.

What can be stated is that over 70% of the data for the sample were obtained after the recommencement of testing, so that our findings may be more representative of the Emergency period. It is possible that the Emergency affected primarily the items concerned with the police, the franchise, firearms, and African nationalism, but our evidence does not give support to this idea. The relation of the Emergency to attitudes will be discussed further in Chapters 9 and 19.

*Sampling Errors.* The procedures adopted to control the sampling, to reduce chance fluctuations and biases, have been described in Chapter 5.

IMPERFECTIONS IN THE QUESTIONNAIRE

Despite the fact that the statements in the questionnaire were gathered by a panel of researchers (both European and African), scrutinized by experts, and tried out in a number of dummy runs, imperfections were not avoided. Each type of imperfection was mentioned by only a few people, however, with the majority finding the questionnaire manageable. The main flaws, as pinpointed by the survey, are listed.

*Equivocality.* A number of the statements appeared equivocal and were misunderstood. Such a statement was the one that read: "Many Africans are required to pay relatively higher costs in travelling to work than are Europeans, as they often must live at some distance from their places of employment." In this are embedded notions of the different levels of income of the Europeans and Africans, the ratio of transport costs to income, and the influence of the Land Apportionment Act. These various factors could not always be unraveled.

*Emotive Terms.* Throughout the questionnaire we used the term "African." To some of those who habitually use the term "Kaffir" (literally, "unbeliever" in Arabic), "munt," "native," "Bantu," or "Black," this was taken as evidence of bias against Europeans. But the term African was adopted for the study because it seemed less open to misinterpretation than any of the other labels; this assumption may not be justified.

*Length.* To some persons, the questionnaire was too long, and discouraged a consistent approach to it.

*Balance in Tone.* Other respondents stated that a greater balance in tone would have been achieved if some mention had been made, for example, of the free services available only to Africans.

*Leading Statements*. In the "Note to persons answering the Questionnaire," we cited a number of reasons commonly given for the differential treatment of Europeans and Africans. The fact that these same reasons were often quoted back to us suggested that their frequency might have been increased by drawing attention to them. However, we felt they were necessary for the establishment of rapport between interviewer and respondent.

## THE DISSEMINATION OF KNOWLEDGE

Since attitudes are often latent, it was not unusual for respondents to comment that they had never given much thought to many of the items in the questionnaire. Comments such as "I didn't realize there were so many problems," and "I didn't know that many of these discriminations existed" were not uncommon. It was pointed out, in response, that the incidence of many of the examples could not be determined, and that changes had rendered some of the statements no longer true. Thus, a side effect of the study was to spread knowledge of the extent of differential treatment.

Another subsidiary effect was to give correct information on a number of subjects on which previous information had been incorrect or hazy. For example, the impressions that Europeans had concerning the size of African farms, the cross-racial sexual privileges that applied only for European men, and the extent of trade training facilities for Africans were often wide of the true mark.

## Marking and Coding the Data

### MARKING

The sixty-six items of the questionnaire were assigned values according to the scoring system described in Chapter 4. The marking was checked for accuracy by an independent panel.

### CODING OF PERSONAL DATA

The personal data recorded on the answer sheets were coded so that they could be punched into a standard Hollerith card. It is hardly necessary to detail the system of coding. Just as we utilized the census returns for constructing a sampling model, so, in principle, we followed the census system of coding.[1] But whereas the Statistical Office often used several columns, we found it necessary for reasons of space to telescope data from some of the stratification areas so that they could be handled on a single Hollerith column. For example, census officials used three columns to code occupations as against our use of only one. However, quite apart from considerations of space, a breakdown of the detailed data in the census would have been inappropriate for a study involving 500 people.

PUNCHING THE CODES

A data sheet was prepared for each questionnaire. Onto it were transferred the values for the sixty-six statements, general attitudes, and the codes for the thirteen items of personal information. A data sheet was used rather than the original answer sheet to reduce the possibility of punching errors, and to keep responses confidential. Then the information from the 500 new data sheets was punched onto Hollerith cards, utilizing a full eighty columns (sixty-six plus fourteen). The punches on each card were verified electronically, as is usual. The cards were numbered serially, and on each the individual's mean score for all statements was recorded.

These steps taken, the calculations and analyses could begin. All the major tabulations and calculations were done on Hollerith machines.

TEST RELIABILITY

The term "reliability" has a mathematical definition that need not concern us here; as an operational concept, it refers to the consistency with which measures on a scale can differentiate the qualities being assessed. As Guilford (1956) stresses, it is the measurements that have the property of reliability rather than the measuring instrument, because reliability depends upon the sample under investigation as well as upon the measuring rod. Thus, when we speak of reliability, we refer to a certain test applied to a certain sample of the population under certain conditions. We have described the test, the sample, and the conditions under which the testing took place. Given these three variables, and the imperfections in each, our task is to determine the degree of reliability of the measures.

However, the concept must be examined further because there are many types of reliability and each has to be calculated and interpreted differently (Cronbach, 1947). It is necessary to glance at the main types to determine which might be applicable to the present study.

TYPES OF RELIABILITY COEFFICIENTS

The internal consistency of a test can be calculated by correlating the scores on the odd-numbered items of the test with those on the even-numbered. This measure of reliability—a split-half method—is more applicable where the test is factorially homogeneous, that is, where it measures only one trait or quality. From evidence to be presented in Chapter 8, we know that one general factor accounts for the great bulk of the variance on the questionnaire. This is sufficient reason, we consider, for allowing us to use two different estimates of internal consistency, namely, those achieved through inter-item correlation, and factor analysis.

Reliability coefficients can also be obtained by correlating the alternate forms of a test. This type cannot be used in the present case, however, as only one form of test was constructed.

The method of test-retest reliability, which is meaningful for heterogeneous tests, was given some consideration. This reliability can be calculated when the same test (or its equivalent) is readministered to the test sample, and when the scores obtained on the two occasions are correlated. Two reasons led us to reject this method, one practical and the other theoretical. In the first place, because of the time-consuming nature of the questionnaire and the scatter of our sample, it was not considered practicable. Secondly, where a considerable period of time elapses between the two administrations of a test, there is the chance that the function being measured may have altered, and yet the test could still possess high reliability of other types. This phenomenon of "function fluctuation" has been treated in full by Thouless (1936).

TEST RELIABILITY THROUGH INTER-ITEM CORRELATION

As we have noted, two variants of internal consistency are available for estimating the reliability of a test, or, more strictly, the measures derived from a test. One of these involves inter-correlating the items of the test, deriving an average correlation for them all, and then correcting the average figure by means of the Spearman-Brown formula to arrive at the reliability of the whole scale. This method is excessively time-consuming and is not usually employed unless the inter-item correlations are to be employed for some purpose other than estimating reliability. In this study, they are to be used for a factor analysis of the scale. The steps are described in brief so that they can be retraced by others.

With the system of scoring used in this study, it was necessary to use some form of tetrachoric r. The number of inter-item correlations involved would also have precluded any other method. As a first step, we telescoped the data into two categories—"maintain" and "discontinue"—and then prepared a four-celled table for each of the 2,145 pairs of items so that Thurstone's computing diagrams could be employed. After this, the entries in the four-celled tables were reduced to proportions of 1.00. Observing Guilford's (1956) strictures, we did not consider further any table in which one part of a dichotomized variable showed a proportion of less than .05. Splits as lopsided as this do not give a satisfactory estimate of linear correlation, and make it difficult to support the assumption that the underlying metric is normal in distribution. By eliminating such tables on statistical grounds, the number of items was reduced to fifty-five.

With the data organized in this manner, it was possible to read off the tetrachoric correlations ($r_t$) from computing diagrams (Chesire, Saffir, and Thurstone, 1933). The 1,485 correlations so obtained were converted into Fisher's (1950) z function and averaged. The average z function was then reconverted to yield a mean correlation of .49. The mean correlation is taken to represent one item, and the reliability of the scale ($r_{tt}$) can be estimated from the fifty-five items retained. This is done by means of a modification of the Spearman-Brown formula:

$$r_{tt} = \frac{n\bar{r}_{ij}}{1 + (n - 1)\,\bar{r}_{ij}}$$

in which n equals the number of items, and $\bar{r}_{ij}$ equals the average correlation of all pairs of items.

From this method, a reliability coefficient of .98 was obtained. This is high, particularly when we note Guilford's (1946) contention that tests with reliabilities of about .80 can be used to advantage. It is true that a few items have been dropped for statistical reasons, but our estimate of reliability would have been impaired rather than improved by their inclusion.

TEST RELIABILITY THROUGH FACTOR ANALYSIS

Another check on the reliability of the scale was possible at the conclusion of the factor analysis reported in Chapter 8. It is convenient to include it here as corroborating evidence.

The method bases its estimate of reliability on the test communalities ($h^2$). To effect the method, use was made of Thurstone's (1947) theorem: "The communality of a test is always smaller than the reliability except in the limiting case where the specific factor is absent, in which case the communality and the reliability are equal." If one turns to the section on factor analysis, the communalities can be seen: on the basis of the theorem, these were accepted as minimum estimates of reliability ($r_{tt}$). Following Guilford's (1956) rationale, we then calculated an index of reliability ($r_{t\infty} = \sqrt{r_{tt}}$) from each of the communalities. These can be interpreted as minimal correlations between the item scores and what they actually measure, in effect, the hypothetical test criterion. The indices of reliability ranged from .58 to .93, an average of .79. This average for the scale is good, particularly when one appreciates that the true value may be considerably higher. The reliability coefficient derived from the inter-item correlations indicates that it is.

The checks on reliability were made to see whether imperfections in sampling and the questionnaire, described earlier, impaired the capacity of the measures to differentiate people on their social attitudes. The evidence indicates they did not.

## Test Validity

Put very simply, a test is valid if it measures what it purports to measure. Thus, our test was designed to measure attitudes toward customs and laws that affected Europeans and Africans differently, and it would clearly be invalid if, for example, it measured barometric pressure. But it is no simple matter to determine whether or not a test is valid. Vernon and Parry (1949) describe three main types of validity, and Eysenck (1954) outlines seven different methods by which validity can be assessed. Mention will be made of the methods that seem relevant to this study.

### THE CRITERION OF PERSONAL KNOWLEDGE

Most of the methods mentioned by Eysenck depend on agreement with some external criteria. One of these is personal knowledge of the sample, or some of it. Some seventy persons in the study were known to the fieldworkers, and there was common agreement between the test scores and their known attitudes. Although we have not made a statistical analysis of these data, it can be stated that in no case did a person whose global attitudes we could judge rather securely furnish a test score that was widely different. As Hutchinson (1949) and Segerstedt (1951) have also found, the interviews assisted considerably to validate the scale by showing that it was in fact measuring European attitudes about Africans.

### THE CRITERION OF SELF-RATING

At the end of the answer sheet to the questionnaire, the respondent was asked to rate his general attitude toward Africans on a five-point scale: very unfavorable, unfavorable, neutral, favorable, and very favorable. Following a procedure described by Vernon (1945), a tetrachoric correlation was run between the self-ratings and the total score on the test, the result being a positive coefficient of .57.

There are a number of difficulties attached to the use of self-ratings as an external criterion of validity. These are analyzed succinctly by Vernon (1953). He shows that self-ratings of traits are generally less accurate than the ratings of associates, and that people overrate themselves on traits they considerable to be more desirable or ethical. Something of this overrating was evident in the scatter diagram prepared for the correlation. There was a noticeable tendency for persons whose total scores were on the conservative (maintain) side to rate themselves as neutral in attitude or even favorable. On the other hand, respondents whose scores were on the social-change (discontinue) side were more prone to judge their attitudes as favorable and to place themselves less into the neutral category. Only seven who had scores on the change side of the dimension rated themselves as unfavorable, reasoning that their stand on discontinuing differential practices was dictated by their appreciation of the future rather than by any personal desiderata.

Our correlation of .57 between self-ratings and total scores can be compared with other researches. Ellis (1946) reviews some 380 studies ranging through many areas of personality and concludes that, for the most part, the validity coefficients of questionnaires are low, that is, .40 and less. Again, Vernon (1953) inspects a large number of personality questionnaires, including some of his own, and shows that validity coefficients using the kind of criterion we are discussing usually fall around the .40 and .50 level, although some go higher. In perspective, an obtained coefficient of .57 is probably as good as can be expected in a study of this nature. Our contention is that other modes of validation (to be described) reveal more sharply the power of the scale to differentiate between groups and to make deductions from hypotheses.

THE CRITERION OF KNOWN FACT

This type of criterion is of advantage inasmuch as it allows one to work from a given hypothesis. MacCrone (1937) employed it to study the social distance between various racial groups in the Union. Evidence is presented elsewhere by Rogers (1959) to show that persons who vote for the Dominion party of Southern Rhodesia are significantly more conservative in their attitude about Africans than the supporters of the United Federal party. As an extension of this measured fact, it is consistent to postulate that on our scale there should be differentiation between the political parties, with the supporters of the Dominion party taking a position more in favor of the status quo. The mean scores for each party were calculated and are shown in Table 26.

Use was made of Gosset's *t* distribution to test the difference between the supporters of the two major political parties. It can be seen that the difference of 1.10 on our test scale is highly significant, and the possibility that the difference could have arisen by chance cannot be accepted. This method of hypothetico-deduction forms one of our most forceful reasons for assuming that the test has validity and discriminative power.

It may be noted in passing that the mean scores of the other parties are in the expected direction, but more will be said of this later. The center of gravity of the scores from persons who did not specify their political preference lies closest to the attitude scores of Dominion party supporters. It would seem from this that persons with more conservative attitudes were more reluctant to express their party choice, just as the more conservative tended to overrate in favorableness their attitudes toward Africans.

TABLE 26. *A* t *Test of Differences in Attitude between Supporters of the Major Political Parties in the Federal Election, 1958*

| Party | No. | S.D. | Mean | Difference | t | H₀ |
|---|---|---|---|---|---|---|
| Constitution | 5 | — | 4.84 | | | |
| United Federal | 290 | 1.03 | 2.88 | U.F.-Dom. ⎫ | | |
| Dominion | 177 | .89 | 1.78 | 1.10 ⎬ | 11.81 | rejected |
| Other | | | | | | |
|   Confederate | 7 | — | 1.87 | | | |
|   Unspecified | 21 | .78 | 2.13 | | | |
| Totals | 500 | 1.12 | 2.45 | | | |

FACTORIAL VALIDITY

A type of validity for which Guilford (1956) argues strongly is that which can be demonstrated through factor analysis. He employs a mathematical rationale to demonstrate that the validity of a test is given by its correlation with the test factors, that is, the factor loadings. It is recognized that the factorial method has its limitations, as Rogers (1956) has mentioned, but the representative nature of the sample and the inclusiveness of the test items would appear to make them minimal.

In brief, Vernon's (1947) method is to calculate the variances of the correlations between test and factor (the factor loadings) to arrive at an index of test validity. When this was done for the fifty items retained in the factor analysis, the validities averaged 62.6%, while the best rose to over 80% (see Chapter 8). These figures can be regarded as good, particularly when it is realized that a large number of investigators are able to work with common-factor variance at a considerably lower level (Guilford, 1946). By a judicious selection of the items with the highest loadings, it should be possible to devise a shorter questionnaire for future use, and to augment further its validity.

The task of sampling to fit a model of the community was attended by a number of difficulties and problems. Not the least of these were the imperfections in the testing situation and the questionnaire. An essential part of the study was to determine whether the imperfections had impaired the capacity of the questionnaire to differentiate people in their attitudes about Africans. For this reason, considerable attention was focused on matters of reliability and validity.

It is appreciated that some of the statistical checks on reliability and validity are based on less than the full number of statements in the scale. This was inevitable because of the skewed nature of eleven of the item distributions; they could not be handled by procedures derived from the known properties of the normal curve. Even so, the scale seems to possess adequate power to differentiate between different qualities of attitude, and supporting evidence for this contention flows through the chapters that follow. It seemed clear to us that some items were highly skewed, not because they could not distinguish between people, but because the population was too single-minded for differentiation. Thus, on statement 59, for example, it would hardly have been a failure to differentiate that only twenty-nine persons advocated the admission of Africans to European dance halls. There were practically no differences in attitude for the item to record. In all, we feel justified in proceeding to the further analysis of the test scores.

# 7

## THE DISTRIBUTION AND STRUCTURE OF ATTITUDES

### THE GENERAL FINDINGS

Attitudes, like much psychological, sociological, and biological data, are often *assumed* to be distributed "normally" throughout a given population. Most people will share similar attitudes, and the frequency of attitudes diverging from the mean or average will decrease as either extreme is approached. When plotted graphically, such a distribution results in the well-known unimodal or bell-shaped curve.

In Chapter 4, we described the system we adopted for scoring European attitudes about Africans in Southern Rhodesia. For each item the possible range of scores is from 0 to 6. A person whose mean score is .18, to give an example, displays attitudes that most strongly favor the maintenance of the status quo. An individual whose score is 5.58 thinks it extremely important to discontinue almost every differentiating practice cited in the questionnaire.

Figure 2 portrays the distribution of the mean scores of the entire sample population of 500 Europeans. Seven persons feel emphatically that it is important to maintain virtually every practice or law cited. At the other extreme, no person wants everything to be changed. The highest mean score obtained was 5.58, indicating a very strong desire for discontinuing or changing almost every law and practice that differentiates between Africans and Europeans.

Also shown in Figure 2 is a normal distribution with the same surface area as the sample distribution, but with a mean score of 3.00. This distribution, a mathematical model, is constructed to illustrate the deviation of the European sample from the normal, Gaussian form. The mean or average score for the sample population is 2.45, illustrating that the majority of persons, in their general attitude, are in favor of retaining the status quo rather than changing it. A further

FIGURE 2. *The Obtained and Theoretical Distributions of Mean Attitude Scores* (*N* = *500*)

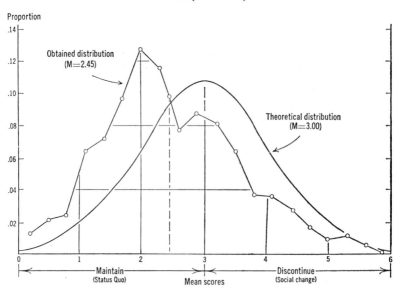

illustration of this fact is revealed through the obtained standard deviation of the mean scores, 1.12. If the obtained distribution were normal—which it is not—then 68.26% of the scores would fall between 1.33 and 3.57. A quick inspection of Figure 2 reveals that within this range the greater proportion of the curve lies within the area of maintaining the status quo. From this finding, it can be educed that the mean scores for the majority of the single statements also show attitudes in favor of the current practices.

## A Chi-square Test of a Normal Distribution Hypothesis

Although the mean for the sample does not coincide with our theoretical center point of 3.00, the obtained distribution could still be approximately normal about its mean value of 2.45. If it is, this will facilitate further deductions about the distribution of European attitudes within Southern Rhodesia.

The obtained distribution of Figure 2 is derived from a sample of 500 people, a mean of 2.45, and a standard deviation of 1.12. Given these data, can the distribution be regarded as significantly different from normal? The hypothesis to be tested is that the distribution of scores can arise by chance from a normally distributed population.

Chi-square may be used to test the hypothesis. The procedure involves comparing the obtained frequencies with the frequencies that can be expected in a normal distribution having the same M, the same $\sigma$, and the same N. The fundamental formula for calculating the expected frequencies is:

$$Y = \frac{N}{\sigma \sqrt{2\pi}} e^{\frac{-x^2}{2\,\sigma^2}}$$

wherein  Y = the expected frequency
          N = the number in the sample
          $\sigma$ = the standard deviation of the distribution
          $\pi$ = 3.1416
          e = 2.718 (the base of the Naperian system of logarithms)
          x = the deviation of a measurement from the mean of the distribution.

Some of the terms in this equation are constants and others can be read from tables. Accordingly, the main computations consist of converting the mid-point of each interval into a standard score (z), finding the height of the ordinate (y) for each z score when read from tables in which N and $\sigma$ are unity, and then employing the derived formula $f_e = \left(\frac{iN}{\sigma}\right)$ y to arrive at the frequency expected for each interval.

The obtained and expected frequencies are then combined into a table, and a chi-square test applied. Chi-square equals 25.86 and, with 14 degrees of freedom (the number in the table), this figure falls at the 3% level of confidence. We are not prepared to accept the null hypothesis ($H_o$) at this level, and conclude that the departure from normality is a significant one which derives from the bias of the population. Furthermore, our sampling includes methods of stratification that should reduce chance fluctuations in distribution, so that $\chi^2$ at the 3% level will in fact indicate a significant divergence of greater magnitude.

## THE RANK ORDER OF STATEMENTS

Turning from the distribution of scores of individuals, we present next the scores for all of the sixty-six statements. If, on the average, the European population scores equally in all the response categories, the mean score obtained for each statement will be the same as the hypothetical mean, 3.00. However, forty-two of the items received scores lower than the mean, while on twenty-four statements the scores were higher than the mean. The scores on the *items* naturally would show the same bias as the scores for the *individuals*. These are simply two parallel methods for examining the same data.

Table 27 presents the sixty-six items included in the questionnaire, gives the mean score for each item, and designates the categories into which they are classified. This classification will be discussed in the next section of the chapter. The mean scores obtained for the individual items range from .41 to 4.83, and the mean of means works out at 2.45, as before. The mean of the standard deviations on the items is 1.87, which is larger than the standard deviation of individual scores, i.e. 1.12. This is because the scores for the items fall only on four points (0,2,4,6), whereas the scores for individuals form a continuous distribution.

The responses show that the Europeans vary widely both in the intensity of their feelings about differentiating laws and customs and in their "policy orientation"—whether these practices ought to be maintained or discontinued. They feel most strongly about maintaining laws and customs that prohibit or reduce intimate and personal contacts with Africans. The items concerned with such opportunities generally receive the lowest scores. In this general context are items dealing with home residence, sexual contacts and marriage, school attendance, the location of businesses, social and recreational facilities, freedom of movement, working under the supervision of an African, the purchase of alcoholic spirits, and the sharing of public facilities in which close physical contacts with Africans can occur.

Europeans feel it important, as indicated by the scores, to equalize sentences for crime, to prohibit sexual contacts between European men and African women, to provide equal but separate educational and vocational training opportunities, to admit Africans to general political meetings, to establish avenues by which Africans can make known their grievances, and to discontinue practices in which Europeans assault Africans or show them little courtesy or respect.

TABLE 27. *European Attitudes about Africans, by Ranked Items*

| Category | Item no. | Statement | S.D. | Mean |
|---|---|---|---|---|
| Legal justice | 61 | Europeans who rape African women sometimes are given lighter sentences than Africans who rape European women. | 1.90 | 4.83 |
| Personal courtesies | 51 | European children generally do not treat African adults with respect. | 1.72 | 4.64 |
| Legal justice | 16 | Africans and Europeans are sometimes not punished equally by the court for the same crimes of violence. | 1.93 | 4.57 |
| African lands | 7 | Many Africans are required to pay relatively higher costs in travelling to work than are Europeans, as they often must live at some distance from their places of employment. | 1.65 | 4.37 |
| Personal courtesies | 14 | Africans are liable to be assaulted by a European employer, whereas European employees are less liable to receive this treatment. | 1.91 | 4.29 |
| Legal justice | 65 | European men may have sex relations with African women without legal penalty, but African men are prohibited by law from having sex relations with European women. | 2.38 | 4.17 |
| Unclassified | 41 | It is more difficult for the Africans in urban areas to find effective and simple means of lodging protests than for Europeans to do so. | 1.91 | 3.91 |
| Unclassified | 28 | From time to time, African voters are refused admission to political meetings open to the general public. | 2.12 | 3.80 |
| Educational opportunities | 9 | Facilities for the training of Africans in the skilled trades and professions are very limited. | 1.96 | 3.78 |
| Educational opportunities | 30 | African children do not receive the same educational opportunities as European children. | 1.96 | 3.77 |
| Educational opportunities | 2 | In general, Africans are not admitted to the technical classes which are an essential part of the apprentice training for a trade. | 2.06 | 3.71 |
| African lands | 38 | African locations are equipped less frequently than European townships with amenities such as tarred roads and electricity. | 1.83 | 3.65 |
| Personal courtesies | 60 | European men and women have on occasion dropped friends when they have discovered them to have non-European ancestors. | 2.13 | 3.62 |
| Educational opportunities | 1 | Africans are not accepted for apprenticeship training for the skilled trades. | 2.10 | 3.57 |
| Personal courtesies | 58 | Africans who question the authority of Europeans often are accused of being 'cheeky' and may be assaulted for such behaviour. | 1.91 | 3.54 |

TABLE 27. *European Attitudes about Africans, by Ranked Items* (cont.)

| Category | Item no. | Statement | S.D. | Mean |
|---|---|---|---|---|
| Personal courtesies | 56 | Generally, Europeans do not treat Africans with as much respect as they do members of their own race. | 1.96 | 3.50 |
| African lands | 5 | No matter how good an African farmer is, under the Land Husbandry Act he cannot obtain more than three standard-sized holdings of land (totalling 18 acres in high rainfall areas). | 2.05 | 3.43 |
| Public facilities A | 50 | There are few opportunities for Africans to participate with or against Europeans in sporting events. | 2.08 | 3.42 |
| Unclassified | 8 | In many instances, Europeans and Africans are not paid the same rates for similar jobs. | 1.63 | 3.36 |
| Personal courtesies | 55 | Europeans generally are served before Africans at shop counters and places of business. | 2.03 | 3.25 |
| Public facilities A | 36 | Most churches do not hold services for multi-racial congregations. | 2.29 | 3.21 |
| Public facilities A | 35 | In many public buildings Africans are not allowed to use lifts. | 2.01 | 3.13 |
| African lands | 19 | Africans in urban areas are not permitted to own land outright, but have up to a 99 year lease, and this only in certain areas. | 2.06 | 3.07 |
| Public facilities A | 3 | Africans may not lawfully buy lottery tickets or bet on horse racing in Southern Rhodesia. | 2.08 | 3.02 |
| Unclassified | 66 | African men have to take more care not to become 'familiar' with European women than do European men with African women. | 2.43 | 2.86 |
| Employment | 10 | Most European trade unions do not accept African members. | 2.13 | 2.82 |
| Personal courtesies | 54 | Africans nearly always are expected to address Europeans as 'Sir,' 'Boss,' 'Master,' or 'Madam,' whereas Europeans usually address Africans as 'Boy' or 'Nanny.' | 1.99 | 2.79 |
| Public facilities A | 42 | In some shops and cafes there is a little window through which Africans are served. | 2.01 | 2.74 |
| Personal courtesies | 53 | Europeans generally do not shake hands with Africans. | 1.96 | 2.66 |
| Public facilities A | 37 | Different entrances are provided for Africans and Europeans in certain shops and banks and in many post offices. | 2.12 | 2.56 |
| Personal courtesies | 52 | Africans normally are expected to stand back and allow Europeans to go first through doorways, into lifts, and so on. | 1.97 | 2.51 |
| Civil order | 27 | African householders living in urban areas have no vote in municipal elections. | 2.06 | 2.49 |
| Employment | 4 | In some businesses and industries only Europeans are employed. | 2.00 | 2.39 |
| European lands | 13 | African organizations cannot rent offices legally in European commercial areas. | 2.05 | 2.39 |

| Category | Item no. | Statement | S.D. | Mean |
|---|---|---|---|---|
| Unclassified | 15 | No provision is made for Africans to serve on juries in Southern Rhodesia. | 2.09 | 2.26 |
| European lands | 33 | Generally there are separate cemeteries for Africans and Europeans. | 1.95 | 2.20 |
| Public facilities A | 40 | At railway stations there are generally separate booking offices for Europeans and Africans. | 2.04 | 2.18 |
| European lands | 6 | The Land Apportionment Act prevents Africans from occupying land for business purposes within the recognized European commercial areas. | 2.06 | 2.10 |
| Civil order | 20 | In general, Africans but not Europeans are forbidden by law to buy alcoholic spirits. | 2.06 | 2.09 |
| Civil order | 25 | Pro-African 'nationalism' is viewed with more suspicion by much of the European community than is pro-European 'nationalism.' | 1.88 | 2.04 |
| Employment | 47 | Africans are not hired often as counter attendants in European shops or businesses. | 1.71 | 1.85 |
| Public facilities B | 31 | Except on specified routes, Africans and Europeans may not ride in the same buses. | 1.86 | 1.79 |
| Employment | 57 | In general, Africans are not placed in charge of Europeans even when equally qualified. | 1.96 | 1.78 |
| Public facilities B | 29 | In some parks there are separate benches for Europeans and Africans. | 1.93 | 1.74 |
| Social facilities | 46 | Many European restaurants and hotels will not accept African clients. | 1.92 | 1.71 |
| Civil order | 17 | African men are obliged by law to carry identity papers, whereas Europeans are not. | 1.84 | 1.70 |
| European lands | 11 | In the main, Africans are prohibited from buying beer and wines from shops in European areas, but must buy beer at the African beer halls or bottle stores. | 1.76 | 1.67 |
| Civil order | 24 | In Southern Rhodesia, Europeans control the election of Africans to the Federal Government, whereas the Africans have virtually no control over the election of Europeans. | 1.89 | 1.58 |
| Social facilities | 45 | European sporting and social clubs are not open to Africans. | 1.85 | 1.58 |
| Social facilities | 48 | Africans generally are not allowed into European theatres. | 1.89 | 1.52 |
| Civil order | 23 | The qualifications for the franchise are such that few Africans have a vote, whereas practically all Europeans are eligible. | 1.75 | 1.44 |
| European lands | 63 | The legal regulations of Southern Rhodesia make it extremely difficult for an African man to live with a European woman to whom he is married legally. | 2.10 | 1.38 |

TABLE 27. *European Attitudes about Africans, by Ranked Items* (cont.)

| Category | Item no. | Statement | S.D. | Mean |
|---|---|---|---|---|
| Public facilities B | 34 | Europeans and Africans are required by law to attend different schools. | 1.63 | 1.28 |
| Public facilities B | 49 | Africans may not try on clothes in most European shops. | 1.67 | 1.24 |
| Civil order | 26 | In the Federal Parliament there are roughly four times as many Europeans as African members, although the European population is about ½₈ the size of the African population. | 1.63 | 1.18 |
| European lands | 18 | Under the Land Apportionment Act, Africans are not allowed to own houses in the same areas as Europeans. | 1.68 | 1.08 |
| Sexual relations | 62 | A European man who is suspected of having sex relations with an African woman is likely to be ostracized socially. | 1.75 | 1.06 |
| Public facilities B | 39 | There are different hospitals and other medical services for Africans and Europeans. | 1.54 | 1.05 |
| Sexual relations | 64 | A friendship between an African man and a European woman is generally viewed with suspicion. | 1.73 | 1.04 |
| Civil order | 21 | Meetings held by African leaders are attended more often by the Police (C.I.D.) than similar meetings held by Europeans. | 1.38 | 1.03 |
| Sexual relations | 22 | If a European woman becomes 'familiar' with an African man, she is almost certain to be ostracized socially. | 1.63 | .85 |
| Public facilities B | 32 | There are different compartments for Europeans and Africans on trains. | 1.41 | .85 |
| Civil order | 12 | Africans are permitted to own or carry firearms only in very exceptional circumstances, while Europeans may do so with relatively fewer restrictions. | 1.17 | .62 |
| Social facilities | 59 | Africans are refused admission to European dance halls. | 1.24 | .57 |
| Social facilities | 43 | Africans and Europeans are not permitted to use the same public swimming baths. | 1.25 | .46 |
| Public facilities B | 44 | Europeans and Africans generally are not permitted to use the same lavatories. | 1.12 | .41 |

N = 66                               Means for all items   1.87   2.45

The territorial segregation of Africans is favored and is combined with strong opinions about discontinuing restrictions on the economic development of areas reserved solely for African use and occupation. In contrast to the *private* level of relationships, Europeans generally wish to discontinue many of the legal and nonlegal restrictions on association with Africans in *public* relationships, although this is sometimes qualified with preferences for "separate but equal" facilities and opportunities.

The degree of European consensus about the differentiating laws and customs can be ascertained by examining the standard deviations of item scores. As noted above, the mean standard deviation ($\sigma$) for all sixty-six items is 1.87. Greatest agreement is shown on items dealing with lavatories (no. 44, $\sigma = 1.12$), firearms (no. 12, $\sigma = 1.17$), and swimming pools (no. 43, $\sigma = 1.25$). The three items that rank next highest in agreement concern the attendance of police at meetings (no. 21, $\sigma = 1.38$), train compartments (no. 32, $\sigma = 1.41$), and hospitals (no. 39, $\sigma = 1.54$).

The items on which opinions range most widely deal with ostracism and legal penalties for sexual relations between European men and African women (no. 66, $\sigma = 2.43$, and no. 65, $\sigma = 2.38$). Then follow items relating to church services (no. 36, $\sigma = 2.29$), the treatment of friends who have been discovered to have mixed racial ancestry (no. 60, $\sigma = 2.13$), and African membership in European trade unions (no. 10, $\sigma = 2.13$).

In general, European attitudes about Africans crystallize around the maintenance of the country's present social system and the removal of those practices that limit opportunities for separate development and equal legal justice. Europeans have strong feelings that it is important to maintain segregation in situations where social relations are more personalized, lasting, and voluntary. They think that contemporary political arrangements must be maintained, as should European moral standards and European dominance in the economic system. There is less concern that Africans should continue to defer to Europeans in situations of personal contact.

Europeans believe that differential rights and privileges for the two culture groups are necessary if the present course of development in Southern Rhodesian society is to continue. Europeans who deviate from the norms of their group, especially with respect to cross-racial sexual contacts, are to be criticized or punished. Endogamous marriages are viewed as essential. Residential segregation is thought necessary both to maintain health standards and to prevent association with Africans which might result in miscegenation, the lowering of property values, and less tranquility and orderliness in European neighborhoods.

To summarize all the responses, Europeans feel that contact with Africans should be minimized and controlled. Preferably, contact should be confined to public settings. Where more direct association is unavoidable, as in the employment of Africans as domestic servants, deference behavior is strongly desired.

## A GROUPING OF TEST ITEMS

It was predicted that the responses and scores on the sixty-six test items would vary. An a priori set of seven categories had been proposed when constructing the questionnaire, but the testing process and further discussion among ourselves suggested that a larger number of categories was essential.

It is difficult to create neat and exclusive categories to which the sixty-six statements may be assigned. Approximately one-third of them, for example, relate directly or indirectly to considerations of health, cleanliness, and disease. Again, about the same number of statements —many of them also relevant to standards of health—involve some component of actual or potential cross-racial sexual relations. (Chapter 8 on factor analysis also indicates the presence and strength of a "sex factor" in the responses to many of the statements.) Further, most of the items in the questionnaire seem to involve attitudes toward maintaining the general "standards of Western civilization" or, more exactly, the "standards of the European community in Southern Rhodesia."

To construct a more satisfactory classification, we not only considered the logical interrelations between items but the emotive factors as well. Attention was given only secondarily to the distribution of the mean scores obtained from the population. In cases where a particular statement could be included in any of several categories, we decided through discussion what seemed to be its outstanding characteristic or connotation. To illustrate this process, let us look at statement 61: "Europeans who rape African women sometimes are given lighter sentences than Africans who rape European women." Sex is clearly one strong and emotive element within this statement, but it seemed to relate more clearly to the differential legal consequences, and we accordingly placed it into the category of legal justice. Statement 20 may serve as a second illustration: "In general, Africans but not Europeans are forbidden by law to buy alcoholic spirits." This could reasonably have been placed in categories in which the main criterion was health, the use of public facilities (shops), or sex (as drunkenness may lead to interracial sexual aggressiveness). We felt, however, that the legal prohibition of the right to purchase spirits was relevant to the general maintenance of civil order—the prevention of criminal behavior of any variety. As a final example, no. 14 states that "Africans are liable to be assaulted by a European employer, whereas European employees are less liable to receive this treatment." Conceivably, this item could be classified in a category relating to job amenities and employment, political control, or legal justice (since assault may result in conviction for a criminal offense). But we decided that it was best classified in a category concerned with patterns of etiquette between Africans and Europeans.

Table 28 summarizes the data by the categories finally established. Eleven categories seem to derive from the sixty-six test items, although we were unable to agree on the classification of five individual statements. The number of items within each category varies from three to nine. The reader may refer to Table 27 for the identification number, the content, the mean score, and the standard deviation of the items included.

TABLE 28. *European Attitudes about Africans, by Ranked Categories*

| Rank | Category | Mean of S.D.s | Mean of means | Items in questionnaire Total | Item numbers |
|------|----------|---------------|---------------|-------|--------------|
| 1 | Legal justice | 2.07 | 4.52 | 3 | 61, 16, 65 |
| 2 | Educational and training opportunities | 2.02 | 3.71 | 4 | 9, 30, 2, 1 |
| 3 | Opportunities on African lands | 1.90 | 3.63 | 4 | 7, 38, 5, 19 |
| 4 | Personal courtesies and etiquette | 1.95 | 3.42 | 9 | 51, 14, 60, 58, 56, 55, 54, 53, 52 |
| 5 | Public facilities, Type A | 2.09 | 2.89 | 7 | 50, 36, 35, 3, 42, 37, 40 |
| 6 | Employment | 1.95 | 2.21 | 4 | 10, 4, 47, 57 |
| 7 | Opportunities on European lands | 1.93 | 1.80 | 6 | 13, 33, 6, 11, 63, 18 |
| 8 | Civil order and political control | 1.74 | 1.57 | 9 | 27, 20, 25, 17, 24, 23, 26, 21, 12 |
| 9 | Public facilities, Type B | 1.59 | 1.20 | 7 | 31, 29, 34, 49, 39, 32, 44 |
| 10 | Social and recreational facilities | 1.63 | 1.17 | 5 | 46, 45, 48, 59, 43 |
| 11 | Sexual relations | 1.70 | .98 | 3 | 62, 64, 22 |
| — | Unclassified | 2.04 | 3.24 | 5 | 41, 28, 8, 66, 15 |
| | Totals | 1.87 | 2.45 | 66 | |

The mean score, and the mean of the standard deviations of each category, are derived by averaging the means and standard deviations of the particular items included in the category. The categories are ranked to indicate the laws and customs that Europeans feel are most important to discontinue. They feel strongest about changing the present laws and practices in the areas of legal justice (M = 4.52) and educational and training opportunities (M = 3.71). Those categories of behavior which they feel are most important to maintain are related to sexual relations (M = .98) and social and recreational facilities (M = 1.17). Of the eleven categories, the mean scores in four of them are above and the remaining seven below the theoretical mean of 3.00.

The standard deviations of scores for the categories range from

1.59 for public facilities Type B to 2.09 for public facilities Type A. These figures indicate that of all the given categories of differential behavior, there is most agreement on the value of maintaining separate buses, park benches, schools, privileges of trying on clothes in shops, hospitals and medical services, train compartments, and lavatories. The least consensus is shown about Africans and Europeans competing in sports and sharing in church services, Africans using elevators, buying lottery tickets, being served in shops and cafes through "hatch windows," having separate entrances in public buildings, and separate railway booking offices.

These two categories, public facilities Types A and B, illuminate some features of attitudes as well as some of the difficulties of classification. All the statements classified into Type A and Type B concern the use of public facilities, if privately-owned commercial businesses that cater to the "public" are included. All of the items in Type B involve real or alleged close physical contact, and considerations of sex and health seem to be of diagnostic importance in the responses given. Only one practice does not involve a type of immobility such as sitting, lying, or sleeping. The situations in Type A, on the other hand, necessitate more mobility—physical proximity is present only for a short span of time.

It is worth noting that in the Type A facilities, Europeans and Africans generally assume standing postures, if indeed there is any contact at all. Thus, we may conclude that Europeans in Southern Rhodesia feel it is very important to maintain "horizontal segregation," but feel less strongly about maintaining "vertical segregation" (Golden, 1958). Despite their common designations as public facilities, the widely divergent mean scores of Type A ($M = 2.89$) and Type B ($M = 1.20$) indicate their relative importance to the Europeans.

The general results of our study show that considerable variation exists within the European population regarding maintenance or change in the laws and customs that differentiate between Africans and Europeans. The range of scores on the test items indicates that the intensity and direction of European feelings are statistically and sociologically significant. The standard deviations for the statements suggest that European opinion is quite homogeneous in some cases, but less so in others. The extent of agreement has important implications for the possibility and probability of social and cultural change within the total society, a topic we will examine later in our study.

On the majority of items, Europeans generally wish to continue the current structure of relations between the two culture groups. Where a desire for change is indicated, this is often qualified in terms of providing "separate but equal" facilities within the segregated and reserved areas. European attitudes differ about the importance of continuing various aspects of social differentiation. They feel strongest about the laws and practices that relate to sex, health, and legal justice. All these involve the maintenance of "standards," the protection of European culture, a minimum of contact with Africans, and the continuation of differential status, prestige, and power for the foreseeable future.

# 8

## A FACTORIAL ANALYSIS OF ATTITUDES

### AIMS AND METHODS OF FACTOR ANALYSIS

The aims of factor analysis have been stated in many publications, but the essential ones have been conveniently summarized by Wolfle (1940). The first objective is that of simplification. The usual procedure is to convert test scores into a table of correlations, and then by means of factor analysis to reduce these to a set of factor loadings. At each step some of the original information is lost but the relations among the tests become clearer. This aim fits well with Burt's (1940) use of factor analysis as a scientific principle of classification. Wolfle's second aim is to find a set of factors that will be fewer in number and more fundamental in nature than the original tests. Most psychologists would agree to these two aims.

The nature of factors in psychological and sociological research has been discussed by a number of writers, and it is hardly necessary to iterate the various positions here.[1] It is sufficient to state that Vernon's (1950) standpoint has been adopted for this investigation; he regards factors "primarily as categories for classifying mental or behavioural performances rather than as entities in the mind or nervous system." Each factor shows the test items that have some component in com-

100

mon which is distinct from the components shared by others. If the items do not correlate, then they have no common elements. In so far as they do, it is possible to factor them out. Thus, a factor is a hypothetical construct; it is a mathematical quantification of a quality held in common by all items in a scale, or by a limited number or group of them. The items that embrace the same component are generally inspected to arrive at an operational definition of the factor, that is, a definition that identifies the function or quality that appears to be involved. These components will be taken as classifications of behavior as it can be observed and measured in Southern Rhodesia, not as invariant entities of the mind. Even though the affective and conative aspects of attitudes seem to have a genetic core, the situation that molds them can change, with a resultant modification of their expression.

The chief methods of factor analysis have been outlined by Vernon (1950). The one chosen for this study is Thurstone's centroid method, a modification of the Burt simple summation technique. As we intend to investigate race attitudes from a hierarchical point of view, it might be asked how the centroid method can be adopted. Thurstone uses it to obtain a multiple factor solution, but Vernon (1946, 1947) has shown how it can be used to arrive at a general plus group factor pattern. It will be shown later why we believe this furnishes the most meaningful psychological solution.

## THE OMISSION OF ITEMS

In Chapter 6, when we were discussing test reliability through interitem correlation, it was pointed out that a number of items had to be omitted because of their lack of variability. Let us consider just one example of this lack of variability. With item 44 (lavatories), 480 respondents affirmed that it was important or very important to maintain separate facilities, while only twenty wished to see this separation discontinued. In all, eleven items had to be omitted on such statistical grounds. In addition, five other items were omitted because they were no longer as relevant as when the study was first planned. Table 29 summarizes the omitted items.

It may be noted that all of the items save one which had to be omitted on statistical grounds are ones that provoke very strong sentiments among Europeans, and on which the attitude is strongly in favor of maintaining the present differential practice. It would be most valuable to include such items in the factor analysis, but inasmuch as the proportion of people desiring the discontinuance of the practice was so small, they could not be handled statistically. The practice described in item 51, concerning the general lack of respect for African adults by European children, is one in which the great majority of our sample wished to see a change.

Item 3 has been changed by law, and Africans now are permitted to buy lottery tickets and bet on horse racing. The Industrial Conciliation Act of 1959 now makes it possible for multiracial trade unions to be established, so item 10 may be irrelevant within the near future. Item 37 refers to different entrances to shops, banks, and post offices. In 1959, the Federal Government instructed that the signs indicating separate entrances to post offices should be removed, and many banks and shops thought this an appropriate time to follow suit

TABLE 29. *Items Omitted from the Factor Analysis*

| No. | Area of differentiation—law, custom, practice | Grounds for omission |
|---|---|---|
| 3 | Gambling on lotteries and on horse racing | Change in law |
| 10 | Membership of trade unions | Change in law |
| 12 | Owning or carrying firearms | Statistical |
| 18 | Area of ownership of houses | Statistical |
| 21 | Attendance of police at (political) meetings | Statistical |
| 22 | Reaction to European woman's "familiarity" with African man | Statistical |
| 32 | Compartments on trains | Statistical |
| 35 | Use of elevators | Less relevant now |
| 37 | Entrances to shops, banks, and post offices | Less relevant now |
| 39 | Hospitals and medical services | Statistical |
| 40 | Booking offices at railways | Change in practice |
| 43 | Public swimming baths | Statistical |
| 44 | Lavatories | Statistical |
| 49 | Trying on clothes in European shops | Statistical |
| 51 | Respect shown by children to adults | Statistical |
| 59 | Admission to European dances | Statistical |

and did so. Similarly, the differentiating signs to elevators in many public buildings in the main cities were removed, so item 35 is now less relevant than it was at the commencement of the study. The same comment is true of item 40 following the Government's instruction that booking offices at railways should be differentiated by class of travel and not by race. Because practices on items 3, 10, 35, 37, and 40 have changed, or are in the process of changing, it is considered that these can be left out of the factor analysis to reduce a little the massive task of computation.

## FACTORIAL PROCEDURES

It is not proposed to outline the factor analysis in detail, as similar treatments have been covered in a wealth of publications. Vernon's (1950a) summary of the centroid method has been followed, and a fuller description will be given only at those points where alternative procedures are available and where some choice has to be made.

## THE PROBLEM OF COMMUNALITY ESTIMATION

The first step in a centroid analysis consists of estimating the communalities ($h^2_1$, $h^2_2$, . . . . $h^2_n$) for insertion in the diagonal cells of the original correlation matrix. In a matrix of unknown rank, Thurstone (1947) adopts the approximation of inserting the largest correlation of the column in the diagonal cell. This is his procedure for estimating what Burt (1951) has called the reduced self-correlation of a test. When the number of tests in a matrix is less than about a dozen, Vernon suggests that the estimated communalities should be corrected by iteration. However, where the number of tests is large, as in this investigation, an exact estimation is not important because the factor loadings are largely unaffected by variations within the original diagonal cell.[2] Before adopting the Thurstone procedure, an examination was made of the nine methods outlined by Medland (1947) for estimating the unknown communalities. His results show that the most accurate assessment is one entitled Centroid No. 1. For this, a sub-matrix is made from several variables that correlate most highly with the test where a communality is wanted, and a simple formula enables one to arrive at an estimation of $h^2$. This method has been tried on several cases but, as the result was largely of the same order and size as the highest correlation in the column, it was discarded, and Thurstone's procedure was followed.

The matrix for analysis consists of 1,225 separate correlations. To economize space, these are not included, and neither are the various matrices involved in the computation.

## THE NUMBER AND SIGNIFICANCE OF COMMON FACTORS

At the outset, it is important to make a distinction between the number of factors that can be extracted from a given matrix and the significance of these factors. For example, American statisticians generally extract more factors than would be deemed significant by British investigators. It is often the practice of the former to rotate much of the general factor onto the minor ones until a substantial alteration in variance gives them the appearance of significance (cf. Vernon, 1950). However, as it is now usual to extract extra factors for rotational elbow-room, some criterion of significance must be kept in mind. It is here that standards vary so much. Vernon (1949) has reviewed about twenty of the possible criteria, mostly based on empirical evidence, and we have given greater credence to the more austere of these.

The criteria formulated by a number of psychologists have been applied, and the evidence from them helps us to judge which factors may be statistically significant.[3] In doing this, we also follow Burt's

(1951) advice that "any factor whose presence seems decidedly more probable than not should be retained," and that it is wise to extract "at least one factor more than those that are fully significant." This allows for the rotational freedom mentioned by Thomson (1948) and considered to be necessary by Thurstone and his followers.

From the criteria it seems that, apart from the general factor that pervades all items, there are four further group factors on which seven significant clusters are lodged in bipolar form; that is, some of the loadings are positive and others negative. So that these can be split from each other, we have taken out further factors that are deemed insignificant but that allow us room for rotating the clusters into positive planes.

## THE ROTATIONAL PROBLEM

When the factors have been extracted from a matrix, some investigators proceed to interpret them as they stand, while others rotate the arbitrary reference frame into a preferred or simplified position. If rotation is employed, a number of guiding principles are available, each mathematically proper, but differing according to the psychological framework the investigator wishes to employ.

(1) The various guiding principles for determining the choice of factors have been outlined by Cattell (1946), Kettner (1952), and others. Kettner gives three that are ordinarily useful in psychological studies, and inasmuch as we have made some use of them, a brief description is called for. The first involves rotation to what Thurstone (1947) has called simple structure. If this is employed, it means that by definition no general first-order factor can emerge; the variance on some items of our general factor will be eliminated by rotating it onto the smaller group factors, thus increasing their size.

But most British factorists retain a "g" or general factor, and they support their stand on the grounds of psychological meaningfulness. We are aware that there are strong differences of opinion on this matter, but we follow Burt's reasoning and do not modify the positive general factor that rolls first out of the matrix. We feel that its retention can be justified on the basis of other empirical evidence.

With the group factors, rotation to simple structure is possible and has been achieved. The method is helpful in maximizing the clusters that show on the unrotated factors, and enable us to identify them with more clarity.

(2) Kettner's second guiding principle is aimed at achieving positive manifold, that is, ensuring that all the loadings on a factor are positive or not significantly different from zero, and none significantly negative. Vernon recommends this because of the difficulty that is met in interpreting negative factor loadings, although as principles of classification they are quite legitimate.

(3) The third principle is that of psychological meaningfulness. This needs some discussion, for meaningfulness can best be expressed through the adoption of a scientific taxonomic framework. Let us start from the premise that the social sciences are concerned with the description and classification of behavioral data, the formulation of hypotheses, and the testing of these hypotheses by the observation and measurement of their consequences. The methods they employ are largely the methods of other sciences.

The history of sciences (Pledge, 1939) suggests that they all begin by classifying the data with which they have to deal. In the biological world, the traditional mode of classification was in accordance with a linear scheme derived from the Aristotelian notion of a *scala naturae,* a single line or ladder of descent. But in the eighteenth century, Linnaeus, the Swedish botanist, introduced the idea of a *systema naturae* which, with some modification, is the forerunner of the modern hierarchical scheme in the social sciences.

FIGURE 3. *The Hierarchical Nature of Attitudes*

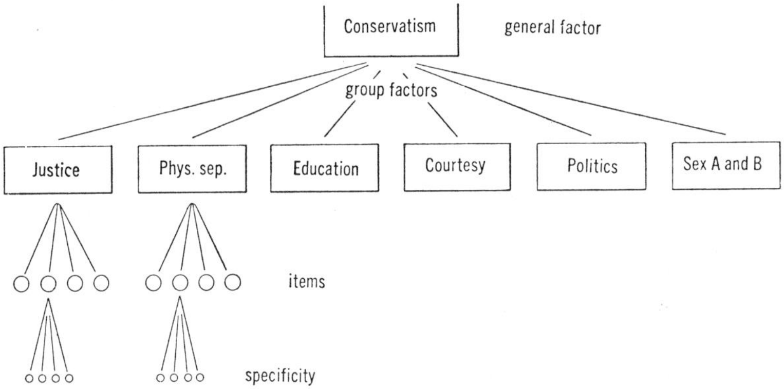

The term "hierarchical" needs some explanation. It is a late Greek word which translates literally into "holy government"; it meant the kind of ecclesiastical organization peculiar to the Church, with descending orders of authority through the officials down to the individual layman. The term is now used to denote a particular kind of logical structure. Described in Burt's (1949) words, "A hierarchical arrangement is a divergent order progressively generated by an asymmetrical one-many relation, much as a serial order is generated by an asymmetrical one-one relation." Pictorially, a hierarchical system of classification resembles a genealogical tree, as can be illustrated from the final solution of the factor analysis. This is shown in Figure 3.

An interpretation of this nature assists considerably in the classification of human behavior. For example, Allport (1937) makes a distinction between different levels of personality structure, each level forming part of a hierarchy in which disparate units of behavior are integrated into larger and more inclusive integers. For this study, the hierarchical interpretation is important because it facilitates an explanation of human behavior in parsimonious factorial terms, and it seems to fit best the results of so much biological and social research. Burt (1949), in drawing together much evidence, shows that Spencer and his followers employed such a system to describe internal organization and control within the individual, while Jackson, Sherrington and McDougall applied the notion to the organization of the nervous system and so of the mind. More recently, Eysenck (1947) has used a hierarchical taxonomy to describe the temperamental side of man's personality, and MacCrone's (1955) factorial work on race attitudes in South Africa can be similarly interpreted.

With a considerable body of evidence before us, from which we have cited but a few examples, it seems clear that the greatest degree of meaningfulness will flow from our study if it is related to a hierarchical system which, though certainly not complete, is gradually being sketched with more precision in the social sciences. Thus, it seems necessary to preserve our important general factor, because it fits in with a widely adopted taxonomy. It is possible that a similar hierarchy can be achieved with the extraction of a general factor at the second order—through the intercorrelation of the group factors—but we do not prefer this solution.

From a glance at Figure 3, the structure of our hierarchy can be observed. At the first level, we can assume the specificity which lies in all items, and from which little can be deduced. At the second level are the individual items that support the group factors. At the group factor level, a considerable degree of organization has entered the structure. At the fourth level is the general type from which the largest number of other qualities can be inferred, and from which the most secure predictions of future behavior can be made. Consequently, in rotating to psychological meaningfulness, a hierarchical taxonomy has been our major guiding principle.[4]

## INTERPRETATION OF THE FACTORS

The ground has now been cleared for an interpretation of the factors. Following Thurstone's (1938) procedure, frontier lines on either side of zero are established, within which we regard loadings as zero or not significantly different from zero. These lines are laid down at $+.25$ and $-.25$. Then, for the purpose of operationally defining and naming a factor, we place greatest weight on the largest projections in a column. The plan of significant loadings, shown in Table 30, will be examined by columns.

TABLE 30. *Plan of the Significant Factor Loadings after Rotation* *

| No. | Area of differentiation—law, custom, practice ** | I | II | III | IV | V | VI | VII | VIII | h² |
|---|---|---|---|---|---|---|---|---|---|---|
| 1 | Apprenticeship training for the trades | .81 | | | | | | | | .73 |
| 2 | Technical classes for trade training | .77 | | .45 | | | | | | .86 |
| 4 | Employment in industry and business | .74 | | | | | | | | .59 |
| 5 | Size of farms (Land Husbandry Act) | .64 | | | | | | | | .48 |
| 6 | Use of land for business purposes | .84 | | | | | | | | .81 |
| 7 | Cost of travel to work | .43 | .33 | | | | | | | .34 |
| 8 | Rates of pay for similar jobs | .66 | | | | | | | | .56 |
| 9 | Facilities for training in trades and professions | .77 | | .36 | | | | | | .81 |
| 11 | Places for buying beer and wines | .65 | .28 | | | | | | | .51 |
| 13 | Rental of offices in commercial areas | .76 | .28 | | | | | | | .74 |
| 14 | Assault by a European employer | .65 | | | .34 | | | | | .57 |
| 15 | Serving on juries | .70 | | | | | | | | .50 |
| 16 | Punishment for similar crimes of violence | .36 | .59 | | | | | | | .54 |
| 17 | Carrying identity papers | .64 | | | | | | | | .46 |
| 19 | Freehold tenure of urban land | .68 | | | | | | | | .54 |
| 20 | Purchase of alcoholic spirits | .60 | | | | | | | | .40 |
| 23 | Effect of the franchise qualifications | .66 | | | | .35 | | | | .59 |
| 24 | Control of election to the Federal Parliament | .77 | | | | .37 | | | | .75 |
| 25 | Reaction to African and European "nationalism" | .55 | | | | | | | | .42 |
| 26 | Number of representatives in the Federal Parliament | .72 | | | | .38 | | | | .72 |
| 27 | Municipal franchise | .77 | | | | | | | | .65 |
| 28 | Admission to some political meetings | .78 | | | | | | | | .68 |
| 29 | Park benches | .80 | .35 | | | | | | | .80 |
| 30 | Educational opportunities for children | .67 | | | .25 | | | | | .55 |
| 31 | Buses | .76 | .25 | | | | | | | .66 |
| 33 | Cemeteries | .78 | | | | | | | | .68 |
| 34 | Schools | .80 | | | | | .28 | | | .74 |
| 36 | Churches | .75 | | | | | | | | .63 |
| 38 | Amenities in townships | .55 | | | | | | | | .41 |
| 41 | Methods of lodging protests | .63 | | | | | | | | .49 |
| 42 | Facilities for obtaining service at shops and cafes | .76 | .30 | | | | | | | .69 |
| 45 | Sporting and social clubs | .71 | | | | | .32 | | | .63 |
| 46 | Restaurants and hotels | .88 | | | | | | | | .85 |
| 47 | Employment as counter attendants in European shops | .76 | | | | | | | | .68 |
| 48 | Theaters | .80 | | | | | | | | .71 |
| 50 | Sporting events | .74 | | | | | | | | .63 |
| 52 | Behavior at doorways and elevators | .77 | | | .25 | | | | | .73 |
| 53 | Shaking hands | .79 | | | | | | | | .66 |
| 54 | Forms or terms of address | .76 | | | | | | | | .72 |
| 55 | Order of service at shop counters | .84 | | | | | | | | .76 |
| 56 | Respect shown to Europeans vs. Africans | .68 | | | .28 | | | | | .60 |

TABLE 30. *Plan of the Significant Factor Loadings after Rotation* (cont.)

| No. | Area of differentiation—law, custom, practice ** | I | II | III | IV | V | VI | VII | VIII | h² |
|-----|--------------------------------------------------|-----|-----|-----|-----|-----|-----|-----|------|------|
| 57 | Supervision of workers of the other race | .82 | | | | | | | | .75 |
| 58 | Reaction to "cheekiness" | .70 | | | | | | | | .58 |
| 60 | Friendship behavior because of (mixed) ancestry | .71 | | | | | | | | .57 |
| 61 | Sentences for cross-racial rape | .37 | .59 | | .27 | | | | | .57 |
| 62 | Reaction to European man's sexual relations (cross-racial) | .48 | | | | | .42 | | | .50 |
| 63 | Place of residence for an interracial marriage | .71 | | | | | .37 | | | .72 |
| 64 | Reaction to European woman's friendship with an African | .69 | | | | | .40 | | | .71 |
| 65 | Legal sanctions on cross-racial sexual relations | .29 | | | | | | | .52 | .42 |
| 66 | Sanctions (implied) on cross-racial "familiarity" | .46 | | | | | | | .56 | .60 |

\*   Insignificant loadings omitted.
\*\* The items are given in full in Table 27.

#### FACTOR I: GENERAL CONSERVATISM

The first factor has significant loadings on all of the items, and its total variance is far greater than that revealed by any other attitude study we have seen. This finding illuminates the high degree of consistency that pervades European sentiments about Africans in Southern Rhodesia. It takes little inspection of the whole of Factor I to bring out that here we have a mathematical "g" factor that can be equated psychologically with conservatism.

The term "conservatism" may need some elaboration. Among others, Eysenck (1954) reserves the term for the general factor common to a whole family of attitudes, not only those that are ethnic in orientation. The term as we use it is thus more restricted, and refers to the universe of European attitudes toward Africans.

In the first instance, we advance an operational definition of Factor I rather than a sociopsychological interpretation. The questionnaire was constructed so that the intensity of attitudes could be measured as well as their direction. As we have said, individuals were given the choice of indicating whether they wished to maintain a practice or to discontinue it, of conserving or changing the status quo. Accordingly, the general factor of conservatism that emerges can be taken as a continuum, as is the general factor of intelligence. Different forms or qualities of behavior will be associated with the two contrasting ends, as is also the case with the "g" factor in human ability. Thus, our identification of the mathematical "g" factor in attitudes as a general factor of conservatism is not an implication that all the population is conservative in its thinking, feeling, and acting. Rather, it implies that individuals can be placed along a fundamental attitudinal continuum to which different behavior is related at different points.

But having operationally defined the general factor, there still remains the task of giving it a sociological-psychological interpretation. In previous chapters, we have examined some of the molding influences on the formation and expression of race attitudes. Where they are held strongly, and are negative or unfavorable, the individuals holding them tend to judge those who do not belong to the same cultural or racial group as in some way different and possibly inferior. These judgments—which may be termed ethnocentric—are common in societies elsewhere. We have noted already how Europeans in Southern Rhodesia have employed their standards—which are seldom applicable—to evaluate the customs and behavior of Africans. As the study unfolds, it should be possible to illustrate in more detail some of the ethnocentric judgments that flow from the negative attitudes held by many in our sample.

TABLE 31. *Contrasting Projections on the General Factor of Conservatism*

| No. | Area of differentiation | Loading |
|---|---|---|
| 46 | Restaurants and hotels | .88 |
| 6 | Use of land for business purposes | .84 |
| 55 | Order of service at shop counters | .84 |
| 57 | Supervision of workers of the other race | .82 |
| 1 | Apprenticeship training for the trades | .81 |
| 66 | Sanctions (implied) on cross-racial "familiarity" | .46 |
| 7 | Cost of travel to work | .43 |
| 61 | Sentences for cross-racial rape | .37 |
| 16 | Punishment for similar crimes of violence | .36 |
| 65 | Legal sanctions on cross-racial sexual relations | .29 |

It is of value to examine a little more closely the items contrasted in Table 31. The highest loadings are on items least likely to embrace additional group factors, and the lowest loadings, conversely, are on items more likely to encompass additional factors. This trend is observable in our table of significant factor loadings. Separation or differential treatment in restaurants and hotels, on land, in shops, and at the apprentice school is explicable, according to our findings, in terms of a single general factor. Thus, a person with a "maintain" score on one of these items will tend to have a "maintain" score on the others, and the individual with a "discontinue" score on one will tend to have the same pattern on the others.

When we turn to the items with small loadings on the general factor, we cannot make the same generalization. Let us consider item 16, which is concerned with different punishments for similar crimes of violence. Here the general loading is small (.36) and contributes less to the total variance of the item than does one of the group factors. The implications can be readily educed from these factorial findings. A "discontinue" score on item 16 will not predict "discontinue" scores on the other items that have a high general factor loading. Put another way, an individual may well choose to maintain a considerable number of the practices listed in our questionnaire and yet wish to discontinue unequal punishments by the courts, on the ground that such practices violate an abstract principle of justice. A similar observation can be made of those items dealing with sexual matters. An individual may wish to discontinue many of the listed practices, but may not be prepared to accept an African into the intimate circle of his family.

These examples—and others will follow—illustrate the use of factor analysis as a principle of classification. As we stressed previously, the reduction of a matrix of correlations to a small set of factors reveals the relations among tests in a manner that cannot be achieved from inspection. Two of the classifying principles described by Burt (1949) are evoked. The successive principles of classification are independent of each other, and, secondly, each factor indicates the distinctive or essential features common to a group of items. The molding forces that combine to forge attitudes in the manner demonstrated here are not revealed by factor analysis; they must be unraveled by other enquiries. What stand revealed more clearly are the major components underlying interracial behavior and attitudes. Given these, the molding forces can be sought on surveyed ground rather than on unexplored territory.

FACTOR II: LEGAL JUSTICE

Two of the three significant loadings on Factor II fall on items clearly concerned with·principles of justice. These are shown in Table 32. Items 16 and 61 are concerned with the different punishments that Europeans and Africans may receive for similar crimes. One of the items involves physical violence, and the other sexual violence; but the concept of differential penalties for both these crimes is, in general, strongly opposed by the European sample. In naming the factor, greatest account is taken of the two highest projections.

TABLE 32. *Factor Projections on Legal Justice*

| No. | Area of differentiation | Loading |
|---|---|---|
| 16 | Punishment for similar crimes of violence | .59 |
| 61 | Sentences for cross-racial rape | .59 |
| 7 | Cost of travel to work | .33 |

Of interest is item 7, which has a moderate loading of .33 on the factor. It is possible that it is a factorial "sport," an occurrence not unknown in statistical work. On the other hand, it may have a genuine place on the dimension. Item 7 reads: "Many Africans are required to pay relatively higher costs in travelling to work than are Europeans, as they often must live at some distance from their places of employment." This statement is interpreted variously by Europeans, but to many it appears to involve an abstract principle of justice, or fair play. Africans cannot live in townships other than those set aside by law for their use, and this law has been passed by a European parliament. In interviews, it is apparent that many Europeans are aware that the effect of land apportionment is to deny Africans any opportunity of choosing a home nearer to their place of employment, and this results in proportionately higher traveling costs. Perhaps of more importance is the fact that African wages are substantially lower than European wages, so that a greater proportion of the African pay packet is spent on travel. This seems unjust to many Europeans who suggest a solution through increased transport subsidies, chargeable to the territorial or local governments or to industry.

FACTOR III: PHYSICAL SEPARATION

Factor III has significant projections on five items, and they all seem to be associated with the physical separation of Africans and Europeans, as seen in Table 33.

TABLE 33. *Factor Projections on Physical Separation*

| No. | Area of differentiation | Loading |
|---|---|---|
| 29 | Park benches | .35 |
| 42 | Facilities for obtaining service at shops and cafes | .30 |
| 13 | Rental of offices in commercial areas | .28 |
| 11 | Places for buying beer and wines | .28 |
| 31 | Buses | .25 |

The items on park benches, shops, and buses are what we have called public facilities, and attitudes toward these items are not explicable in terms of the general factor alone. The other two items do not envisage the use of separate facilities on common ground, but rather separate facilities for Africans in their own areas. The unifying principle running through them all seems to be that of physical separation. It is true that there are other items in our scale that involve separation, but they are expressed through projections on other factors.

FACTOR IV: EDUCATIONAL AND TRAINING OPPORTUNITIES

It is not difficult to pinpoint the underlying principle of Factor IV. All items concern the educational and trade training facilities without which economic advancement is hardly possible for the African people. Once again the implication is that general attitudes are distinct from attitudes that involve economic advancement and ultimately competition for the same employment opportunities. The three significant items are listed in Table 34.

TABLE 34. *Factor Projections on Educational and Training Opportunities*

| No. | Area of differentiation | Loading |
| --- | --- | --- |
| 2 | Technical classes for trade training | .45 |
| 9 | Facilities for training in trades and professions | .36 |
| 30 | Educational opportunities for children | .25 |

When one reviews the interview data, the emergence of this fact is not surprising. Individuals with conservative attitudes who have secure economic positions occasionally express a wish for more extensive trade training facilities and more extended educational opportunities for Africans. Conversely, the European artisan, whose attitudes tend to favor change, at times has second thoughts on educational opportunities for Africans where he can see that the ultimate effect may be competition for the job he holds. It is true that these three items also have considerable loadings on the general factor, thus lending consistency to behavior, but outside the general attitude there is sufficient variance to posit a significant group factor.

FACTOR V: PERSONAL COURTESIES AND ETIQUETTE

The variance of Factor V seems to fall in the realm of what might be called courtesies and etiquette. A quick inspection of Table 35 should reveal this. It would seem to us that these items are concerned with status differences in personal relations. There are certain norms of conduct to which the European community adheres, or which it recognizes as desirable even if it does not adhere to them. To assault an African employee, to show disrespect, and to expect him to stand

TABLE 35. *Factor Projections on Personal Courtesies and Etiquette*

| No. | Area of differentiation | Loading |
| --- | --- | --- |
| 14 | Assault by a European employer | .34 |
| 56 | Respect shown to Europeans vs. Africans | .28 |
| 61 | Sentences for cross-racial rape | .27 |
| 52 | Behavior at doors and elevators | .25 |

back at doors and at elevators are infringements of the codes that normally govern personal relations. The rape of an African is also an infringement of these codes, as well as different punishments, which violate the principle of equal justice before the law.

FACTOR VI: POLITICAL CONTROL

A distinct group factor emerges on the items that clearly involve political control. Political control in Southern Rhodesia, and in the Federation, rests in the hands of Europeans; if the qualifications for the franchise are substantially lowered, or if the number of Africans in the Federal House is made proportional to their number in the Federation, then political control could pass from the European population. It is not surprising, then, that these items, shown in Table 36, should constitute a separate group factor.

TABLE 36. *Factor Projections on Political Control*

| No. | Area of differentiation | Loading |
|---|---|---|
| 26 | Number of representatives in the Federal Parliament | .38 |
| 24 | Control of election to the Federal Parliament | .37 |
| 23 | Effect of the franchise qualifications | .35 |

The general factor of conservatism enters into these three items, but variation occurs frequently among individuals who display high total scores. It was stressed to us that if political control is transferred to Africans, standards will fall, economic development will be retarded, and the way of life of the European community will be disrupted. Given that the majority of the European population feels and expresses itself along these lines, it is not difficult to account for the emergence of the factor.

FACTORS VII AND VIII: SEXUAL RELATIONS

The analysis reveals two distinct factors that have a sexual component, and it is appropriate to examine them together. Let us inspect the most pervasive of these first, that listed in Table 37.

TABLE 37. *Factor Projections on Sexual Relations (A)*

| No. | Area of differentiation | Loading |
|---|---|---|
| 62 | Reaction to a European man's sexual relations (cross-racial) | .42 |
| 64 | Reaction to a European woman's friendship with an African man | .40 |
| 63 | Place of residence for an interracial marriage | .37 |
| 45 | Sporting and social clubs | .32 |
| 34 | Schools | .28 |

It is noteworthy that items 45 and 34 fall on the sexual factor. The reason for this phenomenon is given in the interviews. It is frequently stated that if Africans and Europeans attend the same schools, this can lead to sexual relations between the races. Of particular danger are the coeducational schools. And the same sexual element can be detected in the opposition to the admission of Africans to sporting and social clubs. Sporting and social clubs in Southern Rhodesia commonly are used by both sexes; men take their wives along, and bachelors their girl friends or fiancees. There are undoubtedly other reasons Europeans employ to justify the exclusion of Africans from their social clubs, but an underlying opposition to cross-racial sexual contact runs through this item, and also the others that fall on the factor.

Factor VIII also embraces sexual relations, as can be seen in Table 38, but here some kind of legal sanction on African men is either stated or implied.

TABLE 38. *Factor Projections on Sexual Relations (B)*

| No. | Area of differentiation | Loading |
|-----|------------------------|---------|
| 66 | Sanctions (implied) on cross-racial "familiarity" | .56 |
| 65 | Legal sanctions on cross-racial sexual relations | .52 |

An alternative hypothesis, which appears plausible but which we do not prefer, is that these two factors both involve the physical separation of Africans and Europeans. Such a theme also runs through Factor III, but a study of the interview material leads us to conclude that a sexual component is dominant in Factors VII and VIII.

As a frame of reference for the factorial study, two basic assumptions have been made. The first concerns the organization of attitudes. Our hypothesis is that they can best be described in terms of a hierarchical structure. It is a scientific maxim to prefer the least complex of alternative explanations of phenomena, and we contend that a hierarchical description of personality interprets best the law of parsimony proposed by William of Occam, the scholastic philosopher. Translating this hypothesis into statistical terms, it means that we have accepted the general plus group factor solution of matrices as being more appropriate than other factorial approaches.

The second assumption is that, in principle, it is possible to measure human behavior with a relatively high degree of accuracy. Our hypothesis here is that measurement is fundamental to all descriptions of behavior, and to the prediction of behavior. The task of measurement certainly seems to be less precise in the social sciences than the physical sciences, possibly for two reasons: "First, the phenomena of human nature are more complex than physical phenomena; secondly, our judgements of personality are much more fallible than our observations of objective events in the physical world" (Vernon, 1933). Even so, it is important to assume that measurement is possible and that it can be done with consistency and validity.

But eleven of the measures display little variability, and have to be omitted from the analysis. Yet it seems logical that they should be related to the items that can be handled statistically, and from which the factors are extracted. For example, if variability were less restricted, there is little reason to doubt that the omitted items would also have loadings on the general factor, and that some of them would have affinities with the group factors. However, we will not pursue this nonstatistical argument further than to observe that the omitted items do not fall into conflict with the hierarchical taxonomy adopted for the analysis.

Turning to the results, we have demonstrated that race attitudes or behavior can be measured with some confidence. Within the setting of Southern Rhodesia, the major variance of European attitudes about Africans can be described in terms of a general factor of conservatism. This general factor we conceive as a continuum, ranging from conservative to change-tolerant, and it illustrates the consistency with which Europeans respond and the predictability of their behavior. Toward the two ends of our continuum, behavior does appear very consistent. A person with a substantial conservative score on, for example, five of the items saturated highly with the general factor shows a marked tendency to score the same way on other items with high general loadings. And the same is true of the person obtaining a substantial social-change score.

But not all is consistent in the realm of attitudes about Africans. Our analysis shows that in six areas that have been identified, forces other than general conservatism have some influence. The identification of these areas—justice, physical separation, educational and training opportunities, personal courtesies, political control, and sex —enables us to describe European attitudes with greater precision, and to sketch in later sections some of the forces that determine whether an individual favors changing or maintaining the status quo.

# 9

## THE ATTITUDES OF DIFFERENT SEGMENTS
## OF THE POPULATION

Within the European population of Southern Rhodesia, it has been demonstrated that attitudes about the laws and customs affecting Africans vary greatly. Not only is there variation in total score, but reactions to specific items also differ. These variations are accommodated within a distribution that ranges from very conservative, through a theoretical neutral point, to very change-oriented, even though, as we have demonstrated, the bulk of the scores fall toward the conservative end of the scale.

From the distribution, it seems reasonable to infer that some of this variation stems from subpopulations that have fundamentally different attitudes about contact and association with Africans. Our next task, then, is to fragment the community into a number of *logical* groupings or classifications to see where these differences lie, and to determine their significance.

For the fragmentation, we have followed the subpopulations encompassed within the sampling model. These subpopulations were extracted mainly from the returns of the last census carried out in Southern Rhodesia in 1956. When they are fitted together, the result is a very close approximation of the population as a whole. One reason for adopting a complex sampling design is to minimize the possibility of bias, and various statistical checks show how far this desideratum has been achieved. A further determinant in the selection of the subpopulations is the possibility that they might demonstrate differences in attitude score. The analyses that follow allow us to identify these differences.

## SEX

The division of the population into males and females allows a straightforward analysis. Mean scores and standard deviations are obtained for both groups, and this permits an application of Gosset's $t$ test to determine the significance of the differences between the means. The degrees of freedom are taken as $N_1 + N_2 - 2$. The $t$ values for different levels of confidence are read from tables furnished by Snedecor (1946). The data in Table 39 summarize these steps.

TABLE 39. *Sex and Attitude Score*

| Sex | No. | S.D. | Mean |
|---|---|---|---|
| Male | 269 | 1.07 | 2.51 |
| Female | 231 | 1.17 | 2.39 |
| Totals | 500 | 1.12 | 2.45 |

$M_M. - M_F. = .12$   $t = 1.21$   1 of c $= >20\%$   $H_o =$ supported

The $t$ value of 1.21 falls above the 20% level of confidence, meaning that by chance alone the difference we obtain can occur over twenty times in one hundred samples. Consequently, the null hypothesis is supported. Our finding does not prove that there is no significant difference between male and female attitudes in Southern Rhodesia, but it does state that any difference, if it exists, is not large enough to be revealed by a sampling study of 500 people. If N were substantially larger, a significant difference might emerge. This is so, for example, when one considers the relation of height and intelligence: on small samples no relation emerges, but on representative samples of great size a small but significant correlation of about .10 is found. In terms of this study, one can deduce that the global attitudes of European men and women are very similar. The historic and cultural forces that mold attitudes about Africans seem to have fallen with about equal weight on both sexes, and matters generally of concern to men seem also of moment to women.

## AGE

At the outset, we postulated that there would be a relation between age and attitude score, with older people tending to be more conservative. But an inspection of the analyses under Table 40 reveals that this hypothesis is not tenable for the European population of Southern Rhodesia. The two most disparate intervals in the table are 20–29 years and 60–69 years, but the *t* test demonstrates that the obtained difference of .30 in attitude score may have arisen through chance fluctuations in sampling.

TABLE 40. *Age and Attitude Score*

| Age in years | No. | S.D. | Mean |
|---|---|---|---|
| 20–29 | 129 | 1.25 | 2.56 |
| 30–39 | 146 | 1.15 | 2.50 |
| 40–49 | 115 | 1.05 | 2.30 |
| 50–59 | 63 | .88 | 2.51 |
| 60–69 | 30 | .97 | 2.26 |
| 70–79 | 15 | — | 2.47 |
| 80 and above | 2 | — | 1.66 |
| Totals | 500 | 1.12 | 2.45 |

$M_{20-29} - M_{60-69} = .30$   $t = 1.24$   1 of c $= >20\%$   $H_o =$ supported
$r_{xy} = -.07$   $t = 1.57$   1 of c $= >10\%$   $H_o =$ supported

Further support for the null hypothesis flows from the correlation between age and attitude score. A bivariate distribution has been plotted from the data, and the resultant product-moment coefficient ($r_{xy}$) is —.07. The significance of this coefficient is tested by an application of Fisher's *t* formula: $t = r \sqrt{\dfrac{N - 2}{1 - r^2}}$, in which r stands for the obtained correlation, and N is the number of pairs of measures. The *t* value of 1.57, when read against the appropriate tables in Snedecor (1946), shows that the correlation is an insignificant fluctuation from zero. Thus, one is obliged to accept the hypothesis that age and attitude about Africans are not correlated in this population.

On further analysis, one of the main reasons for this finding, which differs from that displayed in many other Western countries, becomes apparent. It will be recalled that only 14.5% of the residents of Southern Rhodesia over the age of twenty were born inside the Colony. The immigrants came at various ages, from various countries, and with varying value systems. Thus, a person fifty years of age may have been in the Colony for only a short time, and consequently be less likely to have experienced the full force of the particular molding influences within Southern Rhodesian society. In the future, when (and if) a greater proportion of the European population is native-born, the expected relation of age and conservatism may emerge. Again, if one equates both age *and* length of residence for a limited group of people, it is probable that age and attitude will be correlated. But inasmuch as this task falls outside our immediate study, it has not been attempted.

## COMMUNITY OF RESIDENCE

No separate analyses have been made of the communities in which respondents state they live. The term "community of residence" has been variously interpreted by individuals, and it is not possible to equate their entries with the sampling model available.

## CENSUS DISTRICT

It will be recalled that testing and interviewing were carried out within the census districts established by the Central African Statistical Office, and that the data were grouped by the size of the largest urban nucleus within each district. The findings allow us to examine two propositions put forward by individuals in Southern Rhodesia.

The first, which is held with some frequency, is that Europeans who live in Bulawayo tend to be more favorable in their attitudes about Africans than are the residents of Salisbury. Such a tendency is not reflected in our data, however, as an inspection of Table 41 reveals.

TABLE 41. *Census District and Attitude Score*

| Census district by population of largest nucleus | No. | S.D. | Mean |
|---|---|---|---|
| Rural: under 1,000 | 92 | 1.04 | 2.40 |
| Semiurban: 1,000 to 10,000 | 99 | 1.03 | 2.42 |
| Urban: 10,000 to 50,000 (Bulawayo) | 119 | 1.05 | 2.33 |
| Urban: over 50,000 (Salisbury) | 190 | 1.23 | 2.57 |
| Totals | 500 | 1.12 | 2.45 |

$M_{Sal.} - M_{Bul.} = .24$   $t = 1.75$   $1$ of $c = >8\%$   $H_o =$ supported

The second proposition, which is more fundamental to the study, is that the State of Emergency in Southern Rhodesia has systematically altered European attitudes about Africans. A simple test of this hypothesis is possible. The sampling in Bulawayo was done prior to the Proclamation of the Emergency, and at all other places the testing was done during the Emergency. On the Proclamation, testing was discontinued and some time was allowed to elapse because of an apparent unease among Europeans. After five weeks, it seemed that attitudes were more stabilized and the study was recommenced. It is our hypothesis that if the Emergency systematically influenced European attitudes, this would be reflected in significant differences between the Bulawayo and Salisbury scores. The Salisbury mean score

is .24 higher than that of Bulawayo, but the *t* test shows that this difference can have occurred over eight times in a hundred through sampling
fluctuations. It is possible that, with a much larger sample, Salisbury
might emerge as significantly more change-oriented than Bulawayo,
but we can make no such inference from the data.

It may also be argued that the Bulawayo attitudes were significantly
different from the Salisbury attitudes before the Emergency, and that
its effect has been to reduce the gap. But this assumption is untestable
and therefore will not be entertained further. Thus, we conclude that
the attitudes gathered during the Emergency are not significantly different from those gathered prior to it, and that it is legitimate to proceed with the analyses as if the Emergency had not intervened. One
notable fact is that attitudes in Southern Rhodesia are remarkably
similar irrespective of the degree of urban concentration.

## COUNTRY OF BIRTH

A number of beliefs on the relation of country of birth to race
attitudes are common coinage in Southern Rhodesia. It is averred by
some that Southern Rhodesians by birth have a greater understanding
of Africans, know their strengths and weaknesses better, and are therefore less likely to have an unrealistic attitude toward them. In this
context, the term "unrealistic" is generally equated with attitudes supporting social change. Another point of view suggests that persons
from Britain, with their roots more directly in a "liberal" Western culture, are more likely to have favorable relations with Africans. Again,
it is maintained that immigrants born south of the Limpopo are more
prone to carry with them the conservative attitudes about race that
have been described by MacCrone and Starfield (1949). Yet again, it
is postulated that South Africans of a less conservative persuasion
have emigrated because of an antipathy toward the Union's racial
policies. There are many subvarieties and corollaries to these points
of view. Our data, presented in Table 42, give some answer to these
speculations.

TABLE 42. *Country of Birth and Attitude Score*

| Country of birth | No. | S.D. | Mean |
|---|---|---|---|
| Non-Commonwealth | 31 | 1.24 | 2.84 |
| United Kingdom and Eire | 190 | 1.00 | 2.82 |
| Other Commonwealth | 24 | 1.35 | 2.61 |
| Southern Rhodesia | 78 | 1.15 | 2.22 |
| Union of South Africa | 177 | 1.02 | 2.07 |
| Totals | 500 | 1.12 | 2.45 |

$M_{U.K.} - M_{U.S.A.} = .75$   $t = 7.08$   1 of c $= <0.1\%$   $H_o =$ rejected
$M_{U.K.} - M_{S.R.} = .60$   $t = 4.26$   1 of c $= <0.1\%$   $H_o =$ rejected

Tests of significance have been calculated for the differences between the principal countries; the results are shown in Table 42. Because of the small numbers involved, little can be educed about the attitudes of those coming from other Commonwealth countries. The foreign block in the sample—Greeks, Portuguese, Italians, Central Europeans, and others—have attitudes that show almost the same center of gravity as the United Kingdom-born. Clearly individuals born in the British Isles have less conservative attitudes about Africans than persons born in Southern Rhodesia and the Union of South Africa. The most conservative persons are from South Africa, followed by those born in Southern Rhodesia.

But before one draws inferences about the Rhodesian-born, one has to take other factors into account. Of the seventy-eight born in Southern Rhodesia, all save four have spent a minimum of twenty years in the Colony, including the most formative years of their lives. Thus, to keep the relation of country of birth and attitude in proper perspective, it is also important to take length of residence into account. This has been done for the United Kingdom and the Union of South Africa, and the figures are shown in Table 43.

TABLE 43. *Country of Birth, Length of Residence, and Attitude Score*

| Years of residence | United Kingdom and Eire | | Union of South Africa | |
|---|---|---|---|---|
| | No. | Mean | No. | Mean |
| 0– 4 | 56 | 3.15 | 42 | 2.27 |
| 5– 9 | 60 | 2.87 | 31 | 1.89 |
| 10–19 | 36 | 2.63 | 35 | 2.12 |
| 20–29 | 13 | 2.61 | 30 | 1.97 |
| 30–39 | 15 | 2.57 | 17 | 1.77 |
| 40 and above | 10 | 2.14 | 22 | 2.27 |
| Totals | 190 | 2.82 | 177 | 2.07 |
| 20 and above | 38 | 2.47 | 69 | 2.01 |

There are some noteworthy trends in the table. Persons born in the United Kingdom enter the Colony with attitudes on the change side of the dimension, and they are modified in a conservative direction each year they stay. For those persons of British birth who have resided in the territory for twenty years and more, the attitude scores average 2.47. The average score for the Southern Rhodesian-born in the sample is 2.22, illustrating that although individuals from the United Kingdom have become more conservative, they are still not as conservative as the Southern Rhodesians.

It is also possible that recent immigrants from Britain (and elsewhere) are less conservative about racial matters than those who arrived upward of twenty years ago. Yet, from the interview evidence, it did seem clear that the attitudes of the British-born had been modified conservatively over the passage of time. Consequently, the assumption has been made (because we do not possess valid evidence to the contrary) that length of residence in Southern Rhodesia is of more significance than a possible change in the attitudinal climate of the United Kingdom or other countries from which immigrants have come. Our subsequent arguments rest on this assumption.

In contrast to the British-born, those from the Union entered the Colony with more conservative attitudes; for those of twenty years or more residence, the mean score is 2.01. The conclusion to be drawn from the figures is that the United Kingdom-born enter the Colony with change-tolerant attitudes on the whole, and although these are modified in a conservative direction, they still are more prone to tolerate change than either the South African or the Rhodesian-born. Thus, it seems clear that *both* country of birth *and* length of residence are important interlocking correlates of attitudes about Africans.

NATIONAL OR ETHNIC ORIGIN

The relation of country of birth and attitudes is made clearer if one analyzes attitudes in conjunction with the felt national origins of the sample. As we have stressed, the ethnic group to which an individual may feel he belongs does not always correspoond to legal nationality. As an example, many in our sample were born in the Union of South Africa but regard themselves as English or Afrikaner.

TABLE 44. *National or Ethnic Origin and Attitude Score*

| Origin | No. | S.D. | Mean |
|---|---|---|---|
| Rhodesian | 7 | — | 3.17 |
| British, Welsh, and Irish | | | |
| British | 10 | — | 3.08 |
| Welsh | 11 | — | 3.06 |
| Irish | 14 | — | 2.89 |
| Others | 35 | 1.13 | 2.70 |
| English | 302 | 1.08 | 2.57 |
| Scottish | 39 | .84 | 2.54 |
| South African | 12 | — | 2.27 |
| Afrikaner | 70 | .87 | 1.48 |
| Totals | 500 | 1.12 | 2.45 |

$M_{Eng.} - M_{Afrik.} = 1.09$    $t = 7.84$    1 of c $= <0.1\%$    $H_0 =$ rejected

From Table 44, it is clear that 60.4%, the bulk of the European population, regard themselves as English and have less conservative attitudes ($M = 2.57$) than the average for the remainder. By inference it is also clear that, apart from the 14.0% who identify themselves as Afrikaners, the majority of those born in the Union regard themselves as English, as might be anticipated. Also in the expected direction is the fact that the Afrikaners are the most conservative of our sample. Their standard deviation of .87 is almost the smallest of any of the groupings and demonstrates a greater degree of cultural homogeneity than that displayed by Englishmen.

Of interest is the small number who identify themselves as British, Welsh, or Irish, as distinct from English or Scottish. Their composite mean attitude score of 3.00 is substantially less conservative than that of the population mean, although we have no explanation for this trend. We have also telescoped the Jewish-Hebrew and other nationalities together; as a group, they too display less conservative attitudes than the whole population. The Scottish in the sample have attitudes similar to those of the English, except that the former are more homogeneous. A very small number describe themselves as Rhodesian (1.4%) and South African (2.4%), but they are too few to permit valid generalizations.

For purposes of further analysis we have taken the two largest groups, the English and the Afrikaners, and determined the significance of the difference between their mean scores. The $t$ value is significant beyond the 0.1% level of confidence, signifying that the difference in attitude can be taken as genuine and is not a consequence of chance fluctuations in sampling. Accordingly, the null hypothesis must be rejected.

## LENGTH OF RESIDENCE

It has been suggested that length of residence within Southern Rhodesia is related to attitudes about Africans. Our data allow a fairly precise examination of this hypothesis. It can be seen from Table 45 that persons who support the status quo least strongly are those who have been in the Colony for less than five years. Thereafter, attitudes become more conservative until the period of 30–39 years is reached. A $t$ test on the difference in attitude between the two most contrasting periods of residence indicates that it is very significant. However, the standard deviations show that there is much overlap between the intervals displayed in Table 45, and that some individuals who have lived in the country for a short space of time hold attitudes as conservative as those held after a residence of forty years and more. Conversely, some of the long-time residents display attitudes as change-oriented as those of the newcomers. This variation can be accounted for by differences in education, religious affiliation, country of birth, national origin, and many other factors.

The intrusion of other factors may be educed by reference to the correlation that has been run between length of residence and attitude score. The obtained correlation of —.17 is significant at beyond the

0.1% level of confidence, showing that in less than one instance in a thousand such a relation can be obtained through the vagaries of sampling. Thus, we take it as proven that as length of residence increases, attitudes about Africans tend to become more conservative. Although the correlation is highly significant, it is still small, and from this we suggest that other factors, such as those mentioned above, also have some role to play in the molding of attitudes. Accordingly, it is not valid to assess an individual's attitudes about Africans solely on the basis of length of residence.

TABLE 45. *Length of Residence and Attitude Score*

| Years of residence | No. | S.D. | Mean |
|---|---|---|---|
| 0– 4 | 112 | 1.28 | 2.82 |
| 5– 9 | 103 | 1.05 | 2.46 |
| 10–19 | 84 | 1.06 | 2.47 |
| 20–29 | 92 | 1.07 | 2.32 |
| 30–39 | 54 | .94 | 2.11 |
| 40 and above | 55 | 1.03 | 2.18 |
| Totals | 500 | 1.12 | 2.45 |

$M_{0-4} - M_{30-39} = .71$   $t = 3.62$   1 of c = <0.1%   $H_o$ = rejected
$r_{xy} = -.17$   $t = 3.85$   1 of c = <0.1%   $H_o$ = rejected

## OCCUPATION

Studies of socioeconomic status indicate that one's occupation depends on a number of factors, not the least of which are education and intelligence. Inasmuch as there is evidence to suggest that education and intelligence are also related to race attitudes, it is not imprudent to postulate a relation between occupation and attitudes. Table 46 shows the way in which the test scores vary with type of occupation.

The highest scores fall in the professional and technical grouping, the persons who are architects, chemists, engineers, journalists, missionaries, physicians, teachers, and the like. To some extent, their attitudes may be a consequence of higher intelligence and scholastic achievement. But not without influence is the fact that individuals in the professional and technical occupations experience little competition as yet from the emergent Africans, and furthermore, most other occupational groupings are likely to experience this competition first.

At the conservative end of the dimension, we find the craftsmen— the fitters, motor mechanics, metal workers, plumbers, welders, and so on—who are beginning to experience the impact of African competition. In the interviews, the craftsmen continually expressed concern for the future, as did the transport, mine, service, and sales workers. Hence, it is not difficult to forecast that, in such occupational groupings, we will find the most conservative attitudes about the problems posed by African advancement.

It is noteworthy that of the seven occupational groupings four display more conservative attitudes than the farmers. It is a common belief in many societies that farmers are traditionally among the most conservative of occupational groups. This is not so in Southern Rhodesia with respect to race attitudes, although it is true that the farming community does contain persons of very conservative persuasion, as the standard deviation of .98 demonstrates. But the conservative farmers are counterbalanced by others who are less so, these being, for the greater part, immigrants from the United Kingdom or of English origin from South Africa.

TABLE 46. *Occupation and Attitude Score*

| Occupation | No. | S.D. | Mean |
|---|---|---|---|
| Professional and technical | 68 | 1.15 | 3.21 |
| Managerial, admin., and clerical | 117 | 1.04 | 2.70 |
| Farmers, hunters, and lumbermen | 35 | .98 | 2.30 |
| Economically inactive and unstated | 170 | 1.11 | 2.25 |
| Others | | | |
|   Sales workers | 20 | .92 | 2.20 |
|   Operating transport workers | 8 | — | 2.19 |
|   Foremen and skilled | 32 | .94 | 2.17 |
|   Service workers | 10 | — | 2.05 |
|   Mine and quarry workers | 4 | — | 2.04 |
| Craftsmen | 36 | .85 | 1.95 |
| Totals | 500 | 1.12 | 2.45 |

$M_{Prof.} - M_{Crafts.} = 1.26$    $t = 5.78$    1 of c $= <0.1\%$    $H_o =$ rejected

The economically inactive group of 170 persons, of whom 153 were women, proved somewhat more conservative than anticipated. Most of these women were occupied with home duties, although a few were retired persons. We have noted that women collectively obtain a somewhat more conservative score (2.39) on our test than do men (2.51). However, this does not explain the more conservative center of gravity (2.25) of the economically inactive grouping. The data show that women who work, and are therefore classifiable as economically active, are substantially less conservative than those involved solely in home duties or retired. Their respective scores are 2.69 and 2.23.

The *t* test on the difference in scores between the professional and technical class and the craftsmen, the two most contrasting groups, results in a rejection of the null hypothesis at a very significant level of confidence.

## Type of Industry or Business

For the sampling model, a distinction was made between the occupation of an individual and the type of industry or business in which he was employed. The economically inactive persons, it will be recalled, were allocated to the industry on which they were dependent. Thus a miner and his wife, engaged solely in home duties, were both classified under the heading of mining. Table 47 shows the relation between industry and attitude.

TABLE 47. *Type of Industry or Business and Attitude Score*

| Industry or business | No. | S.D. | Mean |
|---|---|---|---|
| Govt. and business services | 95 | 1.17 | 3.15 |
| Industry unstated | 14 | — | 2.68 |
| Economically inactive | 29 | 1.06 | 2.39 |
| Transport and communications | 51 | 1.14 | 2.39 |
| Mining and quarrying | 28 | 1.00 | 2.33 |
| Commerce | 99 | .97 | 2.29 |
| Construction | 50 | 1.04 | 2.22 |
| Agriculture, forestry, and fishing | 59 | 1.00 | 2.20 |
| Manufact. and repair; elect., water, and sanitary services | 75 | 1.08 | 2.20 |
| Totals | 500 | 1.12 | 2.45 |

$M_{\text{Govt. and Bus.}} - M_{\text{Agric.}} = .95$   $t = 5.28$   1 of c $= <0.1\%$   $H_o$ = rejected

One category stands out from all the rest by virtue of its higher mean score. This includes individuals employed in government and business services, as defined by the Central African Statistical Office. The classification embraces three fairly distinct types of occupation, and the standard deviation of 1.17 shows that it is the most heterogeneous of the industrial groupings.

The first subclassification is that of government administrative services, which includes administrators in the Federal, territorial, municipal, and local governments, the police, the defense forces, and so on. The second subclassification is that of community and business services, embracing all schools, the health services, religious services, legal services, government research stations, medical aid societies, and political organizations. It is generally true that these two subclassifications encompass occupations that are professional, managerial, and administrative in nature and display the highest scores in the occupational analysis.

The third subclassification covers private domestic work, restaurants, hotels and boarding houses, and other personal services such as those rendered by barbers, hairdressers, undertakers, and fumigators. It is within the third subclassification of services that we generally find the most conservative attitudes. This is in accord with our theme that individuals whose occupational status is most likely to be affected by African advancement are most likely to resist changes in the status quo. However, the proportion of persons falling within the third subclassification is small, and it is outweighed by the numbers scoring toward the higher end of the scale. This accounts for the change-oriented general attitude in the grouping of services personnel.

It is noteworthy that although the farmers as an occupational grouping obtain a mean score of 2.30, agriculture as a type of business or industry drops to 2.20. This shift occurs mainly through the inclusion of farmers' wives in the industrial classification. In general, they fall more toward the conservative end of the continuum than do their husbands. For purposes of contrast, a *t* test has been applied to the difference in mean score between the classifications of agriculture and government and business services. The *t* value of 5.28 indicates a highly significant difference between the mean scores of 3.15 and 2.20, respectively. Because of this difference, it seems most probable that persons in agriculture will also reflect different attitudes about such matters as education for Africans, the use of public facilities, and African participation in politics.

Apart from the services grouping and the fourteen persons who do not give sufficient information for classification, there is much similarity in the mean attitudes of the people in the remaining occupations. They all fall on the conservative side of the mean for the whole distribution.

## INCOME

In the planning stages of the study, it was felt that an individual's income would bear some relation to his attitudes. Individuals in the higher income brackets, we assumed, would be less threatened by direct African competition and therefore more likely to hold favorable attitudes. But Table 48 illustrates the very uneven nature of the distribution that does in fact emerge.

The most conservative grouping, comprised mainly of women, is that earning no income. This is consistent with our other findings. Following our postulation, we would expect to discover the least conservative attitudes among those earning £1800 and above. But this does not happen. The most change-tolerant persons fall within the £600–899 bracket, but we have not discovered the reasons for this. The standard deviation of 1.29 for those earning between £600 and £899 is the largest shown in Table 48.

Another factor that undoubtedly has some bearing on the asymmetry of the table is that of the working wife. The married woman in

Southern Rhodesia, because of the availability of domestic servants, is able to accept employment which supplements the husband's income, but which is not regarded as a career in itself. The attitudes of the working wife seem more likely to be related to the husband's income and economic prospects than to her own salary.

TABLE 48. *Income and Attitude Score*

| Income in £ | No. | S.D. | Mean |
|---|---|---|---|
| Nil | 148 | 1.09 | 2.19 |
| 1– 299 | 14 | — | 2.57 |
| 300– 599 | 33 | .88 | 2.35 |
| 600– 899 | 74 | 1.29 | 2.92 |
| 900–1199 | 86 | 1.09 | 2.29 |
| 1200–1499 | 69 | 1.03 | 2.57 |
| 1500–1799 | 32 | 1.25 | 2.47 |
| 1800 and above | 44 | .84 | 2.71 |
| Totals | 500 | 1.12 | 2.45 |

$M_{N11} - M_{600-899} = .73$ $\quad t = 4.40$ $\quad$ 1 of c $= <0.1\%$ $\quad H_o =$ rejected
$r_{xy} = -.01$ $\quad\quad\quad\quad\quad t = .22$ $\quad$ 1 of c $= >50\%$ $\quad H_o =$ supported

The largest difference (.73) between any two income groupings has been tested and found to be significant. But the correlation of income and attitude yields a coefficient of —.01 which is statistically not different from zero. Because of this total absence of relation, and the heterogeneous nature of occupations within a single income range, further analyses of income and attitude probably will yield little of value.

EDUCATION

Of the continuous data analyzed in this chapter, the clearest relation that emerges is between length of schooling and attitude score. Attitudes about differential treatment and behavior swing progressively toward the "discontinue" end of the dimension as education lengthens. This trend is shown in Table 49. However, the standard deviations show that at any point on the ladder there is considerable variation in attitude, and that some individuals with extended education show conservative attitudes.

The product-moment correlation of .41 between length of schooling and attitude is highly significant, and it is worth speculating a little on the deductions that can be made from it. From the relation between these two variables, one can calculate that 16.81% of their total variance (i.e., $100r_{xy}^2$) is held in common, and that the remainder is due to other influences.

The correlation may also be employed to show how accurately an attitude score can be predicted from an individual's known length of schooling. To effect this, use is made of an index of predictive efficiency (E). Simply defined, E shows the reduction in error of prediction (expressed as a percentage) because of the correlation that exists between two variables x and y, in this case length of schooling and attitude score. Leaving out the mathematical rationale, it has been demonstrated that $E = 100 \ (1 - \sqrt{1 - r_{xy}^2})$, wherein $r_{xy}$ represents the correlation between the independent (x) and dependent

TABLE 49. *Length of Schooling and Attitude Score*

| Years | No. | S.D. | Mean |
|---|---|---|---|
| 0– 8 | 56 | .96 | 1.83 |
| 9–10 | 150 | .93 | 2.07 |
| 11–12 | 165 | .98 | 2.46 |
| 13–14 | 60 | 1.10 | 2.94 |
| 15–16 | 40 | 1.09 | 3.34 |
| 17 and above | 29 | 1.34 | 3.33 |
| Totals | 500 | 1.12 | 2.45 |

$M_{0-8} - M_{15-16} = 1.51$   $t = 7.19$   1 of c $= <0.1\%$   $H_0 =$ rejected
$r_{xy} = .41$   $t = 10.03$   1 of c $= <0.1\%$   $H_0 =$ rejected

(y) variables. Substituting in the formula, $E = 8.8\%$. This means that, with the given correlation of .41, the amount of error in predicting y (attitude) from x (duration of schooling) is only 8.8% less than that which can be obtained on the basis of chance. From this demonstration, it should be clear that correlations in the order of .41, even though highly significant, cannot be employed for the prediction of an individual's behavior. Consequently, we are obliged to analyze the attitudes of groupings of people on the assumption that deviations on either side of a mean score will tend to cancel out.

## RELIGIOUS AFFILIATION OR PREFERENCE

For the sampling model, religious affiliations or preferences are grouped into broad categories, and subvarieties are not treated separately. Of our respondents, 474 express affiliation to or preference for some religious denomination, and twenty-six specify that they either have no religion or do not adhere to any of the recognized denominations. The mean attitude scores are shown in Table 50.

Persons with the highest mean scores specify no religious affiliation. However, this grouping is something of a mixed bag, as the large standard deviation of 1.38 illustrates. Attitude scores range from very high to extremely low, and there seems to be no genuine center of gravity to the distribution. If the dispersion of scores in the distribution were more restricted, deductions would be possible even with a small group of twenty-six. As this is not the case here, we feel it is wisest to leave the nonreligious grouping out of. further major discussion. Similarly, we are not prepared to draw inferences about the "Other Christian" grouping that lumps together Baptists, members of the Church of Sweden, Greek Orthodox adherents, Jehovah's Witnesses, Quakers, Seventh Day Adventists, and others.

TABLE 50. *Religious Affiliation or Preference and Attitude Score*

| Affiliation or preference | No. | S.D. | Mean |
|---|---|---|---|
| No affiliation | 26 | 1.38 | 3.03 |
| Roman Catholic | 58 | 1.11 | 2.90 |
| Other Christian | 33 | 1.19 | 2.63 |
| Anglican | 194 | 1.04 | 2.60 |
| Jewish | 17 | — | 2.60 |
| Presbyterian | 72 | .89 | 2.31 |
| Methodist | 53 | 1.10 | 2.14 |
| Dutch Reformed | 47 | .79 | 1.38 |
| Totals | 500 | 1.12 | 2.45 |

$M_{R.C.} - M_{D.R.} = 1.52$   $t = 7.84$   1 of c $= <0.1\%$   $H_o =$ rejected
$M_{Ang.} - M_{D.R.} = 1.22$   $t = 7.53$   1 of c $= <0.1\%$   $H_o =$ rejected

It is easy to rank the remainder according to religious affiliation. The least conservative, on the average, are the Roman Catholics. Then, in order of increasing conservatism, are the Anglican, Jewish, Presbyterian, Methodist, and, finally, Dutch Reformed. It should be stressed that the attitudes expressed by the individuals in our sample are not necessarily the attitudes of the church leaders. Not infrequently there is a considerable distance between the views expressed by religious leaders and laymen. As an example, quite a number of the Methodist ministers of British Central Africa express views on race that are change-oriented by our definition, but the members generally hold distinctly conservative attitudes.

In other studies, it has been argued that the Roman Catholic church is conservative by tradition, but within Southern Rhodesia the hierarchy generally does not adopt such a position on race relations. Catholic leaders have advocated the discontinuance of many laws and practices that differentiate between Africans and Europeans. Our evidence suggests that they may have influenced the members of their church to a greater degree than have the leaders of other denominations.

The greatest difference in attitude lies between members of the Roman Catholic and Dutch Reformed churches. A *t* test has been run on the difference between their mean scores, and it is found to be highly significant. Thus it can be postulated that the difference is not due to chance fluctuations in sampling, but stems from basic differences in philosophy or doctrine. The distance between individuals in the Dutch Reformed and Anglican churches is also significant, and cannot be explained on the grounds of sampling fluctuations.

### POLITICAL PARTY PREFERENCE

A division of the population by political party preference results in a number of sharp differences. The center of gravity of each party is displayed in Table 51. By far the most change-oriented grouping

TABLE 51. *Political Party Preference and Attitude Score*

| Preference | No. | S.D. | Mean |
|---|---|---|---|
| Constitution | 5 | — | 4.84 |
| United Federal | 290 | 1.03 | 2.88 |
| Dominion | 177 | .89 | 1.78 |
| Other | | | |
| Confederate | 7 | — | 1.87 |
| Unspecified | 21 | .78 | 2.13 |
| Totals | 500 | 1.12 | 2.45 |

$M_{U.Fed.} - M_{Dom.} = 1.10$   $t = 11.81$   1 of c $= <0.1\%$   $H_o =$ rejected

is that which offers support to the Constitution party. Even though only five such cases are embraced within the sample, their mean score is so profoundly different from that of Federal party adherents that the possibility of chance accounting for the gap cannot be accepted. The least conservative supporters of the two major political divisions prefer the United Federal party; they occupy a position close to the theoretical center of the scale. It will be remembered that the center of the obtained distribution of Southern Rhodesian scores is 2.45, although the theoretical center of the scale is 3.00. Thus, whereas the supporters of the Federal party are substantially less conservative than the adherents of the Dominion party, they in fact occupy a mean position that politicians might feel justified in calling middle of the road.

The Dominion party is the major conservative party of Southern Rhodesia. In Chapter 6, in the section on test validity, we demonstrated that its mean position is significantly different from that of the Federal party. The seven cases indicating support for the Confederate party lie close to the Dominion party, but the difference between them is not large enough to indicate any significance. It is worth observing, however, that political thinking in Southern Rhodesia generally places the Confederate party on the conservative side of the Dominion party. The fact that this does not occur in our study can be regarded as an anomaly.

The mean attitude score for those who do not indicate a political preference is 2.13, which is slightly nearer the position of Dominion party supporters than Federal party adherents. From this, it can be inferred that the more conservative Europeans show somewhat greater reluctance to indicate their political views. However, we have considered neither this unspecified grouping, the Constitution party, nor the Confederate party as large enough to warrant separate analysis. At the Federal election of 1958 there were only two parties that received significant support, the Dominion party and the United Federal party, and it is the supporters of these two that we will examine in subsequent analyses.

For each of the subpopulations of reasonable size, mean attitude scores and standard deviations have been computed. Then, within each of the stratification areas, the most contrasting attitude scores have been pulled out and the differences between them tested by means of Gosset's $t$ formula. A comparable $t$ test has also been made of the correlations between attitude and age, length of residence, income, and length of schooling, respectively. These two sets of data, which are summarized in Table 52, will guide the selection of subpopulations for further analysis.

Of the stratification areas, subpopulations within eight of them are treated in the chapters to follow. Sex, age, and census district reveal no significant correlation with general race attitude; consequently they are not likely to show a relation to attitudes about social and recreational facilities, legal justice, the use of land, and so on. Under the heading of community of residence, we have no valid data, so naturally it cannot be handled. The other area eliminated at this point involves income. Because of the total absence of relation between income and attitude, and the heterogeneous nature of occupations within a single income range, additional examinations will furnish little information of value. The important social and personal characteristics that remain in the study, then, are country of birth, national or ethnic origin, length of residence, occupation, type of industry or business, length of schooling, religious affiliation or preference, and political party preference.

The following chapters contain analyses of the relations between these eight characteristics and European attitudes about the differential laws and customs that affect Africans in such matters as legal justice, sexual relations, the franchise, and educational opportunities. The focus shifts, therefore, from an analysis of attitude scores on the

TABLE 52. *Summary of the t Tests between the Principal Subpopulations and the Correlations on Continuous Data*

| Area of stratification | Contrasted subpopulations | $r_{xy}$ | t | Level of confidence | Null hypothesis |
|---|---|---|---|---|---|
| 1. Sex * | Males : Females | | 1.21 | >20.0% | supported |
| 2. Age * | 20–29 yrs. : 60–69 yrs. | | 1.24 | >20.0% | supported |
| | | −.07 | 1.57 | >10.0% | supported |
| 3. Community of residence * | *no valid data* | | | | |
| 4. Census district * | Salisbury : Bulawayo | | 1.75 | > 8.0% | supported |
| 5. Country of birth | U.K. and Eire : South Africa | | 7.08 | < 0.1% | rejected |
| | U.K. and Eire : S. Rhodesia | | 4.26 | < 0.1% | rejected |
| 6. National or ethnic origin | English : Afrikaner | | 7.84 | < 0.1% | rejected |
| 7. Length of residence | 0–4 yrs. : 30–39 yrs. | | 3.62 | < 0.1% | rejected |
| | | −.17 | 3.85 | < 0.1% | rejected |
| 8. Occupation | Prof. and tech. : Craftsmen | | 5.78 | < 0.1% | rejected |
| 9. Type of industry | Govt. and bus. : Agriculture | | 5.28 | < 0.1% | rejected |
| 10. Income * | £ 600–899 : Nil | | 4.40 | < 0.1% | rejected |
| | | −.01 | .22. | >50.0% | supported |
| 11. Length of schooling | 15–16 yrs. : 0–8 yrs. | | 7.19 | < 0.1% | rejected |
| | | .41 | 10.03 | < 0.1% | rejected |
| 12. Religious affiliation or preference | R. Catholic : Dutch Ref. | | 7.84 | < 0.1% | rejected |
| | Anglican : Dutch Ref. | | 7.53 | < 0.1% | rejected |
| 13. Political party preference | U. Federal : Dominion | | 11.81 | < 0.1% | rejected |

* Omitted from subsequent analyses.

133

*entire questionnaire* to an examination of the responses of various groupings to the eleven *categories* of differentiating laws and customs that have been established.

Each of the chapters will be introduced by a sociocultural discussion of the relevant differential laws and customs in Southern Rhodesia since the beginning of European settlement. Then the reasons given by the sample, either orally or in writing, for wanting to maintain or discontinue the practices cited in the questionnaire will be described. After presenting the data on contemporary attitudes, the scores of various subpopulations will be analyzed according to the eight significant personal and social variables reported in this chapter. Chapters 10 through 17 will conclude with an identification of the themes that appear in the behavior of Europeans in Southern Rhodesia.

# 10

## LEGAL JUSTICE

The concept of justice, in its broad sense, is rooted in philo-sophic, moral, and religious principles, and these provide the ultimate standards, the fundamental human rights from which the common law of a culture group is derived (Tredgold, 1960). The idea of justice, therefore, is difficult to define, and this is particularly so in a society like Southern Rhodesia, with its different peoples and different legal systems. Two culture groups, or even two individuals, may apply divergent criteria for determining what is just or unjust. Justice and law are intimately related to the society in which they operate. As one of many institutions in society, the law is affected by other institutions and activities: family and kinship relations, economic activities, political practices, and other social matters.

The law, in a narrow sense, is one of the principal mechanisms by which a society attempts to control the behavior of its individual members and groups. Thus, while the common law may embrace enduring standards that have evolved through time, the law of the day, the statute law, may reflect divergent standards resulting from institutional and other pressures within society, and so may the courts. For such reasons it is important to draw a distinction between the common law, the statute law, and the attitudes of the courts.

## THE COMMON LAW

European immigrants into the land of the Mashona and Matabele brought their legal system with them. In 1891, Southern Rhodesia adopted the laws in force in the Colony of the Cape of Good Hope, and the 1898 Order-in-Council gave official sanction to these laws. The new legal system contained important differences from the common law of England: its procedures were largely English, but its principles were a mixture of Roman-Dutch and English antecedents. The criminal law was largely derived from England, whereas the civil code was largely Roman-Dutch (Patterson, 1957:89). In view of the differentiating nature of much statute law in Southern Rhodesia, it is important to note that Roman-Dutch law, as modified in the Cape of Good Hope by English law, discountenanced all forms of racial discrimination. It is not without significance that many of the great names in international law are those of the founders of the Roman-Dutch system, and they played a large part in formulating the principles that have become the basis for the modern approach to fundamental human rights. This Roman-Dutch *cum* English system has continued in Southern Rhodesia, even though, since the establishing of the Federal Supreme Court in 1955, appeals are no longer referred to the Supreme Court of South Africa in Bloemfontein.

During the early decades of European settlement, the new legal system had litle influence on the majority of Africans. From the time of the granting of a Charter to the B. S. A. Company, African laws and customs had been partially recognized. Although African customary law has been modified over time, it is still applicable as long as it is not repugnant to European ideas of "natural" justice or morality, or has not been superseded by legislation (Hailey, 1957:595).

Since all criminal cases are tried by Roman-Dutch and statutory law, African customary law applies only in civil cases between Africans and Africans. Africans and Europeans, therefore, can be subject to different sets of legal principles and practices.

African civil cases are heard within a tripartite system of Headmen's or Chiefs' Courts, the Native Commissioners' Courts, and the Native Appeal Courts.[1] As these courts are not concerned with litigation between Europeans and Africans, they are not a major concern in our study. However, it may be noted that, particularly in appeal cases, Native Commissioners will refer to the works of their predecessors (e.g. Posselt, 1927, and Bullock, 1950) or to those of anthropologists familiar with African laws and customs (e.g. Holleman, 1952). But so-called African law is not fixed and static; it has been modified by European contact both in its principles and in its practices (Simons, 1958).

There has been almost no attempt to codify African customary law in Southern Rhodesia. Such an endeavor would raise both theoretical and practical problems for society. It would be difficult to decide which tribe's law, as practiced at which date, should be codified. To do so, Lewin (1947:5) warns, "might tend to crystallize a custom in which a change had become desirable."

In all criminal cases, and in civil cases that involve both European and African litigants, Roman-Dutch law prevails. Jurisdiction rests with either the Magistrates' or High Courts, depending upon the nature and seriousness of the case. In rural areas, the role of magistrate may be filled by the Native Commissioner, but in larger urban centers, judicial and administrative responsibilities are performed by different people. African criminal cases in the High Court are tried before a judge and two special assessors rather than a judge and common jury. Assessors are officials or ex-officials of the Native Affairs Department. In cases where a European is charged with a serious crime against an African, the trial may be held before a judge and specially selected jury.

These details give only a rough outline of how the common law introduced by Europeans and the customary law of Africans are interwoven in Southern Rhodesia's judicial system. In the future, the two may be fused into a single system, but the existing cultural differences make it impossible to forecast when, or indeed if, this will happen.

## THE STATUTE LAWS AND REGULATIONS

In the early days of the Colony, and later, many laws and regulations were passed by Europeans to reinforce their status superiority and control over the conquered Africans. Some of these laws and regulations underlie the statements in our questionnaire; for example, those on apprenticeship training, separate schools, the ownership of land and houses in European areas, the use of certain public facilities, passes, the franchise and the electoral system, firearms, and so on (see Appendix B). In general, these matters are treated more fully in other chapters because, under our classification, they do not flow from the operation of the courts. But it is important to stress their relevance in this study inasmuch as they reflect the European attitudes of the day.

The ordinances on sexual matters, however, should be mentioned in more detail, because, in the minds of many of our sample, the principle of equity is involved. In 1903, an ordinance to suppress immorality was passed. A European woman found guilty of illicit intercourse with an African man was liable to two years hard labor, while the African was liable to five years.[2] Later, in 1916, a further ordinance was passed which made "acts of indecency" between African

males and European females an offense.[3] But, of significance to our
attitude study, no prohibitions were placed upon similar conduct between European males and African females.

Other laws and regulations were introduced in the belief that they
would be for the benefit or protection of Africans. Among them are
the Land Husbandry Act, and those related to the purchase of
lottery tickets and alcoholic spirits. But these were not the only
motives behind the enactments, as some of our later evidence shows.
Another law, which seems clearly protectory, was enacted in the early
years of the Colony. A considerable number of Europeans had with-
held the wages due to their African servants and employees, particularly in the period of economic stress that accompanied the Boer War.
These cases caused concern, and a law was passed making it a criminal offense not to pay such wages. As would be expected, a number
of prosecutions followed, but the frequency declined and the practice
has now virtually disappeared.

Some of the requirements imposed upon Africans seem an inevitable concomitant of the dominant new culture. The spread of Christianity brought many Africans under some of the European laws,
especially in matters of marriage and divorce (Lewin, 1947). Economic expansion and European society have also progressively involved Africans in new activities with legal sanctions behind them.
As a consequence, new kinds of petty and major crimes have been
generated among Africans. Hailey (1957) and Gussman (1952–53)
have instanced some of the new kinds of rules and regulations that
affect Africans: the theft of European artifacts, delinquency in hire-
purchase and insurance payments, riding unlicensed or unlighted
bicycles, and so on.

From this brief inspection, it can be seen that most of the statute
laws, rules, and regulations have no precedents in African customary
law, and the traditional sanctions for conformity do not operate.
The Africans' extended kinship systems, political structures, and relationships with the natural environment can only apply to a limited
percentage of criminal and civil cases arising in an urbanized and
industrialized society. As an increasing number of Africans become
acculturated and integrated into the emergent social system, European
legal principles and procedures will undoubtedly assume greater importance. African involvement in litigation and the legal justice administered to the guilty derive in part from the attitudes and policies
of Europeans toward Africans. Much litigation results, however, from
the unavoidable stresses that accompany the integration of peasants
and tribesmen into "modern" society.

## THE COURTS AND THE LEGAL SYSTEM

A number of problems face those who administer the laws applying in Southern Rhodesia. On the one hand, magistrates, judges, Native Commissioners, and others have had training in, and are familiar with, the fundamental equity of the common law. On the other hand, even though they may do so with misgiving, they are obliged to administer statute laws and regulations that frequently differentiate on the grounds of race. Yet again, they are subject to the attitudes of society outside the courts—a society concerned with its status and, in the case of Europeans, with its control over the African population. For these reasons, we intend focusing our attention on the operation of the courts within the legal structure of Southern Rhodesia.

One method would be to select the anomalies in the administration of justice, and illustrate them by reference to specific cases. These can certainly be found in Southern Rhodesia's history, but by the selection of specific cases the impression could be conveyed that Africans have been subjected to persistent judicial injustice. Furthermore, the norms of independence and impartiality today are markedly different from those of the early pioneering period when legal power was in the hands of people who were not adequately trained or experienced. To give a complete picture, from which valid deductions could be drawn, and to show how norms have changed, would require a separate study on its own, and is outside the scope and intent of our research.

Instead, rather than concentrate on case law, we intend to examine briefly some of the problems that face the administration of justice in Southern Rhodesia. In so doing, we will look at the jury system, the influences on magistrates and judges, the roles played by status, social class, and other factors, the preparation of defense, the review procedures, and the sentences applied. All of these bear on the determination of justice by the courts.

The early European population of Southern Rhodesia included a mixture of rough and ignorant people—the "riff-raff" [4]—and a large number of men who were well-educated and well-mannered.[5] Compared with frontier societies elsewhere, the documentary evidence suggests that the Southern Rhodesian immigrants were relatively more law-abiding. Still, heavy drinking in the 1890's and early 1900's led to a number of unwarranted abuses of Africans, and it was not uncommon for Africans to be intimidated or frightened by gunfire.

Juries play an important role in the administration of justice in the Western world. Prior to 1899, accused persons in Southern Rhodesia were tried in the High Court by a judge and assessors and not by a jury. Since the largest group among the immigrants were of British origin, they pressed for a jury system, and it was introduced by Ordinance 4 of 1899. Both Europeans and Africans indicted in the High Court were then normally tried by a judge and a jury. At first the qualifications of jurymen were theoretically nonracial, but Africans were later expressly excluded from serving on juries, though they were still tried by them.[6]

The jury system seems to have worked fairly as long as racial passions were not aroused. In particular, racial passion erupted over sexual offenses. For example, in 1902 and 1903 a number of "black peril" cases occurred in which African men allegedly attacked European women. The European public reacted quickly and demanded that attempted and actual rape should carry the death penalty. Legislation to that effect was enacted in 1903, though the imposition of the sentence was left to the judge's discretion. Mason (1958:246) observes that the more extreme sentences were given to African rather than to European men.

Some anomalous decisions were also reached in cases of cross-racial assault and violence. In these, the European sentences were comparatively light. It is not suggested that such miscarriages of justice were the norm. Even so, they occurred with sufficient frequency in the early years for the judicial officers, and others, to question the impartiality of the jury system.

The unease over the validity of the jury system, according to Mason (1958:308), "exposed the corporate conscience of Rhodesia at work." Warfare existed "between two contradictory sets of values —on the one hand, justice as betwen man and man, fair play and a fair trial, ideals felt with pride to be part of the English heritage; on the other, the purity and prestige of the dominant race and the preservation of its dominance." The Europeans eventually realized that justice was not necessarily served best by the jury system (Howman, 1949). In 1912, an attempt was made to eliminate miscarriages of justice due to bias by the introduction of the "special" jury. When a European was charged in the High Courts with a serious crime against an African, and vice versa, the trial was before a judge and a jury selected from a special panel of jurors. Even this refinement was considered ineffective, and since 1927 all Africans indicted in the High Court have been tried by a judge and assessors.

Thus, the present position is that in the High Court all Africans are tried by a judge and assessors. Europeans are tried by an ordinary jury, or, where they are charged with a serious crime against an African, a special jury. But in all cases, they may opt for a trial by a judge and assessors.[7]

Another problem concerns the different knowledge that magistrates and Native Commissioners may have of African behavior and customary law. Native Commissioners in Southern Rhodesia benefit from their direct and extensive contact with Africans. Magistrates in urban areas, on the other hand, have generally had less direct contact with African life to assist them in interpreting African motives, honesty, intentions, and the credibility of evidence. Thus urban magistrates are obliged to administer justice to people who distinguish differently, and far less precisely than do Europeans, between civil and criminal law. Indeed, Africans had virtually no criminal law as Europeans understand it. Wrongs were dealt with as an injury to a group to be compensated through payment, the surrender of an individual, or some other way.

Until Holleman's *Shona Customary Law* appeared in 1952, magistrates also had the disadvantage of possessing no serious study of the laws of any indigenous tribe or community. Further, in the absence of codified African laws, the higher courts in Southern Rhodesia have been unable to provide guidance to the lower courts. On the other hand, although such guidance is characteristic of most European legal systems,[8] it can be argued that a codification of African customary law would be of little real help to the higher courts of the Colony.

The status or social class position of judges may also affect legal justice. Like all people, judges participate in a network of social relations. They are subject to the values and interests of individuals of similar status which contrast with those of lower-class position. But, in comparison with many others, the judiciary in British countries has remained relatively independent of the attitudes and opinions of the local electorate. Judges, magistrates, prosecutors, and members of the B. S. A. Police in Southern Rhodesia are not installed through periodic elections. Hence they can take more initiative than their counterparts in, say, the United States (Myrdal, 1944), to restrain the irregular methods that might be used, such as intimidation and violence.

But there remains the possibility that other factors, as everywhere, influence the administration of legal justice. In the rural areas of Southern Rhodesia, for example, the Native Commissioner acts both as magistrate and administrator. In this dual role, he may face a dilemma in deciding whether to interpret Acts as an administrator, i.e. what the legislature *meant,* or as a judicial officer, i.e. what the legislature *said.* Because of possible administrative repercussions, the Commissioner also may be tempted to convict when he is satisfied in his own mind that the accused is guilty, even though the evidence does not clearly support a conviction.

A further problem, which has been touched upon already, stems from cultural, social, and economic differences between Europeans and Africans. The former are generally more familiar with the legal rights they have inherited, and their economic position is more advantageous for securing defense. Most Africans, on the other hand, have little knowledge of the basic rights they possess under the Roman-Dutch system. Minimal incomes restrict the possibility of retaining advocates and the likelihood of raising bail. Africans generally are ignorant of trial procedures even when defended.

As Simons (1949) has indicated also of South Africa, defendants in Southern Rhodesia face a legal procedure in which the prosecutor can utilize police reports, has few limitations on court expenditures, and works with the whole apparatus of the state behind him. The temptation is always present to place greater reliance upon the testimony of Government officials, especially policemen (who sometimes are also prosecutors), than upon the evidence presented by poorer and less educated persons. The courts have been mindful of this latter difficulty, and have declared that it is undesirable for a prosecutor to give evidence except on a formal point (Gardiner and Lansdown, 1957:384). Many convictions have been upset where the prosecutor's evidence appears to have caused prejudice. In addition, the correct interpretation of African testimony poses a problem that is absent where social class differences exist within a linguistically homogeneous society. All of these matters are integral in the delicate process of ascertaining legal justice in Southern Rhodesia.

It is appropriate next to consider the preparation of defense in its relation to legal justice. The law usually assumes that the members of society are equally able to pay the costs of professional services although financial assistance may sometimes be given to needy defendants (Simons, 1949). While no private legal aid society has developed so far in Southern Rhodesia,* provisions for aid in criminal cases are embodied in the Legal Assistance and Representation Act of 1948.[9] A certificate may be obtained under certain conditions which allows legal assistance for the defendant at the Government's expense. In practice in the High Court, such a certificate is invariably granted by the Attorney General in cases where the death sentence may be imposed, i.e. where the charge is murder or treason, and in extremely serious cases of rape. But in other cases, certificates are seldom granted by the Attorney General or judges. The Bar also has an arrangement with the Native Affairs Department whereby some Africans who have less than twenty-five guineas are assisted in High Court (and only there). Many Africans raise the necessary amount by selling a cow in the Reserves. With further urbanization this source of revenue will gradually disappear for many defendants while other sources, such as post office savings accounts, will be used increasingly.

* Following the arrest of members of the African National Congresses in Southern Rhodesia in 1959, sympathetic supporters established a fund to provide legal aid and, secondarily, other amenities to "detainees" and their dependents.

In civil cases, any person in Southern Rhodesia who has property *
valued at less than £10 may apply to the High Court for leave to
sue or defend as a pauper.[10] This figure is very low in view of the
costs of litigation, and the courts have raised it by interpretation.
However, Africans are largely ignorant of the procedure and have
few means of acquiring knowledge of it. Central to the problem is
the fact that, in the majority of cases, Africans are undefended. Thus
the onerous task of ensuring legal justice depends most heavily on
the judicial officers and the vigilance they exercise. This is especially
true in the Magistrates' Courts, and those presided over by Native
Commissioners.

There are review procedures that help to ensure legal justice,
however. Prior to 1950, if an accused person was sentenced to
corporal punishment, a period of imprisonment exceeding one month,
or a fine of £5 or more, his case was sent on review to the High Court
which could set aside the conviction, reduce or set aside the sentence,
return the case for retrial before another magistrate, send it back
for further evidence, etc. In 1950, the sentences were raised to imprisonment for over three months, or a fine of £25 or more (corporal
punishment remained the same) before the case was reviewed.

Those familiar with the review procedures, in much greater detail
than we are, believe it has worked well and enabled the High Court
judges to control the convictions and sentences of magistrates, some
of whom are less well qualified. Even so, it may be conceded that
the review procedures involve at least two difficulties. First, the reviewing judge does not see the witness and therefore cannot assess
credibility from demeanor. Second, magistrates and Native Commissioners often record evidence in longhand, and there have been
instances when it was recorded incorrectly, even where the accused
was defended. Since the review procedure does not cover cases in
which sentences are less than the above-mentioned limits, and considering the number of convictions set aside on review, some legal
officers believe that injustice sometimes does obtain.

The final matter to be considered is perhaps the most difficult of
all, namely, the comparison of court sentences given to Africans and
Europeans. In the first place, we are hampered in our comparison
because no comprehensive survey has ever been made of court sentences handed down in Southern Rhodesia. When this is done, it
seems to us that all of the problems discussed in the previous sections
will have to be taken into account. So will the differentiating nature
of much of the statute law and regulations that limit certain types
of offenses to Africans only.

* "Property" here excludes household goods, wearing apparel, and the tools
of one's trade.

As a matter for discussion, criminal cases before the Magistrates' Courts in 1958 are summarized in Table 53. The first noticeable feature about the data is that although the African population is twelve times larger than the European, the former have, proportionately, been convicted of only half as many crimes. Among other things, however, this may be a reflection of different degrees of law enforcement in rural and urban areas. Since few B. S. A. Police are stationed in the African Reserves, the possibility that guilty parties can be apprehended there is much smaller than it is elsewhere. To some, the figures may be taken to show that the authorities are

TABLE 53. *Criminal Cases in Magistrates' Courts, 1958* *

| | Convicted | | | | | Not convicted | |
|---|---|---|---|---|---|---|---|
| Category | Separate counts | Cuts only | Cuts and imprison-ment | In-dicted | Sentences of 1 year and over | Ac-quitted (trial) | Dis-charged on preparatory examination |
| Europeans | 13,123 | 25 | 8 | 36 | 19 | 828 | 41 |
| Africans | 78,600 | 682 | 528 | 630 | 403 | 3,566 | 227 |
| Others | 599 | 7 | 0 | 4 | 4 | 76 | 1 |
| Totals | 92,322 | 714 | 536 | 670 | 426 | 4,470 | 269 |
| Ratio of Africans to Europeans (12:1 in total population) | 6:1 | 27:1 | 66:1 | 18:1 | 21:1 | 4:1 | 6:1 |

* Excludes petty offenses which are dispensed with by the payment of deposit fines to the police.
Source: Southern Rhodesia, *Report of the Secretary for Justice and Internal Affairs for 1958* [C.S.R. 9-1959], p. 7.

unduly sympathetic toward Africans. Whether or not this is so can hardly be proven, but it is noteworthy that a number of early European leaders, such as Sir Charles Coghlan, enhanced their popularity by attacking the administration for what they claimed was pro-African sentiment. The interview material (to be examined later) indicates that this notion still persists among Europeans. Equally unproven, in our mind, is the selective evidence used by Franck (1960) in a recent book to imply that Africans have been subject to continued legal injustice.

Table 53 also shows that of persons charged with crime in 1958, African cases were half as likely as European to be discharged upon preparatory examination, and a third as likely to be acquitted after trial. These figures probably reflect the differential access of Europeans and Africans to legal representation.

In cases where the accused were convicted, Africans were more likely than Europeans to receive corporal punishment and sentences of one year or more. However, statistics have not been published showing the relation between the charges and the sentences given. Some advocates suggest that Africans may be guilty of violating, with greater frequency than Europeans, those laws that provide sanctions of corporal punishment. This point must be borne in mind because of the stratified nature of Rhodesian society and the different status and economic positions that Africans and Europeans occupy. Thus, to our knowledge, no African has ever been convicted of a company fraud, of an insurance offense, or of share market rigging. So far, such crimes are peculiarly European. Nevertheless, it cannot be gainsaid that some of the penalties fixed by statute apply almost exclusively to Africans; in such cases we have evidence of the pervasive nature of European attitudes and dominance.

A last matter to be discussed in this section relates to the penalties imposed at the discretion of the courts. These have always presented difficulties and have been the subject of considerable polemics. But it would be unfair to suggest that the courts have not been aware of the problems, even though their resolution may be an extra-legal task. For example, Gardiner and Lansdown (1957:673) contend that fines should be "proportionate in amount to the earnings and means of the delinquent and the payment of them in easy stages." Such reasoning clearly lies behind some of the decisions reached in Southern Rhodesia.[11]

As a corollary, other decisions reflect a concern that, allowing for social and economic differences, punishments should be comparable for Africans and Europeans.[12]

To summarize, a considerable number of pressures and problems have influenced the judicial system. As in any society, there have been miscarriages of justice, particularly where juries have been involved. The statute law, too, much of which reflects the status and dominance of the European population, makes full impartiality a goal for the future. Even so, the courts, and particularly the High Court, have frequently set themselves against racial discrimination [13] and have striven to attain a high standard of impartial justice. In a culturally heterogeneous society such as Southern Rhodesia, where African laws and customs are little understood by the European population, such standards are not easy to attain.

## CONTEMPORARY ATTITUDES

As we have previously mentioned, more than half the statements of the questionnaire have some legal sanction behind them. Practices relating to land apportionment, education, the use of many public facilities, the franchise, cross-racial sexual relations, and so on are all sanctioned by the statutes and regulations of the country. But in attempting to set up a category that can be termed "legal justice," we have not been concerned with the statute laws as such. Instead, we have probed contemporary attitudes toward the administration of justice by stating baldly that racial considerations have been reflected in some of the penalties handed down by the courts.

Nevertheless, the definition of legal justice is arbitrary. Two of the statements (61 and 16) in the questionnaire carry the implication that different penalties for similar crimes may have been applied to Europeans and Africans. In terms of our criteria, the classification of these statements seems straightforward. However, a third statement (65) cites the differing penalties that apply for cross-racial sexual behavior, and does not refer to any differentiating role the courts may play. Even so, Europeans as a whole feel strongly that the principle of equity before the law is violated, and this is considered as sufficient ground for its inclusion within the category of legal justice. The three statements classified under the heading are shown in Table 54.

TABLE 54. *Statements Relating to Legal Justice*

| No. | Statement | −1 P.E. | +1 P.E. | Mean |
|-----|-----------|---------|---------|------|
| 61 | Europeans who rape African women sometimes are given lighter sentences than Africans who rape European women. | 3.55 | 6.11 | 4.83 |
| 16 | Africans and Europeans are sometimes not punished equally by the court for the same crimes of violence. | 3.27 | 5.87 | 4.57 |
| 65 | European men may have sex relations with African women without legal penalty, but African men are prohibited by law from having sex relations with European women. | 2.56 | 5.78 | 4.17 |
|  |  | 3.12 | 5.92 | 4.52 |

The category of legal justice is the one on which Europeans express themselves most strongly in favor of equal treatment. A special caution is necessary at this point in case the reader should attempt to equate a high score (above 3.00) with a point of view that might loosely be termed liberal. Each of the items contrasts the fact that there are two classes of penalty, one less severe than the other. The overwhelming majority of respondents advocate equal penalties at the *more* severe level, rather than the less severe. Let us take an example. Statement 61 suggests that a European who had raped an African woman was sometimes given a lighter sentence than was imposed on an African who had violated a European woman. In no case does the sample population suggest that Africans should receive a lighter penalty; rather, it argues that a heavier penalty should be placed on Europeans. The same implication comes out in much of the discussion on statement 65. It is not often contended that the law should be changed to allow cross-racial sexual relations for African men. Instead, it is argued that the prohibitions and penalties leveled against African men should also apply to Europeans. For these reasons, we do not interpret a high social change score as necessarily indicating what a Rhodesian would identify as a liberal viewpoint. For some statements it may be correct to interpret the response as liberal, but for others it would be incorrect. Much depends on the reasons given for an answer, and the type of change advocated. On the other hand, it seems proper to equate the lower scores on the scale (below 3.00) with conservatism, in that they refer to the maintenance of the status quo and resistance to change.

### A Statistical Rationale for the Selection of Comments

For purposes of content analysis, each separate comment on each statement has been written out, along with the individual's scoring response for the statement. In this way, it is possible to group together the persons who wish to maintain a practice and to examine the reasons advanced for maintenance. Similarly, we are able to collate the scores and arguments that support the change of a practice.

It is obviously impossible, however, to reproduce more than a fraction of the hundreds of pages of comments and interview material gathered, so some selection has to be made. To make the selection, the known properties of the normal curve are utilized, and a fairly detailed account may be necessary to illustrate the procedure.

Let us commence the illustration by reference to statement 61, which has a mean score of 4.83 and a standard deviation of 1.90. From these data, limits can be calculated between which 50% of the scores should lie. The limits are fixed at one probable error (P.E.) on either side of the mean, and are calculated from the known formula of $.6745\sigma_s$. Thus, the points $-1$ P.E. and $+1$ P.E., which are 3.55 and 6.11 respectively, are those between which half of the sample scores should be found. But the procedure is most secure where the scores fall roughly into the form of a normal bell-shaped curve. Where a distribution is skewed, either positively or negatively, we can be less certain about the proportions falling at different P.E. distances from the mean. For example, if the distribution on statement 61 were normal, then we could assume that 25% of the respondents would gain scores greater than $+1$ P.E., i.e., greater than 6.11; and conversely, 25% would display scores smaller than 3.55. But the distribution on statement 61 is not normal; it is decidedly skewed. We know it is impossible for any score to fall above 6.00, which is the highest value that can be received for a response to a statement on the questionnaire.

The skew in a distribution clearly affects the conclusions that can be made about a statement. For every statement within a category, and for the category as a whole, we will endeavor to sift out the principal reasons why the sample wants a practice maintained or changed. We take the 50% of the sample who fall about the mean as the most representative group. Where the distribution is approximately normal, with a mean of about 3.00, it is possible to assume that the 25% with scores greater than one probable error above the mean are less typical in their attitudes favoring social change than is the sample as a whole. Again, the 25% who obtain scores that are smaller than −1 P.E. are also atypical; their stand on the maintenance of the status quo will be more conservative than that of the bulk of the population.

But with a distribution like that on statement 61, a different type of conclusion must be educed; namely, that over half of the population are strongly in favor of changing the status quo, most of the remainder also wish to change it, and a small number wish to maintain the practice. Again, where the bulk of the scores falls heavily on the maintain side of the distribution, as in statement 44 (M = .41; see Chapter 14), it can be inferred that well over half the population are strongly in favor of continuing the status quo, others also wish to maintain it, and almost nobody wishes to change the practice.

It is known that the distance of −1 P.E. to +1 P.E. (a total of two probable errors) encompasses different areas of a curve, depending on the skew in the distribution. However, with each of our sixty-six distributions, the area covered is closer to 50% than the area under any two other probable errors. We take this as a sufficiently powerful reason for equating the area −1 P.E. to +1 P.E. with the attitude that is most representative of the population. Accordingly, we present these two probable error limits with all of the statements, and with the categories of statements, that are to be described. The scores and statements between these limits are then used to identify the principal reasons people advance for wanting to maintain or change a given law or practice.

Let us illustrate further. The two P.E. limits for statement 61 are 3.55 and 6.11 respectively, showing that the persons who score 4 or 6 (important, discontinue; very important, discontinue) represent the dominant sentiment of the sample. With this established, the statements showing 4 or 6 scores can be marshaled together, and the reasons people give for these responses may be taken as the most representative ones in the population. This method, it seems to us, is to be preferred as the most objective technique for the selection of illustrative material.

The illustrative material, however, will not be confined solely to that which appears representative of the bulk of the sample. Where it is statistically feasible, some contrast will be made between the statements of persons who most strongly wish to maintain the status quo and those who most emphatically desire to change it. These smaller groups of people will have scores on a statement below $-1$ P.E. and above $+1$ P.E., respectively. In the case of statements 61 and 44, and others with similarly skewed distributions, such a contrast will not be possible. But with those that show distributions in the form of statement 3 (see Chapter 14), contrasts between the ends of the distribution are feasible and can be made. Thus, where the scores 0 and 6 fall outside the range of minus and plus one probable error, the reasons people advance for these scores can be educed.

*Statement 61* ($M = 4.83$), which suggests that Europeans and Africans on occasion received different sentences for the crime of cross-racial rape, is one on which the sample opts most strongly for social change. Typical of the majority viewpoint are statements such as "The law should be equally *severe*," "The penalties should definitely be the same," and variants of these sentiments. No respondent feels impelled to argue for lighter penalties for Africans and Europeans.

Among persons with high scores, both on the single statement and on the whole questionnaire, there is some doubt that differential punishments have ever taken place in Southern Rhodesia. As one person puts it, "Such cases are surely rare." Another person with a maximum change score on the item states, "I have not witnessed the partiality of the courts in favor of Europeans. Realizing their less civilized backgrounds, courts have, on occasion, dealt less severely with Africans in cases of this nature." However, if an African rapes an African woman, the sentence imposed is frequently less severe than that given when a European rapes a European woman. Here we measure severity strictly in terms of the size of the fine or the length of prison sentence imposed. But there is no absolute standard by which one can equate sentences. For example, a fine of one hundred pounds that has to be met by an African may represent his entire wages for two years or more, and may be more severe on his dependents than a jail sentence of six months. It is not unlikely that an awareness of this problem prompted one of the respondents to comment, "A sentence for any crime must take into account the circumstances of the crime and also those of the criminal." However, to sum up, the outstanding sentiment is that the penalties for cross-racial rape of either variety should be equally severe.

An important distinction can be observed in the comments of individuals who, although they wish to maintain the status quo, also advocate strongly that punishments should not differ. Their emphatic opinion is that penalties should be very severe for either Europeans or Africans who rape a member of the other group. A number advocate the death penalty, and one supports sterilization.

At the tail end of the distribution, and certainly not typical of the community, are those who advocate heavier penalties for Africans on the grounds that "Native women are generally of loose morals, and a native must be treated hard or else he will not learn." The rape of a white woman by an African is not only a violation of the individual, it is also an attack on the established system of European control and this, it is maintained, warrants a more severe penalty for the African. While such thinking may have been typical around the turn of the century, it does not seem to receive much support from Europeans today.

Statement 61 is an interesting one because the advocacy of equal and severe penalties for rape not only satisfies the principle of equal legal justice, but it also expresses the sample's very strong disapproval of cross-racial sexual contact.

*Statement 16* (M = 4.57) can be interpreted in two ways. It states that Africans and Europeans are sometimes not punished equally by the courts for the same crimes of violence. To some, this is taken to mean that Africans are punished more severely, and to others that they are punished more leniently.

One respondent affirms that "during the last ten years or so, it is the African who has been favored," and another suggests that the African "gets away with it because he does not fully understand the seriousness of crimes of violence." Yet another feels that lighter penalties for Africans are justifiable because a European expects juvenile rather than adult behavior from Africans at their "present stage of development."

As on statement 61, there are a number of individuals who wish to see equality on this item although they generally want to maintain the status quo on others. They contend that Africans receive lighter sentences for crimes of violence. One individual, whose mean score of .87 on the questionnaire is clearly on the conservative side of the mean, gives as his reason for equal sentences: "Generally it seems that the law and justice are on the side of the Native. A lot is said about racialism, but my impression is that if your skin is black you'll be alright." One very forceful point of view is that "Kaffirs get only three years for murder. There is no hanging in Southern Rhodesia. If necessary, they are sent to Pretoria for hanging." On the other hand, a number interpret our statement to mean that Africans receive more severe punishment for violent behavior. One such respondent puts it this way: "Our magistrates, Native Commissioners, and police have done a wonderful job, and are doing a wonderful job in handling the African. The Africans have great confidence in them; if their punishments appear harsh, remember that they are the best judges. They have examined the evidence."

The bulk of our sample, however, comes out strongly in favor of equal punishment for equal crimes of violence, irrespective of the racial characteristics of the offender. This stand can be taken as the most representative one in the population. But when the comments that advocate equal punishment are inspected, it is clear that the motives underlying them are by no means uniform or mutually consistent.

*Statement 65* (M = 4.17) contains both a legal and a sexual component: the notion that European men may have cross-racial sexual relations without legal penalty, but that African men may not. Responses to this statement depend little upon whether the over-all attitude of the individual is conservative or change-oriented. Most respondents favor the prohibition of *all* cross-racial sexual contact, and equal punishment for Europeans and Africans who infringe this item in the European moral code.

It is the opinion of some that the statement is incorrect and that European men are also prohibited by law from having sexual relations with African women. This is true in the Union of South Africa. The misconception also seems to have been reinforced by the fact that the Southern Rhodesian Parliament, in 1957, debated a motion that it should introduce a new law prohibiting sexual relations outside marriage between a European man and an African woman. Although the vote went in favor of such a law, no bill has been brought before the House.

Typical responses to this statement are: "Both should be prohibited," "European men should also be penalized," "Both are equally bad," "There should be the same legal penalty for both races," "I am absolutely against any mixing of the races under any circumstances," and so on. The death penalty and euthanasia are advocated by a few in the population, the latter as a cure for what is assumed to be mental illness. The only genuine difference that appears between the end segments of our sample is that the more conservative generally advocate severer penalties for such activities.

Having surveyed the reasons people advance in favor of equal justice, it is appropriate to observe that no single theme underlies them all. Indeed, if the reasons had been taken into account, a completely different scheme of classification would have been necessary. The themes underlying legal justice will be postulated when we have examined the area from the viewpoint of different segments of the sample.

## The Sample Characteristics

The most significant relations between individual characteristics and general attitude about Africans were discussed in Chapter 9. The next task is to determine whether attitudes about legal justice vary with differences in occupation, country of birth, and so on. Five criteria—age, sex, community of residence, census district, and income—are omitted from further consideration because they are not significantly related to general race attitudes. In the following analyses, the subpopulations that contain few people are either combined or left out; otherwise the data are complete.

Table 55 is a summary of the calculations that have been made concerning attitudes about legal justice. The first column indicates the social characteristics used in the analysis, and the second column shows the number of persons who have these characteristics. The graphical display in the middle of the table facilitates a comparison of the mean scores of aggregates or subpopulations on the category of legal justice. The means from which the bar graphs have been plotted are given in the right column. The heavy line through the graph denotes the mean score on legal justice. From this table, the individual reader can make as many comparisons as he wishes, although we will restrict our comments to the most significant of the differences.

Before we embark on a dissection of the characteristics, a note on tests of significance is necessary. In Chapter 9, we selected the major differences that emerged between characteristics and established that they were significant. These tests are valid for the whole questionnaire. From this point on, the comparison will be made not on the basis of the whole scale, but of a portion. Tests of significance will not be run on the differences that emerge on portions of the scale, as we feel that the evidence accumulated in Chapter 9 makes this unnecessary. Even so, we are aware that reliability may be less secure when comparisons are made within a category, such as legal justice, which includes only a small number of items. Equally, we are cognizant that the differences are likely to be less significant than when they are based on the whole scale. These two cautions are kept in mind in the analyses that follow.

COUNTRY OF BIRTH

In the analysis of the whole scale, there were substantial and significant differences between the attitudes of individuals born in the United Kingdom and those born in the Union of South Africa and Southern Rhodesia. Individuals in the two latter groupings displayed much more conservative attitudes than those born in the United

## TABLE 55. *Scores Relating to Legal Justice* $(M = 4.52)$

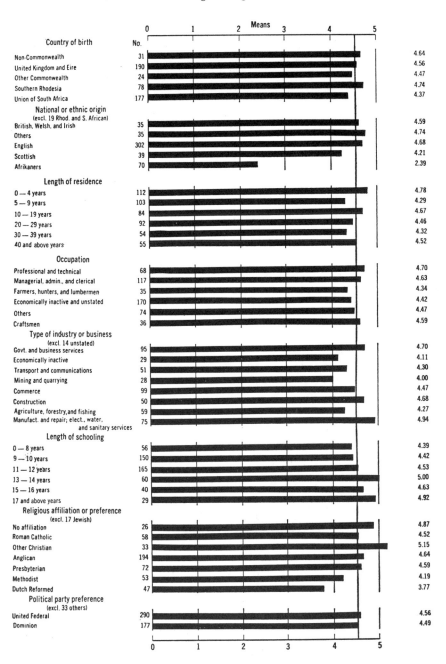

| | No. | Mean |
|---|---|---|
| **Country of birth** | | |
| Non-Commonwealth | 31 | 4.64 |
| United Kingdom and Eire | 190 | 4.56 |
| Other Commonwealth | 24 | 4.47 |
| Southern Rhodesia | 78 | 4.74 |
| Union of South Africa | 177 | 4.37 |
| **National or ethnic origin** (excl. 19 Rhod. and S. African) | | |
| British, Welsh, and Irish | 35 | 4.59 |
| Others | 35 | 4.74 |
| English | 302 | 4.68 |
| Scottish | 39 | 4.21 |
| Afrikaners | 70 | 2.39 |
| **Length of residence** | | |
| 0 — 4 years | 112 | 4.78 |
| 5 — 9 years | 103 | 4.29 |
| 10 — 19 years | 84 | 4.67 |
| 20 — 29 years | 92 | 4.46 |
| 30 — 39 years | 54 | 4.32 |
| 40 and above years | 55 | 4.52 |
| **Occupation** | | |
| Professional and technical | 68 | 4.70 |
| Managerial, admin., and clerical | 117 | 4.63 |
| Farmers, hunters, and lumbermen | 35 | 4.34 |
| Economically inactive and unstated | 170 | 4.42 |
| Others | 74 | 4.47 |
| Craftsmen | 36 | 4.59 |
| **Type of industry or business** (excl. 14 unstated) | | |
| Govt. and business services | 95 | 4.70 |
| Economically inactive | 29 | 4.11 |
| Transport and communications | 51 | 4.30 |
| Mining and quarrying | 28 | 4.00 |
| Commerce | 99 | 4.47 |
| Construction | 50 | 4.68 |
| Agriculture, forestry, and fishing | 59 | 4.27 |
| Manufact. and repair; elect., water, and sanitary services | 75 | 4.94 |
| **Length of schooling** | | |
| 0 — 8 years | 56 | 4.39 |
| 9 — 10 years | 150 | 4.42 |
| 11 — 12 years | 165 | 4.53 |
| 13 — 14 years | 60 | 5.00 |
| 15 — 16 years | 40 | 4.63 |
| 17 and above years | 29 | 4.92 |
| **Religious affiliation or preference** (excl. 17 Jewish) | | |
| No affiliation | 26 | 4.87 |
| Roman Catholic | 58 | 4.52 |
| Other Christian | 33 | 5.15 |
| Anglican | 194 | 4.64 |
| Presbyterian | 72 | 4.59 |
| Methodist | 53 | 4.19 |
| Dutch Reformed | 47 | 3.77 |
| **Political party preference** (excl. 33 others) | | |
| United Federal | 290 | 4.56 |
| Dominion | 177 | 4.49 |

Kingdom. But with legal justice, these differences virtually disappear. Individuals born in Southern Rhodesia have a slightly higher social-change score than persons born elsewhere, and South Africans have a slightly lower score than the rest, but none of these differences are substantial enough to warrant the drawing of conclusions from them. The one conclusion that seems legitimate is that the majority of Europeans in Southern Rhodesia, from whatever country they come, agree that legal justice should not fall differentially on Africans and Europeans. It is felt that, if there are different sentences imposed by the courts, this practice should be changed immediately.

NATIONAL OR ETHNIC ORIGIN

When one turns to national or ethnic origin, some striking differences emerge. The two major ethnic groups in our sample are the English and Afrikaners, and the difference in attitude between them is very significant. Judging from the scores and the interview material, the English generally are less inclined to advocate very severe penalties for cross-racial sexual contacts, although they wish to see them restricted or prohibited. They are significantly in favor of equal penalties for equal violations of the law.

Afrikaners, on the other hand, obtain a significantly lower score because of their general stand on two of the statements. Firstly, on the average, they feel that a differential punishment for rape should stand: it is more serious for a European than an African woman to be raped. Secondly, although cross-racial sexual contacts are strongly deprecated, it is considered more necessary to impose a legal prohibition on African men than on European men. About crimes of violence, however, the Afrikaner position is practically the same as the English.

Differences between the other groupings are of little moment. Persons who classify themselves as British, Welsh, and Irish have attitudes about legal justice little different from those held by the English. The scores are a little lower, but not significantly so, and they fall distinctly on the side of social change.

LENGTH OF RESIDENCE

On the whole scale, it was found that the Europeans who least favored maintaining the status quo had lived in the Colony for fewer than five years. On the category of legal justice, this grouping has the highest score. Then, for an unknown reason, come the individuals who arrived from ten to nineteen years ago. This was a period of rapid immigration from Britain. Although there is a correlation between length of residence and attitude score on the whole scale, this is not reflected in attitudes about legal justice. The reasons advanced in favor of equal treatment by the law seem much the same for all groups.

## OCCUPATION

Because the previous analysis had shown very substantial variations in general attitude between different occupational groupings, particularly the professional men and the craftsmen, it was anticipated that differences would emerge on the category of legal justice. This does not happen, however, as Table 55 shows. All of the groupings express attitudes in favor of social change, and little variation is shown.

## TYPE OF INDUSTRY OR BUSINESS

As with occupations, men in different types of industry or business do not reveal any striking differences in attitude about legal justice for Africans. There is more fluctuation around the mean than in the case of classification by occupation, but the very large difference (government and business versus agriculture) revealed on the full questionnaire does not emerge in this category.

Somewhat surprising is the high score of those engaged in manufacturing, repair work, and electrical, water, and sanitary services. An analysis of the scores on the individual statements shows that these individuals have the highest score of all (5.28) on statement 61, relating to different penalties for cross-racial rape. The higher score on this item is reflected in the high mean for the category.

## EDUCATION

One of the clearest relations that emerged in the study was between length of schooling and general attitude about the differentiating practices. The greater the length of time spent at school, the more change-oriented the attitudes tended to be. Length of schooling was one of the best single predictors of attitudes about Africans. On the subject of legal justice, however, a clear relation of this kind does not emerge. There are fluctuations in sentiment, but they cannot be reckoned as significant trends.

## RELIGIOUS AFFILIATION OR PREFERENCE

The highest scores are obtained by individuals in the "Other Christian" category; a complex of Baptists, Greek Orthodox, Jehovah's Witnesses, Quakers, and others. Then follow those persons who specify "No affiliation." These two groupings are too heterogeneous and too small to justify detailed analysis. Despite major differences in general attitude, the Roman Catholic, Anglican, and Presbyterian adherents have practically identical attitudes about legal justice. Also showing social-change scores, but less strongly than the other religious groupings, are the members of the Methodist and Dutch Reformed churches. It will be recalled that members of these two denominations also displayed the most conservative attitudes toward the whole range of differential laws and customs in Southern Rhodesia.

POLITICAL PARTY PREFERENCE

Little comment is needed on the score obtained by the supporters of the United Federal and Dominion parties. Although there are highly significant differences in general attitudes, within the category of legal justice the scores for those who prefer one or the other party are virtually identical. Both positions are on the "discontinue" side of the continuum.

## THE PRINCIPAL THEMES

From the enumerative and descriptive data, we have endeavored to extract the principal themes that run through the attitudes expressed about the treatment of Africans. In doing so, it is appreciated that we leave the world of numbers and venture into an area that is less quantitative and more open to alternate interpretations. But we consider such formulations as proper if we are to understand more fully the cultural influences that have helped to shape present Southern Rhodesian society. Some of these forces dip deep into history, and we have attempted to trace their geneses and development to the present day. Thus the inferences we make, the themes we identify, are supported by historical documentation and contemporary data. But while we believe it legitimate to go beyond the data, we do so with caution. As far as possible, we allow the data to speak.

It is usual to find complementary and conflicting themes in any society, and Southern Rhodesia is no exception. Indeed, because of its culturally heterogeneous character, it may embrace more conflict, actual and potential, than is common to other Western societies. Instead of seeking for the more ephemeral themes and the minor chords, we have tried to record those that are representative of most of European society, and that show some permanency. The task has been aided by the comments and interview material. It is described elsewhere how the probable error limits were arbitrarily fixed to mark off the portion of the sample whose expressions we took to represent the majority of the population. Within these defined limits, and drawing on the different types of data, the principal attitudes and motivations have been sought.

It has been contended by many, including Bertrand Russell (1949), that the rule of law is fundamental in English-speaking societies. If this can be taken as true, it is apposite to examine the reasons advanced by people in our sample in support of equal justice for Africans and Europeans. To some, legal justice is based upon a theme of moral idealism that is an integral part of European culture. Europeans have a duty to "uplift" Africans, and one of the ways in which this may reach fruition is through an appreciation of the fact that legal justice should be equally available for all men.

But to many, the advocacy of equal legal justice reflects motives that appear to be less idealistic. European society must be kept "pure," and the weaker members of society must be protected from themselves. In the arguments advanced to us, few appreciate the possible incongruity in the viewpoint that stresses the superiority and vitality of Western culture, and yet shows little faith in the capacity of Europeans to retain that culture without a great deal of protection. Not only do many feel it is necessary to protect their own way of life, but they also feel morally obliged to protect Africans until they can participate fully in Western society. To achieve this, firm but just treatment is called for. To the theme of idealism, then, it is necessary to add at least the theme of protectionism before one begins to appreciate the motivations that lead Europeans to support the principle of equal legal justice in Southern Rhodesia.

# 11

## OPPORTUNITIES FOR EDUCATION, TRAINING, AND EMPLOYMENT

Every society maintains its identity and coherence in part through the transmission of knowledge, skills, and values from one generation to the next. The educational system, whether it includes formal or informal institutions, is influenced by other aspects of the whole: the size and character of the population, its means for making a living, and its system of social relations. In a plural society such as Southern Rhodesia, the educational system is influenced by differences in culture and social organization.

The opportunities for formal schooling or training, and the application of the acquired knowledge and skills, have traditionally been unequal for Africans and Europeans. As in many colonial societies, different educational structures have developed in Southern Rhodesia. The facilities for European children have been more highly subsidized than for Africans. European children lived in family and other groups in which the normal process of socialization involved the learning of motivations, work habits, knowledge, and skills that were compatible with efficiency in the industrial, commercial, and other activities of Western society. It was easier, and more natural, for European children and young adults to be integrated into the occupational and economic structures than would have been true for individuals from different cultural backgrounds. Africans were thought to be most easily included in the new economic structure as unskilled laborers. It was felt to be an unnecessary and costly luxury to provide elementary education for the African populace.

Southern Rhodesia's economic history began with the arrival of European hunters, traders, and prospectors. It was they who contributed to the conquest and initial economic development of the country. During the early decades of settlement, the farmers' and miners' political interests greatly influenced the development of the laws, sentiments, and symbols of the new colony. Job opportunities and educational facilities developed to serve the mines and plantations, the earliest capitalistic enterprises. An economic system emerged in which the managers, directors, and capital were European, and the mass of the labor supply was African.

From the beginning, Southern Rhodesia's economy has not operated *in vacuo,* for its products relied on export markets. Currently there is more foreign capital invested in Southern Rhodesia than in any sub-Saharan territory except the Union of South Africa. Today Southern Rhodesia's rate of industrialization is second to none in Africa (Neumark, 1958:99). Secondary industry has replaced mining and agriculture as the largest producing sector of the economy. Southern Rhodesia's economy has increasingly become a part of the world economy: production, consumption, wage levels, investments, and tariffs cannot be understood isolated from the international context. For both specific and general reasons, economic self-sufficiency has never been, and may never be, characteristic of Southern Rhodesia.

All the early educational efforts for Africans were sponsored by religious missions, most of whom were supported by funds and personnel from other countries. At first, educational goals were subordinated to evangelism; a primary aim was to detach Africans from the tribe rather than to teach them to utilize better their own environmental and human resources. The missionary system of education aimed to replace or supplement the traditional African patterns of belief, ceremonial organization, family and marriage practices, and system of tribal teachers. The first training school operated at Hope Fountain Mission from 1898 to 1909. Another was started at Morgenster in 1902. By 1924, seven missions were providing training opportunities with the aid of Government subsidies. In 1958, there were thirty-three teacher-training institutions in Southern Rhodesia, all but one being operated by missions (Fletcher, 1958:11). Altogether, forty-seven teacher-training courses were being offered in 1959.

In addition to and greatly exceeding the number of teacher-training institutions, the missions were enlarging the educational opportunities for African children. An Education Ordinance of 1899 allowed the Government to grant small annual subsidies to African mission schools. In 1910, the number receiving grants was 110. By 1958 the number had risen sharply to 2,741, and only a minority remained unaided by Government funds. Prior to 1947, the Government did not accept responsibility for the salaries of all approved teachers. Since that date, the size of Government subsidies has equaled or surpassed the contributions made by mission churches.[1] For many years, African taxes helped to subsidize the development of the entire country, since they aggregated more than the Government returned in the form of school grants.

Today, more than 80% of the African population of school age get some schooling, the highest proportion of any country in Africa (Fletcher, 1958:12). In addition to the 2,741 mission schools that received grants in 1958, the Government also operated fifty-seven schools. The Government now has accepted the responsibility for providing primary and secondary schools in urban townships. Schooling is not compulsory for Africans, in contrast to the regulations that affect European, Colored, and Asian children. The level of educational attainment for Africans has been much lower than for Europeans and others, though the disparity is gradually diminishing. Even so, fewer than 1% of the Africans proceed beyond eight years of schooling. Less attention is being given to secondary education, although expanded facilities are planned for the next few years. In 1957, the first University College opened to receive students of any background who could meet the academic qualifications.

As early as 1892, a Jesuit mission near Salisbury began the first systematic training of Africans in agricultural and technical skills.[2] By 1915 this Order had established three other schools which provided similar opportunities, but its emphasis on industrial training declined with the replacement of German and French by English priests. Some Protestant denominations also gave practical or technical training to Africans; these included the London Missionary Society, Anglicans, American Methodists, and Congregationalists. Generally, however, the Protestants stressed literary education more than did the Catholics. The Dutch Reformed church generally opposed the training of African artisans. Almost all denominations thought towns were sinful places, and opposed the idea of Africans flocking into them.

The Africans' desire for education was "extraordinary" even in the first decade of this century.[3] Limited funds and personnel obviously prevented all wants from being fulfilled. In addition, the prevalent attitudes of Europeans opposed the quick expansion of educational facilities for Africans, especially for technical training. Many Europeans preferred to keep the Africans as "raw, untutored menials," uncontaminated by the knowledge and values of Western cultures. They argued that all the necessary training of Africans could be provided through the personal efforts of European artisans and farmers. Little was provided, however, and it soon became an issue between the European population and the Administration.

A Commission of Enquiry into Native Affairs was appointed in 1910 to examine the question. It recommended that the Government establish industrial and agricultural schools. Widespread opposition was expressed by Europeans. An editorial in 1912 aided the Government's position when it was pointed out that Africans could utilize their new skills in their *own* segregated areas.[4] The resistance had lessened sufficiently by 1919 for the European public to approve the establishment of trade training schools for Africans. In the following two years, the Government built the technical schools at Domboshawa and Tjolotjo. But the new schools worked under the handicap of smaller subsidies than those provided for general African education.

In the 1920's, Emory Alvord was instrumental in introducing many innovations into African life. One of his programs involved the training of Africans to assist in demonstrating improved agricultural techniques. He was so successful that the African farmers who followed his advice began producing greater yields than the Europeans. The latter raised objections and highly criticized Alvord for making competitors out of the Africans. Consequently, the growth of general educational facilities for Africans was not paralleled by an increase in agricultural and technical training programs. Many, but not all, Europeans resisted the introduction of such programs for more than two decades; only in the past year or two have European attitudes changed sufficiently to permit the resumption of developments that looked promising to Africans in 1920.

Industrial practices in Southern Rhodesia during its first fifty years followed those of the Union of South Africa. The Masters and Servants Act, Wage Act, Industrial Conciliation Act, pass regulations, and the establishment of labor compounds, locations, and rural reserves all derived from the Union's legislation. The enactment of these laws and regulations tended to come some ten to twenty-five years later in Southern Rhodesia. The legal reservation of jobs for Africans and Europeans began in the Union in 1911. This was illegal in Southern Rhodesia according to the provisions of the Constitution. Yet an unofficial segregation of jobs and training facilities developed that restrained Africans from learning and using new skills.[5] Most Europeans believed it necessary to stick together. In 1910, for example, a group of European artisans protested against the employment of African artisans in Salisbury, and the Town Council was asked to forbid this practice.[6] Europeans tended to be hired even though Africans who could be employed for smaller wages were available.[7]

Resistance to the training of Africans increased during the depression of the 1930's, and European artisans demanded greater protection from African artisans. Under the leadership of the late "Jack" Keller, the Rhodesian Labour party put .pressure on the Government to solidify the Europeans' status. When Godfrey Huggins and the Reform party came into power in 1934, he fulfilled his promise to protect European artisans from competition. The Industrial Conciliation Act was passed which permitted the employment of African artisans, but only at the same rates of pay as stipulated for Europeans. Employers were reluctant to take advantage of this permitted innovation, however, because of opposition and threats from European trade unions and associations. Consequently, the employment of African artisans continued to be prevented. Thus the reservation of jobs between Africans and Europeans seems to have resulted more from the pressure of European labor unions than from the provisions of the Industrial Conciliation Act.

Higher wages for Africans were opposed by Europeans as far back as the 1890's. The Farmers Union and the Chamber of Commerce suggested in 1902 that liquor should be given to African employees rather than higher wages, as it was "the only thing that will civilize them." Public reaction to this odd proposal prevented its adoption.[8] Moreover, there was much opposition from employers against allowing Africans to drink liquor since a sober labor force was usually desired. Barber (1957:423–43) has tried to show that there was little real increment in African wages until after World War II, when some increases came in the mining and secondary industries. This resulted, he says, because of a greater demand for labor in the money economy than could be provided by the natural increase of the African population. No minimum wages were laid down by the Government until the Labour Boards Act was promulgated in 1949. African pay scales for various industries are now established by national councils, which have no African membership.

European trade unions have generally insisted on equal pay for equal work. Often the effect of this principle has been to exclude qualified Africans from employment in the more highly paid positions. The interests of shareholders, the assumed endless supply of cheap labor, the desire to prevent a too rapid change in the Africans' way of life, and the wish to preserve European standards of living have been given as reasons in support of this principle (Broomfield, 1944:73). European workers generally have believed that if Africans could be hired at lower rates of pay, the result would be the effective exclusion of Europeans from these positions. The unions have often been less willing to modify the rate and job structures than have the owners and managers of industry.

"In no other dependency" in Africa, according to Lord Hailey

(1957:1446), "is the problem of trade disputes so complicated by the competitive claims of European and African labour." The first European labor union in Southern Rhodesia was formed in 1915 by railway workers. At that time, labor was short as a result of World War I, and the workers were able to strengthen their position on the railways and to control possible competition from an increasing number of Africans. A series of railway strikes helped to bring into being the Industrial Conciliation Act of 1934. Africans were excluded from the Act's definition of "employee," hence only the European unions received *de jure* recognition. Thus, in all of colonial Africa, Southern Rhodesia ranked first in the percentage of the population who were wage earners, but last in the number of trade unionists (Hodgkin, 1956:118).

The high percentage of alien and migratory African workers in the economy had been a deterrent to the development of trade unionism.[9] Not until 1946 was the first African trade union formed, and it likewise was among railway workers. Three years later a special Act gave legal recognition to this association. Prior to this, Africans on the railways had "carried out a widespread and successful strike in 1945" (Luyt, 1949:16). Following these disturbances the Government also created a National Labour Board to establish minimum conditions of service and to provide for the arbitration of individual disputes. The railway strike had shown that, whether permitted to or not, African workers were now willing and able to act collectively. Thereafter African unions increased in number and strength, and were increasingly given *de facto* recognition. They represented a new form of organization for Africans which "involved a radical break with time-hallowed ideas of authority based on lineage, age, or the possession of certain esoteric knowledge" (Epstein, 1958:97).

Prior to 1959, the legality of African trade unions rested only on the early Masters and Servants Act. European unions have been consistent and successful in excluding Africans from membership; only journalists and typographers are jointly organized.[10] The Industrial Conciliation and Apprenticeship Acts of 1959 will allow new opportunities for African occupational mobility and for the joint participation of Africans and Europeans in collective bargaining. New kinds of social relations are probable between Africans and Europeans if the expected changes occur. One of these may be the gradual appearance of qualified Africans in supervisory positions over Europeans. Heretofore, the status and prestige of particular occupations have resulted in their being partly filled through nonrational and uneconomic considerations.

The Commission of Enquiry of 1910 had advocated that positions should be filled according only to the criterion of ability. This criticism of the practice of job reservation reflected a minor thread of dissent about the traditional occupational structure that has existed through-out the history of Southern Rhodesia. Bray's (1958) report on tech-nical training facilities also argued that Europeans must maintain their future position on the basis of competence alone. This will involve, he says, a change of attitude toward work among many European arti-sans: they must welcome competition in the world market, which will involve greater efficiency in production, and they must welcome com-petition from Africans within the country for the jobs Europeans traditionally have held. Bray was especially critical of the frequently cited practice of Africans doing the work of European artisans while the latter "merely looks on" (Bray, 1958:11).

In Government employment, Africans are excluded from the pro-visions of the Public Services Act. No African holds a major position in the Southern Rhodesian administration. McGregor (1940:383) has observed that "even the Native Department is a white preserve." A basic complication has been the absence of a cadre of trained or skilled Africans. Since federation, more opportunities to attain higher positions have come, especially in the Federal Government. The Federal Civil Service is equally open to Africans and Europeans, but the grading (there are four grades) thus far has meant different rates of pay and other conditions of service for individuals of the two culture groups. "Suitability" for the job is the chief criterion that will affect the promotion of civil servants.

The growth of industry has been a "grand mixer of people"; but it also has sorted and segregated individuals from different racial and cultural backgrounds into specific jobs. Frankel (1953:120) charac-terizes such an industrial system as one employing a "multi-racial" team. With industrial growth the size of the team has varied, but not the proportionate racial composition, the different pay scales, or the designated tasks.

In no colonial territory does the indigenous population supply the entire working force.[11] In Southern Rhodesia highly paid Europeans have always been the nucleus of the industrial organization. This was unavoidable in the earliest years; in time the system of quasi-caste relationships became institutionalized. The absence of an African middle class at the time of European immigration did not lead to strong efforts to establish one. Such an undertaking, many Europeans argued, was uneconomic and impractical. Individuals with the cultural and educational qualifications necessary for middle-class status in an industrial society have generally been part of the continuing stream of European immigrants rather than indigenous Africans. Industry has not been guided completely by goals of efficiency and rationality. Hughes and Hughes (1952:78) succinctly describe the situation of Southern Rhodesia: "Industry in the Western world promoted an ideology of mobility; that is, of ambition. In the colonial world ambi-tion is often regarded as unjustified and dangerous."

In summary, then, the capitalist economy brought by Europeans to Southern Rhodesia provided Africans with limited occupational choices and opportunities for upward mobility. Although these limitations have been less severe since 1945, there has been little change in the range of occupations open to Africans *relative* to Europeans. Whatever changes have occurred seem explicable by reference to the general increase in occupational skills required throughout the economic system. It would appear that Africans have benefited primarily because industrialization has improved the general level of the European position. The division of labor remains closely in harmony with the power structure of Southern Rhodesian society. And Africans are more numerous in occupations and industries where less direct contact with Europeans occurs.[12]

Opportunities for Africans to obtain positions with higher status have been resisted from the beginning by organized interest and pressure groups in all spheres of the economy.[13] Intergroup relations and attitudes have been influenced by European trade unions, industrial councils, and business associations in commerce, manufacturing, mining, and agriculture (Leys, 1959). Europeans have felt it necessary to maintain dual systems of education, wages, pensions, and collective bargaining. Africans were not only conceived to be an endless source of relatively cheap labor, but also opponents in a power struggle. Although limited personal contact was permissible in economic activities—unlike other areas of social life—it was to remain structured in terms of superordination and subordination.

Nevertheless, changes have occurred, and the preferred ideals of many Europeans have never been fully realized. The seeds of social and cultural change came partly from the idea transmitted by missionaries that, among other things, the individual has a right to enjoy the products of his own efforts (Mair, 1957). Pressures for modifications in the economic system thus have increased in proportion to the spread of education. Increased industrialization has also provided a slowly increasing number of opportunities for Africans to acquire new kinds of wealth, property, and prestige unknown before Europeans began to settle and develop the lands north of the Limpopo River. Collective trade or employee associations have appeared among Africans as a sign of their newly felt confidence within the larger society of Southern Rhodesia. The arguments and activities of European artisans half a century ago for the total exclusion of, or protection against, African competitors have been compromised on the principle of the "rate for the job."

Different pay scales and job segregation—long practiced by mission schools and Government as well as industry—have also been more seriously examined and alternatives sought. The traditional practice of employing a high percentage of nonindigenous Africans has been debated and slightly modified. The growth of the African population to a size greater than can be supported on reserved lands, with peasant farming as the means of subsistence, has necessitated the recognition of permanent urban settlement, which was irrelevant in the past.[14] Rapid industrialization, and the desire to increase the efficiency [15] of African and European workers, have encouraged many to endorse efforts to improve the quality and quantity of educational and technical facilities. Extraterritorial opinions also have generally operated in a similar direction; these have come not only from the United Kingdom, but perhaps most importantly (for the future, if not now), from inhabitants of the two other territories in the Federation.

CONTEMPORARY ATTITUDES

Although the initial foundations were laid by the missions, and although the bulk of African education is still carried on by them, the Government now contributes over two million pounds per year to education, and its support is constantly increasing. The acceleration of African education, flowing from idealistic motives and a hard-headed recognition of the need to tap African resources and skills, has implications in the field of employment and economics that are not always appreciated by the European population. After legal justice, the next category in which the European community wishes to see differences narrowed or discontinued is that of educational and training opportunities. There is much support for an increase in technical training for the skilled trades, better opportunities for professional education, and more African schools. That these facilities should be separated, and used to advance Africans in their own areas, is another argument that will emerge in due course.

Increased educational opportunities are intimately linked with the necessity and demand for increased employment opportunities. Because of this intimate relation, both education and employment are juxtaposed for analysis. In the study, there are four statements that relate to educational and training opportunities. As an inspection of Table 56 will show, the mean scores on all of these items lie toward the high end of the distribution; that is, the general wish of the population is for changing the status quo.

Although the means indicate that the bulk of the population wants to improve the educational facilities available to Africans, the probable error limits illustrate that Europeans are by no means single-minded on the matter. At one end of the scale, where the scores indicate a wish for change, are those who advocate a crash program to bring Africans to European levels of achievement; at the other end are those who feel that Africans are getting as much as they deserve, if not more. Our analysis shows that individuals in the former group tend to be removed from the more immediate threat of African competition, whereas the latter are not. The problem of finance is continually stressed by people of widely differing attitudinal persuasions.

TABLE 56. *Statements Relating to Educational and Training Opportunities*

| No. | Statement | −1 P.E. | +1 P.E. | Mean |
|---|---|---|---|---|
| 9 | Facilities for the training of Africans in the skilled trades and professions are very limited. | 2.46 | 5.10 | 3.78 |
| 30 | African children do not receive the same educational opportunities as European children. | 2.45 | 5.09 | 3.77 |
| 2 | In general, Africans are not admitted to the technical classes which are an essential part of the apprentice training for a trade. | 2.32 | 5.10 | 3.71 |
| 1 | Africans are not accepted for apprenticeship training for the skilled trades. | 2.15 | 4.99 | 3.57 |
| | | 2.35 | 5.07 | 3.71 |

As with the analysis of legal justice, we have endeavored to get at the typical reasons underlying attitudes on education by returning to the interview and recorded material. Greatest attention is focused on the scores that lie within the band of −1 P.E. to +1 P.E. However, for purposes of contrast, some reference is made to the statements that accompany scores outside this band. The reasons are gathered together below.

*Statement 9* (M = 3.78) grasps the thorny nettle of the availability of training for Africans in the skilled trades and professions. Among persons with typical change-oriented scores, the sentiments are reasonably clear-cut. Their position can best be summed up by drawing directly from the pool of responses: "Give ability a fair chance." "There should be equal facilities." "Facilities are also limited in this country for Europeans. Advanced education is always costly here and involves long journeys apart from other expenses." "A percentage [of training] should be allowed, but the Europeans should not be expected to carry the burden." The dominant themes in these responses are a willingness to expand trade training and professional education, but a concern with the cost this might entail to the European population.

A smaller group, with scores above the +1 P.E. limit, generally advocates a more radical and rapid revision of African trade and educational facilities. The comment of one individual may be taken as reasonably characteristic of this segment of the distribution.

It is just as important for the educated African to acquire professional qualifications as it is for the manually skilled to acquire journeymen status. Indeed, the skilled and professional African can make as great a contribution to the general development of his fellow Africans as the European. . . . Provided

that the African is sufficiently intelligent to undertake apprenticeship for the skilled trades, he should receive every encouragement to do so, even if the ultimate result is the ousting of the
European tradesman—whose standards in this country are pretty
mediocre anyhow.

Turning to the opposite segment, in favor of maintaining the status
quo, qualitative differences in response can be detected. Characteristic
comments are: "They should be trained in their own areas," "These
facilities should be allowed for their own separate development," and
"The European should not be expected to carry the burden." Among
these individuals, who are more frequently in the line of African advancement, there is some awareness of the influence that increased
educational facilities may have upon employment opportunities. Hence
the proviso that African skills should be utilized in African areas.

*Statement 30* (M = 3.77) encompasses educational opportunities
for African children, an area in which Southern Rhodesia has made
considerable progress. Among representative individuals, it is generally accepted that the educational opportunities available to Africans
should be raised to those of Europeans, but few fail to mention the
financial implications of this task. As one person puts it, "Lack of
finance is the main reason for this [difference]." Others comment in a
similar vein: "If Africans were taxed more realistically they could have
these facilities." "This is not so much a question of policy as one of
economics." "There is not enough money in the country to give equal
education now, but we must keep improving the facilities."

All of these statements are those of persons who advocate social
change. A thread running through them all is that improvement is
necessary, advance should be steady, and Africans should assist more
with the financing of their education. On the first two points, there is
a profound shift from the prevailing attitudes of the turn of the century.
There is sober recognition now of the fact that Africans cannot and
should not be kept as "untutored menials." The right to education
is recognized by most to include Africans as well as Europeans.

The reasons and qualifications coincident with the high social-
change scores are not greatly different from those that are representative for the statement. As one person (item score of 6) says, "In
theory I believe that all races should have equal opportunity, but considerations of money, buildings, and teachers must be taken into account." A further comment is, "To realize this ideal in education
would mean prohibitive taxation at the present state of development
of the country." Yet another states, "This is partly a financial issue.
If possible, all children should have equal chances—but how?"

Among the scores supporting the status quo, the comments are
usually clear-cut and leave little room for misinterpretation. A number

deny that educational opportunities are fewer for Africans, and others state that "they are getting enough education as it is." Some doubt that the mentality of Africans will benefit from more education, and one person puts it succinctly: "A nation cannot be barbarians today and civilized tomorrow." A consistent theme embedded in the comments of these respondents is that if the Africans want further education, they should be taxed more heavily to pay for it themselves. These persons give little weight to the fact that even without the burden of increased taxation the average wage of an African laborer is such that he has difficulty in supporting himself and his family.[16]

*Statement 2* (M = 3.71) relates to the separation of facilities for technical education. This separation is traditional, as we have pointed out, both in the mission technical schools and in Government institutions. There has been a wider range of technical classes available for young Europeans than for Africans, and this is realized, as an examination of the representative responses will show.

The center of gravity of the scores on statement 2 is definitely on the side of change, but it is often qualified by the rider that facilities in technical education should be equal but separate. This theme occurs with greatest frequency: "They should have classes in their own schools." "They should have classes separate from Europeans." "They should have separate classes for the African, as a lot can't understand English." Some representative individuals believe that technical schools should be nonracial, either now or in the future: "I suggest nonracial technical colleges." "Those that show promise should be accepted." "Gradual change." Thus, although the bulk of the population advocates change, there is not common agreement on the kind of change. Most want separate facilities but a sizable number think in terms of nonracial technical classes.

At the high end of the distribution, practically all the comments display support for equal opportunities for all. Most suggest that technical colleges should be completely nonracial. From the respondents with low scores, the major theme is for separate but not necessarily equal facilities and classes. Few persons wish to deny Africans technical training, but it is suggested time and again that classes should be separate, and that the skills so learned should be employed in African communities rather than in competition with European workers in European areas.

*Statement 1* (M = 3.57) relates to apprenticeship training for the skilled trades. At the moment there is no recognized system whereby Africans may be apprenticed to a trade, but this will be altered when the Government implements the Apprenticeship Act of 1959, which is designed to make apprenticeship training available to all Southern Rhodesians.

The comments from the most typical section in the population are fairly homogeneous. Representative statements are: "The need for skilled tradesmen and technicians in this country is acute, and I feel that as yet, there is a great deal of undiscovered talent and skill amongst the African people. I feel that it would be of great advantage to the country if this talent were developed to the full." "Those that show promise should be accepted." "No one would stand in their way, surely, if they do so at their own expense and in their own areas, and under their own tutors."

Among those who advocate change more strenuously than the representative group, the theme is clearly in favor of accepting Africans and Europeans for apprenticeship training on an equal basis. One individual insists that "the standard of entry should be lowered especially for the African."

At the other end, the themes are also consistent: "Advance the Native gradually" is one comment. Another believes, "They are not quite ready for skilled trades. We must try and not let them advance too fast." A further theme is that Africans should have apprenticeship training only if they are paid the same wages as Europeans when they are qualified. The principle of equal pay for equal work is considered essential by many to prevent the African tradesmen from undercutting the wages and status of European workers.

The data indicate, therefore, that Europeans are generally in favor of extending education and trade training opportunities for Africans. However, among craftsmen, skilled workers, and others likely to be affected first by the extension of facilities, there is some disquiet about the result this will have on European employment. These groups recognize that African advancement may be inevitable; if so, however, it should be channeled into the service of Africans, and controlled so that Africans will not come into direct competition with the European labor market.

The theme of separation in the labor market is perhaps more clearly revealed when one turns to the employment category. So, too, are European attitudes about the employment of Africans in jobs traditionally reserved for Europeans. Whereas the category of educational and training opportunities is ranked second by our sample, the category of employment is ranked sixth. The mean score of the category is 2.21 which is on the maintain side of our distribution, and the probable error of 1.32 indicates that the sample predominantly opposes unrestricted African participation in the Southern Rhodesian economy. An examination of the items included under employment will make this more clear.

A quick inspection of Table 57 shows that Europeans are divided on the issue of accepting Africans into European trade unions; slightly less than half support the notion, and something more than half are opposed to it. The population is less divided, however, about placing qualified Africans in positions of responsibility over Europeans. Generally, the stand is against this, as is seen from a study of the interview material.

TABLE 57. *Statements Relating to Employment*

| No. | Statement | −1 P.E. | +1 P.E. | Mean |
|---|---|---|---|---|
| 10 | Most European trade unions do not accept African members. | 1.38 | 4.26 | 2.82 |
| 4 | In some businesses and industries only Europeans are employed. | 1.04 | 3.74 | 2.39 |
| 47 | Africans are not hired often as counter attendants in European shops or businesses. | .70 | 3.00 | 1.85 |
| 57 | In general, Africans are not placed in charge of Europeans even when equally qualified. | .46 | 3.10 | 1.78 |
| | | .89 | 3.53 | 2.21 |

*Statement 10* (M = 2.82) brings into focus a vexing problem in Southern Rhodesia, namely, whether trade unions should be integrated. The governing political party of Southern Rhodesia has given much thought to this matter. In the northern territories of the Federation, the principle of parallel development has usually been followed, with Europeans and Africans forming and belonging to separate unions. For example, in Northern Rhodesia there is a European Mineworkers Union and an African Mineworkers Union, and although they display unity of interest on some issues, they come into conflict on others. Separate unions have also grown up in Southern Rhodesia, but unlike the North, they have not had *de jure* status. The Southern Rhodesian Government has decided that nonracial unions will ultimately benefit all workers and promote the best interests of the country. With this as background, it is of value to see how Europeans feel on the matter.

The probable error limits around the mean of the distribution embrace both maintain and change scores, with the former predominating. This makes it difficult to find a theme representative of the population. Let us consider first the reasons affixed to the maintain scores of this middle group: "They are not yet ready for it." "Africans should have their own labor organizations." "Africans can get better representation in their own trade unions." These sentiments are paramount in the maintain wing of the middle group. On the social-change side, although it is felt that Africans should be admitted to European trade unions, qualifications are normally placed on their admission: "The voting power should not pass out of European control." "Africans should be properly educated on the ethics of trade unionism." "This is now being discussed."

Outside the middle group and at the low end of the distribution, the opposition is more clear-cut. One states his reasons clearly: "European unions will take in Africans when the same rates [for the job] are paid, but not otherwise. Each member gets one vote, so if the unions are swamped with Natives they will run it." Thus fear motivates many comments. In particular, the skilled tradesman or craftsman sees the establishment of nonracial trade unions as an ultimate threat to his standard of living. By keeping trade unions separate, he feels that he can bargain with the employing body over his own wages, and at the same time have some control over the entrance of Africans into occupations traditionally reserved for Europeans.

*Statement 4* (M = 2.39) states that in some businesses and industries only Europeans are employed, that some jobs and positions are not open to qualified Africans. Comments on this item vary, but a theme running through them all is that the greater skills of the Europeans make it inevitable that they will be preferred in many occupations, and for some time to come.

Typical comments are: "It depends on skill or qualifications." "In some businesses, only Europeans *can* be employed because of the skills needed." "In Britain only people of a certain class are employed in some positions. The same must apply here regardless of color." "Why not?" Even an individual with a high social-change score feels it necessary to say, "Probably in industries involving food preparation and handling, or where special educational or technical skills are involved, this is inevitable at the present stage of African development."

*Statement 47* (M = 1.85) is clearly related to statement 4, but it specifically names an occupation in which few Africans are found, namely that of counter attendant. This item is of interest because few Europeans feel very strongly that the present practice should be discontinued. From the middle of the distribution through to the most conservative scores, it is common for Europeans to maintain that African hygiene is inadequate, that Africans are irresponsible in money matters ("Very few can be trusted with the handling of money") and that they are not qualified ("Not capable"). These themes also occur within the area of social change on the scale, but not with the same emphasis.

*Statement 57* (M = 1.78) touches a sensitive area: "In general, Africans are not placed in charge of Europeans even when equally qualified." As the statement implies, there are exceptions. At Umtali, there is an African teacher-training school with an African as principal and a staff that is both African and European. Again, in one of the major newspaper establishments, senior Africans hold positions of responsibility that are graded more highly than posts held by Europeans. Further examples can be found in the churches and the Federal civil service. Even so, the situation is unusual and, although Africans can be found in many highly qualified positions, in general the Europeans on lower grades are responsible to other Europeans rather than to Africans.

Of the items in the employment category, this statement is the one on which Europeans most clearly wish to maintain the status quo. Even at the change end of the scale, it is felt that very few Africans are qualified to handle positions of responsibility in charge of Europeans. The general feeling can be summed up by taking comments from the pool: "Such circumstances are likely to remain for some time." "It prevents friction at present." "Africans are usually unreliable." "Not many Africans are qualified, so this generally is inapplicable."

At the conservative end of the scale, the expressions tend to be more definite. "Public sentiment wouldn't stand for it." "This can't be helped. We have made the country as it is." "There is plenty for them to do for their own backward people." The matter of qualifications is stressed at all levels, but among the more conservative it is implied that to place Africans in charge of Europeans would undermine the whole structure of European authority, control, and prestige.

## THE SAMPLE CHARACTERISTICS

The picture that emerges from the interview material is now reasonably clear. The European population on the whole supports or is prepared to see changes in educational and trade training that will lead to a higher standard of living among Africans, but it does not sanction the use of these acquired skills to displace Europeans from their traditional avenues of employment. Of course, on both education and employment there is a wide range of attitudes, but the center of gravity of the former clearly denotes tolerance of change in the status quo, and the latter implies resistance to change.

With this dilemma in front of us, we turn to a comparison of education and employment as they are viewed by different segments of the population. As before, an analysis is made principally of those subpopulations that reveal significant differences in total scores. Thus, in the analysis of the whole scale, we determined that there were statistically significant differences in the attitude of those born in Britain on the one hand, and those born in the Union of South Africa and Southern Rhodesia on the other. In the sectional analyses our task is to see whether or not these differences in attitude re-emerge.

Table 58 presents a breakdown of the data on educational and training opportunities, and Table 59 does the same for employment. These two tables are presented together to facilitate a comparison of the material.

TABLE 58. *Scores Relating to Educational and Training Opportunities* ($M = 3.71$)

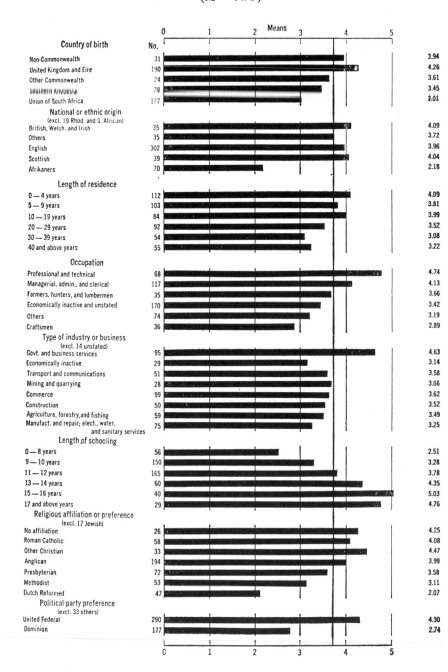

| | No. | Means |
|---|---|---|
| **Country of birth** | | |
| Non-Commonwealth | 31 | 3.94 |
| United Kingdom and Eire | 190 | 4.26 |
| Other Commonwealth | 24 | 3.61 |
| Southern Rhodesia | 70 | 3.45 |
| Union of South Africa | 177 | 3.01 |
| **National or ethnic origin** (excl. 19 Rhod. and S. African) | | |
| British, Welsh, and Irish | 35 | 4.09 |
| Others | 35 | 3.72 |
| English | 302 | 3.96 |
| Scottish | 39 | 4.04 |
| Afrikaners | 70 | 2.18 |
| **Length of residence** | | |
| 0 — 4 years | 112 | 4.09 |
| 5 — 9 years | 103 | 3.81 |
| 10 — 19 years | 84 | 3.99 |
| 20 — 29 years | 92 | 3.52 |
| 30 — 39 years | 54 | 3.08 |
| 40 and above years | 55 | 3.22 |
| **Occupation** | | |
| Professional and technical | 68 | 4.74 |
| Managerial, admin., and clerical | 117 | 4.13 |
| Farmers, hunters, and lumbermen | 35 | 3.66 |
| Economically inactive and unstated | 170 | 3.42 |
| Others | 74 | 3.19 |
| Craftsmen | 36 | 2.89 |
| **Type of industry or business** (excl. 14 unstated) | | |
| Govt. and business services | 95 | 4.63 |
| Economically inactive | 29 | 3.14 |
| Transport and communications | 51 | 3.58 |
| Mining and quarrying | 28 | 3.66 |
| Commerce | 99 | 3.62 |
| Construction | 50 | 3.52 |
| Agriculture, forestry, and fishing | 59 | 3.49 |
| Manufact. and repair; elect., water, and sanitary services | 75 | 3.25 |
| **Length of schooling** | | |
| 0 — 8 years | 56 | 2.51 |
| 9 — 10 years | 150 | 3.28 |
| 11 — 12 years | 165 | 3.78 |
| 13 — 14 years | 60 | 4.35 |
| 15 — 16 years | 40 | 5.03 |
| 17 and above years | 29 | 4.76 |
| **Religious affiliation or preference** (excl. 17 Jewish) | | |
| No affiliation | 26 | 4.25 |
| Roman Catholic | 58 | 4.08 |
| Other Christian | 33 | 4.47 |
| Anglican | 194 | 3.99 |
| Presbyterian | 72 | 3.58 |
| Methodist | 53 | 3.11 |
| Dutch Reformed | 47 | 2.07 |
| **Political party preference** (excl. 33 others) | | |
| United Federal | 290 | 4.30 |
| Dominion | 177 | 2.74 |

TABLE 59. *Scores Relating to Employment* $(M = 2.21)$

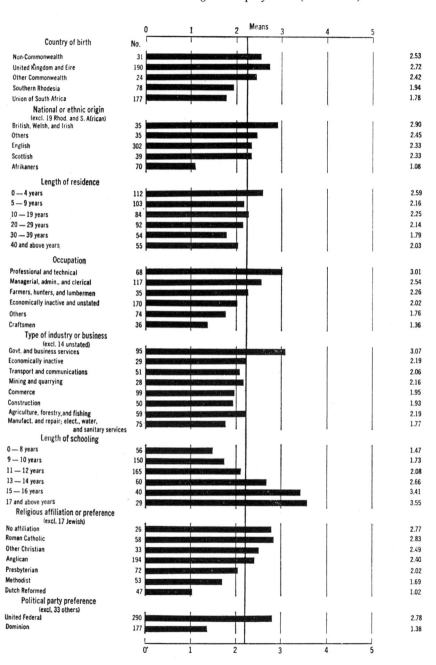

| | No. | Mean |
|---|---|---|
| **Country of birth** | | |
| Non-Commonwealth | 31 | 2.53 |
| United Kingdom and Eire | 190 | 2.72 |
| Other Commonwealth | 24 | 2.42 |
| Southern Rhodesia | 78 | 1.94 |
| Union of South Africa | 177 | 1.78 |
| **National or ethnic origin** (excl. 19 Rhod. and S. African) | | |
| British, Welsh, and Irish | 35 | 2.90 |
| Others | 35 | 2.45 |
| English | 302 | 2.33 |
| Scottish | 39 | 2.33 |
| Afrikaners | 70 | 1.08 |
| **Length of residence** | | |
| 0 — 4 years | 112 | 2.59 |
| 5 — 9 years | 103 | 2.16 |
| 10 — 19 years | 84 | 2.25 |
| 20 — 29 years | 92 | 2.14 |
| 30 — 39 years | 54 | 1.79 |
| 40 and above years | 55 | 2.03 |
| **Occupation** | | |
| Professional and technical | 68 | 3.01 |
| Managerial, admin., and clerical | 117 | 2.54 |
| Farmers, hunters, and lumbermen | 35 | 2.26 |
| Economically inactive and unstated | 170 | 2.02 |
| Others | 74 | 1.76 |
| Craftsmen | 36 | 1.36 |
| **Type of industry or business** (excl. 14 unstated) | | |
| Govt. and business services | 95 | 3.07 |
| Economically inactive | 29 | 2.19 |
| Transport and communications | 51 | 2.06 |
| Mining and quarrying | 28 | 2.16 |
| Commerce | 99 | 1.95 |
| Construction | 50 | 1.93 |
| Agriculture, forestry, and fishing | 59 | 2.19 |
| Manufact. and repair; elect., water, and sanitary services | 75 | 1.77 |
| **Length of schooling** | | |
| 0 — 8 years | 56 | 1.47 |
| 9 — 10 years | 150 | 1.73 |
| 11 — 12 years | 165 | 2.08 |
| 13 — 14 years | 60 | 2.66 |
| 15 — 16 years | 40 | 3.41 |
| 17 and above years | 29 | 3.55 |
| **Religious affiliation or preference** (excl. 17 Jewish) | | |
| No affiliation | 26 | 2.77 |
| Roman Catholic | 58 | 2.83 |
| Other Christian | 33 | 2.49 |
| Anglican | 194 | 2.40 |
| Presbyterian | 72 | 2.02 |
| Methodist | 53 | 1.69 |
| Dutch Reformed | 47 | 1.02 |
| **Political party preference** (excl. 33 others) | | |
| United Federal | 290 | 2.78 |
| Dominion | 177 | 1.38 |

COUNTRY OF BIRTH

Of the three groups selected for analysis, persons from the United Kingdom show the greatest desire to change the opportunities for African educational and trade training. There is positive support for more schools and better equipment to tap more effectively the human resources of Southern Rhodesia. Similarly, there is recognition of the need for better and more extensive training to produce skilled tradesmen—carpenters, bricklayers, electricians, mechanics, and other craftsmen. The Southern Rhodesian-born are also on the side of change, but more cautiously so, and with more qualification. The South Africans fall almost exactly on the theoretical middle of the distribution (3.00), and approximately 50% wish to maintain the status quo, a bigger proportion than in any other grouping.

When we turn to the practical use of educational achievements and trade skills in occupations traditionally filled by Europeans, the scores for all groups drop strikingly. Those born in the United Kingdom, on the average, are now on the side of maintaining the present situation, though by no means as decisively as the other two groupings. Their standard deviation shows that about one-third are on the side of discontinuing the status quo in employment. The Southern Rhodesian and South African-born swing from the side of change in education to a position decisively in favor of maintaining the present pattern of employment, with the latter taking a slightly more conservative stand.

NATIONAL OR ETHNIC ORIGIN

In total score, a very large difference in attitude was measured between the individuals of English and Afrikaner background. In fact the Afrikaners' score was more conservative than that obtained by any other subpopulation in the analysis. On matters of education and trade training, the difference between them is still large, with the Afrikaners again obtaining the lowest score in the category. However, there is an important variation in the Afrikaner scores that should be noted. The Afrikaner mean score on the whole questionnaire is 1.48 as compared with 2.18 on the category of education. From this fact, it can be deduced that although Afrikaners strongly wish to maintain the differentiating customs and laws of Southern Rhodesia, they do not display the same reluctance to change educational facilities for Africans. Quite a proportion state that they favor the improvement of African education, but this is generally linked with the qualification that the acquired skills should be used in intra-African competition rather than in competition with Europeans.

The change in attitude from education to employment is greater with Englishmen than with Afrikaners. The former show a shift from 3.96 to 2.33, whereas the Afrikaners drop from 2.18 to 1.08. In part, this may be a reflection of the greater homogeneity of Afrikaner thinking about Africans.

Although few in number, and of little weight numerically in Southern Rhodesia, individuals who classify themselves as British, Welsh, and Irish (as distinct from English) display attitudes on both education and employment that are more tolerant of change than any other group. The reason for this is not known.

LENGTH OF RESIDENCE

The periods 0–4 years and 30–39 years were chosen for analyzing attitude and length of residence in Southern Rhodesia. As in total scores, those who have been in the country for fewer than five years display most enthusiasm for extending and improving African education and trade training. Individuals who have been resident 30–39 years, although just on the side of change, are not so sure of the effectiveness or desirability of such changes.

When one turns to job competition, the trends are similar but all at a lower level. Individuals in the 0–4 group are now weighted slightly against nonracial trade unions and the acceptance of Africans into positions normally held by Europeans. However, the proportion of new arrivals who opt for change in employment practices is substantially smaller than the proportion supporting change in the provision of educational facilities for Africans.

Within the 30–39-year bracket, the center of gravity is definitely on the side of the present system, and the proportion favoring change is small. The vehicle of change within Southern Rhodesia, on this evidence, seems to be motivated by more recent immigrants. Naturally, it is possible to find exceptions to this rule, but the observation is still generally true.

OCCUPATION

Inasmuch as occupation has some correlation with general intelligence, length of education, and scholastic achievement, it would be proper to postulate some relation between occupation and attitude score. This is as it turned out. Those who would be rated highest on a socioeconomic scale—individuals in the professional and technical class—show a very strong desire for changes in African education. Then, in lessening strength, come the managerial personnel, farmers, economically inactive, skilled and sales workers, and, finally, the craftsmen. The craftsmen are the only ones to opt for the status quo.

There is a very significant gap between professional persons and craftsmen, with the latter sensing and expressing fear that they are likely to take the first impact of the advancing Africans. Even so, nearly half of the craftsmen are prepared to countenance change in African education although, with their own livelihood more clearly at stake, they are prone to qualify the use made of it.

TYPE OF INDUSTRY OR BUSINESS

When we analyzed general attitude in relation to industry, one classification stood out from the rest, that of government and business services. The occupations falling into this group are somewhat varied, but on the whole they can be classified as professional, managerial, and administrative. On the category of education, persons in the services again stand out from the rest. The mean position is very significantly on the side of change and, if one looks at the scores, it is clear that only a small proportion support the status quo. The other industrial subpopulations are also oriented toward changes in African education, but their scores are nearer the mean and approximately of the same value.

On employment, the one valid comparison is between those classified in the services and the remainder. The former, on the average, reject the status quo whereas all the others support it. There is some significance in this fact. Although "services" is a heterogeneous mixture of occupations, it includes all the administrative branches of the Federal, territorial, municipal, and local governments. It is not unreasonable to infer that the differentiating laws promulgated by these governments have to be administered by individuals who are fundamentally in favor of changing them.

EDUCATION

There is a significant relation between length of schooling and attitude about both education and employment. As schooling increases, so does attitude score about the education of Africans. Status quo scores are obtained only by those who have been to school for eight years and less. Thereafter, the mean scores show increasingly heavy loadings on the change factor until a peak is reached with those who have received fifteen and sixteen years of education. This peak score of 5.03 is among the highest displayed on any personal or social variable selected for further analysis.

On employment the trend is clear. With individuals who have fewer than fourteen years schooling, the mean scores fall on the side of reserving for Europeans the positions outlined in the questionnaire. Fourteen years seems to be the critical threshold in the scores. As schooling extends above this level—advanced secondary or early undergraduate at University—the scores become progressively stronger for changing the employment situation to one of competitive equality.

RELIGIOUS AFFILIATION OR PREFERENCE

It has been stressed that the history of African education in Southern Rhodesia is very much the history of mission endeavor. Not infrequently, there has been a considerable difference between the thinking of the church leaders and the European church members about African education. For this analysis, comparison is made between the attitudes of Roman Catholics, Anglicans, and Dutch Reformed. There is little difference between the scores obtained by members of the Catholic and Anglican churches; both are on the side of change in African education. Conversely, the mean obtained by those who specify the Dutch Reformed church as their preference is distinctly on the side of the status quo. This mean score of 2.07 on education is more conservative than that obtained by any other group in the analysis. There is some historical reason for this. Although the Dutch Reformed church reached Morgenster in 1891 and began a school almost at once, it has generally, from the beginning, been opposed to the training of African artisans. This corporate view is expressed through the responses to statements on the questionnaire. Statement 9 is concerned with training for the skilled trades, and items 1 and 2 elicit responses toward the apprenticeship system. Consequently, the stand taken on education and employment by adherents of the Dutch Reformed church can be understood.

On employment, several major differences can be observed. The Roman Catholics take the least emphatic stand in favor of the status quo, and they are more positive than the members of any other church in favoring the admittance of Africans to European trade unions. The wish for social change is noteworthy because it illustrates that the traditional conservatism of the Catholic church is not reflected in attitudes toward African advancement and employment. The greater internal discipline of the church may enable it to influence its members toward a view closer to that of church leaders than is possible in other churches.

The Anglicans' mean is stationed on the side of present employment practices, while the Presbyterians, Methodists, and Dutch Reformed take a more decisive stand in favor of the status quo. The mean score of members of the Dutch Reformed church (1.02) is the most conservative of all. Consequently, it can be inferred that they will object most to the presence of Africans in trade unions and in industrial and commercial positions now filled by Europeans. In particular, the opposition of the Dutch Reformed to Africans being placed in charge of Europeans (M = .38) stands in sharp contrast to the Catholics' score of 2.69.

POLITICAL PARTY PREFERENCE

Differences between supporters of the two major political parties are also clear. The great majority of Federal party supporters are in favor of more schools, better schools, and increased trade training facilities. On employment, the same people lean toward the status quo, but more than a third of them wish to see changes here as well as in education.

Supporters of the Dominion party, on the average, are prepared to retain the present system of African education, though some support its improvement. On employment, they firmly endorse the status quo, and generally do not approve of the employment of Africans in traditionally European jobs.

## THE PRINCIPAL THEMES

From the evidence, both historical and empirical, one can detect a continuity to the themes that run through European society in Southern Rhodesia, and witness to some extent the molding influences that are changing them. The motivations that brought Europeans to Southern Rhodesia were many. In some it was lofty idealism, the challenge to uplift the heathen, to "win souls for God," and to lessen the harsh realities of disease, tribal war, and famine. Set properly in time and place, the deeds of the early missionaries and the examples they set display a quality of moral idealism that has left a permanent mark on African communities. They recognized that the pathway to the African's soul was through his mind, and schools were established to tap his intellectual resources and physical skills. To this day, these schools form the backbone of African education.

Other immigrants were more materialistically motivated to find the minerals that lay locked in the ground and to till the fertile soil. These men came initially to explore, then to settle and to conquer. They also realized that schools for Africans were necessary, but often for a different reason. Mines must be worked, industries established, and trades developed. These goals were difficult to achieve without supporting the schools the missionaries had built, hence the first government grants to African education around the turn of the century.

The development and extension of African education has never received the whole-hearted support of Europeans, and does not today. Some argued in the early days, and still argue, that to start education·is never to finish. The demand is created, and never stops; indeed it accelerates. So, in starting the first schools and in supporting them, the early immigrants—religious and secular—started Southern Rhodesia on an almost irreversible vector of social change.

Historical documents show that the Europeans have been of two minds about education, on the one hand, and employment on the other. While education has come to be recognized as necessary (perhaps an evil necessity) to furnish skilled African workers and to reduce disease, the protection of Europeans from the competitive consequences of this education has been considered essential. Our empirical data demonstrate the same duality in thinking. Hence the pressures, both social and legal, to protect Europeans and to keep Africans in segregated areas. It is argued that this separation also benefits the Africans because it allows them to use their knowledge and skills for their own benefit.

Thus, to some extent, several themes interlock in the realm of education and employment. Within them are the seeds of further cooperation or future conflict. Education and employment may well represent the Scylla and Charybdis between which the Government may have to steer a perilous course in the years ahead.

# 12

## THE OCCUPATION AND USE OF LAND

An understanding of the history and structure of any society requires an appreciation of the relationships individuals and groups traditionally have had with their natural environment. The characteristics of the natural environment—soil, climate, water supply, topography—have considerable bearing on the way of life which a group develops. Some areas permit few alternatives for those who live in them, while others allow many choices to be made. The importance of the natural environment is most clearly seen in relation to aspects of material culture such as houses, food, transportation devices, tools, and clothing. But it also affects the content of religious beliefs, the system of economic activities, the territorial or political organization, and even the family and kinship structures of a society.

Man's knowledge and skills, of course, allow him to modify and partially control his natural environment. Since some type of modification always occurs, the products of human initiative—cities, railways, highways, skyscrapers, cemeteries, mines, and so on—must be considered in analyzing the relationships a particular society has developed in interaction with nature. Urban and rural areas throughout the world testify to the success of human endeavor in manipulating the physical environment.

When the Europeans first arrived in Southern Rhodesia, most

Africans resided in stream-fed valleys amidst broken outcroppings of rock. The terrain, relatively poor soils, and the Africans' limited ability to utilize fully the natural resources resulted in a dispersed population (McGregor, 1940:6). Their political communities were small, organized on the basis of both kinship and locality, and subject to periodic raids from neighboring or distant groups. Some mining was done, but in general the land was used only as a source of crops and game.

The European occupation of the country was stimulated primarily by the prospect of finding gold. Others came later and were more interested in agriculture, but both of these groups settled chiefly in the high veld. This area was above 3,000 feet in elevation and contained most of the known gold resources. It promised the least danger from malaria and the tsetse fly, offered the best climate, and had the lowest density of African population. With the discovery of new minerals, better methods of controlling diseases, and the development of irrigation schemes, Europeans gradually settled in other sections of the country, but the vast majority have continued to this day to live in the high veld.

The growth of towns and cities in Southern Rhodesia, as in much of Africa, depended upon mineral wealth and an adequate labor supply living near subsistence levels. But unlike most other colonies, the European population has always been more urban- than rural-centered, as Table 7 indicates. Expanding industrialization, which will be stimulated by cheap electricity from the new vast Kariba Dam, has also brought an increasing urbanization of the African population. Thus Western culture has come to play a progressively more important part in the location of the Rhodesian population, and in its economic and social organization. The beliefs, feelings, and values of the two culture groups have combined with the potentialities of the natural environment largely to determine the spatial distribution of residences, businesses and industries, and recreational and social facilities. The use of African and European lands, and the patterns of social interaction that takes place thereon, are thus greatly affected by other aspects of culture.

The Order-in-Council of 1894 established the rights of an individual African to "acquire, hold, encumber and dispose of land on the same conditions as a person who is not a native." It also called for a commission to establish the first Reserves in Matabeleland. Another Order-in-Council reaffirmed this right in 1898, and requested the B. S. A. Company to assign land to Africans as they needed it. Apart from the gold-bearing lands, and a twenty-five mile strip along the railways, Africans were able to remain on lands of their own choosing until 1910. The lands assigned to them were often in the hotter, drier, and more isolated regions of the low veld. But in most cases, aboriginal settlement patterns were used as a basic criterion in the apportionment of land. These allocations did not always result in conflict-free situations, however.[1]

The B. S. A. Company's search for gold failed to fulfill expectations, and it became increasingly interested in land and agriculture. It began to encourage greater immigration in 1907 in order to expand European agricultural production. This development hastened the establishment of African Reserves, and the construction of telegraph and power lines, railways, and roads. Wilson Fox, the Company Secretary in London, thought the idea of Reserves was retrogressive, but his view was not officially accepted.[2] The Company wanted a final demarcation of the land in order to define the amount that could be sold to immigrants to increase its meager profits, and to help pay the costs of administering the Colony.[3]

A Native Reserves Commission was appointed in 1914, and its report [4] served as the basis for further assignments of land in 1920. About one million acres were withdrawn from African occupation, a move that provoked much controversy. The papers of the Commission [5] indicate its close cooperation with the B. S. A. Land Settlement Board. In the settlement, Europeans were allocated thirty-two per cent of the total lands. Twenty-three per cent was assigned to Africans, and the remainder was reserved to the Crown for future disposal.

The question of title to the lands of Southern Rhodesia was not fully determined until 1918, however. In that year, the Privy Council decided that the Colony's land belonged to the Crown, by virtue of conquest, rather than to the Administration. After Self-Government was attained in 1923, all land that had been assigned to Africans, or had not been alienated, was reserved for the Crown. The B. S. A. Company was paid a cash settlement of £3,750,000 when it ceased to administer the Colony.

A belief developed over time, and still persists,[6] that Africans could buy land anywhere in the country. Although legally entitled to do so under the Orders-in-Council of 1894 and 1898, and the Constitution of 1924, in practice very few Africans took advantage of this. The B. S. A. Company made few sales to Africans because European farmers protested that the value of their holdings would be jeopardized,[7] and also because freehold title was a novelty to Africans. By 1925, Africans individually owned 44,251 acres, but they had been acquired despite opposition in the Legislative Assembly, the *Rhodesia Herald,* and the Agricultural Union. Europeans increasingly began to call for the segregation of African and European lands. Many missionaries and the Native Affairs Department joined them in advising segregation, though they did so for different reasons (Cripps, 1927). The general European population wanted to protect themselves from the Africans, while the missionaries and the Native Affairs Department sought to safeguard the Africans from the Europeans. At the time, territorial segregation was widely advocated in many African colonies, and it was a Colonial Office policy which Lord Lugard, among others, accepted.

In 1925, another Land Commission was established. Its recommendations embodied the principle of territorial segregation and "separate development" which became the keystones of subsequent Government policy.[8] In addition to a continuation of the system of Reserves, specific areas also were designated in which Africans might acquire land individually. The Commission's report served as the basis for the important Land Apportionment Act of 1930.* It encouraged social, economic, and political segregation: socially, by reducing intergroup contact and opportunities for voluntary cooperation; and economically, by regulating competition between African and European businessmen and farmers. A subsequent political effect was to prevent Africans from voting in municipal elections.

The Land Apportionment Act was welcomed by "liberals" and missionaries both in Rhodesia and overseas, and also by some Africans. At the time, over one-third of the African population was living within designated European areas. The Act prohibited Africans from owning or occupying land in European areas, except under specified clauses such as labor contracts with European farmers. Africans are permitted to occupy unalienated Crown lands under conditions specified by the Government. Thus, a new chapter began in the history of European-African relations, and in their occupation and use of land. For almost another three decades, there were few signs of discontent about the wisdom of this system of land apportionment and use.

Over the years, various alterations were made in the total acreages of land assigned to Europeans and Africans. In 1959, there were 42,000,000 acres in African areas and 48,000,000 acres in European areas, while the remaining 8,000,000 acres were designated as forests and national parks.[9]

The history of land use and ownership in the urban areas is similar to that in the rural areas. African families were encouraged to settle near mines, on farms, and in towns during the early years, but in areas separated from the homes of Europeans. Segregation received legal sanction in Salisbury in 1906, when an ordinance required Africans, especially for sanitary reasons, to live in locations outside the town unless they were domiciled on their employers' lands. The idea of strict segregation did not materialize until about 1925, however, when European fears of African competition increased. The growing percentage of European women in the urban population probably contributed to this change in attitude as well.[10]

* At the time of going to press, the Government is debating far-reaching amendments to, and the eventual repeal of, the Land Apportionment Act.

The residence of Africans in towns and cities was thought to be transitory and at the convenience of Europeans. This is illustrated by the high percentage of single men and nonindigenous workers among the African urban population. Several measures for registering and controlling the movement and employment of Africans had been characteristic of Southern Rhodesia for many years. Numerous others were passed following the enactment of the Land Apportionment Act in 1930. In 1946, another innovation was made: the municipalities, over their objections, were required to provide housing for all Africans working therein (Comhaire, 1950). Africans were not allowed to acquire title to land; they could only lease it and only in some areas. In a few urban centers, they have been permitted since then to buy and own their houses but not the land on which they stand.

The places where Africans and Europeans reside provide some interesting contrasts with the Government's policy on land titles. Outside their Reserves and Purchase Areas, Africans have lived in designated areas while they worked in industry or commerce, or upon European lands if they were farm laborers or domestic servants. To cite McGregor (1940:403), "Commencing with segregation on the land, the State largely breaks down this policy by its taxes and rebuilds it in the markets, industry, agriculture, and domestic service."

The small "plantation" was one of the first new institutions to develop from the interaction of Europeans and Africans in Southern Rhodesia (cf. Thompson, 1939). In the early years, some coercion was used to secure African laborers. In other cases, European farmers allowed laborers to bring their families with them, and sufficient land was supplied for them to raise their own food. There was little need for occupational specialization among the laborers. The employers retained extensive political control over their employees, though in time the Government replaced much of the farmers' authority. But even today, the Government is less effective in bringing conformity with legal norms in the rural than in the urban areas. The plantation system, although it had only a limited development in Southern Rhodesia, had much in common with the system of indirect rule introduced elsewhere by British and other colonial administrations (Frazier, 1953:299). Nevertheless, the farms or plantations provided a few opportunities for Africans—especially the men—to learn European techniques, customs, and values. Patterns of reciprocity began to emerge, as the European farmers usually supplied a measure of medical care, education, religious instruction, and technical training to their employees and their families. Many farmers continue, often with small Government subsidies, to provide the elements of formal schooling where mission schools have not been established.

The early European immigrants believed that the residential segregation (or isolation) of Africans encouraged idleness, a judgment they later modified. The Private Locations Ordinance of 1908 legally sanctioned the residence of Africans on European farms where they were employed.[11] Not until after the Land Apportionment Act was passed in 1930 was the growth in the number of private locations halted. In 1959, a total of 14,881 African families were reported to be living on European farms under labor agreements.[12]

European mining interests have also restricted Africans from owning and working land that contained valuable minerals. Cecil Rhodes obtained the mineral rights in Matabeleland from Lobengula through the Rudd Concession in 1888, and these rights were extended to Mashonaland in 1890. When it was freed from the administration of the Colony in 1924, the Company stimulated the development of the two other large mining trusts, the Rhodesian Selection Trust, Limited, and the Anglo-American Corporation of South Africa, Limited. In 1933, the B. S. A. Company finally sold its mineral rights in Southern Rhodesia to the Government for £2,000,000 (Hailey, 1957:1521).

It seems clear that Africans have done little working of the territory's mineral resources since the decline of the Monomotapa kingdom. At the present time, Africans may obtain a special grant to pan for gold in the Reserves, and they are legally entitled to secure a prospecting license, as are Europeans.

However, in its discussion prior to the passage of the Mines and Minerals Act of 1935, the Chamber of Mines pressed for a "gentleman's agreement" that Africans should not be granted permission to prospect for minerals: it recognized that any discriminatory clause in the legislation would bring objections from the Imperial Government.[13]

Africans in the mining industry, almost uniformly, have been unskilled laborers. The mining companies have provided "compounds" for their African workers, a high proportion of whom have always been of nonindigenous origin. In 1956, more than 69% of the 60,658 African mine workers came from outside Southern Rhodesia, and they tended to be young and unmarried, or to have left their families behind.[14] The mine compound is an institution similar to the plantation in Southern Rhodesia, since many mines (especially gold) are small in size. Food, medical attention, recreation, and some schooling are provided. Social and recreational activities are planned for the Africans, and the general supervision and discipline of off-work behavior lies with the mining companies. Nowhere in the country may African mine workers acquire freehold title to the land on which they reside. Thus the mines, like plantations, tend to assume or exercise political responsibilities over their employees. The companies control more of the workers' day than is spent in strictly economic activities, a pattern found in other areas of the world.[15]

In other spheres of industry and commerce, the residence of Africans is also regulated. But in urban areas, more than in most sections of the economy, opportunities have been created for residence away from the scene of work. Housing is provided for African employees either by the employers, the municipalities, or the Government. Some of them reside in licensed private premises, but most of them live in townships or locations especially created for Africans. The acquisition of accommodation depends on employment and the availability of quarters. Traditional priority has been given to single men's quarters, as indicated earlier. Most Africans employed by the Government also live in these townships and are subject to the same control of their movements, political expression, and off-duty activities as are the others. Contact between the outstanding professional Africans and Europeans is greater than for Africans at other status levels. Yet relatively infrequent contacts are made with Europeans since Africans are employed in predominantly African institutions or services, and reside in African townships.

The closest spatial proximity between Europeans and Africans comes through the pervasive institution of domestic service. In 1956, there were 71,000 Africans employed as servants in Southern Rhodesia.[16] Traditionally they have been males, although an increasing number of women have taken domestic employment. Servants are generally housed immediately to the rear of their employers' residences, and are provided with rations, clothing, and medical care in addition to their wages. A high percentage are of nonindigenous origin. They are subject to the provisions of the Masters and Servants Act, and may bring other members of their families to live with them only if approved by the employer and the local government authorities. The territorial integration generated by domestic service, however, has not led to support for the permanent residence of Africans near their employers.

African farmers in the Reserves can acquire only a limited acreage of land for their crops and cattle. When the Europeans first arrived, and presumably for many years afterward, there was sufficient land for all Africans to support themselves. An increasing population, and the alienation of the majority of the land to non-Africans, have increased the pressure upon what remains, some of which is useless for agriculture, and some which has deteriorated through unsound methods of tillage. In 1929, the Government began centralizing villages and demarcating arable and pasture lands in an attempt to halt the advance of desert conditions (Hancock, 1942). Since then, "revolutionary" changes have been introduced in the relationships between Africans and the land.

Measures designed to conserve the soils, and to teach Africans better methods of land use, commenced as far back as 1926. In 1941, the Natural Resources Act was legislated. The Government found later that "propaganda, instruction and voluntary acceptance of new methods were inadequate," mainly because of African conservatism, an increasing population, and a shortage of technical staff. In 1944, the new post of Director of Native Agriculture was created, and more Land Development Officers were engaged to further the work commenced by Alvord and his colleagues in 1926. Then an important measure, the Land Husbandry Act, was passed in 1951. It aimed to improve the quality and quantity of crops, reduce the number of excessive stock, introduce better husbandry practices, allocate minimum rights to arable land, and ensure security of tenure for individual Africans.

It will be recalled that approximately 42 million acres have been assigned for use by Africans. This figure embraces three categories of land:

(a) Native Reserves (set aside in terms of the Constitution)— approximately 21 million acres;
(b) Special Native Areas (set aside by Act of Parliament)— approximately 13 million acres;
(c) Native Purchase Areas—approximately 8 million acres.

Within the Native Purchase Areas it is estimated that between 17,000 and 18,000 freehold farms will ultimately be transferred to African farmers.

Of the 34 million acres encompassed in the Native Reserves and Special Native Areas, it is estimated that something over 3 million acres are arable. Under the Land Husbandry Act, all Africans who at a given date are cultivating land or depasturing stock are being allocated fixed acreages of arable land, below which fragmentation is not permitted. In areas with a high rainfall, the standard size of an allocation for growing crops was six acres (later increased to eight acres); in areas with less rainfall, the acreage is correspondingly greater. In an attempt to consolidate these standard holdings into more economic units, and to move away from the traditional system of free land usage, any African is permitted to acquire, by purchase or negotiation, up to three such holdings.

The land in the reserved areas, however, is insufficient to support an expanding African population with this system of allocation. Under the Act, it is envisaged that about 307,000 African families (at five per family, over 1,500,000 people) can be carried in the Reserves and the Special Native Areas, with the present methods of agriculture. But if planning is based on a market economy, in which a family produces double its subsistence requirements, then, without better methods of husbandry and further irrigation, it is not likely that more than 200,000 families can be stabilized in the reserved areas.

Either way, a new generation of adult Africans will find that they cannot become agriculturists on the standard-sized holdings. They will be required to seek wage work (e.g. in the urban areas or as agricultural laborers) or, if they can afford to buy land, to acquire either a standard holding or a freehold title in the Native Purchase Areas. Estimates vary considerably but it is expected that up to 250,000 men —mostly young—will move into wage employment during the next five to ten years; almost as many as the number of Southern Rhodesian-born Africans now employed in the money economy.[17] Of course, Africans have been moving into the wage economy for many years; in the future, the number seeking full-time employment should increase slowly at first, but at an accelerating rate.

The comprehensiveness of the five-year plan for "revolutionizing" African agriculture has aroused some misunderstandings and dissatisfactions both among peasant farmers and others.* For a variety of reasons, the expected total allocations under the Land Husbandry Act have been increased from 2.2 million to 3.5 million acres.[18] But unless there are drastic changes in the traditional methods of grazing stock, the increased allocation will not eliminate the shortage of land.[19] At the moment, animal grazing accounts for far more of the 34 million acres of African land than does the tilling of crops, and, by comparison, the economic return is meager.

When the Land Husbandry Act has been fully implemented, it is hoped that the African cultivators will produce about twice their subsistence needs. The surplus half will be marketed in the money economy. However, because they lack financial security, African farmers have had more difficulty than Europeans in obtaining credit and loans, and in subsidizing their capital improvements.[20] Plans are under way, though, to ameliorate this problem.

The implementation of the Land Husbandry Act will necessitate the absorption of the excess population from the Reserves into the urban areas. But considerable discontinuity exists in the Government's rural and urban plans for African residence and employment, and opposition comes from local governments and from individuals, neighborhood groups, and other associations. Europeans have consistently opposed the idea of removing the legal barriers in order to permit Africans and Europeans to live where they choose.

Two events in 1959 illustrate the continuing strength of attitudes among Europeans. One African had returned with a Dutch wife following a period of technical training in Europe. The Land Apportionment Act, in its neat dichotomy, provided no definition for the area

* The program of the Southern Rhodesian African National Congress during 1957–59 called attention to various shortcomings in the land husbandry scheme. The rapid growth in Congress membership was, according to some observers, due to African grievances about the scheme.

in which the couple could legally reside, other than at a mission station. Public reaction, mostly from Europeans, effectively precluded any other alternative. This and other difficulties eventually resulted in their returning to Holland. No other case is known of an African husband and European wife living together in Southern Rhodesia.

The other situation was created when the Federal Government proposed buying a home in a European area for its newly appointed Parliamentary Secretary to the Minister of Home Affairs, Mr. Savanhu. Since he is an African, a special amendment to the Land Apportionment Act would have been required from another parliament, that of Southern Rhodesia. Europeans in Salisbury were outspoken in their dislike of the innovation, and were especially wary of possible sequels and other implications. For reasons other than this opposition, according to Mr. Savanhu, he chose to live in an African township.

In addition, Europeans are strongly against the presence of African beer halls and recreational grounds in European areas. Proposals for expanding these facilities, put forth by the Southern Rhodesian Government, have been opposed by local governments and newly organized protest groups (citizens' councils and property-owners' associations). Thus, the future growth of the urban African population, which is predicted to be high, will raise further questions about the Land Apportionment Act. Not only will the location of African and European residences be of continuing concern, but the further provision of transport and other social services must also come under review.

The Land Apportionment Act, in sum, is one of the basic pieces of legislation in Southern Rhodesia, and affects the whole social system of the country. Europeans traditionally regard houses as very desirable forms of property, and they retain a self-interest in all events that might affect their financial value. But in addition, like most people elsewhere, they think of neighborhoods as more than mere collections of buildings. In them they seek to relax and to associate with their most intimate kin and friends.[21] Those who are not included within their moral and social order are expected to remain outside their homes and neighborhood—unless they are legitimate servants and/or will conform to the established pattern of personal and social deference.

These sentiments are widespread among human groups. In the culturally plural society of Southern Rhodesia, they have been supported by legal enactments and sanctions. Separate and parallel facilities and systems have arisen, or been encouraged, virtually since European settlement began. Africans cannot rent offices or carry on business in European areas, and Europeans are restricted from doing the same in African areas, although permission can be granted. Beer and wine must be purchased in their own areas. The dead generally must be buried in separate cemeteries. In brief, virtually all activities that involve the extended or permanent use of land must be carried on in racially segregated areas. Anomalies to the pattern, such as marriage between an African and a European, are rare. They are not generally approved by European attitudes or values, and they create strains on the formally defined social system.

The future of territorial segregation in Southern Rhodesia is not clear. Sir Godfrey Huggins wrote in 1941, "We have possessory segregation as an essential feature of our policy at this stage, and I say at this stage because there is nothing static in our policy." [22] Since World War II, a small but seemingly expanding minority of Europeans, together with some Africans, have argued that the "stage" has been altered by the dynamic changes in the country. European opinion and Governmental policy have altered enough to acknowledge the necessity to accommodate a stable, married African labor force in urban areas. Important steps have been taken to ameliorate the problems that have derived from the growth of the African population upon a restricted land base. There are signs of minor changes being made in the system of land apportionment: amendments have been passed in the principal Act to allow Southern Rhodesia's only African advocate to occupy an office in the European business area, and to permit the new University College to house students and staff irrespective of race or culture. The use of rented quarters by an interracial social club in the European area of Salisbury has been criticized, but no legal action has been taken. New regulations were passed in 1959 which, with the consent of the owners, remove the legal restrictions on access to and use of hotels.

More important, the keystone of land apportionment is being discussed, analyzed, and argued with increasing frequency. It is a critical issue, as most Rhodesians recognize. At issue are fundamental questions about the country's future: What spatial arrangement of the total population is desirable, practical, and possible? What new types of relations will arise between Africans and Europeans, and should they be welcomed? Should social contacts be legally regulated or left to the customary choices of individuals? Would such radical changes necessitate a basic reorientation of the dominant patterns of culture and social organization?

These matters, which often are felt only implicitly and are not verbalized in rational terms, lie at the base of European attitudes toward the use of "African" and "European" lands. Together with industrial legislation and practices, the patterns of land use have shaped a social system in some ways unique in the world. How it will change in the future remains one of the major questions which divides Rhodesian society.

## CONTEMPORARY ATTITUDES

Because the Land Apportionment Act is one of the basic pieces of legislation in Southern Rhodesia, it was felt that its operation, and the effects that flow from it, should be examined in the study. To this end, a number of statements were constructed for inclusion in the questionnaire. Some of these relate to the use of land set aside for Africans by various Acts and regulations, and others refer to land reserved for European occupancy and use. The juxtaposition of attitudes toward African and European land provides us with some of our most striking contrasts, and illustrates to a degree a problem that may not be resolved by the mere passage of time. The first set of attitudes to consider is that relating to the use of land by Africans, and some of the outcomes of spatial segregation. We can focus attention on these attitudes through the statements of Table 60.

TABLE 60. *Statements Relating to the Use of African Lands*

| No. | Statement | −1 P.E. | +1 P.E. | Mean |
|-----|-----------|---------|---------|------|
| 7 | Many Africans are required to pay relatively higher costs in travelling to work than are Europeans, as they often must live at some distance from their places of employment. | 3.26 | 5.48 | 4.37 |
| 38 | African locations are equipped less frequently than European townships with amenities such as tarred roads and electricity. | 2.42 | 4.88 | 3.65 |
| 5 | No matter how good an African farmer is, under the Land Husbandry Act he cannot obtain more than three standard-sized holdings of land (totalling 18 acres in high rainfall areas). | 2.05 | 4.81 | 3.43 |
| 19 | Africans in urban areas are not permitted to own land outright, but have up to a 99 year lease, and this only in certain areas. | 1.68 | 4.46 | 3.07 |
| | | 2.35 | 4.91 | 3.63 |

These cover the cost of travel to work, the amenities available in the African locations, the size of African land holdings in the Reserves, and the system of land tenure available to urban Africans. Of the ranks of categories, this one comes third on the list, and it falls on the side of those practices Europeans generally wish to have changed. However, to appreciate the nature of the changes envisaged in land usage, it is necessary to inspect the verbal comments on the statements.

*Statement 7* (M = 4.37) reflects one of the consequences of the geographical separation of the races. Apart from those who reside

on their employers' property, Africans are required to live in locations or townships separated from European residential areas. This
means that many are obliged to live considerable distances from their
place of employment, and transport costs can be considerable. Although there is divergence of opinion on how to redress this position,
one fact is recognized by all, namely, that the location of African townships away from European residential areas has been imposed by
Europeans.

The cost of travel to work is an item on which many Africans feel
strongly, whether they travel by bus or on bicycle. Even where bus
fares are subsidized, the proportion of the total wage packet they
represent can be considerable, and so too is the cost of a bicycle. At
all levels of attitude score, there are Europeans prepared to contest
the statement and maintain that the various subsidies bring the African proportion for travel to that of the European level. A few persons
with very high scores recommend the repeal of the Land Apportionment Act but, for the most part, this is not considered desirable. A
few extracts will serve to illustrate typical sentiments: "If Africans
are expected to live in set areas, then perhaps travel could be subsidized." "Municipalities or employers should correct this." "If we
make them live in the bush, I reckon we will have to pay for their
transportation."

The reason for this repetitive theme seems clear. The majority of
Europeans accept responsibility for the separation of residential areas,
and, while they do not want the system changed, they are prepared
to accept some responsibility for alleviating the financial burden this
may place on Africans.

*Statement 38* (M = 3.65) states that African townships have fewer
public amenities such as tarred roads and electricity. The mean score
on this item is for change, but the individual comments show that
the over-all concern is who shall pay for the amenities. Persons with
high social-change scores, and persons with status quo scores, continually stress the financial and economic factor. A typical response
is "Who pays for such amenities?" Another maintains that "this question ignores the fact that amenities are paid for by taxes and rates
which come in the main from Europeans." A somewhat different
theme can also be identified among those with typical scores: "No
doubt these [facilities] will come with time, but at present it should
be remembered that the present amenities are much more than the
Africans themselves are used to." On the other hand, one person with
a high score (6) believes that an "increase in basic social amenities
would inevitably result in improved social standards and greater
social awareness." However, this point of view is not common. At the
low end of the distribution, the reaction, "Who pays?" is common.

To sum up, there is concern about the physical condition of African townships and locations, and a general desire to see them improved. It is held, however, that Europeans should not be taxed further to effect this.

*Statement 5* (M = 3.43) concerns the size of African land holdings under the Land Apportionment Act; the scores indicate substantial sentiment for increasing the allowable acreage. But the suggestions offered in the interview material vary widely and make it difficult to pinpoint an over-all theme.

At the social-change end of the scale, the more representative end, there is some concern because "Europeans hold excessive units of arable land." Others feel they cannot answer or understand the question. Yet again, a number believe the practice should be discontinued when it can be shown that Africans are qualified and can make good use of extra land. To illustrate: "Originally this was needed, but now improved methods of farming have been introduced. I think that if they prove their skills, they should be allowed more land." Another individual, perhaps echoing the sentiment of Sir Godfrey Huggins, suggests that "this will change as the country grows up."

In the moderately conservative area of the scale, one person comments extensively and seems to summarize the disquiet many Europeans feel about modifying the Act: "The Land Husbandry Act can be seen as a protection against soil erosion. . . . Can the African farmer, with the equipment he has, manage more land, or will he go back to his old system of working a big area, and leave it to nature and good luck to determine whether the same area can be used again?"

Where the scores are strongly for the status quo, the reasons are usually clear-cut. "The native is not capable of looking after more land." "I don't think a native is capable of working large farms." "The real problem is population growth. When land apportionment began, the size of the allotments to Africans was adequate."

It is apparent that this statement created considerable unease among our European respondents. The mechanism of rationalization is frequently invoked to explain why Africans cannot be given more land, even though this may be favored in principle. Few people seriously consider a reallocation of land among Africans and Europeans, and fewer still envisage the sale to Africans of land in the European areas. Yet the disquiet and unease—not infrequently a moral unease—about the future is there.

*Statement 19* (M = 3.07) reads: "Africans in urban areas are not permitted to own land outright, but have up to a 99 year lease, and this only in certain areas." The legal restriction upon Africans in the purchase of land freehold has already been described. The development of a leasehold system in the African townships is a more recent innovation.

The probable error limits to this item (1.68 and 4.46) demonstrate that Europeans are divided on the matter, but the nature of the division must be examined further. Among the half who wish to see Africans given the right of freehold tenure in urban areas, it is common for the rider to be attached that the land should be within African townships. The other half, who support the status quo, do so on the ground that to permit unqualified tenure might be tantamount to letting the camel's nose into the tent. Once he gets that far, he will push harder to get right in—in this case, into the European residential areas. If it is guaranteed that tenure be granted only in the African areas, then there is much support for an amendment.

At the high social-change end of the scale, a group of individuals advocate the repeal of the Land Apportionment Act and the granting to Africans of freehold tenure in European areas. This group, however, is not typical.

All of the statements reviewed so far have had some relation to the occupation and use of land by Africans in African areas. Both the mean score (3.63) and the statements demonstrate that Europeans are oriented toward change as long as the change does not affect European land. There is strong feeling that geographical separation bears heavily upon the African who has to travel a long way to his work, and that Europeans should help with the extra costs involved. Also there is a desire to improve the amenities in African locations, to make more land available for African farmers, to raise the standards of living, and to give Africans freehold tenure to land as long as it is confined to the African areas. The proffered solutions to these problems generally do not violate the basic theme of separation.

A contrasting picture is unveiled immediately when one contemplates the use by Africans of European lands, either for residential or business purposes. Six items of this type fall into the category, and the center of gravity of responses (1.80) lies distinctly on the side of maintaining the present segregation. Set in its historical context, this is as we might expect it to be, but the reasons advanced are worthy of scrutiny. The statements are shown in Table 61 and the comments follow.

As with the other tables in the analyses of categories, the items are presented in descending order on a change-maintain continuum. The highest score concerns the renting of offices to Africans, and, on this one, while Europeans generally support the status quo, they are least emphatic about it. The lowest score is associated with the ownership of houses in European areas, and on this item the sample is emphatic that it does not wish to see any change in the status quo. The practice of separation is too well established, and is reinforced by such strong feeling, that it is difficult to conceive of any other response.

TABLE 61. *Statements Relating to the Use of European Lands*

| No. | Statement | −1 P.E. | +1 P.E. | Mean |
|-----|-----------|---------|---------|------|
| 13 | African organizations cannot rent offices legally in European commercial areas. | 1.04 | 3.74 | 2.39 |
| 33 | Generally there are separate cemeteries for Africans and Europeans. | .88 | 3.52 | 2.20 |
| 6 | The Land Apportionment Act prevents Africans from occupying land for business purposes within the recognized European commercial areas. | .71 | 3.49 | 2.10 |
| 11 | In the main, Africans are prohibited from buying beer and wines from shops in European areas, but must buy beer at the African beer halls or bottle stores. | .48 | 2.86 | 1.67 |
| 63 | The legal regulations of Southern Rhodesia make it extremely difficult for an African man to live with a European woman to whom he is married legally. | −.04 | 2.80 | 1.38 |
| 18 | Under the Land Apportionment Act, Africans are not allowed to own houses in the same areas as Europeans. | −.05 | 2.21 | 1.08 |
| | | .50 | 3.10 | 1.80 |

*Statement 13* (M = 2.39) relates to the fact that, as a result of the Land Apportionment Act, Africans are prohibited from renting offices in European commercial areas. This statement falls on the physical separation dimension of the factor analysis and can be interpreted as a device to minimize contact. The interview material does not reveal apprehension about commercial competition but this may be a motive underlying the comments. Certainly the matter of competition emerges in the responses to statement 6. The typical responses support the status quo, but for varying reasons and with different emphases: "There is not enough room even for Europeans." "Nor can Europeans rent places in African areas." "Exceptions might be made." "This [separation] can be relaxed on African progress." "They have and should be given their own areas as in America where there are Chinese areas and so on."

The probable error limits indicate that there is a substantial minority in favor of relaxing this aspect of the Land Apportionment Act. It is not unlikely that this segment will be augmented by the effects of a slower rate of expansion in Southern Rhodesia's economy since the study commenced. In the period of boom, when skyscrapers soared majestically into the air, almost overnight it seemed, there was little doubt that all of the office accommodation would be utilized by the expansion of industry and commerce. But as the growth curve has tapered off, there are some second thoughts on the wisdom of excluding Africans when they could inject further finance into the economy of the country. Whether such pressures will result in the modification of the present practice remains to be seen.

*Statement 33* (M = 2.20) falls more firmly on the side of the status quo than the last statement. In the main, the sample wishes to retain separate cemeteries. "Perhaps, bearing in mind differing religions and tribal beliefs, this should be maintained for a little." "This is accepted on a denominational basis the world over." The latter theme is predominant in the statements advocating the status quo.

Those who wish to have nonracial cemeteries adopt a rather cavalier attitude to the question: "What does it matter? We both make equally good mummies," and "When I am dead I do not care whether the neighboring bodies belong to Africans or not" are characteristic. At the very conservative end of the scale, on the other hand, one individual queries strongly, "Cannot even the dead be left without *forced* federation?"

*Statement 6* (M = 2.10) reflects a further consequence of the Land Apportionment Act. Africans are not permitted to own land in the European commercial areas, nor are they permitted to occupy it for business purposes either through gift, lease, or rent. Exceptions can be made, and are sanctioned, to permit the more itinerant type of African trader to set up a stall on public land (such as a roadside) and to sell from a truck or van. Trading of this kind is licensed, and is not taken to infringe the letter of legal separation in commerce.

The representative feeling of the community is against relaxing this aspect of land apportionment, and it is noteworthy that one of the reasons given for its retention is that "competition would be too strong." Inasmuch as few of our respondents will be likely to experience direct African competition, this comment is as surprising as it is frank. Another argument, possibly a rationalization, is that the law is fair because it applies equally to both races. If Africans are forbidden to carry on business in European commercial areas, so too are Europeans prohibited from trading in African areas. Parallel development and intraracial competition are the dominant themes.

*Statement 11* (M = 1.67) is viewed in two distinct ways. On the one hand, it is realized that although Africans cannot purchase beer and wine from shops in European areas, they can buy both in African beer halls and bottle stores, and so drink them in their own areas. This practice is generally regarded as tolerable. The other viewpoint is concerned with the fact that a change in law, by making alcohol more easily obtainable, will permit Africans to drink (and consequently be more troublesome) in European areas in which they are employed. This viewpoint can be detected in the following extract: "At the moment the majority of Africans are unaware of the social implications of drinking. It has been said that a civilized man is one who knows his capacity and stops one drink short of it. Few Africans can be said to fit this definition. It is something that grows out of education and social experience. Drinking amongst Africans [rooted in the tribal orgy?] springs from a different source than the social drinking of Europeans, and for the time being should in some way be restricted." The second viewpoint is reinforced in a number of typical interpretations. Others argue that "it is in the Africans' interest to maintain this at present, since the profits return to them in the form of welfare and sports facilities." It is true that municipalities do utilize the beer hall profits in this manner, and that private enterprise is not allowed to compete for the liquor trade.

To most of our sample, drinking is regarded as a social activity that should be carried on in racially segregated areas. The attitude is much the same as that expressed about activities included in the category of social and recreational facilities.

*Statement 63* (M = 1.38), while it involves the occupation and use of land, also encompasses a strong sexual element as was revealed in the factor analysis of items. Because of the Land Apportionment Act, it is extremely difficult for an African and a European, even if legally married, to live together. When the marriage involves an African man and a European woman, both the social and legal sanctions are most powerful. The greatest disapproval is expressed of cross-racial marriage, and it makes little difference whether or not the individual is generally in favor of change on the other items.

"They should be able to live in an area located especially for them, but Europeans shouldn't marry Africans." "I don't agree with the intermarriage of any races. The more difficult it is made the better." "These cases are few at present and should be kept so." "We feel that their children suffer more than they do." "What does he want to marry her for?" "Right. The African man knows the position and should not contract such a marriage, especially with a European woman from outside the country. It is as much against the traditions and wishes of his own people as against ours." "No mongrelization, please." "This should *never* be allowed." And so the theme of racial purity is repeated again and again.

It is our feeling that this item would have received a still lower score if the matter of residence had been excised. The opposition to cross-racial marriage is almost complete; but inasmuch as it is not against the law of the land, it is contended that some concession should be allowed in the Act to permit the contracting parties to live together. More desirable, from the viewpoint of Europeans, is the discouragement or prevention of cross-racial marriages.

*Statement 18* (M = 1.08) needs little comment. Africans are not allowed to own houses in the European areas, and this is the way the sample wishes to keep it. The segregation of residential areas (except for domestic African servants) is interwoven with the fabric of Rhodesian history, and the reasons offered in 1906 or 1925 differ little from those offered today. Different living habits, health, hygiene, and the devaluation of property values were and are the common reasons. To these can be added the thought that it would be unfair to allow Africans to own houses in European areas because so few could afford them. Not infrequently the practice is viewed as protective because, if the Land Apportionment Act is repealed, Africans will then be subject to the inroads of powerful European speculators.

A small group wishes to change the pattern of residential separation. It is felt that segregation can be discontinued by proper planning, but the details are frequently missing and the ramifications unrealized. The arguments of these individuals are idealistic and egalitarian, but they are seldom invoked by the bulk of the population.

## The Sample Characteristics

The duality of European thinking on the occupation and use of land emerges from the contrasts that have been drawn. The Land Apportionment Act stands enshrined as basic to and necessary for the preservation of European culture. Without it, economic and commercial practices would have to be modified, the possibility of social and sexual contacts would be enhanced, and even the rites associated with burial might be interfered with. Any alteration in the status quo on these matters would vitiate the superior, dominant culture. There is a group which contends that the Act should be repealed or modified, but it is very small.

Although the population defends the occupation and use of European lands by Europeans, it is aware of some of the effects of separation upon Africans. It shows disquiet on the cost to Africans of travel to work, the amenities available to Africans, the amount of land set aside for their use, and other matters. To these we will return in due course. Before doing so our task is to inspect the attitudes of different segments of the population toward these two aspects of land use. Table 62 gives the data on the use of African lands, and Table 63 does the same for the use of European lands by the Africans.

### COUNTRY OF BIRTH

Of the countries selected for further analysis—the United Kingdom, the Union of South Africa, and Southern Rhodesia—the sample from the first shows the strongest sentiment for an improvement in the opportunities and facilities available to Africans on African lands. The scores of South Africans and Rhodesians are also on the side

TABLE 62. *Scores Relating to Opportunities on African Lands* ($M = 3.63$)

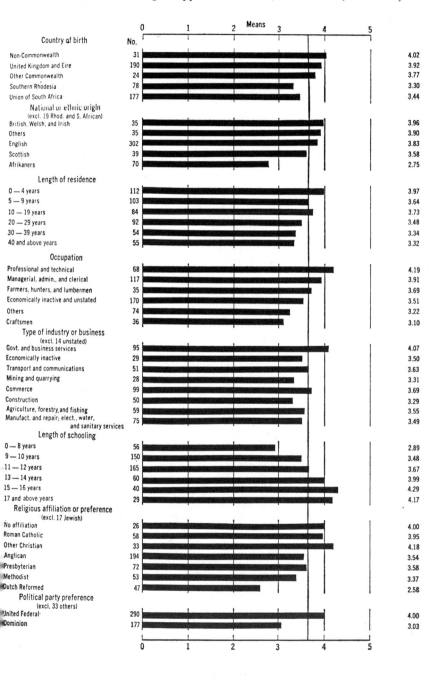

| | No. | Mean |
|---|---|---|
| **Country of birth** | | |
| Non-Commonwealth | 31 | 4.02 |
| United Kingdom and Eire | 190 | 3.92 |
| Other Commonwealth | 24 | 3.77 |
| Southern Rhodesia | 78 | 3.30 |
| Union of South Africa | 177 | 3.44 |
| **National or ethnic origin** (excl. 19 Rhod. and S. African) | | |
| British, Welsh, and Irish | 35 | 3.96 |
| Others | 35 | 3.90 |
| English | 302 | 3.83 |
| Scottish | 39 | 3.58 |
| Afrikaners | 70 | 2.75 |
| **Length of residence** | | |
| 0 — 4 years | 112 | 3.97 |
| 5 — 9 years | 103 | 3.64 |
| 10 — 19 years | 84 | 3.73 |
| 20 — 29 years | 92 | 3.48 |
| 30 — 39 years | 54 | 3.34 |
| 40 and above years | 55 | 3.32 |
| **Occupation** | | |
| Professional and technical | 68 | 4.19 |
| Managerial, admin., and clerical | 117 | 3.91 |
| Farmers, hunters, and lumbermen | 35 | 3.69 |
| Economically inactive and unstated | 170 | 3.51 |
| Others | 74 | 3.22 |
| Craftsmen | 36 | 3.10 |
| **Type of industry or business** (excl. 14 unstated) | | |
| Govt. and business services | 95 | 4.07 |
| Economically inactive | 29 | 3.50 |
| Transport and communications | 51 | 3.63 |
| Mining and quarrying | 28 | 3.31 |
| Commerce | 99 | 3.69 |
| Construction | 50 | 3.29 |
| Agriculture, forestry, and fishing | 59 | 3.55 |
| Manufact. and repair; elect., water, and sanitary services | 75 | 3.49 |
| **Length of schooling** | | |
| 0 — 8 years | 56 | 2.89 |
| 9 — 10 years | 150 | 3.48 |
| 11 — 12 years | 165 | 3.67 |
| 13 — 14 years | 60 | 3.99 |
| 15 — 16 years | 40 | 4.29 |
| 17 and above years | 29 | 4.17 |
| **Religious affiliation or preference** (excl. 17 Jewish) | | |
| No affiliation | 26 | 4.00 |
| Roman Catholic | 58 | 3.95 |
| Other Christian | 33 | 4.18 |
| Anglican | 194 | 3.54 |
| Presbyterian | 72 | 3.58 |
| Methodist | 53 | 3.37 |
| Dutch Reformed | 47 | 2.58 |
| **Political party preference** (excl. 33 others) | | |
| United Federal | 290 | 4.00 |
| Dominion | 177 | 3.03 |

TABLE 63. *Scores Relating to Opportunities on European Lands*
*(M = 1.80)*

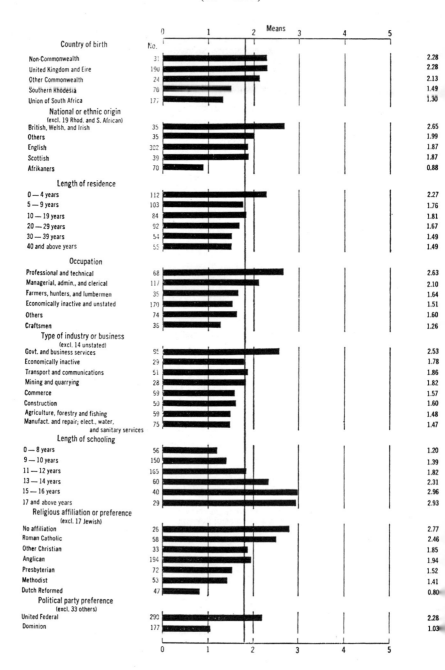

| | No. | Mean |
|---|---|---|
| **Country of birth** | | |
| Non-Commonwealth | 31 | 2.28 |
| United Kingdom and Eire | 190 | 2.28 |
| Other Commonwealth | 24 | 2.13 |
| Southern Rhodesia | 70 | 1.49 |
| Union of South Africa | 177 | 1.30 |
| **National or ethnic origin** (excl. 19 Rhod. and S. African) | | |
| British, Welsh, and Irish | 35 | 2.65 |
| Others | 35 | 1.99 |
| English | 302 | 1.87 |
| Scottish | 39 | 1.87 |
| Afrikaners | 70 | 0.88 |
| **Length of residence** | | |
| 0 — 4 years | 112 | 2.27 |
| 5 — 9 years | 103 | 1.76 |
| 10 — 19 years | 84 | 1.81 |
| 20 — 29 years | 92 | 1.67 |
| 30 — 39 years | 54 | 1.49 |
| 40 and above years | 55 | 1.49 |
| **Occupation** | | |
| Professional and technical | 68 | 2.63 |
| Managerial, admin., and clerical | 117 | 2.10 |
| Farmers, hunters, and lumbermen | 35 | 1.64 |
| Economically inactive and unstated | 170 | 1.51 |
| Others | 74 | 1.60 |
| Craftsmen | 36 | 1.26 |
| **Type of industry or business** (excl. 14 unstated) | | |
| Govt. and business services | 95 | 2.53 |
| Economically inactive | 29 | 1.78 |
| Transport and communications | 51 | 1.86 |
| Mining and quarrying | 28 | 1.82 |
| Commerce | 59 | 1.57 |
| Construction | 50 | 1.60 |
| Agriculture, forestry and fishing | 59 | 1.48 |
| Manufact. and repair; elect., water, and sanitary services | 75 | 1.47 |
| **Length of schooling** | | |
| 0 — 8 years | 56 | 1.20 |
| 9 — 10 years | 150 | 1.39 |
| 11 — 12 years | 165 | 1.82 |
| 13 — 14 years | 60 | 2.31 |
| 15 — 16 years | 40 | 2.96 |
| 17 and above years | 29 | 2.93 |
| **Religious affiliation or preference** (excl. 17 Jewish) | | |
| No affiliation | 26 | 2.77 |
| Roman Catholic | 58 | 2.46 |
| Other Christian | 33 | 1.85 |
| Anglican | 194 | 1.94 |
| Presbyterian | 72 | 1.52 |
| Methodist | 53 | 1.41 |
| Dutch Reformed | 47 | 0.80 |
| **Political party preference** (excl. 33 others) | | |
| United Federal | 290 | 2.28 |
| Dominion | 177 | 1.03 |

of change, although lower by comparison. The Rhodesian-born, who have been in contact with Africans of this area longer than any other group, display the least optimism about the chances of improving African land husbandry and the effect of increasing the facilities in African townships. Similarly they are less convinced, by and large, of the wisdom of introducing a European system of land tenure into African urban areas. This muted optimism runs through the reasoning of many Rhodesians: the necessity to help Africans help themselves is accepted, even though the task carries little reward and often, within the vortex of nationalism, much misunderstanding and resentment.

None of the three groups support the use by Africans of lands set aside for Europeans. On this subject, the most entrenched redoubt protecting the status quo is held by the South Africans. The most powerful palisade is that of residential separation, and the feeling is strong that this must not be breached.

NATIONAL OR ETHNIC ORIGIN

The difference between the English and Afrikaner groups can be detected as soon as one inspects attitudes toward the use of African land. The former group wishes to change the status quo while the latter, in the main, supports it on matters such as the restriction of African land holdings and the denial of freehold tenure to land. On land tenure, the Afrikaners show the greatest resistance to change even though the statement makes clear that it is African urban land that is under consideration, not European land.

Much the same gap exists between English and Afrikaner thinking on whether or not Africans should be permitted to occupy or use lands legally reserved for Europeans. Both groups wish to keep things as they are, but the Afrikaners' score (.88) is far more definite. On residential separation, they have a lower score (.37) than that obtained by any other group or any other item in the section. The British-Welsh-Irish conglomerate displays the highest score of any group, but no explanation of this fact can be offered.

LENGTH OF RESIDENCE

Just as length of residence is correlated with attitudes about other characteristics, so is it related to the occupation and use of African land. Those who have been in the territory for the shortest time show the greatest desire to change the status quo. The strength of feeling for change diminishes the longer an individual remains in Southern Rhodesia, and it reaches its lowest point among those who have been in the Colony for forty years and more. Even so, residents of forty years' standing still advocate, on the whole, that some change should be effected. They feel that there is still room for lessening the burden of African travel costs and for improving amenities in townships.

The idealism of the newcomers does not carry over to the use of European lands and competition in commercial spheres. Even recent imigrants take a stand on the side of the status quo, and this stand generally becomes more resolute with the passing of years.

OCCUPATION

On the evidence from the scores on the full scale, it can be predicted that attitudes toward the use of African land will vary with the occupation of the respondents. This is as it turned out. The very high score of 4.19 for the professional and technical persons indicates their willingness to have changes made. Then in descending order come the managerial and administrative personnel, farmers, economically inactive, skilled and sales workers, and craftsmen. The latter are only slightly in favor of changing the status quo; they propose some relief in the costs of traveling to work, and some improvement in African townships, but the bulk of them do not support an increase in the size of African land holdings, or the granting of freehold tenure in urban areas. It is noteworthy that all groups display the greatest concern about the financial implications of enforced residential separation.

All occupational groups are opposed to Africans occupying land and earning a living within the European areas. But a significant fact emerges when one examines the pattern of responses of farmers. All other groupings insist that the most important practice to maintain is that of separated housing. But farmers feel most strongly against cross-racial marriage, and wish to see the present restrictions on housing remain or even increase. This feeling may be so intense because such marriages can find no haven other than in the missions, which, of course, are located in rural areas. However, although the score is clear, we recognize that the reasons for it are not.

TYPE OF INDUSTRY OR BUSINESS

On the total scores, individuals who work in government and business services come out as the most change-oriented, and agricultural persons as most firmly rooted in the status quo. While individuals in the services still show the highest scores, those in agriculture no longer obtain the lowest. An interesting switch has occurred. Farmers often hold the more conservative attitudes in society; but in Southern Rhodesia the farming population, which forms the greater part of the agricultural group, evinces concern about the size of African land holdings, and expresses a wish to enlarge them. To some extent this may be enlightened self-interest, as it is commonly held that inefficient African farming can adversely effect the quality and value of adjoining European land.

But if the farmers advocate greater opportunities on African lands, they certainly do not intend to alter the status quo within the European areas. This is true of the other occupational classifications. If the items are analyzed separately, however, one striking fact emerges. More than 60% of those employed in government and business services wish to see offices in European commercial areas thrown open to African organizations and business concerns. It has been suggested previously that decreasing rates of economic growth may have buttressed this shift in traditional attitudes. It seems reasonable to infer that men in government and business, many of whom have their fingers on the pulse of the economy, see the financial advantages of leasing empty office space to Africans.

EDUCATION

The clear relation of education and general attitude about the treatment of Africans re-emerges when land usage is considered. Less than half of those with under nine years of schooling wish to advance African opportunities on the land. Then, as education increases so does the emphasis on discontinuing the present restrictions. Particularly noteworthy is the manner in which the more educated groups reinforce their scores for altering the system of land tenure in the urban areas. They argue time and again that Africans must be given a permanent stake in the land on which they live and in their homes.

When one turns to the occupation and use of European lands, the same consistent relation with education is found, although all the scores are at a significantly lower level. It is only within the segment with at least fifteen years of education that more than half are prepared to advocate rental of offices to Africans, and occupancy of land for business purposes, within the European commercial areas.

RELIGIOUS AFFILIATION OR PREFERENCE

Roman Catholics advocate discontinuing all of the practices that relate to restricting opportunities on African lands; so too, at a somewhat lower level, do the adherents of the Anglican faith. Members of the Dutch Reformed church, on the average, advocate change only on the matter of costs incurred in traveling to work. They take a stand on the status quo on all other items, and present a unified front against the granting of freehold tenure on urban lands. This is in keeping with the church's traditional attitude that urbanization is not in the best interest of Africans.

Members of all religious groups wish to reserve European lands for use by Europeans, although the supporters of the Dutch Reformed church are much more immovable on this point than any of the others. If the items are inspected singly, it is clear that a majority of Catholics support the right of Africans to occupy European offices ($M = 3.21$) and business premises ($M = 3.10$); they also support burial by religion rather than by race. This outlook is not matched by the majority of the adherents of any of the other major churches.

POLITICAL PARTY PREFERENCE

The differences between individuals who support the two major political parties are in the expected direction. The supporters of the United Federal party opt strongly for augmenting the opportunities on African lands, whereas Dominion party adherents are split almost fifty-fifty on the issue.

On the use of European land, although the centers of gravity of both groups are on the side of the status quo, a significantly larger proportion of Federal party adherents urges a modification of the traditional separation of races in Southern Rhodesia.

## THE PRINCIPAL THEMES

The occupation of Southern Rhodesia fits into a familiar pattern of European expansion overseas: men came to explore, to conquer, to settle. As in so many other overseas colonies, conflict with the indigenous population was probably inevitable, and for the most part it arose over ownership and use of land. Southern Rhodesia never became the El Dorado that Rhodes hoped it would be, and the possession of large tracts of land became imperative if Europeans were to establish themselves and flourish. But though land was important to the Europeans, it was vital to the existence of the Africans. Consequently, much of the tension between the two culture groups was and still is over the use and possession of land.

The methods by which land was apportioned have already been examined. Within a framework of racial separation, Europeans have achieved a measure of security to maintain and develop their way of life, to protect themselves from African competition, and to isolate themselves from the rigors of communicable disease. But there are two sides to the theme of protection. It is argued that separation is necessary to protect Africans, to allow them freedom for "separate development." If land divisions had not been stabilized by law, it seems clear that much of that assigned to the Africans could have been acquired by the immigrants because of their superior bargaining power. In Canada and New Zealand—there are others—the indigenous peoples are not forced to live on reserved lands; they may and do acquire property rights outside the reserves and can enter into direct competition with Europeans in the commercial areas. This was not envisaged by most immigrants in early Southern Rhodesia, and our data show that there is little enthusiasm for the plan today. Whereas the reserve system in other countries has been applied to protect the indigenous people from the newcomers, in Southern Rhodesia it is argued that both need protection from each other.

Materialism flows strongly through European society. But materialism is not the exclusive stream in Rhodesian history. The tributaries of moral idealism flow into it at many points, and at the junctions are the cross-eddies of moral conflict. The missionaries often dug open the first springs of moral idealism, and these have never ceased flowing into Southern Rhodesian society. This is demonstrated by the data, both enumerative and descriptive, on the use of African lands.

The Europeans accept responsibility for "possessory segregration," and they are concerned about its consequences. Africans must be assisted and encouraged within their own areas; their standards of living must be improved. If these advances can be effected, then there may be less disquiet over the separation and protection of European commercial and residential areas.

But there is no guarantee that the stream will remain in its present channel. As the Colony has matured, initial reappraisal has gathered force. The majority advocate changes in some aspects of land usage, and sizable minorities argue for changes in others. However, it is not likely that most Europeans will easily surrender the basic philosophy of separate development.

# 13

## PERSONAL COURTESIES AND ETIQUETTE

Every society has a system by which personal relations are organized. Elders are usually respected by the young, the learned by laymen, and rulers by subjects. Even when associating with individuals of another society, certain kinds of relations become traditional. Most social relations involve some measure of respect, or other types of reciprocity, and deference to individuals of superior status is common. When contact between two strange societies occurs, however, no system of tacit understandings to regulate behavior exists. In a conquest situation, the victors have the power to determine when, where, and how individuals should behave. These patterns of behavior are not only affected by the existing situation, but also by the values, ideas, and feelings of each group.

European immigrants into Southern Rhodesia established their dominance over the indigenous population through a superior technology, military conquest, and more comprehensive means for regulating political relations. Many had come from a society characterized by a rather rigid system of social classes, in which an Englishman traditionally knew to whom and on what occasions to show deference. The African societies had their own systems for showing respect and politeness to individuals of superior status. The cultural backgrounds of the Africans and Europeans combined to support the new system in which dominant or superior status was assumed by Europeans in almost all instances of cross-cultural contact.[1] Had there been no customary "natural politeness" among Africans, Southern Rhodesia's history could easily have been bloodier and more violent.

The new society that arose after European conquest thus embraced European and African status differences rather easily and naturally. It was similar to the class system of England except that it now included people with greater cultural and physical differences than existed in the British Isles. Patterns of dominance occurred not only in politics and the economy, as instanced by plantations and mine compounds, but were paralleled in most social activities. Obedience and deference were expected of Africans when interracial contact occurred, even after territorial segregation was introduced to minimize the frequency of such contacts. Africans knew that Europeans would not tolerate "cheeky Kaffirs," and that a failure to show sufficient respect might be interpreted as a threat of aggression. Consequently, they felt it was necessary to defer in order to "validate" their submissiveness, and to reduce or avoid friction and conflict.

The European expectation that Africans should display proper respect and deference was in large part a manifestation of the Victorian attitudes of Englishmen and South Africans.[2] Africans were conceived to be "primitive, backward, outdated heathens." Progress could occur only if the "superior" standards and status of the Europeans were recognized and preserved (Leys, 1959). African culture and society would need to be changed in time, but in the meantime their lowly position had to be symbolized through deference in situations of personal contact.

Yet the new legal and social structure encouraged the development of tensions and prohibited the complete realization of the Europeans' conception of society. Dozens of laws and regulations were enacted with which no African, whether educated or not, could always hope to comply. The Masters and Servants Act, borrowed from the Colony of the Cape of Good Hope, was of major importance in structuring the relations between Europeans and Africans. Thus, many kinds of new situations were created which had legal sanctions behind them to assure conformity. There was indeed a simple compounding of situations in which a misbehaving African was liable to be prosecuted and punished.

Intimidation and beating of Africans were common despite checks by the Administration (Rolin, 1913:260). Whippings, assaults, and shootings were frequent between 1890 and 1910, though less so after that. In these early days, serious assaults on Africans averaged about one per week. Even policemen, many of whom were Africans, were guilty of intimidation in the early years.[3] This was encouraged in part by the Europeans' need for cheap and plentiful labor. The recruitment of Africans was often attended by the use of force. Africans lacked the "Protestant ethic" or "the spirit of capitalism" within their own culture, hence they seldom volunteered to work for their conquerors.

The beating of docile servants was disapproved, but it was acceptable for "cheeky Kaffirs" to be chastised.[4] Africans who attempted to imitate the Europeans as a peer group, especially in the wearing of clothes, provoked scorn and hostility. Wearing a hat was like carrying a chip on the shoulder—an invitation to get it knocked off.[5] For many decades, Africans were prohibited from walking on pavements or sidewalks. When entering doorways, they were expected to allow Europeans to go first. Similarly, in shops and other places of business, Africans were expected to wait for service until any Europeans present had completed their transactions. The terms Africans and Europeans used in addressing one another likewise symbolized the differences in status and power.

During the early years of settlement, many Europeans drank heavily, and they were generally contemptuous of the Africans. As a small group which had conquered a population many times its size, the European population was concerned with its own safety. The difficult conditions of the frontier, and the possession of extensive power, frequently tempted individuals into acts of violence. The public's tolerance of these acts, and the relative lack of legal restraints, sometimes made a man almost a king. Unfortunately, however, a stereotype has developed that virtually all European immigrants were cruel, sadistic, domineering tyrants who "sjamboked" (whipped) their "boys" on the slightest provocation. The record clearly shows that there was a high incidence of maltreatment, abuse, and violence, but this declined as the social system changed.

Since the "Pioneer Column" arrived, many processes have served to check the frequency of such incidents—education, urbanization, industrialization, the extension of law and order, and economic growth. The B. S. A. Company, as a chartered commercial firm, felt the need to prevent such abuses in order to allay suspicions that it was exploiting Africans. The eternal eye of the Imperial Government, an integral part of the social system of Southern Rhodesia, also helped the relatively quick development of orderly government and habits of compliance with the authorities. In comparison with European settlers in the early colonial periods of countries such as Australia, Mexico, and the United States, Southern Rhodesians were among the least abusive and law-breaking.[6]

Law does not regulate all personal contacts between Europeans and Africans, however, and many of the deference patterns of the early period still persist. In part, this is due to the general tenacity of habits; but it also results from European race and social-class attitudes, and from the traditional ways in which Africans have shown respect and subservience. In some contemporary Reserves, it is not uncommon to see Africans take off their hats and stand aside when Europeans drive by. Also, Africans traditionally have sat on the floor of the Native Commissioner's office, just as they traditionally have shown deference to their tribal chief. African workers or hawkers must call at the rear rather than at the front door (as do many Europeans performing equivalent tasks). Africans must not take the initiative in shaking hands with Europeans if embarrassing situations are to be avoided, and must be much more cautious in making physical contact with Europeans than vice versa.

As the new social structure of the country has taken shape, personal contacts between Africans and Europeans have slowly but gradually increased in number. Forthright European dominance has been replaced by paternalism and separatism. This pattern in turn is being modified, and it may be safely predicted that future relations will be less paternal and more impersonal. The growth of cities and secondary industries gives singular emphasis to this well-nigh irreversible process. More educational and training opportunities for Africans are appearing. To the extent to which these opportunities diminish status differences between Europeans and Africans—a necessary condition for the maintenance of deference behavior—more chances will correspondingly occur for quasi-social class contacts. In brief, as the total social system of Southern Rhodesia changes, so will the pattern of personal courtesies and etiquette.

## CONTEMPORARY ATTITUDES

At various points in the questionnaire, statements were included dealing with the relations of Europeans and Africans, the courtesies observed, and the behavior regarded as proper. All the situations alluded to involve some form of contact, usually face-to-face, and through these the dominant attitudes have been measured. An assumption was made that the rules of behavior would follow certain conventional forms when Europeans came into contact with other Europeans, and take other conventional forms when the contact was with Africans.

The practices described in these statements are somewhat different from practices that have a legal basis or can be quantified. For example, the ramifications of the Land Apportionment Act are definite and observable, and racial differences in trade opportunities are not difficult to establish. But with matters of courtesy and etiquette, it is more difficult to substantiate practices. Nor are practices as invariant as they are when based on law. To take another example: one can state flatly that Africans do not own land in the European residential areas of Salisbury, but it is incorrect to state that Europeans do not shake hands with Africans. Some do. Because we have not determined the frequency of behavior of any of the practices, all are qualified. Nor are the frequencies of behavior uniform. From our observations, it seems likely that the majority of Europeans expect Africans to display deferential behavior at doorways and in elevators, but it appears most unlikely that more than a few sanction assault on an African by a European employer. It is possible, although not verifiable from our data, that the scores many indicate the frequency of the practice.

After pruning and weeding, nine statements remained that seemed worthy of inclusion in the questionnaire. These are given in Table 64.

TABLE 64. *Statements Relating to Personal Courtesies and Etiquette*

| No. | Statement | −1 P.E. | +1 P.E. | Mean |
|---|---|---|---|---|
| 51 | European children generally do not treat African adults with respect. | 3.48 | 5.80 | 4.64 |
| 14 | Africans are liable to be assaulted by a European employer, whereas European employees are less liable to receive this treatment. | 3.00 | 5.58 | 4.29 |
| 60 | European men and women have on occasion dropped friends when they have discovered them to have non-European ancestors. | 2.18 | 5.06 | 3.62 |
| 58 | Africans who question the authority of Europeans often are accused of being 'cheeky' and may be assaulted for such behaviour. | 2.25 | 4.83 | 3.54 |
| 56 | Generally, Europeans do not treat Africans with as much respect as they do members of their own race. | 2.18 | 4.82 | 3.50 |
| 55 | Europeans generally are served before Africans at shop counters and places of business. | 1.88 | 4.62 | 3.25 |
| 54 | Africans nearly always are expected to address Europeans as 'Sir', 'Boss', 'Master', or 'Madam', whereas Europeans usually address Africans as 'Boy' or 'Nanny.' | 1.45 | 4.13 | 2.79 |
| 53 | Europeans generally do not shake hands with Africans. | 1.34 | 3.98 | 2.66 |
| 52 | Africans normally are expected to stand back and allow Europeans to go first through doorways, into lifts, and so on. | 1.18 | 3.84 | 2.51 |
|  |  | 2.10 | 4.74 | 3.42 |

It can be seen that while the mean for the category (3.42) stands on the side of change, there are three forms of behavior that the population is generally in favor of retaining. Thus the category swings within itself from change to maintain, and different deductions must be made from different points within it. Before generalizing about the category as a whole, it is important to examine the variations between the statements.

*Statement 51* (M = 4.64) asserts that European children generally do not treat African adults with respect. This item received the second highest score on the whole scale, and is one that nearly every-. one wishes to see discontinued—if the statement is generally true. However, a considerable number who vote for change insist that the statement is not true, and that children who are disrespectful to African adults in all probability show no respect to European adults either. To those who accept that the statement contains some truth, typical responses depict clear disapproval: "It will not improve until adults treat Africans with more respect." "European parents, whose children do not treat African adults with due respect, are not bringing their children up properly." "Civility costs nothing. Children should be taught to give respect if they expect to receive any in return."

A discordant note is heard from some: "Very few Africans command respect." "African nannies mistreat their own children and European children too." Among the few who do not believe in respect for Africans, one contends that respect will lead to familiarity. However, apart from the aberrant few, the sample insists that its children should show respect toward Africans.

*Statement 14* (M = 4.29), a contentious one, refers to a practice that has declined with the passing of years and changes in Southern Rhodesian society. Although it is not possible to make any estimate of frequency, our records indicate that Africans are much less likely to be assaulted by employers today than fifty years ago. They have direct recourse to law and frequently use it. Because cases of this type of assault still come before the courts, however, we considered it important that the attitude of the population should be determined.

There is little doubt where the Europeans stand. They are strongly opposed to assault, although they state that Europeans are frequently driven to extremes of exasperation by the behavior of Africans. This thought is contained in the statement:

> Usually one European is in charge of a large gang of natives. In their lazy, good-natured way they do as little as possible and have to be told the same thing over and over. A European is often driven to extremes of exasperation. European employees are usually more conscientious and the most usual punishment is to dismiss them. A man with a family doesn't want to lose his job. An African could not care less.

Other comments associated with the scoring range of plus and minus one probable error illustrate the typical thinking: "An African has the same recourse to law as the European." "Europeans should only assault an African when really necessary." "This must surely be dying out." "Natives now know how to run to the police. Europeans just don't get away with it." "All assault of employees should stop."

The theme of provocation is stressed at all points on the scale, but at the level where corporal punishment is felt to be good and necessary for the African, the emphasis is weighty. "For disobeying a lawful order, a hiding is a greater deterrent than two weeks or so in gaol to the average African." "Africans are likely to aggravate you more than the European."

*Statement 60* (M = 3.63) is difficult to quantify. During the planning stage of the study, several instances were cited where friends had been dropped when it was suspected that they had some non-European ancestry. However, the frequency of such behavior seems to be very small because miscegenation has not been widespread in Southern Rhodesia, certainly not as widespread as in the Cape Province (Patterson, 1953). Generally, it is considered wrong to victimize children because of their ancestry: "They can't help it; it is unfair to blame them. This is the tragedy of miscegenation." However, a sizable minority think that to continue the friendship will be to condone cross-racial sexual relations. Therefore, there is no alternative but to impose some form of social control.

*Statement 58* (M = 3.54) is related to number 14. Both involve the chastising of Africans, but in statement 58 it is the "cheeky" Africans who receive the assault. It is notable that whereas the mean score of statement 14 is 4.29, it drops to 3.54 for statement 58. Historical documents show that in the frontier days of the Colony, an African who questioned the authority of a European—who talked back—ran the risk of being physically chastised. But the rule of law has been strengthened and such cases have obviously declined. Most Europeans now insist that disobedient Africans should be fined, not assaulted, though some feel that physical punishment is still the most effective way of instilling discipline. Europeans must not abrogate their authority.

Comments drawn from the middle range of the distribution illustrate some ambivalence in European attitudes: "I do not believe in physical assault." "Most 'questioning of authority' takes a surly form, but I feel that few Africans are assaulted for this, but just fired." "Africans now run to the Native Commissioner." "In cases of this nature the law favors the African." There is the implication that, while physical assault is generally deplored, it is disapproved by some because of the consequences of violating the law.

*Statement 56* (M = 3.50) reveals some duality in European thinking. Whereas the sample insists very strongly that children should treat Africans with respect, it is not so imperative that adults should behave similarly: "It should be left to one's discretion." "We do—when we find them worthy of it." "This is a matter of class distinction." "One can't respect people unless they have a sense of responsibility." "I've just seen a boy come out of the (tobacco) grading shed and blow his nose on the ground where his kids will be crawling the next minute. If this commands respect, I'll give it." "The African must try and obtain the respect of the European first." These responses, and the scores with which they are associated, show that, although Europeans generally feel it desirable to show respect toward Africans, many assert that it is difficult to accord.

*Statement 55* (M = 3.25) reads, "Europeans generally are served before Africans at shop counters and places of business." The records show that in the pioneering days Africans almost invariably waited until Europeans had been served at shop counters, if indeed they were allowed into the shops at all. The mean score of 3.25 indicates that a substantial shift has occurred in the European attitude, and less than half would now insist on receiving preferential treatment. But the custom of serving Europeans first still seems to prevail and people fit into the practice rather than take the initiative to change it. They may not approve of the custom, but they accept it, since the status quo is convenient.

While the mean for the statement expresses a wish for change, the range of plus and minus one probable error embraces scores both for the status quo and for change. We have endeavored to select representative comments of both types: "This should be a matter of common courtesy." "This could be corrected by having African counter attendants." "Not true, I've often stood back for Africans. In any case they push in and demand to be served." "The European's time is more valuable than the African's." "A matter of custom." "Where they are allowed to enter, they should be served in their turn."

At the two extremes of the scale, the attitudes are unambiguous. One segment wants all preferential treatment eliminated and the other insists upon its maintenance.

*Statement 54* (M = 2.79) has occasioned more comment than any other statement in the category. The middle group lies on both sides of the maintain-change continuum, but more than half favor the status quo—with qualifications. Many individuals feel that the titles used to address Europeans are proper for the different status positions of the two groups, and are at a loss to think of alternatives. The terms "Sir," "Boss," "Master," and "Madam" seem appropriate from servants, but the labels "Boy" and "Nanny," although customary, are not generally favored.

Let us consider some of the arguments put forward by the representative group: "It depends on the relationship involved. It is not unusual for a subordinate to address his business superior as 'Sir.'" "Standards of courtesy should apply. People are entitled to be addressed by their names." "It wouldn't happen if the European and African were of equal education, i.e., a European wouldn't call an

educated African 'Boy,' or an educated African woman 'Nanny.' "
"Don't forget that *most* Africans are still very low in social status."
"As long as I have been in the country it has been the custom."
"I prefer to be addressed as Mrs. and I make a point of using my
servants' names." "This is a master and servant, not a color relationship." "If you could suggest a good alternative to 'boy' or 'nanny'
we would use it. What do you call an African whom you do not know?
Americans use 'lad.' Egyptians called British soldiers 'George.' 'Boy'
and 'Nanny' are kind-sounding words."

Dozens of statements were collected reflecting the sentiments we
have cited. If one can educe a common theme, it is that "Sir" and
"Master" are normal because they reflect the superior status of Europeans, but that proper names should be employed when addressing
Africans.

In the smaller group with high social-change scores, the sentiment
is not significantly different from that expressed by the larger group.
At the other end of the scale, however, there is a feeling that the status
of the two groups must be sharply defined, and the correct terms
used: "Europeans are superior to Africans as regards civilization."
"The African is generally uneducated and irresponsible."

*Statement 53* (M = 2.66) examines whether or not Europeans
will shake hands with an African. The majority consider it unnecessary or undesirable, although an exception will usually be made for
a Member of Parliament, a minister of religion, or an African with
some other high status. The common argument is that handshaking
is not traditional among Africans, and that Africans do not prefer it.
Some say they decline on the ground of hygiene.

*Statement 52* (M = 2.51) describes the deferential behavior ac-
corded Europeans when they meet Africans at doorways and at the
entrances to elevators. As with handshaking, the majority express a
preference for the practice to continue, although about a third want
its elimination.

"It makes for good manners. Europeans should be due a certain
respect for what they are contributing to African education." "This
is a matter of class distinction. We find it in all walks of life—a junior
gives way to a senior in the army, in hospitals, etc." "I have found they
usually do stand back for me, and I thank them." "This should
continue, as Africans push, shove, and are rude." These opinions fall
within the normal range.

Among those with high change scores the usual feeling is that "common courtesy should apply to both races." At the other end of the
distribution we find, "It is a sign of respect, the same as when a child
gives up a seat for a grown-up." It is among the conservative scores
that the historic pattern of European dominance is most clearly revealed.

## The Sample Characteristics

Before analyzing the data according to the different characteristics of the population, it is necessary to focus attention once more on the distribution of means within the category. In the categories studied so far, the item means are all on one side or the other of the theoretical neutral point of 3.00. But this is not so with personal courtesies and etiquette. The means range from far above neutral (4.64) to the side of the status quo (2.51). Thus when one generalizes about the category, this statistical divergence will have to be taken into account. Just as the scores on the statements vary for the whole population, so they are likely to vary for segments of it. The data showing the breakdown of items by social characteristic are far too extensive to be reproduced here, but we have drawn on this material to illustrate significant trends or differences. The relations of courtesies and etiquette to the characteristics of the sample are given in Table 65.

### COUNTRY OF BIRTH

A substantial majority of persons from the United Kingdom advocate greater courtesy toward Africans and more respect for them as individuals. A small majority of the Southern Rhodesians opt for the status quo, while the South Africans split fifty-fifty on the maintain-change continuum of the category.

When we turn to the scores on the individual items, striking differences emerge. Persons from the United Kingdom opt for change on every item; and on statement 51 (children not treating African adults with respect), their score of 5.14 is the highest in the category for discontinuance. On the other hand, both the South Africans and the Southern Rhodesian-born maintain, on the average, that Europeans should be served before Africans at shop counters, that the customary titles of address should not be altered, that Europeans should not shake hands with Africans, and that Africans should show deferential behavior at doorways and at the entrances to elevators. It seems evident that individuals born in southern Africa are closest to the traditions of the past, and have been influenced most by them through the home and the community. Individuals from Britain, on the other hand, seem to have been molded by different traditions. Although their attitudes shift as they live longer in the Colony, some of their original attitudes survive.

TABLE 65. *Scores Relating to Personal Courtesies and Etiquette*
$(M = 3.42)$

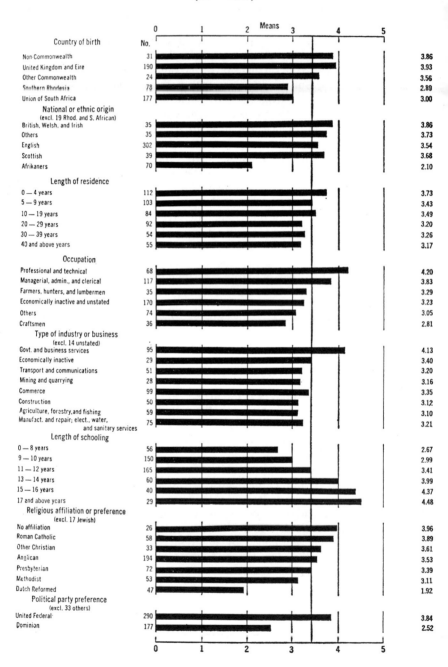

| | No. | Mean |
|---|---|---|
| **Country of birth** | | |
| Non-Commonwealth | 31 | 3.86 |
| United Kingdom and Eire | 190 | 3.93 |
| Other Commonwealth | 24 | 3.56 |
| Southern Rhodesia | 78 | 2.89 |
| Union of South Africa | 177 | 3.00 |
| **National or ethnic origin** (excl. 19 Rhod. and S. African) | | |
| British, Welsh, and Irish | 35 | 3.86 |
| Others | 35 | 3.73 |
| English | 302 | 3.54 |
| Scottish | 39 | 3.68 |
| Afrikaners | 70 | 2.10 |
| **Length of residence** | | |
| 0 — 4 years | 112 | 3.73 |
| 5 — 9 years | 103 | 3.43 |
| 10 — 19 years | 84 | 3.49 |
| 20 — 29 years | 92 | 3.20 |
| 30 — 39 years | 54 | 3.26 |
| 40 and above years | 55 | 3.17 |
| **Occupation** | | |
| Professional and technical | 68 | 4.20 |
| Managerial, admin., and clerical | 117 | 3.83 |
| Farmers, hunters, and lumbermen | 35 | 3.29 |
| Economically inactive and unstated | 170 | 3.23 |
| Others | 74 | 3.05 |
| Craftsmen | 36 | 2.81 |
| **Type of industry or business** (excl. 14 unstated) | | |
| Govt. and business services | 95 | 4.13 |
| Economically inactive | 29 | 3.40 |
| Transport and communications | 51 | 3.20 |
| Mining and quarrying | 28 | 3.16 |
| Commerce | 99 | 3.35 |
| Construction | 50 | 3.12 |
| Agriculture, forestry, and fishing | 59 | 3.10 |
| Manufact. and repair; elect., water, and sanitary services | 75 | 3.21 |
| **Length of schooling** | | |
| 0 — 8 years | 56 | 2.67 |
| 9 — 10 years | 150 | 2.99 |
| 11 — 12 years | 165 | 3.41 |
| 13 — 14 years | 60 | 3.99 |
| 15 — 16 years | 40 | 4.37 |
| 17 and above years | 29 | 4.48 |
| **Religious affiliation or preference** (excl. 17 Jewish) | | |
| No affiliation | 26 | 3.96 |
| Roman Catholic | 58 | 3.89 |
| Other Christian | 33 | 3.61 |
| Anglican | 194 | 3.53 |
| Presbyterian | 72 | 3.39 |
| Methodist | 53 | 3.11 |
| Dutch Reformed | 47 | 1.92 |
| **Political party preference** (excl. 33 others) | | |
| United Federal | 290 | 3.84 |
| Dominion | 177 | 2.52 |

### NATIONAL OR ETHNIC ORIGIN

The English ethnic group supports change whereas the Afrikaner group endorses the status quo. Statement 51 (M = 3.14), on European children not showing respect for Africans, is the only one on which more than half the Afrikaners vote for a change. On Africans being assaulted by European employers, slightly more than half the Afrikaners (M = 2.94) believe this permissible. The means for the other items then drop more substantially on the side of maintenance. Of all the practices in this category, the one about which Afrikaners feel most strongly is that of shaking hands with an African.

On the other hand, Englishmen generally wish to change all the practices save those associated with titles of address, handshaking, and deferential behavior at doorways and elevators (nos. 54, 53, 52). They are strongly against (M = 4.46) physically chastising Africans. It should be observed that the English group cannot be equated with those born in the United Kingdom. Of those born in South Africa, and emigrating to Southern Rhodesia, the majority regard themselves as of English origin. While their attitudes are generally not as conservative as those held by Afrikaners, they are still less inclined to countenance change than are their kinsmen from Britain. It is this fact that accounts for the difference in attitudes between the United Kingdom-born and the English ethnic group.

### LENGTH OF RESIDENCE

There is a relation between length of residence in Southern Rhodesia and observance of the niceties of etiquette. Newcomers are much more willing to change the Rhodesian pattern of deferential behavior than are those who have resided in the country for forty years and more. Not without influence, however, is the fact that the new immigrants are also younger than those who came forty years ago, and it is the younger individuals in the population who display a greater desire for change. Most strongly deplored at all levels are the lack of respect shown by European children toward African adults and the assault of African employees by European employers. Somewhat surprising is the finding that, irrespective of length of residence, over half of the individuals feel that Africans should stand back and allow Europeans to go first through doorways, into elevators, and so on.

### OCCUPATION

On the full scale, the greatest difference emerged between professional and technical persons, on the one hand, and craftsmen. The same situation occurred on that part of the scale devoted to etiquette, the former being very inclined toward change (M = 4.20), and the latter not (2.81). Professional and technical people are inclined to change all the practices in the category, whereas craftsmen opt for change on only three: lack of respect by European children, the assault of African employees, and an individual's loss of friends because of his hitherto undiscovered non-European ancestry (nos. 51, 14, 60).

The item that received the lowest score for all occupational groupings, except farmers, concerns the behavior to be observed at doors and elevators. Surprisingly, perhaps, farmers do not feel strongly on this issue, as more than half wish to see such deferential behavior dropped. Perhaps with fewer public buildings with doors and elevators in the rural areas, this statement has less meaning to farmers.

#### TYPE OF INDUSTRY OR BUSINESS

As with some of the former analyses, when the data are broken down by industry or business, the significant difference is between persons in the government and business services and the rest. The mean score gathered by the service personnel (M = 4.13) is strongly for change; all the other means are moderately so. Alone among the groups, more than half of the former advocate change on every one of the practices described in the nine statements. It will be remembered that the administrative personnel of the Federal, territorial and local governments, and doctors, ministers of religion, and other such professional and administrative workers comprise the majority of the classification. Their backgrounds seem to have some bearing on the high change score.

#### EDUCATION

The relationship between education and attitudes about etiquette is in the expected direction. Where schooling has been meager, individuals generally want to maintain present practices. Those with eight years of education and less wish to change only two practices in the category. They feel that children should show more respect for African adults, and that Africans should not be assaulted by their employers. Otherwise, the remaining differentiating practices should not be removed.

Attitudes about personal courtesies and etiquette shift across the dividing line at twelve years of schooling, and from then on a majority of all the groups disapprove of distinctions on the basis of race.

#### RELIGIOUS AFFILIATION OR PREFERENCE

Of the religious groups selected for study, the Roman Catholics are most in favor of change; there is only one practice (elevators and doorways) which they are inclined to continue. They feel most strongly that Africans should not be assaulted by their employers. The Anglicans stand also on the side of change, and they express most concern over the disrespectful attitude of European children toward African adults.

Members of the Dutch Reformed church, on the other hand, score conservatively on all the statements except number 51, and they feel most strongly $(M = .98)$ that Europeans should not shake hands with Africans. Individuals who affiliate with the other religious denominations advocate changing the whole category of practices, and so do those who have no religious affiliation.

POLITICAL PARTY PREFERENCE

Differences between individuals who back the two major political parties need little description. Viewing the category as a whole, supporters of the United Federal party advocate changes in the system of deference, whereas adherents of the Dominion party do not. Naturally the two distributions show overlap, and a minority in both parties display similar attitudes. However, the means are distinct and reveal significant differences in attitude.

An analysis of individual statements uncovers the specific areas where differences lie. Dominion party supporters disapprove of disrespectful behavior by European children $(M = 4.16)$ and the assault of African employees $(M = 3.57)$, but for the remaining seven practices in the category more than half wish to see no change. On the other hand, those who back the Federal party prefer to see changes in all the practices except preferential treatment at shop counters and places of business. On shaking hands with Africans, while Dominion party supporters strongly oppose its adoption $(M = 1.48)$, most Federal party adherents do not $(M = 3.36)$. Summing up, the interview material illustrates that those who prefer the Dominion party believe firmly in 'the status quo, whereas Federal party adherents are inclined toward change.

THE PRINCIPAL THEMES

The ways in which men behave toward each other, the customs they observe, and the manners they display are seldom determined by legal fiat. Rather, they are determined by the molding influences within society—by culture, status, and so on. In the frontier days of Southern Rhodesia, with the establishment of European dominance through conquest, it is not surprising that modes of behavior should have been linked with differences in power. The immigrants demanded, and obtained, deferential behavior from Africans, behavior that acknowledged the superior status of the newcomers.

European settlement in Southern Rhodesia is sufficiently recent for it to be possible to document with some accuracy the attitudes about Africans, and the behavior that was prevalent. This is not to say that Europeans acted uniformly—they did not—but Africans were generally considered inferior. They clearly had less military power and fewer technological skills. With these disadvantages, real and alleged, Africans were hardly likely to be accepted as peers; they had their status in the new society and they were expected to keep it. Evidence in support of this view has to be gleaned from diaries, letters, newspapers, the testimony of living pioneers, and both official and unofficial records. It does not come to us from the measurement of attitudes and behavior.

Even so, some comparison is possible between the historical data and the data accumulated from measurement. At the turn of the century, the forms of behavior we have described seemed much more widespread than today—except that there were no elevators, and shops were fewer. Africans had to be disciplined, it was insisted, and they were obliged in many ways to recognize their inferior status. The picture is fundamentally different today. Even though the links with the past can still be traced, a different society has emerged. The gap between the cultures has been narrowed through the efforts of both Africans and Europeans. It is not suggested that Africans now have equal status; they have not, but the responses of our sample show the modifications that might be permitted by the European population.

The European population is not singleminded in its attitude about change, as we have shown. Some of the links with the past have rusted away, but others have been retempered to last in the future. Many Europeans still expect their dominant status to be recognized in a variety of ways; but their numbers have diminished and their attitudes are not enforced with the finality of the past.

It would seem that changes are inevitable as long as Europeans hold to their traditional ideal of "equality." Herein lie the seeds of moral conflict. Africans are not regarded as peers, and yet many feel they may become so through education and other processes. Europeans are torn between their vested interest in maintaining a dominant status in Southern Rhodesia and humanitarian ideals to extend their version of civilization to the African population. The data suggest that most Europeans support changes in the deferential aspects of the system by which personal relations are organized. Whether this is possible without other significant modifications in Southern Rhodesian society and European culture is a critical question that can be answered only by time.

# 14

## PUBLIC FACILITIES

When colonies are founded, not only are people transplanted but so is much of their customary way of life—their values, beliefs, technology, and social structure. Europeans who emigrated to Southern Rhodesia were accustomed to various public facilities and services in their home countries, and it was natural to duplicate or parallel these in the new country. Railways, school buildings, post offices, banks, and hospitals were already an integral part of the European social system. In contrast, the Africans had no experience of such institutions and services prior to European contact.

The provision of medical services and hospitals was typical in many ways of the growth of public facilities in Southern Rhodesia. Few knew the malevolence of the new climate and the diseases that would be met. But an early concern developed, principally among the Administration rather than the general population, about European health and sanitation. Gelfand (1953) reports that it was often difficult to get the Europeans to act for their own health in the early days, and epidemics were frequent. Latrines were not compulsory until 1908, and general health services developed slowly even in towns; the largest, Bulawayo, did not appoint a health officer until 1918. Prior to 1900, Africans who lived in towns received little medical attention except in emergencies, although upon occasion they were admitted

223

to European hospitals.[1] In 1908, the residential segregation of Africans in towns was implemented, being motivated in part by a desire to protect Europeans from the diseases that presumably had high incidence among Africans.[2] Even so, it was still another decade or more before efforts were made to improve sanitary conditions in the African locations.

From the beginning, missionaries had provided for rural Africans a modicum of medical services, along with schools and evangelism. The bad health of Africans caused much anxiety to both missionaries and Native Commissioners. In 1903, smallpox vaccinations were given to 80,000 Africans. Later, in 1909, the B. S. A. Company Administration recommended systematic innoculations for the entire African population.[3] However, there were great obstacles in getting Africans to cooperate and use these services during the early decades. After World War II, their use of medical facilities became very extensive.

Apart from epidemics, one of the earliest concerns of the Administration was over the health of the African mine workers, a concern that arose chiefly from European economic motives (Gelfand, 1953: 132 ff.). Not only was the efficiency of the African workers impaired, but their poor health also threatened the European population.[4] Despite the opposition of the smaller mine owners, the Administration introduced measures to improve health standards in recruiting and transporting workers, as well as in the conditions in mines. In the latter, the Administration was gradually able to enforce better housing, sanitation, nutrition, and the construction of hospitals.

The majority of European immigrants into Southern Rhodesia, as suggested earlier, came from a society with strongly marked differences in social class. People usually lived in spatially demarcated areas, and the place of residence affected access to and use of various public facilities: hospitals, parks, retail shops, churches, taverns, inns, and public lavatories. Class differences also supported the growth of distinctive school systems and membership in various religious denominations. Cricket was a game reserved for gentlemen, and competitive sports were rare between individuals of different social classes. Banks and shops often had separate entrances and counters to serve clients and messengers. Costumes and dialects varied sufficiently to enable the identification of one's class position and to regulate the use of facilities and services.

In Southern Rhodesia, cultural differences between Europeans and Africans were even greater than those between social classes in England and the Union of South Africa. The development of dual facilities and services seemed normal and "natural" to the Europeans, since they conceived themselves to be "more advanced," and they also assumed most of the financial responsibilities. Europeans made conscious efforts to maintain their customary way of life; this implied limited access for Africans to the new facilities and services, and deferential behavior in their personal relations with Europeans.

In order to protect Africans from harmful influences, legislation was passed to prohibit them from participating in the state lottery, betting on races, and consuming alcoholic spirits. However, the provision of separate facilities and services more often reflected European ideas about sanitation, health, and disease, and the felt need to pro tect European women from sexual contacts with Africans.

Separate hospitals and medical services seemed natural because of dissimilar customs relating to convalescence—the expression of pain, food habits, techniques of childbirth and child care—and the ability to pay for services. The widely held belief, though unsupported by science, that biological characteristics were inherited through the blood stream gave rise to separate blood-donor services. European ideas about cleanliness and the communication of disease were fundamental in contributing to the appearance of separate prisons and correctional institutions, barbering and hairdressing services, funeral and undertaking agencies, and booking offices and compartments in the railway system. Standards of health were also basic in the growth of separate schools and the absence of sports competitions between Europeans and Africans; both were contact situations involving the possibility of sharing physical facilities.

The appearance of different facilities and services, however, was not due solely to the Europeans' values and wishes. In many societies one group dislikes accepting or granting responsibility to others in services such as haircutting and hairdressing, treatment of the sick (at least for some maladies), burial of the dead, and ministering to religious and moral needs. Where Europeans in Southern Rhodesia have traditionally wanted to maintain separate facilities, they have been willing to subsidize uneconomic schemes for separate schools, hospitals, housing, lavatories, swimming pools, and so on. The need for subsidies, as indicated in an earlier chapter, derives from the difference between African and European wage levels, a gap sufficiently large for few Africans to have the financial resources to contribute directly to the support of these services and facilities.

It may be noted that those segregated facilities and services Europeans felt most strongly about maintaining in the early years involved small and intimate groups, particularly kinsmen and close friends. This was clearest in the attendance of schools, confinement in hospitals, trying on clothes in shops, sitting on park benches, riding in closed train compartments, and participating in church services. Among Christian groups, tensions arose between the ideal—the doctrine of brotherhood—and the real situation of cultural differences. It was not rare for congregations to object to Africans participating in their services, or even to being near their church buildings. On one occasion, for example, the Presbyterian and Dutch Reformed churches of Salisbury protested to the Native Affairs Department when the office for issuing passes to Africans was moved near their churches. The members not only referred to the danger of disease to women and children, but also said that it was "extremely unpleasant to the members . . . for so many natives to be in the vicinity of the church." [5]

The integration of disparate cultural groups into the same sacred institutions seldom occurs readily. Christian churches and doctrine are broadly based on the family, hence relations among communicants of the faith tend to be more intimate and permanent than in secular (economic and political) institutions.[6] Even when European denominations have welcomed African participation, the latter have often preferred to establish their own organizations in order to maintain distinctive cultural traditions. However, many Africans have totally or partially rejected Christianity as a result of their nonacceptance by Europeans. Other Africans have broken away from European religious supervision by seeking to establish and control their own Christian sects and denominations. "Separatist" sectarian leadership and doctrines from the Union of South Africa have given impetus to this development. Thus, separation of religious organizations has resulted from the values and wishes of both Europeans and Africans.

In sum, the location and use of public services and facilities have been largely determined by two basic factors: the fundamental policy of territorial segregation or land apportionment, and cultural differences between Europeans and Africans. Today, Africans are using these facilities with increasing frequency and are more aware than previously of restrictions upon their use. If the educational and income levels of Africans continue to rise, and if acculturation is not slowed down, the present trend toward fewer separate facilities and services may continue on its own momentum. Slow but certain changes in European attitudes have occurred about the use of public facilities by Africans, and an increasing number of people inside and outside Southern Rhodesia have expressed opinions about the efficiency and morality of such practices.

The social system of the country is undergoing change, and within it are differing ideas and practices about the use of public facilities and services. The Federal Government has eliminated the separate railway booking offices and entrances to post offices, and some private firms have followed suit. Africans are now permitted to buy lottery tickets and to bet on horse races. Changes have been advocated in the sale of beer, wine, and alcohol to Africans. Sporting events between Europeans and non-Europeans have just begun, and their number may expand in the near future. With rising African incomes, commercial firms may be inclined to seek more customers among the

African population, who would be attracted to shops without hatch windows and segregated entrances and counters.

Public facilities and services thus have become less differentiated and segregated during Southern Rhodesia's short history, but most of the change has taken place only in the past few years. The degree to which the traditional social system of Southern Rhodesia will be modified, and in what manner, will be greatly influenced by both contemporary attitudes and cultural differences between Europeans and Africans.

### CONTEMPORARY ATTITUDES

It is possible to classify in different ways the facilities and services available to a community. In some societies, facilities owned by the state or a local government would be considered as belonging to the "public" and classified accordingly. The taxonomy we have favored is broader than this; we have embraced within the category any facility which, in a Western society such as Britain, would normally be available to members of the public. Included, then, are state- and municipal-owned facilities and services, commercial enterprises, and institutions such as churches which are of more limited reference. Tables 66 and 67 show the facilities which, by our definition, are deemed to be public, and the nature of the differentiation attached to their use.

Since the first settlement of the Colony, the facilities available to the European public have altered profoundly both in type and extent. In the beginning, there were no elevators, few shops and banks, no buses, and certainly no airports. Therefore, the problem of differing treatment or separate facilities could not arise in these contexts. However, as such facilities were developed, the prevailing philosophy of separation usually made itself felt. Elevators were used by Europeans alone, or separate ones were provided for Africans; shops, banks, post offices, and railway stations, while providing services for Africans, generally had separate entrances or counters; and buses, hospitals, schools, lavatories, and the like were separated by race.

In our analysis of attitudes, it is possible to detect two fairly disparate types of differentiation; these are distinguished as Type A and B. All the items included in Type A involve physical proximity of a transient nature. Individuals are together for only a short period of time and are usually standing as they make use of the facility. If there is any physical contact at all it is fleeting. Situations of this nature are viewed with more tolerance by the European population. On the other hand, the situations described in Type B involve the possibility of closer physical contact, and considerations of health and sex loom larger in support of separate facilities. It has been noted, not facetiously, that situations of this second type generally place the individual in a sitting, prone, or supine position, a position of greater immobility in which the attendant attitudes are all more strongly in favor of the status quo. It is not suggested that the vertical or horizontal position of the body per se generates the attitudes; but where the individual is sitting or lying, as in a bus or a hospital, he is less able to remove himself from a situation he regards as undesirable, unhygienic, or offensive. Thus, whereas more than half of our sample feel that Africans should be permitted to use elevators, nearly all of the same people have no wish to share a train compartment with an African, or to sleep in a bed that may have been used by one.

The reasons advanced will emerge more definitively as we examine the practices classified under Type A and Type B.

TABLE 66. *Statements Relating to Public Facilities, Type A*

| No. | Statement | −1 P.E. | +1 P.E. | Mean |
|---|---|---|---|---|
| 50 | There are few opportunities for Africans to participate with or against Europeans in sporting events. | 2.02 | 4.82 | 3.42 |
| 36 | Most churches do not hold services for multiracial congregations. | 1.67 | 4.75 | 3.21 |
| 35 | In many public buildings Africans are not allowed to use lifts. | 1.77 | 4.49 | 3.13 |
| 3 | Africans may not lawfully buy lottery tickets or bet on horse racing in Southern Rhodesia. | 1.62 | 4.42 | 3.02 |
| 42 | In some shops and cafes there is a little window through which Africans are served. | 1.38 | 4.10 | 2.74 |
| 37 | Different entrances are provided for Africans and Europeans in certain shops and banks and in many post offices. | 1.13 | 3.99 | 2.56 |
| 40 | At railway stations there are generally separate booking offices for Europeans and Africans. | .80 | 3.56 | 2.18 |
| | | 1.48 | 4.30 | 2.89 |

Table 66 shows that over half the population are in favor of changing four of the Type A practices, while less than half support change on the other three. When the items are pooled, the mean position of the category (2.89) is slightly on the side of the status quo, as contrasted with the mean for Type B (1.20) which is heavily against change. If we take the area of minus one probable error to plus one probable error as representing the attitudes of the population, it will be seen that it is neither completely for nor against change; the typical attitude is a compound of both viewpoints. The fluctuation of the majority is pinpointed more accurately by an analysis of each separate statement.

*Statement 50* (M = 3.42) strides into an arena where change has been notable in the last year or so. In the past, it was uncommonly rare for Africans and Europeans to compete in sporting events. But in recent years, some outstanding African athletes have thrust their way to the top, and have competed successfully with European sportsmen of world standing. The crowds of the Colony have witnessed visiting American Negroes in action, and European schoolboys have been coached at "clinics" by them. Also, since the founding of the University College of Rhodesia and Nyasaland, African students have participated in growing numbers in athletics and the major sports.

There is little concrete evidence to show how Europeans would have viewed these contests before they took place, but today it is clear that the majority support the idea. "Sporting events encourage Africans to improve themselves." "The barriers in sport will probably be relaxed as Africans progress." One remarkable young African athlete received wide acclaim from both black and white Rhodesians prior to his sudden accidental death while abroad.

However, there is some qualification to African participation in sporting contests, and there is some opposition. One individual with a high social-change score suggests that "rugger" should be excluded because it is too exciting. Generally submerged, but breaking surface on occasion, is the opposition felt toward including Africans in contact sports such as rugby and boxing. Among the contact sports, rugby in particular is disapproved. At the other end of the scale, a few are opposed to all nonracial sporting events, and one advocates their banning on the ground they would be riot-provoking. In summary, however, it seems safe to predict that Africans and Europeans will participate with increasing regularity in the sporting events of the Colony.

*Statement 36* (M = 3.21) observes that most churches do not hold services for multiracial congregations. This statement is contested by a number of people at different attitudinal levels, but the expressions of some in the middle 50% illustrate the disagreement: "Most churches within my experience are perfectly willing to admit Africans to European services, but any clergyman I have spoken to feels that the African is probably far happier in his own service in his own language; even their singing of English hymns differs from ours. But certainly Africans should be allowed in any service they wish." Other comments similarly challenge the validity of the statement: "Africans can attend all Anglican churches." "Untrue. Catholic churches in Bulawayo and Queen's Park do have multiracial congregations."

It is not our intention to enter the lists to refute the challenges. Some churches may be willing to admit Africans to the services held in European areas, but it is an observable fact that most Africans worship elsewhere. Nor are we disputing that the reasons in favor of separate facilities may not be valid. Some mention the language barrier, others for reasons of health object to communion from the common chalice, and still others feel they will be crowded out of their churches if all the Africans in European areas decide to attend. Despite these objections, the majority insist that the Christian ethic of equality before God means equality to worship with Europeans in church.

*Statement 35* (M = 3.13) is one of the most clearly defined of the "vertical" facilities; it refers to the use of elevators. Since the study was planned, the practice of providing separate elevators for Africans, or none at all, has undergone much modification. When in 1959 the Federal Government eliminated separate entrances to post offices, similar restrictions were eliminated in many public buildings. Almost overnight, it seemed, the signs on elevators stating "Europeans Only" came down. It is now difficult to find the remaining ones in the capital city of Salisbury. A similar trend can be detected in other centers of the Colony. Thus, a practice more than half of the population wish to see changed has in fact changed considerably. Support for separate facilities is generally on the grounds of hygiene.

*Statement 3* (M = 3.02) needs little comment because it no longer applies. An alteration in law now permits Africans to bet on horse racing and to participate in lotteries, and some African ticket holders have recently had the heady experience of winning thirty thousand pounds in a national lottery. It is notable that Europeans split almost exactly over the advisability of change. Those who wish to discontinue the law generally invoke the principle of equity; those who support its retention express concern for the families of Africans who gamble. As an example, one respondent deplores the idea of change because of the "inherent gambling instinct of the majority of Africans, and in the interest of their wives and children."

*Statement 42* (M = 2.74) is the first in the category where the majority shift to the side of the status quo. Linked with the past is the practice of building shops and cafes with a separate window or hatchway so that Africans, who are obliged to remain outside, can still make purchases. Separate facilities of this kind generally are not included in the larger urban shops being built today. Consequently, it is of interest to find that the greater portion of the sample favors the retention of separate windows or hatchways, particularly for cafes. In the factor analysis, this feeling was reflected through the significant loading on the physical separation factor.

In the majority of cases, it is argued that Africans should be served outside shops and cafes because of their failure to observe adequate standards of hygiene. As one person from the typical group phrases it, "These things are dependent on an improvement in the African's personal hygiene." But not all employ the argument of hygiene. One person contends there will be no objection to the well-dressed, well-behaved African being served inside a shop; it is the "raw" African to whom people object. Another suggests that hatches are provided so that Africans can obtain service without encountering language difficulties. Some of the respondents, on the other hand, feel more strongly about the matter than those cited above:

> A neighbour has a Native store in his farm. Natives come in large numbers—they seem to have so much time to spare. They lean on the counter and gaze at the shelves. They ask to be shown this and that and end up by getting a pound of sugar. Quite often something they asked to see disappears off the counter; it can be passed from one to the other very quickly. To deal with Europeans and Africans in the same store would require a lot of handling.

It is noteworthy, however, that this theme of African dishonesty is not employed by many of the respondents. Generally they object to poorly-dressed Africans solely on the ground of hygiene.

*Statement 37* (M = 2.56) is a corollary of the last one. If the general sentiment is in favor of keeping Africans—particularly the poorly-dressed—outside shops and cafes, then it is safe to predict that where they are let inside, separate doorways and entrances should be provided. The sample, on the average, is in favor of separate entrances to shops, banks, and post offices. The finding is of particular interest in the case of post offices, because during the course of the survey separate entrances were discontinued. Many of our comments relate to post offices, and it seems clear that the majority dislike their present nonracial character. Hygiene is again the principal objection, with "delay in service" a close second.

"This morning I went into the post office. A native had his piccanin with him and his nose was running and pressing against people's dresses. Would you like that?" "It is sometimes impossible to get near enough to post letters because of Africans gossiping." "Separate facilities are more convenient for Africans." "Separate facilities are more convenient for Europeans." These are responses from the representative half of the group. There seems little doubt that in eliminating separate entrances to post offices the Federal Government acted contrary to the majority wish of the people. It led rather than followed public opinion.

*Statement 40* (M = 2.18) speaks of the railway stations, where booking offices are differentiated by class of travel rather than by race. However, inasmuch as most Africans travel fourth class and Europeans do not, the separation by class in fact largely achieves separation by race. And this is the way the sample population wishes to keep it. Far more Africans than Europeans travel by rail, and the latter feel it would be most inconvenient as well as unhygienic to have to stand in a queue to purchase a first-class ticket while crowds of Africans were waiting to buy fourth-class travel. It is felt that separate booking offices are speedier and more to the advantage of both Africans and Europeans.

These, then, are the attitudes about sharing the public facilities of the Colony, the facilities in which physical proximity between the races is most transient and contact brief, if it occurs at all. The majority of the European population is attuned to the greater participation of Africans in athletics, to the admission of Africans into European places of worship, and to nonracial elevators. Furthermore, the majority is prepared to let Africans gamble on horses and lotteries even though it feels the consequences might well be disastrous for Africans, particularly women and children. On the other hand, most of the sample advocate some kind of physical separation in shops, cafes, banks, post offices, and railway stations. As the advocacy becomes stronger, so does the frequency with which hygiene is mentioned. The theme of protection from contagion grows stronger as we turn to the second type of public facility, where there seems to be a greater possibility of direct or indirect contact.

The Type B facilities are shown in Table 67, along with the scored responses of the sample population. An immediately observable feature of the table is the heavy sentiment in favor of the status

TABLE 67. *Statements Relating to Public Facilities, Type B*

| No. | Statement | −1 P.E. | +1 P.E. | Mean |
|-----|-----------|---------|---------|------|
| 31 | Except on specified routes, Africans and Europeans may not ride in the same buses. | .54 | 3.04 | 1.79 |
| 29 | In some parks there are separate benches for Europeans and Africans. | .44 | 3.04 | 1.74 |
| 34 | Europeans and Africans are required by law to attend different schools. | .18 | 2.38 | 1.28 |
| 49 | Africans may not try on clothes in most European shops. | .11 | 2.37 | 1.24 |
| 39 | There are different hospitals and other medical services for Africans and Europeans. | .01 | 2.09 | 1.05 |
| 32 | There are different compartments for Europeans and Africans on trains. | −.10 | 1.80 | .85 |
| 44 | Europeans and Africans generally are not permitted to use the same lavatories. | −.35 | 1.17 | .41 |
| | | .13 | 2.27 | 1.20 |

quo. Indeed, opinion against sharing lavatories with Africans can hardly be more definite. The reasons offered for retaining the status quo emerge from an analysis of the interview material.

*Statement 31* (M = 1.79) focuses attention on travel by bus. Here there are local variations that should be noted. In Salisbury, it has been and is the general practice to provide separate buses for Africans and Europeans. In Bulawayo, however, both groups frequently ride in the same buses, but in different sections. Some of the residents of this city take pains to draw attention to their "more liberal" attitude in the matter.

Some qualification can be detected in the comments to the statement. The bulk of the population is firmly against sharing buses if it means sitting next to an African; but, in the interest of economy, some support separate sections within the same bus. The reasons in support of separate facilities leave little room for misinterpretation. The greatest fear is of contagion and infection. "When Africans have learnt to maintain cleanliness of body and practice clean habits, then only do I think that this practice should be discontinued." "This is not purely a question of color. It involves health considerations, general standards of conduct, and so on." "Africans often smell highly, hence the objection to riding in the same bus." These are typical of the reasons given by the European population. A few express themselves more circuitously and others more bluntly, but the themes are the same.

*Statement 29* (M = 1.74) has a higher loading than any other on the factor that we called "physical separation." Most Europeans do not wish to share their park benches with Africans; they should have their own, preferably in separate areas. This stand is characteristic of 75% of the population, and the reasons for it center principally around hygiene. It is a widespread conviction that diseases and vermin can be picked up from park benches, hence there is a clear case for separate facilities.

*Statement 34* (M = 1.28) reads, "Europeans and Africans are required by law to attend different schools." There are no exceptions to the legal requirement, but in practice some interracial schools exist. The most notable one is the newly established University College where the Royal Charter affirms that "no test of religious belief or profession or of race, nationality, or class shall be imposed upon or required of any person in order to entitle him to be admitted as a member, professor, teacher, or student of the University College . . ." For the most part, it is accepted that the College should be nonracial, but the preference is clearly for separate facilities at lower levels of education. The arguments advanced by the representative half of the sample are varied.

Some stress the problem of language: "Segregation in schools is inevitable when most African primary education is carried out in the vernacular. Even at the high school level, the European child would have an unfair advantage when instruction is given in English." Others emphasize that the methods of teaching Africans are different: "Africans usually need different methods of approach." As might be expected, some are concerned about health and hygiene, while a fourth group maintains that the inferior mental equipment of the African makes separate schooling inevitable. A fifth group insists that Africans prefer their own schools in any case, so the present system really reflects the dominant wish of both cultural groups.

It is noteworthy that only one person openly expressed concern at the possibility of mixed friendships and marriages, and yet this reason probably lies at the back of much European thinking. Positive support for such a hypothesis comes from the factor analysis, which indicates that statement 34 has a significant loading on one of the sex factors. If the races are mixed in school, the friendships formed may be other than Platonic and can lead to marriage. As we have determined already, cross-racial sexual contact is most strongly deplored by the European population, and any step that may lead to the removal of barriers will encounter massive resistance.

*Statement 49* (M = 1.24) returns to the dominant theme of protection from disease. Very few Europeans are prepared to purchase clothes if it is suspected that they have been previously tried on by an African. This sentiment prevails despite the general attitude of the individual. Persons with high scores on the entire questionnaire are just as concerned about health and hygiene as are persons who strongly support the status quo. A few individuals state that they have no objection to Africans trying on clothes before they are bought, but this group is very much in a minority.

*Statement 39* (M = 1.05) probes attitudes about the separation of hospitals and other medical services. The mean and probable error limits reveal how strongly the sample supports the status quo, and the comments bring into focus the reasons why people take this stand.

To some, differences in culture and custom are paramount: "Many Africans have a completely different way of life." "Africans have different customs so the medical services are more easily administered separately." "It is easier to cope with differences of food, etc., in separate establishments." To others, the overriding consideration is that of hygiene: "Africans generally do not have the same standards of hygiene as Europeans." "Who would like to sleep in a bed where a Native has?"

Shot through the comments at all levels, however, is concern with the cost of medical attention. It is stressed again and again that whereas medical treatment for Africans is free, for Europeans it is not. The most modern hospital in Salisbury cares for the African population without charge, yet Europeans are obliged to pay heavily for the services they receive. This being so, it is felt that Africans have little cause for complaint. The financial burden of medical services is almost entirely carried by the European population, many feel, and it is high time that some of the burden should be shouldered by Africans.

*Statement 32* (M = .85) is concerned with travel facilities, just as is statement 31. But the sentiment against mixed compartments on trains is much heavier than that against mixing on buses. Travel by train generally involves a greater time span, so all the objections to nonracial travel by bus receive reinforcement. At the core of practically all objections are the differences in standards of health, hygiene, and social status. "This is not really a color bar, it is a hygiene bar, as most Africans do not have facilities for proper cleanliness." "The longer period of tenure in trains [as compared to buses] may render infestation more likely." "I think that this will be abolished in time, but the time is not ripe for it now."

Some of the comments are more forthright than those cited, and others less so, but the attitudes are consistent. Many feel and say that the solution to the difficulty lies in providing separate compartments of equal standards for Africans who can afford them.

*Statement 44* (M = .41) covers one of the most emotive areas in the whole questionnaire. By social custom, sanctioned in law, Europeans have always insisted upon separate lavatories. Municipal regulations enforcing separate lavatories not only apply to shops, hotels, factories, theaters, and the like, but theoretically are also applicable. to individual homes.

Thus, although an African can be welcomed as a guest into one's household, he is not legally permitted to use the same toilet as his host. In recent months, however, discussions in the Salisbury City Council have stressed the difficulty that might be experienced if an attempt were made to enforce this by-law.

There is no doubt about attitudes on the use of public or private toilets. They have been racially separate in the past, they are separate now, and custom if not law will help to keep them separate in the future. If public toilets are made available to everybody, the European population, on our evidence, will mostly refuse to use them. Typical comments are associated with maximum maintain scores: "The local health authorities would think that the time is not yet ripe." "I don't like sharing my toilet with anyone." "It is more healthy to use separate lavatories." In particular, tuberculosis, venereal disease, and leprosy are singled out as diseases that might be communicated through the use of common toilets. Many also feel that the African methods of achieving hygiene leave much to be desired. All the reasons put forward add up to the same conclusion—maintain separate toilets.

## THE SAMPLE CHARACTERISTICS

The picture that emerges from the interview material now seems reasonably distinct. Toward Type A public facilities, there is a con-

siderable body of opinion in favor of social change; in four out of
seven items, the majority wish to see current practices discontinued
or modified. Very much the reverse is true of all the areas examined
in the Type B category. Here attitudes are generally much more homogeneous and strongly on the side of the status quo. The standard
deviation of 1.59 for the Type B category, as compared with 2.09 for
Type A, illustrates this greater solidarity in thinking and feeling. From
buses to toilets, the arguments are strongly in favor of separate facilities. In the latter case (toilets) the standard deviation of 1.12 displays
greater unity of attitude than that achieved by any other item on the
scale.

With these attitudes before us, the next task is to see whether they
vary with different segments of the population. Table 68 presents a
breakdown of the data on the first group of facilities, and Table 69
gives the attitude scores for the Type B category.

### COUNTRY OF BIRTH

Of the three countries that have provided the majority of the European population of Southern Rhodesia, the United Kingdom group
—with a mean score of 3.44—is most clearly on the side of changing
facilities of Type A. In fact, the greater portion of them advocate
change on all the items save one, that of booking offices at the railway
stations. On this item, it is felt that separation by class of travel should
be retained. The United Kingdom-born are strongly in favor of multi-
racial sport (M = 4.19) and nearly as strongly in favor of accepting
Africans into European places of worship. The majority support unrestricted elevators, the sharing of gambling facilities, and the abolition of separate windows and entrances to shops, banks, and post
offices.

Standing in sharp opposition to the United Kingdom segment are
those born in the Union of South Africa. A majority opt for the status
quo on every single item in the Type A category. Very similar are the
attitudes of Southern Rhodesians who wish to maintain all the practices except that relating to sporting contests. On this item, the mean
score of 3.03 demonstrates how evenly the Southern Rhodesians are
split, with the scales tipped just slightly in favor of change.

With the Type B facilities, however, there is not one grouping that
wishes to change any of the practices, although, as before, those born
in South Africa and Southern Rhodesia are more firm and united in
their opposition to change than are persons from the United Kingdom. Among all groupings, the lowest maintain scores are reserved for
separate lavatories.

TABLE 68. *Scores Relating to Public Facilities, Type A (M = 2.89)*

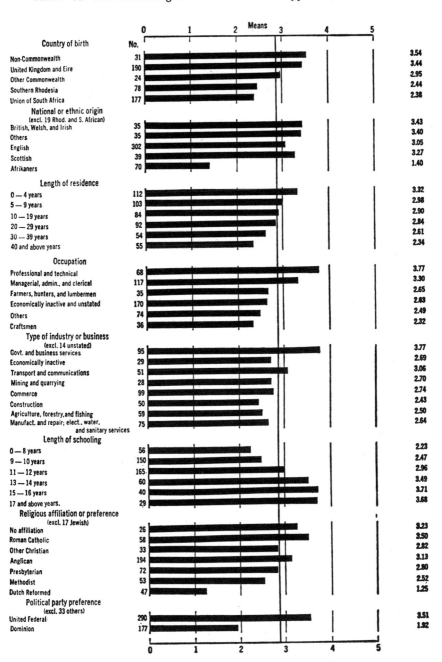

| | No. | Mean |
|---|---|---|
| **Country of birth** | | |
| Non-Commonwealth | 31 | 3.54 |
| United Kingdom and Eire | 190 | 3.44 |
| Other Commonwealth | 24 | 2.95 |
| Southern Rhodesia | 78 | 2.44 |
| Union of South Africa | 177 | 2.38 |
| **National or ethnic origin** (excl. 19 Rhod. and S. African) | | |
| British, Welsh, and Irish | 35 | 3.43 |
| Others | 35 | 3.40 |
| English | 302 | 3.05 |
| Scottish | 39 | 3.27 |
| Afrikaners | 70 | 1.40 |
| **Length of residence** | | |
| 0 — 4 years | 112 | 3.32 |
| 5 — 9 years | 103 | 2.98 |
| 10 — 19 years | 84 | 2.90 |
| 20 — 29 years | 92 | 2.84 |
| 30 — 39 years | 54 | 2.61 |
| 40 and above years | 55 | 2.34 |
| **Occupation** | | |
| Professional and technical | 68 | 3.77 |
| Managerial, admin., and clerical | 117 | 3.30 |
| Farmers, hunters, and lumbermen | 35 | 2.65 |
| Economically inactive and unstated | 170 | 2.63 |
| Others | 74 | 2.49 |
| Craftsmen | 36 | 2.32 |
| **Type of industry or business** (excl. 14 unstated) | | |
| Govt. and business services | 95 | 3.77 |
| Economically inactive | 29 | 2.69 |
| Transport and communications | 51 | 3.06 |
| Mining and quarrying | 28 | 2.70 |
| Commerce | 99 | 2.74 |
| Construction | 50 | 2.43 |
| Agriculture, forestry, and fishing | 59 | 2.50 |
| Manufact. and repair; elect., water, and sanitary services | 75 | 2.64 |
| **Length of schooling** | | |
| 0 — 8 years | 56 | 2.23 |
| 9 — 10 years | 150 | 2.47 |
| 11 — 12 years | 165 | 2.96 |
| 13 — 14 years | 60 | 3.49 |
| 15 — 16 years | 40 | 3.71 |
| 17 and above years. | 29 | 3.68 |
| **Religious affiliation or preference** (excl. 17 Jewish) | | |
| No affiliation | 26 | 3.23 |
| Roman Catholic | 58 | 3.50 |
| Other Christian | 33 | 2.82 |
| Anglican | 194 | 3.13 |
| Presbyterian | 72 | 2.80 |
| Methodist | 53 | 2.52 |
| Dutch Reformed | 47 | 1.25 |
| **Political party preference** (excl. 33 others) | | |
| United Federal | 290 | 3.51 |
| Dominion | 177 | 1.92 |

TABLE 69. *Scores Relating to Public Facilities, Type B* (*M* = 1.20)

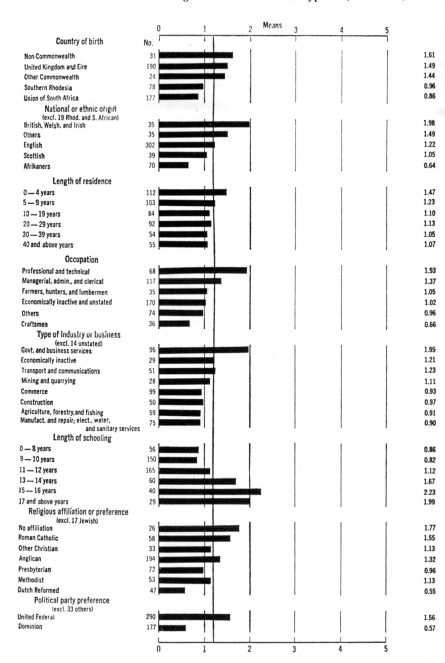

| | No. | Mean |
|---|---|---|
| **Country of birth** | | |
| Non-Commonwealth | 31 | 1.61 |
| United Kingdom and Eire | 190 | 1.49 |
| Other Commonwealth | 24 | 1.44 |
| Southern Rhodesia | 78 | 0.96 |
| Union of South Africa | 177 | 0.86 |
| **National or ethnic origin** (excl. 19 Rhod. and S. African) | | |
| British, Welsh, and Irish | 35 | 1.98 |
| Others | 35 | 1.49 |
| English | 302 | 1.22 |
| Scottish | 39 | 1.05 |
| Afrikaners | 70 | 0.64 |
| **Length of residence** | | |
| 0 — 4 years | 112 | 1.47 |
| 5 — 9 years | 103 | 1.23 |
| 10 — 19 years | 84 | 1.10 |
| 20 — 29 years | 92 | 1.13 |
| 30 — 39 years | 54 | 1.05 |
| 40 and above years | 55 | 1.07 |
| **Occupation** | | |
| Professional and technical | 68 | 1.93 |
| Managerial, admin., and clerical | 117 | 1.37 |
| Farmers, hunters, and lumbermen | 35 | 1.05 |
| Economically inactive and unstated | 170 | 1.02 |
| Others | 74 | 0.96 |
| Craftsmen | 36 | 0.66 |
| **Type of industry or business** (excl. 14 unstated) | | |
| Govt. and business services | 95 | 1.95 |
| Economically inactive | 29 | 1.21 |
| Transport and communications | 51 | 1.23 |
| Mining and quarrying | 28 | 1.11 |
| Commerce | 99 | 0.93 |
| Construction | 50 | 0.97 |
| Agriculture, forestry, and fishing | 59 | 0.91 |
| Manufact. and repair; elect., water, and sanitary services | 75 | 0.90 |
| **Length of schooling** | | |
| 0 — 8 years | 56 | 0.86 |
| 9 — 10 years | 150 | 0.82 |
| 11 — 12 years | 165 | 1.12 |
| 13 — 14 years | 60 | 1.67 |
| 15 — 16 years | 40 | 2.23 |
| 17 and above years | 29 | 1.99 |
| **Religious affiliation or preference** (excl. 17 Jewish) | | |
| No affiliation | 26 | 1.77 |
| Roman Catholic | 58 | 1.55 |
| Other Christian | 33 | 1.13 |
| Anglican | 194 | 1.32 |
| Presbyterian | 72 | 0.96 |
| Methodist | 53 | 1.13 |
| Dutch Reformed | 47 | 0.55 |
| **Political party preference** (excl. 33 others) | | |
| United Federal | 290 | 1.56 |
| Dominion | 177 | 0.57 |

## NATIONAL OR ETHNIC ORIGIN

Two of the most disparate groupings in the population are those of English and Afrikaner background, with the former significantly more change-oriented than the latter. Within the Type A category, the English advocate changing four of the practices (those associated with athletics, churches, elevators, and gambling) whereas the Afrikaners strongly resist change on all items. Indeed the *lowest* English score of 2.32 on item 40 (railway booking offices) is greater than the *highest* Afrikaner score of 1.91 on item 3 (gambling). In all of our analyses, the Afrikaners display conservatism in their attitudes about social change.

Within the Type B category, both Englishmen and Afrikaners are on the side of the present, with the latter generally twice as emphatic as the former. The two groupings come closest together in their attitudes toward lavatories; neither wishes to share them with Africans.

## LENGTH OF RESIDENCE

The greatest contrast in this analysis comes between those who have lived for less than five years in the Colony and those who have been there forty years and more. The differing attitudes toward public facilities can be gleaned from an inspection of the scores given in Table 70.

TABLE 70. *Length of Residence and Attitude about Public Facilities*

| | Type A | | | | Type B | | |
| --- | --- | --- | --- | --- | --- | --- | --- |
| Statement no. | 0–4 years | 40+ years | | Statement no. | 0–4 years | 40+ years | |
| 50 | 3.89 | 2.58 | | 31 | 2.04 | 1.67 | |
| 36 | 3.98 | 2.40 | | 29 | 2.21 | 1.24 | |
| 35 | 3.38 | 2.47 | | 34 | 1.70 | 1.16 | |
| 3 | 3.43 | 2.40 | | 49 | 1.48 | .95 | |
| 42 | 3.07 | 2.40 | | 39 | 1.30 | 1.24 | |
| 37 | 2.82 | 2.29 | | 32 | 1.02 | .80 | |
| 40 | 2.64 | 1.85 | | 44 | .54 | .40 | |
| Means | 3.32 | 2.34 | | Means | 1.47 | 1.07 | |

The largest gap occurs on the Type A facilities, where the newest immigrants generally favor an end to differentiating practices, and the persons of forty years' residence do not. With Type B, the gap is reduced but never closed, and the most recent arrivals are again the least conservative. Such findings support the hypothesis that the longer one lives in Southern Rhodesia, the more one accepts and supports the status quo. The newcomer's angry cry of protest against the social system becomes muted as the years pass, and in the end it often returns as a protest against the protest.

OCCUPATION

The segment that would be rated highest on a socioeconomic scale, the professional-technical, is on the side of changing all the practices of category A. Managers, administrators, and clerical workers take a similar stand. The other occupational groupings, however, fall generally on the side of the status quo. Farmers advocate the discontinuance of two practices, separate sports meetings and gambling facilities, while the economically inactive and craftsmen are in favor only of common gaming.

With the Type B practices, all the occupational means fall against change. As might be expected, the professional and technical people are not as resolute on the matter as the others, particularly the craftsmen, who obtain the very conservative mean score of .66. As we have noted in other sectional analyses, the differences between the subpopulations are smallest about the sharing of toilets. Professional and technical individuals display a mean score of .88, and the craftsmen an average figure of .22. The difference of .66 between these high and low means is the smallest within the occupational analysis.

TYPE OF INDUSTRY OR BUSINESS

It has been noted previously how persons in the government and business services stood apart from the other industrial groupings. This also happens with the use of various public facilities. The services personnel are the only ones in which a majority opt for change on all the items classified as Type A. Their mean score of 4.59 in favor of nonracial sport meetings is the highest in the category under analysis. At the other end of the continuum, those in the construction industry wish to maintain all the practices, while the agricultural people want to alter only one, that concerned with gambling. The general attitudes of individuals in the other industrial classifications fall at various points between the high and low limits described.

With the Type B category, a similar difference emerges between persons in the services and in agriculture, but this time all the mean scores are on the side of the status quo. The nearest approach to the theoretical center of 3.00 occurs in the attitude of services personnel toward riding in mixed buses. The mean score for this item is 2.95, which demonstrates that nearly half are for altering the present separation. It might be argued, however, that few of the services personnel

—doctors, teachers, administrators, lawyers, etc.—are obliged to ride in buses, so their attitudes may be largely theoretical.

EDUCATION

There is a steady change in attitudes toward the use of public facilities as length of schooling increases. Those who have attended school for eight years or less wish to alter none of the Type A facilities, and neither does the nine- to ten-year grouping. With eleven and twelve years of schooling, change is advocated on four items (50, 36, 35, 3); with thirteen and fourteen years the status quo is supported only once (item 40); and with a minimum of fifteen years of education, the present practices receive no majority support.

Turning to our tables of figures on category B, the mean scores are on the side of separation. The sole exception is that a majority of those with fifteen or sixteen years of schooling wish to discontinue the system of separate buses. Once again, it can be argued that these highly educated persons have little recourse to buses, hence may not feel strongly about them.

RELIGIOUS AFFILIATION OR PREFERENCE

Of the major religious affiliations selected for further analysis and contrast, the Roman Catholics consistently support the abolition of all the Type A differentiations except the one at railway stations. A majority of Anglicans wish to abolish four of the practices but to retain separate entrances to shops, banks, post offices, and booking offices. Members of the Dutch Reformed church want to retain the lot. The mean attitudes of Presbyterians and Methodists both fall on the maintain side of the continuum, although the scores for the latter more generally support the status quo.

In none of the religious affiliations, however, do we find a majority advocating the abolition of the separate facilities listed in category B. Table 69 illustrates that the pattern of scores for each item is much the same. The greatest differences emerge between individuals in the Catholic and Dutch Reformed churches, as we would expect from our earlier data.

POLITICAL PARTY PREFERENCE

Those who favor the two major political parties display significantly different attitudes toward both types of public facilities. On Type A, the bulk of Dominion party supporters advocate the retention of all the differentiating measures, while a majority of the Federal party want the abolition of all practices except that connected with railway stations.

On Type B, both groupings stand for the status quo, but the responses to the particular items illustrate how different is the thinking of individuals who support each party. It is only on the subject of toilet facilities that attitudes come close together. On the other practices, Dominion party supporters range from .94 to .32, in contrast to the Federal party supporters' range from 2.38 to 1.16. Such differences indicate fundamentally dissimilar attitudes about the use of public facilities.

## THE PRINCIPAL THEMES

It is now possible to draw together the common threads and to identify more precisely the major themes that underlie attitudes about the sharing of public facilities. In the beginning, the cultural gap between Africans and Europeans was extensive and, although smaller today, it is still evident. It is known that attitudes depend at least partly on observable differences between people. Even if differences in customs, standards of living, and language are bridged or eliminated, visible dissimilarities in color and physical appearance will still remain. In such circumstances, over most of the world, attitudes have been resistant to modification. Thus, in the United States, while it has been relatively easy through educational processes to modify attitudes about disparate groups of European immigrants, it has been demonstrably difficult to do the same about persons of African descent. A not dissimilar problem exists in Southern Rhodesia.

When the first immigrants arrived in the Colony, they set about establishing a way of life they generally knew elsewhere. Certain public facilities, such as shops, post offices, banks, hospitals, schools, and trains, were normal in their way of life, whereas they were not in African societies. These facilities were established in the first instance for themselves; if they were to share them with Africans, they believed they would be swamped. But it was not only the weight of numbers that perturbed Europeans; vicious, unknown diseases were encountered among Africans, and it was felt desirable, even imperative, that the two cultural groups should be separated. As European society became more established, the lines of geographical demarcation between them and the indigenous societies were more clearly drawn and eventually enacted into law. Thus the major themes, it seems to us, have been physical separation and protection from communicable disease, the former being necessary to achieve the latter.

But while Europeans for various reasons have preferred to keep contact with Africans to a minimum, they have appreciated that in a developing economy Africans should be able to travel to and from work without undue financial hardship, that health standards should be improved, that some support should be given to mission schools, and that the money Africans earn should be spent in shops and deposited in banks. Consequently, many public facilities have not been denied to Africans, but separate ones established. It cannot be gainsaid that facilities for Africans are generally less munificent, but they have been extended in scope and quality with the passage of years.

Nor has the extension of public facilities been dictated solely by hard-headed economic materialism. Idealistic motivations have always been present: it would be immoral to leave Africans to fight their diseases unaided, or to deny them the education that will roll back the frontiers of ignorance. And just as Europeans have considered it necessary to protect themselves from contagion and infection, so have they believed it necessary to protect Africans from some of the consequences of the new society. Gambling has seldom been accepted as a virtue in European society, and its possible effects upon untutored Africans have been realized and deplored. In this realization, we can witness much of the opposition to the extension of gaming facilities among Africans.

Europeans established themselves in Southern Rhodesia by virtue of their knowledge and power. Upon their differences from Africans —color, class, and culture—and the attitudes accompanying them, a social philosophy and social system based on physical separation were erected. But change can be witnessed and modification in attitudes measured. It seems clear that where the social contacts with Africans are limited and impersonal, the population is increasingly willing to share rather than duplicate its public facilities. Such facilities fall into our Type A category. On the other hand, Europeans generally do not countenance the sharing of Type B facilities. Social relations would be too intimate, too embarrassing, and even offensive if this were to happen. Differences of class and culture in Southern Rhodesia have been modified since the turn of the century, but they are still profound enough to echo George Orwell: some men are yet more equal than others.

# 15

## CIVIL ORDER AND POLITICAL CONTROL

Every society seeks to regulate both its internal relations and its contacts with outsiders or foreigners. Procedures must be developed by which decisions are made, power is exercised, and individuals are required to conform sufficiently with the customs and laws of the group so that a measure of order and security is maintained. Political communities are commonly organized on the bases of consensus, genealogy, and territory. With the expansion of numbers that generally comes in time, the importance of kinship for structuring political relations declines. Spatial or territorial divisions become more relevant, as can be attested by the terms commonly used in the English-speaking world: village, town, ward, city, district, province, and state.

A political system cannot function effectively, however, unless there is a moral order or a consensus in ethics among the members of the community or society. Individuals must share a measure of common loyalties and values if government is to carry out its responsibilities. In conquest situations, or when there are divergent cultural, linguistic, or religious groups, there may be multiple and perhaps conflicting moral orders. The difficulties that arise from the presence of minority groups in various political systems are well-known: Basques in Spain, Germans in Czechoslovakia, and overseas Indians, Chinese, and Englishmen. Thus it is possible to agree with Frankel (1953:13) when he says that a nation "is but a symbolic expression for a society which harbors within it innumerable social structures" and moral orders, some of "which are linked directly and indirectly to complementary structures in other societies throughout the world . . ."

The contact of Europeans and Africans in Southern Rhodesia brought a meeting of two unlike political systems and moral orders. In time, the dominance of one group necessarily had to emerge, given the assumption that both culture groups wanted to live in the territory. The earliest European immigrants were traders and concessionaires who adapted themselves to the control of the various tribal and clan communities among the African population. But these contacts were replaced by conflicting ones when larger numbers of Europeans began to occupy Southern Rhodesia and to establish a competitive political system. Since the Europeans sought to exploit the country's mineral and agricultural resources, it was necessary to develop extensive political institutions to maintain their dominance, civil order, and internal peace. If a new society were to be built upon the British or South African model, the immigrants needed a stable, adaptable, efficient, and responsible government.[1]

The required stability for a political system involves not only common loyalties and institutions for making decisions, but also an establishment for controlling deviant or potentially disruptive behavior. In the African Reserves, the Government has traditionally relied upon the self-policing of Africans to preserve law and order. There are many Reserves today in which no B. S. A. police are stationed. The size of the country's police establishment is relatively small, and most offenses are heard by the courts of the chiefs, headmen, and Native Commissioners. The Matabeleland Order-in-Council, 1894, allowed the Company to impose conditions, disabilities, or restrictions upon the right of Africans to possess firearms or ammunition.* But even so, many Europeans felt insecure enough to carry firearms, and go to sleep with guns under their pillows or at their bedsides. This practice was more frequent in rural than in urban areas, perhaps because of the absence of policemen. Yet it apparently has diminished but slightly, for in 1959 more than 60,000 guns were registered in the names of Europeans, an average of about one per household.†

The Order-in-Council of 1894 also allowed the Company or the Administrator to prohibit the sale of alcoholic spirits to Africans in order to minimize civil disturbances and irresponsible behavior against the Europeans, the Government, and fellow Africans. But in

---

* Today, Africans can obtain special permits to possess firearms, particularly when they are needed for such tasks as slaughtering or protecting stock.

† On Nov. 30, 1959, a total of 64,978 firearms were registered in Southern Rhodesia—about one for every three Europeans. Information provided by the Ministry of Justice and Internal Affairs, Dec. 30, 1959.

the 1890's, it was a common offense for a European to sell liquor to Africans. There were twenty-nine such cases in Bulawayo alone in 1894.[2] In fact, the practice became so prevalent that the Administration raised the fine to £300. However, by 1901 the fine had been lowered to £50.[3] Africans still are forbidden by law to manufacture or consume alcoholic spirits.

In the early years of settlement, the B. S. A. Company assumed direct rule over the indigenous population, unlike British colonial practices elsewhere in Africa (Hailey, 1951:9). Lands were reserved for the sole occupation and use of either Europeans or Africans, and numerous measures were introduced to prevent further rebellions and to maintain law and order. Dual branches of the administration were established to regulate the political affairs of the two different culture groups. The Administration sought to preserve much of the traditional political structure of the African communities, but the Native Commissioners replaced the chiefs and headmen as the principal holders of power. The Commissioners assumed the major executive and judicial functions, while the indigenous political leaders became agents of the Government's developing administration. In addition, particularly outside the Reserves, political control was exercised widely by mining companies, European farmers, and individual employers, as has been discussed in earlier chapters.

The chiefs' powers to organize warfare were discontinued by the Government. In addition, new responsibilities, such as helping to control the drinking of beer, were added to their traditional duties of collecting taxes or tribute, preventing crime, and apprehending criminals. Although some of the religious and ceremonial functions were lost to the Christian missionaries, many spiritual and moral sanctions continued to support the chiefs. Thus, the chiefs served as effective intermediaries between their followers and the Government.

Africans were not included in the wider political system of the territory, however. As in other colonial situations where wide cultural differences existed, the Crown generally ignored the problem of integrating indigenous and immigrant populations into a single political system. The devolution of power to the Europeans in Southern Rhodesia in 1923 therefore was not radically different from the previous practices of the Imperial Government (Coleman, 1958:33–37). In obtaining Self-Government, the Europeans became a legalized oligarchy in a country where differences of color and culture were theoretically irrelevant.

The passive or "caretaker" attitude toward African participation in Government in the early years slowly began to modify. The preservation of indigenous African political institutions had generated an unwanted psychological dependence upon European initiative and decisions which was accompanied by apathy, suspicion, and hostility.

Gradually, a new policy took shape that was designed to maintain territorial segregation and European dominance, and yet to provide opportunities on the Reserves for African local government. The growth of schools, hospitals, taxation, roads, and other services came gradually. Since many of these services were unknown before the coming of the Europeans, the idea that the Africans should systematically join in providing them was new (Hailey, 1951:42). To encourage more participation, the creation of new kinds of political organization was necessary, as a reliance upon the authority of the chiefs did not hasten the adoption of nontraditional measures.

The Government, through a strong central administrative organization, sought to stimulate African initiative, cooperation, and the formation of local councils. The Constitution Letters Patent of 1923 provided for the creation of African consultative and advisory councils, but not until 1930 were the first "Native Boards" formed. In 1937, the Native Councils Act allowed for executive powers and responsibilities to devolve on the Councils. Then in 1943 they were given the right to levy taxes, and the Government began to match the Councils' revenues with £ for £ grants. Although the formation of Councils was to follow from the Africans' voluntary decisions, many Native Commissioners encouraged them to choose affirmatively.

The policy of the Government was to create no artificial unifications of territorial groupings. Southern Rhodesian chiefs were not transformed into heads of large "Native Authorities" (local governments) and equipped with Native Treasuries, as was done in other British colonies. Rather, the Government relied more upon demonstration and persuasion than upon legal compulsion to change the traditional structure of African society. In this process, the institution of chieftainship has been gradually transformed. The chiefs today are primarily concerned with symbolizing clan, tribal, and council unity, judging civil cases among Africans, performing ceremonies, and acting as executive agents of the Government. Although the chief's powers have changed, his commands are still "as constitutional as those of a modern parliament—in the sense that he takes for granted the whole social organization of which he is a part" (Mair, 1957:39).

Since the implementation of a revised Native Councils Act (1957), members of the Council are elected by the people. Native Commissioners become presidents of the Councils, and also, in the initial stages, chairmen, but they may be succeeded as chairmen by Africans when the councillors are deemed to be adequately trained in local government.[4] Chiefs are vice-presidents of the Councils, and all headmen in the area are included as members. By 1960, the idea of Councils had proved sufficiently popular for sixty-one of them to have been formed.[5]

Local rural government, Europeans felt, provided opportunities for

Africans to learn the procedures, financial implications, and values of British democracy.[6] The theory has been that, following a period of experience in local Councils, Africans should be allowed to broaden their participation until they can enter into full political partnership with Europeans at the territorial and Federal levels. In 1941, Provincial Assemblies of Chiefs were established to discuss common problems on the Reserves, but although they usually meet twice annually, it is doubtful that they are completely representative of African public opinion. On the other hand, neither Provincial Councils and electoral areas nor—the climax of this system—an African National Assembly, or Legislature, have been established to coordinate the activities of various local Councils. It seems clear that the present Government does not support such a pyramidal structure.

Southern Rhodesia's traditional policies have provided even fewer opportunities for political participation by Africans in urban areas. This was a logical consequence of the assumption that Africans were temporary sojourners. The extensive use of nonindigenous labor —usually unmarried or unattached males—required considerable governmental control and appeared to obviate an extension of political rights and responsibilities to urban Africans. The intentional drawing of municipal boundaries to exclude African residential areas, the practice of "tied" housing, and the restrictions placed upon the movement of Africans reflected the Europeans' intentions to direct and control urban growth and political activities. The separate European and African townships were linked economically and administratively, but politically the latter were subordinate to the former. Municipal governments traditionally resisted the idea that Africans should administer their own political affairs in urban areas. No attempt was made to bring tribal political structures into the urban context; hence the development of local government in urban African townships had to come through a newly created political organization.

With the increasing number of Africans who were becoming rather permanently urbanized in the late 1930's, and especially after World War II, the Europeans' complete control and management of African townships began to be examined, especially by Native Welfare Societies. Although these societies included more European than African members, they began to make recommendations to the Government for political, social, and economic changes. But it was not until 1951 that Africans were allowed to elect urban Advisory Councils.[7] These Councils were chaired by appointees of local (European) governments. In the following year, provisions were made that limited voting powers to persons who had resided continuously in the township for at least a year. Several extra-legal African trade unions and interest groups tried to introduce party politics into these elections, but the electorate remained very small. One writer attributes this to the system of migratory labor and the lack of home security for urban Africans, a condition incompatible with a sense of community.[8] Another reason for the lack of African participation might be that these Councils were assigned relatively unimportant duties and responsibilities. Not until 1959, for example, did the Salisbury City Council finally accept in principle that the African Advisory Councils could raise and spend money in their townships with fewer restrictions.[9] Recently, an Advisory Boards Congress has been formed, and they have demanded both greater responsibility for administering their own townships and for representation on Town Management Boards and City Councils.[10]

The right to vote, or to stand for election in the larger Municipal Councils, is confined to individuals who pay water or electricity rates. But since these rates are generally paid by their employers, most urban Africans are automatically ineligible. In 1959, some rate-paying Africans in Salisbury decided to test these regulations by attempting to register for the municipal elections. Their petition was not accepted by the town clerk, however, on the ground that although the area was administered by the Salisbury City Council, it lay outside the boundaries of the Municipality.[11]

Thus today none of the 175,000 Africans who reside in the Greater Salisbury area are eligible to participate directly in municipal government. The same situation is true in all of the other cities, towns, and villages in Southern Rhodesia. No African has ever stood for or been a member of a Municipal Council. In contrast to their growing participation in the governing of their own townships, Africans legally are still an undifferentiated mass of temporary visitors who need no franchise rights in the wider context of municipal politics.

Turning our attention to the Colony as a whole, Africans have shared the right to vote since 1898, when Southern Rhodesia introduced a single voters' roll modeled after that of the Colony of the Cape of Good Hope. The Orders-in-Council of 1894 and 1898 had proscribed "any conditions, disabilities, or restrictions which do not equally apply" to Europeans and Africans—except for liquor, arms and ammunition, and matters authorized by a Secretary of State. Although Cecil Rhodes had opposed the extension of the franchise to Africans in the Cape Colony (cf. Plomer, 1933), his view of "equal rights for every civilized man" (he was actually referring to Coloreds) was officially adopted in Southern Rhodesia by Proclamation No. 17 of 1898. Conflict immediately arose in the Legislative Council between the ideas of Cape liberalism and Dutch paternalism. The B. S. A. Administration, being sensitive to British opinion, had to steer a middle course to satisfy both the European immigrants and the Imperial Government. The 1898 Order-in-Council had provided for specific qualifications of property or income and the ability to write one's name, address, and occupation. In 1912, these were judged by Europeans to be too low, and higher qualifications were enacted.

When Self-Government was obtained in 1923, a Legislative Assembly of thirty members was introduced. Members were elected by a continuation of the common roll, even though Europeans widely advocated its discontinuance, being fearful of the presence of even a few Africans on the roll. No changes were made until 1944, however, when the qualifications were raised once more. These assured the Europeans of the protection they desired without the bad name of *apartheid* or white *baaskap,* an interpretation that would have been given overseas to the separate voters' rolls.[12] In 1951, the same reasons, and a sharp drop in the purchasing power of money, were important factors in raising the qualifications once again.

Then, in 1957, new legislation was enacted providing for higher and lower rolls. The requirements differed in terms of the amount of income, value of property owned, and/or education.[13] Whereas few Europeans have had difficulty fulfilling the conditions of the higher roll, most Africans have been able to meet only the lower set of qualifications. Even so, it has been estimated that only one-tenth of the Africans who have the necessary qualifications have taken the initiative to enroll. The law stipulates that when the number of voters on the lower roll reaches one-sixth that of the total electorate, it will be closed to further registrations, and the relevant clauses of the Act will be repealed. Thereafter, all future voters will have to meet the requirements for the higher roll.

The European fear of being "swamped" by the African voters (see *Rhodesia Herald,* 1900 to 1959) can be compared to the actual number of African voters in Southern Rhodesia: 51 in 1906, 139 in 1946, 560 in 1956, and 1,812 on both rolls prior to the last territorial election in 1958.[14] Paradoxically, Europeans fear that Africans will vote "racially," just as the former apparently have done from the first elections. Leys (1959) has argued that European politics in Southern Rhodesia have basically reflected a "one-party system." Although various political parties have existed, a majority of the electorate has preferred those that were ideologically and historically related. Inasmuch as these parties have agreed sufficiently upon fundamentals— i.e., maintaining dominance and control over Africans—no real opposition (from Africans) has existed in Parliament.

The Administration's attempts to nourish African local government in the rural areas has been conceived to be separate from African representation in the central government. The Government's decision not to provide a comprehensive political structure for articulating local African Councils with the central government has resulted in little opportunity for Africans to secure experience and training in public administration. Another factor has been the administrative division of former units of tribal government, a reversal of the normal process by which larger territorial units become politically organized and integrated. This policy has not been free from criticism in Southern Rhodesia as well as elsewhere.[15]

Immediately after World War II, the number of Africans interested in territorial politics began to increase. Many of them were journalists, teachers, and welfare workers, and they were politically active outside the traditional framework of African political organization. Earlier, an African National Congress had been formed though it became defunct in a few years. Then a Youth League began and, in 1957, a second Southern Rhodesian African National Congress was formed. The activities, roles, and responsibilities of the League and Congress were defined more by the Government and the social system of the country than by the Native Affairs Department or the traditional African political structure. The program with which they attracted followers was designed to bring about changes in urban areas— in housing, amenities, and allotted political responsibilities—to remove discrimination in public facilities, to resist the implementation of some provisions of the Land Husbandry Act, to replace the authority of the chiefs, and to change the provisions restricting their right to vote. Lord Hailey has commented on the African point of view in Southern Rhodesia:

> Their outlook is at the moment directed to securing an increase in the proportion of political representation now accorded to them. This, as they see it, can eventually be used by them to obtain a larger share in the social and other services provided by the State.[16]

African nationalists in Southern Rhodesia, like European nationalists, have aimed to obtain eventual independence from Great Britain. In contrast to the Europeans, however, Africans have argued that their great superiority in numbers demanded a larger absolute share in representation, and therefore control. Conflict with the Europeans and the Government was almost inevitable because, given a plural society, the final goal of African self-government the nationalists sought could not be extended to them (Coleman, 1955:251).

The Congress had no role in parliamentary affairs, but rather it was a pressure group seeking to influence the course of government.[17] It shared the characteristics of many congresses in Africa: loosely structured, aggressive, and claiming to represent all the people (Hodgkin, 1956:144). About a dozen Europeans joined the second Southern Rhodesia A. N. C., but their influence seems to have been small. In general, Europeans thought the movement and its leaders were too immature, inexperienced, and aggressive to undertake legislative and executive powers in the foreseeable future. Africans were expected to develop their political interests and to go through "the usual apprenticeship of democratic aspirants" within the constitutional and parliamentary framework of the country. Here, like Europeans, they would have their particular qualifications for assuming responsibility subjected to practical tests.[18]

The postwar growth of African nationalism was met with a strengthening of security legislation in Southern Rhodesia. In addition to the traditional measures of internal control—pass regulations, exclusion from compulsory military service, restrictions on firearms and alcoholic spirits, franchise regulations, and spatial segregation—Native Commissioners were given further powers over rural Africans. The police began to tighten their surveillance of African public meetings. Some Africans and Europeans were deported for their political activities; others found themselves unable to obtain passports, or were refused citizenship or admission to the country. New laws or amendments, some restrictive but others not, were enacted to deal with sedition, passes, liquor, firearms, public order, police powers, subversive activities, and African affairs.[19]

Books, magazines, and films judged to be dangerous either to the security of the country or to the moral standards of Africans were censored or prohibited. The Native Affairs Department stepped up a counter-propaganda drive to offset an increasing number of inflammatory speeches by Congress leaders. The newspapers of the Federation, which are almost totally owned and controlled by one firm, continued their traditional support of the governing party. Except for one weekly newssheet, and one newsletter on current affairs, no communication facilities were owned by Africans. Hence, the Government had little difficulty in gaining access to the mass media in its attempt to maintain public order and cooperation from all sections of the population.

These security measures are common to a number of countries, but their enactment in Southern Rhodesia reflected the concern of the European population with African political aggressiveness. The attempt of some Africans to improve their status, or to disregard the class-caste pattern by asserting political initiative, was sometimes thought of as mass "cheekiness." The enthusiasm of Congress leaders and the restrictions imposed by the Government eventually brought a climax to the clash of interests.

The critical turning point in Government policy came in 1958, when it initiated discussions about declaring a State of Emergency in terms of the Public Order Act of 1955. Since 1957, the Congress had reportedly used intimidation to increase its membership, to reduce and silence African opposition, and to generate an *élan vital* in the new, nontraditional organization. The Government believed, on evidence, that Congressmen were also inciting defiance of the law, abusing and ridiculing Government officials, and suborning the loyalty of Africans to the Government.[20] These reasons, combined with the Nyasaland disturbances, a strike for higher wages among African workers at the Kariba Dam, and a rumored general strike among Africans in Southern Rhodesia, were judged sufficient to warrant the declaration of a State of Emergency on February 26, 1959.[21]

Early on the morning of the 26th, with the gazetting of the Proclamation and other regulations, officials and active members of the Southern Rhodesian African National Congress, and of the branches of three other Congresses of Northern Rhodesia and Nyasaland, were arrested. A total of 510, including two African women and one European man, were placed in detention. Of this number, 311 persons were Southern Rhodesians. The State of Emergency lasted eighty-four days while the Legislative Assembly deliberated on new security legislation. A number of new Acts or amendments were passed, the principal ones being the Unlawful Organizations Act and the Preventive Detention (Temporary Provisions) Act.[22]

Under the provisions of the latter Act, each detainee's case was reviewed by a special Tribunal, but no trial was permitted. Upon the Tribunal's recommendations, the Governor then decided whether individuals should be released with or without restrictions. The remainder were liable to detention for the duration of the Act, five years, or longer if the Act were extended. The 199 Africans from Northern Rhodesia and Nyasaland were not the direct responsibility of the Southern Rhodesian Government. Prior to the final recommendations of the Review Tribunal, 286 Africans were released after inquiries, and 124 were repatriated to the two northern territories of the Federation. Thus 100 Africans were still in detention when the Tribunal began its sittings. The final recommendations of the Tribunal were made in October 1959. One African was deported to Bechuanaland, and another was permitted to leave the country with his family. Forty were recommended for continued detention in prison, while another 50 were to be restricted to a rural area where the Government had constructed special facilities for them. Eight were recommended for unconditional release.[23]

The growth of African nationalism, or "Africanism," in Southern Rhodesia is not only due to the high franchise qualifications and other political circumstances. It is also partly the product of African reading of the European press, and of the economic system created by the immigrants. The need for unskilled laborers resulted in a high rate of African labor mobility, and these movements in turn allowed for the development of political consciousness and loyalties among individuals of differing tribal and cultural backgrounds. Friendships and new organizational plans often resulted despite the continuation of strong tribal identities—as manifested in the incidence of fighting and quarreling reported by social workers, employers, policemen, and the newspapers.

The creation of the Federation of Rhodesia and Nyasaland also contributed to an increasing frequency of intertribal and interterritorial contacts between Africans. The growth of the various Congresses cannot be understood if this factor is ignored. Reports generally have stressed the widespread African opposition to the idea of Federation since the first exploratory discussion in 1951. Overt opposition in the two northern territories was so serious that it culminated in disturbances and hostilities in 1958 and 1959. A State of Emergency was also declared in Nyasaland after weeks of tension and conflict. Both in Nyasaland and Northern Rhodesia, specific Congresses were proscribed and their officials and leaders arrested and prosecuted.

A final topic to be discussed is the role of Africans in Federal politics. Unlike the dichotomy in local government and the limited restrictions in territorial political activities, the Federal Constitution of 1953 contained specific provisions for the participation of Africans in Parliament. Seventeen of the thirty-five seats were assigned to Southern Rhodesia. Three of these seventeen were to be filled by specially elected members to represent African interests, two of whom were to be Africans and one European. In 1957, the Constitution was amended to enlarge Parliament to fifty-nine members.[24] Twenty-nine were to come from Southern Rhodesia; of these, four Africans and one European were specially elected. Under the new law, as Clegg (1957:16–17) has observed, the proportion of seats in the Federal House "which purports to represent African interest remains as before, namely 25 per cent."

The franchise qualifications of the two Federal voters' rolls in Southern Rhodesia are similar to those in force for electing the territorial Legislative Assembly. Yet in spite of reserved African representation in the Federal Parliament, Africans have been slightly less enthusiastic about registering for Federal than for territorial elections. For the Federal election of 1958, only 1,014 and 628 Africans were registered on the general and special rolls in Southern Rhodesia, compared to 62,124 and 132 Europeans, respectively. Despite efforts made to step up the number of registrations, there were still only 1,212 Africans on the general roll and 974 on the special roll in August 1959.[25]

The Federal Constitution also established an African Affairs Board in Parliament whose main responsibility is to watch for legislation that might affect African interests. If the Board believes that any Bill differentiates against Africans disadvantageously, it can reserve the measure for assent by the Crown. The Board classed the Constitution

Amendment Bill and the Federal Electoral Bill as differentiating measures, but its objections to their enactment were not upheld in the British Parliament.[26] The Board today enjoys but limited support from Africans in the Federation, including those in Southern Rhodesia.

Steven-Hubbard (1955:259) has noted that the concept of "partnership," embodied in the Preamble to the Federal Constitution, "is sophisticated and Western-centred and has little meaning for any of the groups involved [and] . . . raises no enthusiasm from anybody, least of all from Africans." It may be questioned, however, whether partnership is simply "a desperate line of defence against the dangers perceived as a consequence of nationalism." Sociologically, it appears that Federation occurred prior to the emergence of three relatively well-integrated states. Most of the problems raised by the Federation are due to the absence of common loyalties among Europeans and Africans, and the fact that the decision was made without a positive consensus among the majority of the inhabitants. With the passage of time, Africans may change their aspirations and self-conceptions and come to accept Federation more fully. But the future of the experiment will depend largely on the choices made by Africans and Europeans to find a better modus vivendi.

To conclude, communication and political relations between Europeans and Africans in the early years were primarily confined to the Reserves. Later, a change in Government policy was expressed in a program of "parallel development." But dual administrative services and high franchise qualifications deterred the growth of a common set of values and loyalties upon which any stable political system must be founded. Local and central governmental institutions were not articulated, hence no central forum for debate and cooperation was established.[27] Yet the growth of political consciousness among Africans came naturally with increasing education, urbanization, industrialization, and population growth. The social and cultural changes in Southern Rhodesia since World War II have, in sum, had ramifications throughout the entire sphere of civil order and political control.

"Southern Rhodesia," says Sir Godfrey Huggins (1954:1), "has always maintained that the advancement of the Abantu would have to be on evolutionary lines and, therefore, comparatively slow." The current difficulties are largely due, however, to the fact that Africans in the territory are increasingly dissatisfied with this policy for their political enfranchisement. The decisions that will be made about the extension of the franchise are viewed by Lord Hailey (1958:5) and others as a fundamental test of "partnership." Population growth, urbanization, education, and the implementation of the Land Husbandry Act forecast an increasing number of Africans who will become qualified to vote. As more political sophistication develops among Africans, the Colony faces the problem of developing an acceptable party system that will enable all sections of the population to express and work for their interests.[28] Unless the present party structure is made sufficiently flexible in the future to encompass emergent African ambitions, the maintenance of loyalty and respect for the Government will be fraught with greater difficulties than in the past.*

There also remains the problem of working out a political system for the Colony and the Federation that satisfies the British Government as well as the various cultural groups in the country. Although many individuals and governmental officials criticize "interference from Whitehall," Europeans generally would be reluctant to minimize their allegiances to British parliamentary traditions and legal ideas. This is illustrated by their sensitivity to censures both inside and outside the United Nations by India, Ceylon, Egypt, Ghana, Guinea, and other ex-colonial or Commonwealth nations. International criticism of the Union of South Africa's policy of *apartheid* is, by inference, interpreted as applicable to Southern Rhodesia. Given their geographical location, Rhodesians are increasingly aware that their future in Africa will impose obligations to develop a society in which "partnership" is more than a theoretical moral ideal lacking practical application.

Sir Andrew Cohen (1959:38) has said that Britain's colonial policy has traditionally been one of reacting to situational pressures as they arise, and making one compromise after another to minimize or prevent civil disorder and hostilities. The use of specific timetables to assist the colonies toward self-government and independence has not been favored. In some measure, this approach also seems to have characterized the Southern Rhodesian Government's policy toward Africans. Many Africans in the Colony (and elsewhere in the Federation) are pressing for greater political rights and responsibilities, and timetables are often a part of their thinking. The members of the Monckton Commission and other officials reviewing the Federal Constitution in 1960 and 1961 have assumed responsibilities for the furtherance of efficient, adaptable, stable, and representative government that have rarely been duplicated in history.

### Contemporary Attitudes

From the evidence offered, it can be seen that the achievement and maintenance of civil order and political control are not restricted

* In the 1958 Federal election, for example, of 43,449 recorded votes in Southern Rhodesia, 6,134 ballot papers were rejected by returning officers. This was believed to be due principally to the high number of Europeans who deliberately invalidated their ballot papers by refusing to vote for an African candidate. *Rhodesia Herald.* (Nov. 14, 1958).

to voting power. The ballot box is not the only method of disturbing the tranquillity of society and the orderly progression of established government. Firearms can also be disturbing, particularly when they are in the hands of men who do not understand or believe in the constituted machinery of government. Again, alcoholic spirits can inflame the individual into acting rashly. Offenses against the peace are not viewed with equanimity by many people, and neither are political meetings that may lead to more serious consequences. Accordingly, we have considered it necessary to adopt a more catholic classification of political control than matters just concerned with franchise. We are aware that there can be disagreement with the classification, but, from the evidence, we are prepared to defend it as reasonable.

TABLE 71. *Statements Relating to Civil Order and Political Control*

| No. | Statement | −1 P.E. | +1 P.E. | Mean |
|---|---|---|---|---|
| 27 | African householders living in urban areas have no vote in municipal elections. | 1.10 | 3.88 | 2.49 |
| 20 | In general, Africans but not Europeans are forbidden by law to buy alcoholic spirits. | .70 | 3.48 | 2.09 |
| 25 | Pro-African 'nationalism' is viewed with more suspicion by much of the European community than is pro-European 'nationalism.' | .77 | 3.31 | 2.04 |
| 17 | African men are obliged by law to carry identity papers, whereas Europeans are not. | .46 | 2.94 | 1.70 |
| 24 | In Southern Rhodesia, Europeans control the election of Africans to the Federal Government, whereas the Africans have virtually no control over the election of Europeans. | .31 | 2.85 | 1.58 |
| 23 | The qualifications for the franchise are such that few Africans have a vote, whereas practically all Europeans are eligible. | .26 | 2.62 | 1.44 |
| 26 | In the Federal Parliament there are roughly four times as many European as African members, although the European population is about ⅛th the size of the African population. | .08 | 2.28 | 1.18 |
| 21 | Meetings held by African leaders are attended more often by the Police (C.I.D.) than similar meetings held by Europeans. | .10 | 1.96 | 1.03 |
| 12 | Africans are permitted to own or carry firearms only in very exceptional circumstances, while Europeans may do so with relatively fewer restrictions. | −.17 | 1.41 | .62 |
|  |  | .40 | 2.74 | 1.57 |

In Table 71, statements relating to civil order and political control are presented with their means and probable error limits. The first noticeable feature about the data is that all of the mean scores lend support to the status quo, to the maintenance of civil order and political control through the established mechanisms. The second feature relates to the considerable variation between the mean scores. It is clear that on some matters, such as extension of the African vote to municipal areas, the sample population does not feel strongly that current restrictions should be inviolate. But on the matter of firearms, few Europeans wish to see these in African hands—that would be tempting fate too far. Explicit reasons for keeping political control are revealed from the interview material; the implicit reasons are not always so easy to uncover.

*Statement 27* (M = 2.49) is the first that ventures into the controversial area of the franchise. At the moment, Africans who are bona fide payers of municipal rates (taxes) are not able to vote, although Europeans, Coloreds, and Asians may. This avenue of influencing municipal policy is not open to Africans, as we have shown. When we probe the European population, however, we discover that 41.6% advocate a change in the practice. The middle half of the distribution do not feel strongly either way on the matter, although the majority are just on the side of supporting the present system.

A small number doubt that there are any Africans who pay rates, and some disqualify them on grounds of political immaturity and insufficient education. Generally, however, the feeling is that "if they pay rates they should vote," although some qualify the sentiment by maintaining that "African householders should have some say in their own areas." But there is some doubt at both ends of the continuum about the wisdom of extending even the municipal vote.

One individual with a high social-change score expressed his opinion literately: "On matters concerning the franchise, government, etc., in spite of my moderately liberal views, I believe that the African as a whole is incapable of sustaining responsibility (everyone knows of notable exceptions), and therefore he must *not* be allowed to oust the European from positions of authority for a long time to come." Much the same reason is advanced by another individual who wishes to maintain the status quo. "Africans need to be trained and given equal civil rights—including the vote—in time, perhaps in ten to fifty years. But voting should not be the privilege of uncivilized people." Underlying many of the arguments is the fear that should the franchise be extended to municipal elections, it would increase the pressures for an extension at the territorial and Federal levels.

*Statement 20* (M = 2.09) distinguishes between Europeans who are permitted to buy alcoholic spirits and Africans who are not. In fact, Africans who are university graduates may buy spirits upon producing their diplomas or some equivalent evidence, but very few fall into this special category.

Two themes emerge from the interview material—the first concerned with protection for Africans and the second with preservation of public order. Much concern is expressed about the damaging influences of alcoholic spirits and the need to restrict their use: "The practice should be continued not because I think it desirable that there should be discrimination between the races, but because I believe the unrestricted sale of spirits to be undesirable. If it is restricted at present, this is probably to the advantage of the Africans." "Alcohol is an abomination and has destroyed the Red Indians in America and very nearly the Maoris [of New Zealand]; why encourage it?" "This is for their own protection." "It is bad enough that Africans are allowed to buy beer, let alone spirits, on an average salary of five pounds per month." These expressions are typical of many others.

Concern with public order is also implied in many of the arguments: "Many Africans become savage when they have consumed spirits." "Never let them have it [spirits] as they go crazy." "They have no limit and what will happen?" "Note their general reaction to their own brews." These two themes can be found in both the maintain and discontinue halves of the distribution, but the emphasis on public order is stronger among those who support the status quo.

*Statement 25* (M = 2.04) achieved particular significance in Southern Rhodesia when the Government, viewing with alarm the activities of the African National Congresses, declared a State of Emergency in February 1959, and proscribed these organizations. The Government's action is generally supported by the European population which, from our evidence, also observes with deep suspicion the vigorous pro-African nationalism that has arisen. This suspicion is undisguised in the interview material: "At the present time it is impossible not to view pro-African nationalism with greater suspicion." "After the riots in Nyasaland, it is no wonder!" "Pro-African nationalism is akin to Communism." "Africans are more susceptible to Russian broadcasts, outside influences, etc." "In view of the threat of communism, I feel that until the African people (the mass) have been educated, and hence been granted the power of positive thinking, political power should remain in the hands of responsible people, whether African or European."

Embedded in these comments, and others too, is the belief that African political agitation is inspired from outside, most likely by Russian communism. Nowhere in the argument is it accepted that African nationalism might be a logical consequence of social and political forces generated within Southern Rhodesia; the blame is primarily attributed to outsiders. Some individuals, perhaps with greater insight, state categorically that they view pro-African nationalism with unease because it is "dangerous to the existence of the White population." A few deplore both pro-European and pro-African nationalism on the ground that they destroy the possibility of future cooperation and "partnership" between the races.

*Statement 17* (M = 1.70) draws attention to the fact that African men are obliged by law to carry identity papers, whereas Europeans are not. The item evokes considerable comment, and only 21.4% vote to change the present system. A majority of the typical group stress the importance of maintaining civil order within Southern Rhodesia by means of political or administrative control over the African population. Let us examine a few of the typical comments:

"Identity papers are necessary for security reasons." "There are no other means of checking on the Africans." "This is necessary for administrative reasons." "There would be too many unqualified and lazy rural Africans wandering in [to the urban areas] if this were changed now." "Because we are the minority, there must be some check." "Necessary, or else the Government will have no control over the Africans." "They usually have no fixed address and cannot be found if they have committed a crime." "I imagine that for rural Africans some form of identification would counteract any feelings of bewilderment and confusion in themselves, and be an aid to police direction." Further comments are proffered in different wordings but with the same theme of control and regulation.

A small percentage of the sample invoke the principle of equity: "Europeans must enter the Colony on passports, Africans can just walk in." "Europeans have to produce identification references, birth certificates, X-ray plates, etc., before entering the country." "It is easier to identify a European without papers." "Most Europeans have passports. Also, the local police have a tab on each of us. Every detail concerning us is just as carefully recorded; more so."

Others still feel that identity papers are of definite help to the African: "It gives them protection in many respects, particularly those who have difficulties in reading and writing, or in making themselves understood." "It is necessary for Africans to have some means of identification for their own protection, as much as for any other reason."

The reasons we have given as illustrations are the main ones; and dominant among them in frequency and emphasis is the idea that, for the public good, careful surveillance of the African population must be maintained.

*Statement 24* (M = 1.58) shows a significant loading on the political control dimension of the factor analysis. Under the present Constitution, five Southern Rhodesians have been elected to the Federal Parliament to represent African interests, and four of these are Africans. The Africans are elected from two voters' rolls, the general and the special. The general roll, which is much the larger, is comprised mainly of Europeans who can meet the specified qualifications;

the special roll, which is small even though it requires lower qualifications, is overwhelmingly African. Any African who stands for election in one of the special constituencies of Southern Rhodesia must receive the support of the European voters if he wishes to take a seat in the House. Hence the controlling influence of the Europeans mentioned in statement 24. It is true that Africans on the general roll can also vote for any person who stands for a general constituency, but there are too few African voters to have much bearing on the result.

It must be noted that a considerable number of our respondents do not fully grasp this statement until the electoral machinery is explained to them. As the mean and probable error limits reveal, the population is firmly opposed to any relaxation of European control. But most of the representative group concede that change is inevitable in the future. As might be expected, "the future" means different periods of time to different people. "This should disappear with the abolition of racial representation." "This should be maintained for the present." "The law on the subject seems fair and the position will correct itself." "As the Africans advance, control by race will disappear." "The African generally is still very primitive and looks to the European for guidance." "Until there are more responsible Africans, it must stay this way—it will take two generations." These are typical arguments.

A few persons advocate an immediate revision of the franchise laws so that Africans can elect their representatives uninfluenced by the European vote, while another group feels that the African advance to political maturity will be so slow that the present system may have to remain indefinitely. However, the bulk of the sample foresees change ahead, but not now. In a sense, theirs is a philosophy that votes should be weighed, not counted. With superior education, experience, mental maturity, and sense of responsibility, the Europeans consider it natural that their votes should count for more.

*Statement 23* ($M = 1.44$) examines an effect of the franchise regulations: "The qualifications for the franchise are such that few Africans have a vote, whereas practically all Europeans are eligible." Even greater support is given to this practice than to the last one. Overwhelmingly the sentiment is against any lowering of "European standards" and many insist that the franchise qualifications are too low already: "The African has to rise to the standard of education of the European, and it is not for the European to drop to his low standard." "In most cases I don't think that the African is ready to vote yet. If they have sufficient schooling and are able to think for themselves, then yes, but not as long as they behave like a lot of sheep." "If anything, qualifications should be made stiffer to disfranchise many poor quality whites." "The majority of natives are not yet ready to vote."

Some go beyond an insistence on adequate standards to analyze what might happen if they were lowered: "If this were not so, Africans would rule the country and the Whites would be ousted." "Europeans must remain dominant." "We would lose our country if they had our vote." Such apprehensions as these may well be more pervasive than the overt expressions indicate.

*Statement 26* (M = 1.18) is another of the three statements that emerged on the political control dimension of the factor analysis. In the statement, we observe that although the European population is but a fraction of the African population, there are roughly four times as many Europeans elected or appointed to the Federal House. With a predominantly European electorate it can hardly be otherwise, and from the scores and arguments given, Europeans think that the situation should be maintained, at least for the foreseeable future.

Very few dissent from the opinion that "universal adult franchise would be quite impractical at present." It is stressed time and again that Africans are not educated or mature enough to undertake a controlling role in affairs of state. But although few wish to tamper with the status quo, a genuine difference can be observed between individuals whose general attitudes are on the side of social change and those whose attitudes are not.

With the first group, it is argued that change will and should take place in the future: "Until such time as there are more educated and responsible Africans, I think this should be maintained." "This is not a permanent state of affairs." "This should continue until the African is able to run the country on democratic lines." "This will be eradicated in the course of time. It is essential that Government remains in responsible hands." "The ratio will alter as the African becomes more civilized." Such responses are typical of individuals who support the status quo on this item, but who speak in favor of eliminating a majority of the other differentiating practices.

When we turn to the group which wishes to maintain this practice, and most of the others as well, qualitative differences in response can be detected: "If people like 'Banda,' etc. are examples of educated Natives, it is just as well." "We still hope to retain a white Rhodesia." "The native will not work for the European interest as does the European for the native." "The majority of Africans are irresponsible." "The African has not $\frac{1}{28}$th the amount of civilization behind him that the European has." "When the Africans are qualified to vote properly, they can elect more members." In these and other responses typical of the group, little reference is made to the leavening influences of education and economic development. The notion that Africans might play an increasingly significant role in the political life of the Federation is not seriously (or openly) entertained.

*Statement 21* (M = 1.03) was particularly relevant during the events that led to the proclaimed Emergency in the Colony. With the growing aggressiveness of the African National Congresses, there were few political meetings held by African leaders unattended by the police. Transcripts of speeches were obtained, and notes were taken of those who attended either as participants or observers. That the Europeans regard this surveillance as imperative is clear from our records:

"This is necessary until incitement to sedition and violence is eradicated." "It is essential for the police to know what is happening for security reasons." "Necessary because most political meetings are conducted by fanatics who are seeking power." "Attendance by the police is not simply because the leaders are African, but because they may be subversive. The police protect the public present from injury by possible riotous behavior." "The activities of the African National Congress made this necessary." "Africans are easily incited." There is little deviation from responses of this nature. It is clear that Europeans regard the African National Congresses as particular threats to public order, even to the security of the state, and therefore it is logical that the police should keep a close watch on their activities.

*Statement 12* (M = .62) is one of the most strongly supported on the questionnaire. In the interests of security it is essential that Europeans should be permitted firearms, but that Africans should not. This is the dominant theme in most of the responses. "In view of the present emergency I think this practice should be continued for the security of society." "Africans cannot be trusted with firearms."

Some insist that Europeans carry guns because of their great love for hunting, but this argument is not supported by other responses to the statement. Neither is the argument that the only reason for which Africans are forbidden firearms is because they will indiscriminately shoot down wild game. Some insist, however, that although firearms may be necessary for security reasons, far too many Europeans already possess them. They should be subjected to much more stringent control than is exercised at present because their indiscriminate use can also imperil the peace and security of Southern Rhodesian society.

## THE SAMPLE CHARACTERISTICS

These are the attitudes of Europeans toward matters of civil order and political control, and the methods by which they hope to maintain them. The sample is against change at the moment, but generally appreciates that it will come in time. When it does, it must be through proper educational processes, achievement of European standards, acceptance of the established method of government, and conformity with constitutional methods of changing governments. Europeans are generally agreed that to allow political control to pass out of their hands at this time would be reckless folly.

It has been observed that while the European population generally speaks with one voice, dissenting notes can be heard. The areas into which these fall can be identified from a breakdown of the social characteristics of the population. Table 72 presents the relevant data for this task.

COUNTRY OF BIRTH

The majority of no subdivision wish to change any of the practices of the category, although individuals born in the United Kingdom approach it in two instances. Nearly 50% of them are in favor of extending the municipal vote to African householders ($M = 2.95$), and about 40% feel that Africans should be permitted to buy spirits ($M = 2.47$). This latter mean stands in sharp contrast to the attitude of those born in South Africa ($M = 1.56$). It is of interest that individuals born in the United Kingdom express themselves more strongly than any others in the analysis against permitting Africans to carry arms.

Of the three groups selected for further analysis, the South African-born are most strongly on the side of the status quo; the Rhodesians show much the same attitude, while persons from the United Kingdom support it least strongly. Even so, all groups fall significantly on the maintain side of the continuum.

NATIONAL OR ETHNIC ORIGIN

While there are substantial differences in attitude between the English and the Afrikaners in other analyses, on the subject of civil order and political control the difference (.54) is small. Throughout the analysis of this category, Afrikaners return a more conservative score except on firearms. Here the roles are reversed, with the English taking a more conservative stand than the Afrikaners. As before, we have no empirical data to support a hypothesis on the matter.

The Scottish attitudes are nearly identical with the English, while the puzzling aggregate of British-Welsh-Irish once again displays the least conservative score. It may be worth observing that Afrikaners express less concern about pro-African nationalism than about any of the other forms of behavior. This may stem from their longer contact with Africans, their more extensive experience of other nationalistic movements, and greater confidence in their ability to contain them.

TABLE 72. *Scores Relating to Civil Order and Political Control*
($M = 1.57$)

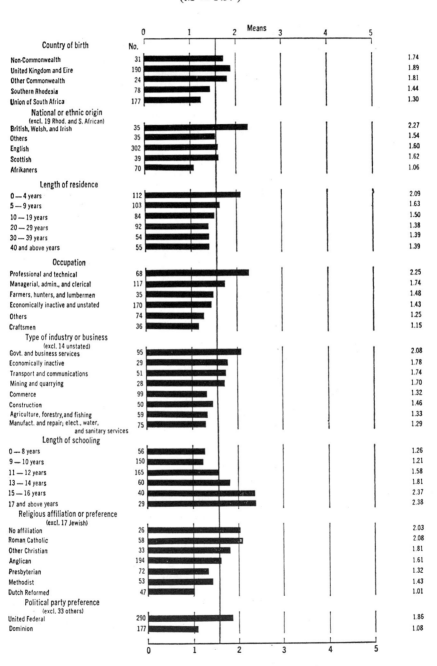

| | No. | Mean |
|---|---|---|
| **Country of birth** | | |
| Non-Commonwealth | 31 | 1.74 |
| United Kingdom and Eire | 190 | 1.89 |
| Other Commonwealth | 24 | 1.81 |
| Southern Rhodesia | 78 | 1.44 |
| Union of South Africa | 177 | 1.30 |
| **National or ethnic origin** (excl. 19 Rhod. and S. African) | | |
| British, Welsh, and Irish | 35 | 2.27 |
| Others | 35 | 1.54 |
| English | 302 | 1.60 |
| Scottish | 39 | 1.62 |
| Afrikaners | 70 | 1.06 |
| **Length of residence** | | |
| 0 — 4 years | 112 | 2.09 |
| 5 — 9 years | 103 | 1.63 |
| 10 — 19 years | 84 | 1.50 |
| 20 — 29 years | 92 | 1.38 |
| 30 — 39 years | 54 | 1.39 |
| 40 and above years | 55 | 1.39 |
| **Occupation** | | |
| Professional and technical | 68 | 2.25 |
| Managerial, admin., and clerical | 117 | 1.74 |
| Farmers, hunters, and lumbermen | 35 | 1.48 |
| Economically inactive and unstated | 170 | 1.43 |
| Others | 74 | 1.25 |
| Craftsmen | 36 | 1.15 |
| **Type of industry or business** (excl. 14 unstated) | | |
| Govt. and business services | 95 | 2.08 |
| Economically inactive | 29 | 1.78 |
| Transport and communications | 51 | 1.74 |
| Mining and quarrying | 28 | 1.70 |
| Commerce | 99 | 1.32 |
| Construction | 50 | 1.46 |
| Agriculture, forestry, and fishing | 59 | 1.33 |
| Manufact. and repair; elect., water, and sanitary services | 75 | 1.29 |
| **Length of schooling** | | |
| 0 — 8 years | 56 | 1.26 |
| 9 — 10 years | 150 | 1.21 |
| 11 — 12 years | 165 | 1.58 |
| 13 — 14 years | 60 | 1.81 |
| 15 — 16 years | 40 | 2.37 |
| 17 and above years | 29 | 2.38 |
| **Religious affiliation or preference** (excl. 17 Jewish) | | |
| No affiliation | 26 | 2.03 |
| Roman Catholic | 58 | 2.08 |
| Other Christian | 33 | 1.81 |
| Anglican | 194 | 1.61 |
| Presbyterian | 72 | 1.32 |
| Methodist | 53 | 1.43 |
| Dutch Reformed | 47 | 1.01 |
| **Political party preference** (excl. 33 others) | | |
| United Federal | 290 | 1.86 |
| Dominion | 177 | 1.08 |

LENGTH OF RESIDENCE

As in the other analyses, the least conservative individuals are those who have been in the Colony for the shortest time. But whereas on the other categories it takes thirty and sometimes forty years before the most conservative attitudes are reached, in the category of political control the lowest scores are reached after twenty years. There are practically no variations in attitude with further lengths of residence. Among the newest (0–4 years) immigrants, six of the item scores are greater than 2.00, whereas no other subpopulation contains more than two of this magnitude. As we have remarked before, the movements of change within the community receive most support from those who have lived in this part of Africa for the shortest period of time.

OCCUPATION

The two most disparate occupational groups are the professional-technical class and the craftsmen. Both are on the side of the status quo, but whereas the former exhibit seven scores greater than 2.00, the craftsmen display none. Indeed, more than half of the professional and technical persons contend that African householders should be given the vote in municipal elections (M = 3.29). Even at the territorial level, nearly 40% advocate a modification of the present electoral system, a further relaxation of the requirements for the vote, and an increase in African representation. The craftsmen, on the other hand, entertain no such ideas; neither do the farmers, the economically inactive, or other skilled and sales workers. We interpret the attitude of the professional and technical people as a reflection of superior education, economic status, and security; such an hypothesis is consistent with our other evidence.

TYPE OF INDUSTRY OR BUSINESS

More than 50% of the service classification are in favor of extending the municipal vote to Africans, and over 30% argue for changes in the franchise at the territorial and Federal levels. As in the last chapter, individuals in government and business show the least conservative scores and the greatest willingness to tolerate change. With their superior socioeconomic background, this is as we would predict.

Three industrial groupings come out at very much the same attitudinal level—those in commerce, agriculture, and manufacturing. They support the status quo on all items, least strongly on the municipal franchise and alcoholic spirits and most strongly on firearms.

EDUCATION

The relationship between education and racial attitude is apparent when civil order and political control are examined. Those with the least amount of schooling—ten years and less—are most concerned that the established order should not be upset. Such attitudes are not difficult to understand. It is partly because of education that Africans are entering employment in areas closed to them a few years ago. Education is perceived as the key to the future. But if this is so for the African people, it is hardly less so for the Europeans. The competitive position of the Europeans will become less enviable if their education, or capacity to benefit from it, is slight. Thus, if Europeans lose political control in Southern Rhodesia, they will perhaps not receive much protection from the Africans. But the highly educated Europeans can view the situation with greater equanimity. Even with a substantial shift in political power within the Colony, any threat to their security is more likely to be remote than immediate. It seems that this disparity in bargaining power is mirrored in the variations in attitude at different educational levels.

RELIGIOUS AFFILIATION OR PREFERENCE

A majority of the Catholics favor giving African rate-payers a vote in municipal elections, but none of the other religious groups follow suit. Supporters of the Dutch Reformed church are opposed to an extension of the vote at either the municipal, territorial, or Federal levels, and to any alteration in the modes of African representation. On statements 23, 24, and 26, which deal with franchise beyond the local level, the mean attitude of the Dutch Reformed (.78) is more conservative than that of any other subpopulation.

Between the limits demarcated by the Catholics and the Dutch Reformed, supporters of the other denominations generally take their positions. The Anglicans lie closer to the Catholics in their attitude toward civil order and political control, while the Presbyterians and Methodists lie closer to the Dutch Reformed. Taking the category as a whole, a majority in all the religious groupings support the established political system, and its continuation for some time to come.

POLITICAL PARTY PREFERENCE

A clear difference emerges between the attitudes of the supporters of the two major political parties. Those who favor the Dominion party are, without exception, more conservative on every item than those who prefer the Federal party. This fact is displayed in Table 73. Some of the differences are striking and although both parties

TABLE 73. *Mean Attitude Scores about Civil Order and Political Control, by Political Party Preference*

| No. | Area of differentiation | D.P. | U.F.P. |
|---|---|---|---|
| 27 | Municipal franchise | 1.65 | 2.99 |
| 20 | Purchase of alcoholic spirits | 1.42 | 2.49 |
| 25 | Reaction to African and European "nationalism" | 1.63 | 2.26 |
| 17 | Carrying identity papers | 1.37 | 1.97 |
| 24 | Control of election to the Federal Parliament | .84 | 2.01 |
| 23 | Effect of the franchise qualifications | 1.01 | 1.69 |
| 26 | Number of representatives in the Federal Parliament | .53 | 1.53 |
| 21 | Attendance of police at (political) meetings | .84 | 1.08 |
| 12 | Owning or carrying firearms | .45 | .68 |
|  | Means | 1.08 | 1.86 |

stand for the status quo, individuals who prefer the Federal party support the discontinuance of these practices much more frequently. About 50% of them advocate an extension of the municipal franchise to African rate-payers, and their attitudes about the territorial and Federal franchise are significantly more flexible. It is only on police attendance at African political meetings, and the possession of firearms, that the two parties come close together.

## THE PRINCIPAL THEMES

All societies, if they are to persist, protect themselves from internal disorder and external threats. In Southern Rhodesia, because of the protecting shield of the Imperial Government, there has been no direct threat to the safety of the territory from outside. Southern Rhodesian history reveals that more thought has been given to protecting the State from threats within its borders. An efficient police force has been developed with the power to nip in the bud any movement that seems likely to challenge the established political system by unconstitutional means. A close watch is kept on militant African organizations, and the possession of firearms is carefully regulated. It is argued that such measures are as necessary for the safety of the African people as for the smaller European population. If Africans possessed firearms on any scale, it is felt that they might be used to bolster the power of a pressure group such as the African National Congress. It may be assumed that even if the head of every household in Britain possessed a rifle, these would not be used to menace the security of the State; the political system is too well established and respected for this to happen readily. But few Europeans in Southern Rhodesia would be prepared to make a like assumption if arms were in the hands of the African population. Similarly, both races must be protected from the possible consequences of Africans consuming alcohol.

Both our historical and empirical data suggest that these measures are aimed at securing the State, and preserving the ballot box as the legitimate method of changing the political order. Africans are to be brought into the established system as they attain the franchise qualifications, and thereby the balance of power will shift slowly over the years. Our evidence suggests that this is appreciated by the majority of Europeans, but it is never more than a small minority who advocate political change here and now. Nearest to change is the sentiment that African rate-payers living in the urban areas should have some direct voice in municipal government. But even though such an extension of the municipal franchise will not have a direct influence on elections at the territorial and Federal levels, there is concern that Africans may not vote responsibly.

African agitation for increased political power is viewed with considerable suspicion. This ferment is believed to be inspired largely from outside by the expansionist doctrines of international communism. The reasons given are significantly extra-punitive; the internal methods of civil and political control are not blamed for the increasing pressures, and neither are the forces of education and economic development. Accordingly, it is felt to be most important that Europeans should have some say in, if not control over, the election of Africans to the Federal Parliament. Similarly, the franchise qualifications must be kept high because "the untutored Africans" cannot be expected to use their votes wisely or nonracially. And more important still, it is felt that to increase substantially African representation in Parliament would be to place the future security of the European population in jeopardy. Whatever the stated aims of the governing party of Southern Rhodesia, the people who have placed them in power believe these things to be true.

Power and consensus are necessary for protection. With an African majority in Parliament, it is unlikely that the social system would remain unaltered. Territorial segregation, separate educational and public facilities, and limited opportunities within industry and commerce might well be swept away. Thus, changes in the system of civil and political control, if they are to be countenanced, must be gradual and reserved mainly for the future. It seems to us that although few Europeans have heard of it, and fewer still have read it, the main theme in their attitudes is inscribed on the base of a statue to Kwame Nkrumah in Accra: "Seek ye first the political kingdom, and all things shall be added unto it."

# 16

## SOCIAL AND RECREATIONAL FACILITIES

In previous chapters we have noted the infrequent occasions, aside from occupational activities, in which Europeans and Africans have associated together. On the bases of land apportionment and cultural differences, separate farming and residential areas were developed; these in turn fostered a system of deferential behavior toward Europeans and the emergence of a number of public facilities and services that bifurcated the total society. The desire to minimize social contact with Africans was most evident in the use of restaurants, cinemas, theaters, swimming pools, dance halls, hotels, and sporting and social clubs.

Restrictions on access to social and recreational facilities are not unique to Southern Rhodesia. Virtually every society has a number of places that may be used or visited by only a restricted segment of the population. These include churches, temples, the Holy of Holies, social clubs, sites for initiation rites, abodes of ancestral spirits, chiefs' homes and kings' palaces, lovers' rendezvous, women's menstruation huts, men's sweat lodges, and the hideouts of children's play groups. In places where exclusive membership or association occur, participation is usually selective or voluntary. Recreational and "socializing" facilities are, by definition, places where people may relax, seek the warmth and pleasure of close emotional ties, and act more informally

than is often possible elsewhere. Play and recreation provide a thera-
peutic function by permitting the release of tensions, hostilities, and
aggressions generated in the ordinary daily affairs of life. Greater
solidarity and cooperation may also be encouraged through such
activities. The beginnings of personal friendships, sometimes even
leading to marriages, are often made in this relaxed atmosphere.

It is not surprising then, since Europeans and Africans in Southern
Rhodesia have traditionally shared few social interests, that European
social and recreational facilities have not been open to Africans. Intimate groups that share tacit understandings seldom welcome in-
truders and uninvited guests, but not all of them have the sanction
of law to maintain their exclusiveness and intimacy. In Southern
Rhodesia, we have noted, the choice to avoid social contact with
Africans resulted from mixed motives: maintaining "standards,"
protecting personal health, and minimizing opportunities for contacts
that might lead to sexual relations between African men and European
women.

In Southern Rhodesia, individual municipalities have the power to
control the kinds of audiences in town halls, theaters, and cinemas,
and admission to hotels, restaurants, and swimming pools. The admission of Africans to some of these facilities is prohibited by regulations
or by-laws, but in other cases the decision rests with the individual
proprietor and manager. Several municipalities have by-laws that
require separate lavatories for Europeans, for Africans, and for Asians
and Coloreds. Local authorities have used these by-laws to discourage
or prevent interracial gatherings, since few places have, or could
afford to build, three sets of lavatories. This question was debated by
Parliament in 1959 after the municipalities were asked to submit a list
of their by-laws containing discriminatory clauses.

European public opinion has been sufficiently strong during most
of Southern Rhodesia's history to preclude any substantial modification of the way people traditionally made use of their social and
recreational facilities. For many years, however, a small minority
of Europeans have inaugurated and encouraged the growth of voluntary interest groups that include both Europeans and Africans, though
the number of such associations is small compared to the hundreds
whose membership is exclusively European or African. Included are
women's groups organized by various missions, and the homecraft
clubs started by the wives of Native Commissioners and their colleagues. Several interracial African Welfare Societies,[1] and activities
sponsored by the Women's Institutes, Boy Scouts, League of Student
Parliamentarians, and other associations, also bring Africans and
Europeans into contact with one another. The number of educational,
religious, political, and labor union conferences open to all seems
to have steadily increased. A handful of interracial social clubs and

associations have also appeared, some lasting only a relatively short period of time.*

For several years, the Federal Art Gallery and some museums have admitted all visitors. One or two libraries are considering making the same move. Non-European visitors from outside the Federation may now be lodged in "European" hotels.† In 1959, a few theaters and cinemas began to accept Asian, Colored and, less frequently, African patrons.‡ Two Salisbury night clubs employed Africans as entertainers for their European audiences. One cafe in Salisbury began serving meals to both Europeans and Africans at different prices and in divided sections of the room. A number of private dances and parties have been attended by Europeans, Africans, Asians, and Coloreds, and although criticized by some people, no legal sanctions were applied. Asians and Coloreds succeeded in getting a circus company to eliminate its policy of discriminatory admissions. Thus far, no joint sharing of public swimming pools or attendance at public dance halls has taken place, although they have not been legally proscribed in all municipalities.

The system by which social and recreational facilities have been used in Southern Rhodesia appears to be undergoing some modification. Not many Europeans would traditionally have approved the degree of social contact that has occurred in the past few years. They believed it was necessary to keep a wide "social distance" between the two culture groups "to prevent integration from coming about." To be seen mixing socially with Africans was a symbol of abnormality; and, as for the African, he was simply being insolent or "cheeky." Whether the current trends of voluntary social contact between Europeans and Africans will continue, and at what pace, depends not only upon the wishes of the two culture groups in Southern Rhodesia, but also upon the opinions and actions of people outside the territory.

* The Land Apportionment Amendment Act, No. 51 of 1954, allows interracial clubs to use land in European or African areas, with the consent of the local authority, if the members confine their activities to religious, welfare, or "cultural" activities.

† Also permitted by the Land Apportionment Amendment Act, No. 51 of 1954. Another amendment, Act 12 of 1959, allows the Government to grant permission, upon application and if certain conditions are met, for a hotel in a European area to provide accommodation to an African. As of early 1960, other changes in regard to the use of hotels, restaurants, and other facilities seemed probable in the near future.

‡ Films are censored in Southern Rhodesia, and are subject to approval for African viewers. The judgments of the analogous board in the Union of South Africa are often accepted ipso facto. This procedure was attacked in 1959 (*Rhodesia Herald*, Oct. 30, 1959) by the Director of Native Administration for the municipality of Salisbury. In 1960, a committee was appointed to review the entire question of film censorship.

## CONTEMPORARY ATTITUDES

It is hardly practicable to include for specific study all the separate social and recreational facilities established in Southern Rhodesia. However, we do feel that an adequate sample of European attitudes can be obtained by including in the scale those facilities that come under periodic scrutiny in the press. Any mention in the press, particularly by an outsider, that perhaps Africans should be allowed into restaurants, hotels, theaters, or public swimming pools is sufficient to draw fire in the "Letters to the Editor" on the folly of such action. Such correspondence was found helpful in determining areas in which European opinion is particularly sensitive to change in the status quo. The areas selected are reproduced in Table 74.

TABLE 74. *Statements Relating to Social and Recreational Facilities*

| No. | Statement | −1 P.E. | +1 P.E. | Mean |
|-----|-----------|---------|---------|------|
| 46 | Many European restaurants and hotels will not accept African clients. | .41 | 3.01 | 1.71 |
| 45 | European sporting and social clubs are not open to Africans. | .33 | 2.83 | 1.58 |
| 48 | Africans generally are not allowed into European theatres. | .25 | 2.79 | 1.52 |
| 59 | Africans are refused admission to European dance halls. | −.27 | 1.41 | .57 |
| 43 | Africans and Europeans are not permitted to use the same public swimming baths. | −.38 | 1.30 | .46 |
|  |  | .07 | 2.27 | 1.17 |

The first noticeable feature is that separation in social and recreational activities is even more strongly supported than is the present mechanism of ensuring civil order and political control. It is our hypothesis that this stems from the more intimate nature of social activities, from the fact that women and children may be present in situations where social barriers are likely to be relaxed. In addition, matters of hygiene assume considerable importance, as we shall see from a study of the interview material.

The mean attitudes of Table 74 are all on the side of the status quo, none more strongly than those on the separation of public swimming pools. All of the distributions to these five statements are strongly skewed, with only a small, unrepresentative number advocating the partial or total integration of social facilities. The probable error limits give some idea of how skewed the distributions are.

*Statement 46* (M = 1.71) has been subjected to the clash of debate in the Federal and territorial parliaments, in municipal councils, and in the press. At the moment there are very few hotels and restaurants—European by tradition—where Africans can receive service, although special arrangements are made on occasion to accommodate visiting American Negroes or prominent Africans from other territories. This state of affairs has been of concern to Governments in the past, and with the formation of the Federation of Rhodesia and Nyasaland it is certain to be of considerable embarrassment in the future if change is not effected. Hotel proprietors can point with truth to a decline in their trade when non-Europeans have been accepted as clients. After all, they insist, they are in the trade to make money rather than to implement the Constitution's stated philosophy of "partnership." An added financial burden is the municipal requirement of separate toilet facilities for different races. But the Federation looks forward to international trade fairs, the Empire games, cultural festivals, and the like, and it will be difficult to hold these without modification of the present restrictive system.

The problems are appreciated by some of the European population, and their sentiment is to retain the status quo but to make exceptions when the need arises. "Maintain, with exceptions in special cases." "I feel that exceptions should be made for the few Africans who are on an equal social, educational, and cultural standard with the European." Others who also are within the typical range make no special provision for the exceptional cases that arise at the present time, but feel the situation will rectify itself in the future. "This is essential until Africans have reached European standards." "Progress has got to be a long and slow process, and is best left to the individual European, not the politician or the church." "This is being gradually adjusted."

Still others are not prepared to envisage the sharing of facilities now or later. "Why not build their own restaurants and hotels?" "Facilities should be given to the native in the native areas." "This is a matter of hygiene. Let the European have *something* of his own." And so on. At the social-change end of the dimension are a number who contend that economics will control the situation, and that only Africans who enjoy European standards of living will be able to avail themselves of hotel and restaurant services. Economics plus the "right of admission" will ensure that proper standards of conduct and hygiene are maintained. These opinions, however, are outweighed by the other points of view.

*Statement 45* (M = 1.58) applies to clubs of various kinds where membership is generally associated with sporting activities and the social occasions that go with them. European Rhodesians are sportsminded people; and although we have no figures to support us, we would hazard a guess that there are as many, if not more, sports clubs than in other communities of comparable size.

The attitude about the admission of Africans to such clubs is clear and unequivocal: "I strongly oppose legislation to enforce the opening of clubs to all races. Clubs are not public places and members should be free to make their own rules about admission." "Private clubs have a right to restrict membership—they do among Europeans." "Jewish clubs are not open to the non-Jewish."

A number make a distinction between the sports and the social sides of a club, and are prepared to share the former but not the latter: "I would like to compete with Africans at sport, but not socially." "Africans should be allowed to compete in sports, but I wouldn't fancy belonging to the same club and sharing facilities."

As in the case of statement 46, it is vigorously stressed within the typical group that Africans should have their own clubs: "The African would feel more at home in his own social and sporting clubs." "Natives could and should develop their own recreations." "Let them have their own clubs in their own townships." Health and hygiene do not go unmentioned as reasons for exclusive membership.

It is significant that not one of our respondents mentions the possibility of cross-racial sexual contact as a reason for restricting membership to Europeans. Yet the factor analysis of data showed that a sexual component was significantly embedded in this item. Men take their wives along to the sports club, and bachelors invite their girl friends and fiancees. Consequently even the remotest possibility of sexual interest or contact with Africans must be proscribed.

*Statement 48* ($M = 1.52$) makes specific mention of European theaters, and the term is interpreted to mean both the live theater and the cinema—or bioscope, as it is often called in Rhodesia. As the enumerative data depict, the general attitude of the community is against the admission of Africans, and the central reason offered is protection from contagion. A few consider that separate seating will provide the protection, but for most respondents such a division is inadequate. A further danger is that Africans might see plays or films that are "unsuitable," and this can be avoided if they are kept to their own places of entertainment.

Although we have not probed the matter specifically, it is likely that Europeans carry different attitudes toward the admission of Africans to the drive-in cinema. Four of these in the two main cities admit anyone as long as the board of censors has not ruled to the contrary. There is little possibility of cross-racial contact while sitting in a car; on our evidence, this would account for the more permissive attitude toward the attendance of Africans.

*Statement 59* ($M = .57$) conjures up emotions of considerable intensity. It is rare indeed for Africans and Europeans to attend the same dances, although in some nonracial institutions—the University, one or two political parties, some mission stations—it is regarded

as a violation of principle to segregate Africans and Europeans. But
there is no mistaking the general attitude of the sample.

"In the present social climate in this country there is no alternative." "Uneducated Africans associate dancing with sex, and are
therefore likely to form the wrong opinion of the female European
dancers and act accordingly." "Never admit them. The native does
not take a woman out unless he intends to have intercourse with
her." "In general it would be against their own inclinations and the
traditions of their people to wish to do so." "Dancing is closely associated with sex. They naturally think that the same applies to European
dancing." "What decent European girl would like to dance with a
black?" These are but a few of the responses that illustrate the European abhorrence of any form of association that may lead to intimacy
with Africans. A few others, while wishing to maintain the restrictions, feel that some exceptions might be made. "I think that an
exception should be made for an African who educationally, socially,
and culturally is equal to the European—at the moment, few."
"There are no European dance halls here. There are restaurants for
dining and dancing. An African's admission to these should depend
on his general appearance and behavior, rather than on the color of
his skin. I think it is correct to say that most restaurant managers
have the authority to 'throw-out' anyone, black or white, if his
behavior does not come up to standard."

Summing up, the European population insists that it is clearly undesirable to allow any mixing with Africans at dances. Should this
happen it might expose the participants, particularly the women, to
sexual temptations, and these are to be strongly deplored.

*Statement 43* ($M = .46$) evokes even stronger sentiments than
the one on dancing, possibly because some of the African pressure
groups have proclaimed their hostility at being refused admission
to European public swimming pools. Overwhelmingly the opposition
to mixed bathing is based on grounds of hygiene and health. Also
present is an opposition to African men being present when European
women are clad only in brief swimming costumes.

## The Sample Characteristics

Within this category variability is compressed, and there are very
few segments of the population where a majority is in favor of dis-
rupting the status quo. Consequently the analysis of attitudes by social
characteristics will be relatively brief; it resolves into a comparison
of the degrees to which there is opposition to change. The comparison
would be more straightforward if there were space to include all the
tables that have been computed, but inasmuch as this is not so, the
more striking differences will be made to suffice. Table 75 gives the
attitudinal scores on this category.

TABLE 75. *Scores Relating to Social and Recreational Facilities*
(*M* = 1.17)

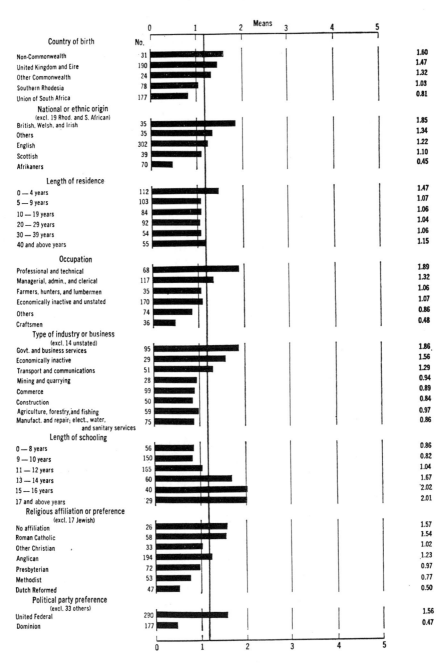

COUNTRY OF BIRTH

Irrespective of country of birth, the scores on the category are against change, with those from South Africa taking a far more conservative line than those from the United Kingdom. Over a third of the United Kingdom-born favor the admission of Africans to European hotels and restaurants, a greater number than that from any other group. It is only on the two items concerned with dancing and swimming that the scores from the United Kingdom group drop to much the same level as those held by persons born in southern Africa. Only a small and very unrepresentative number are prepared to countenance change in these two situations.

NATIONAL OR ETHNIC ORIGIN

The two largest groups, the English and the Afrikaners, display similar attitudes on mixed dancing and swimming, and dissimilar attitudes on the admission of Africans to the traditionally European hotels, restaurants, and clubs. The Afrikaner score of .45 is the most conservative we encountered in the analysis of social and recreational facilities. In particular, the notion of mixing at dances is anathema to them. As in other sections, the enigmatic British-Welsh-Irish aggregate is the least conservative of all.

LENGTH OF RESIDENCE

When attitudes are broken down by length of residence, a different pattern emerges for this category as compared with others. Previously, it was found that attitudes became more conservative with the passage of time, reaching the lowest point after about 35–40 years. But in the case of social and recreational facilities, it takes only five years in the Colony for attitudes to drop to near their lowest level. There are no significant variations after this point. It might be deduced from this that it requires a shorter span of time for people to decide whether or not they wish to share their social activities with people of African origin. The decision, as we have noted, is in the negative.

OCCUPATION

Variations of attitude by occupational classification are revealed in Table 75. The professional-technical grouping is the least conservative and craftsmen the most. Three of the item scores of the professional and technical personnel are above 2.00, namely 2.59, 2.62, and 2.53, thus showing a substantial segment of approximately 40% who support the notion of opening hotels, restaurants, theaters, and even clubs to certain Africans. It is their contention, in the main, that the economic barrier will select the proper people for admission. On the other hand, the mean scores of the craftsmen range from .89 to .00, a very solid stake in the status quo.

## TYPE OF INDUSTRY OR BUSINESS

A similar result emerges from the breakdown by industrial classification. Government and business services (mainly professional) are the least conservative, while those in mining, commerce, construction, agriculture, manufacturing, repairing, etc., are uniformly the most conservative. For an unknown reason, the economically inactive and the transport employees come out with somewhat higher scores than we would have expected from the previous data.

## EDUCATION

Although length of residence makes little difference to attitudes about social facilities, length of schooling does. Attitudes become less fixed in the status quo as education is extended, and at the more advanced levels they spill over into the area of social change. After fifteen years of education, a majority of individuals opt to eliminate restrictions on hotels and restaurants; they feel that economic forces will govern the situation. Over 40% of the highly educated also wish to drop the barriers at theaters and social clubs. Quite the contrary attitudes are held by those whose education has been terminated early.

## RELIGIOUS AFFILIATION OR PREFERENCE

The two most contrasting religious groupings are the Catholic and Dutch Reformed. Catholic attitudes average 2.17 on three items (hotels, restaurants, clubs, and theaters), whereas the highest score of adherents of the Dutch Reformed church is .85 on statement 45. Of individuals in the other churches of significant size, the Anglicans fall closer to the Catholics, the Methodists average out closer to the Dutch Reformed, and the Presbyterians score almost halfway between the two most contrasting groups. The mean positions of all the religious groupings are on the side of the status quo, with the Catholics, however, showing a greater proportion of social-change scores than persons who prefer or are affiliated with the other denominations.

POLITICAL PARTY PREFERENCE

Differences between the two major political parties are substantial and significant. Perhaps they can be illustrated best in tabular form (Table 76).

TABLE 76. *Mean Attitude Scores about Social and Recreational Facilities, by Political Party Preference*

| No. | Area of differentiation | D.P. | U.F.P. |
|---|---|---|---|
| 46 | Restaurants and hotels | .61 | 2.34 |
| 45 | Sporting and social clubs | .84 | 2.01 |
| 48 | Theaters | .49 | 2.13 |
| 59 | Admission to European dances | .27 | .68 |
| 43 | Public swimming pools | .12 | .62 |
| | Means | .47 | 1.56 |

The scores of the Dominion party and the United Federal party are reasonably close on the matter of dance halls and swimming pools, but they are wide apart on the other items. A sizable minority of Federal party supporters advocate the relaxation of restrictions on restaurants, hotels, clubs and cinemas, but their attitude is not matched by supporters of the Dominion party. It seems that social change is more likely to be effected through the Federal party than through the opposition party of the Federal and territorial parliaments.

THE PRINCIPAL THEMES

From the begining of European settlement in Southern Rhodesia, men have gathered together to share their leisure time, to enjoy a quiet pipe on the *stoep,* and to quaff a "sundowner." It was natural that these groups should embrace kith and kin, people whose language was understood and whose customs were familiar. As the frontier days receded, the ways in which a man could enjoy his leisure time increased.

Small hotels and restaurants, then larger ones, catered to the growing European population and the traveler far from home. Clubs were established where like-minded men could participate in their favorite sport, and debate afterward the result of the match or the state of the Colony. Women and children were often included in these clubs, and they discussed their own affairs and played their games. In a sense, social clubs represented a retreat from the world of work, from grappling with Africans who did not share the European culture, and from the tensions that arise when any small community adopts the task of ruling a larger one. The newcomers established their theaters, went to dances, and partook of their recreations in much the manner of other Europeans abroad.

But it was not contemplated that these social groupings should be widened to include even a fragment of the indigenous population. They had their own recreations they could enjoy in their own way. On this evidence, then, we conclude that there has been a considerable shift in thinking and practice because Africans now share some of the social facilities Europeans have regarded traditionally as their own, even if the number involved is very small. Furthermore, a percentage of Europeans, even though generally in the minority, advocate the modification, if not the elimination, of some of the current restrictions. Such advocacy would have been less likely at the turn of the century.

But if there has been some shift in attitudes, it is still true that the European population as a whole is against an intrusion into its kinship and interest groups. They feel uncomfortable if Africans in any number are admitted to hotels, restaurants, and clubs; extra precautions would have to be taken against contagion, and to prevent embarrassment of European women. Even so, attitudes on hotels and restaurants are nowhere nearly as intense as they are on mixed dancing and swimming. In the former, the situation can be more impersonal, some degree of spatial separation can be achieved voluntarily, and physical contact can be avoided.

Dancing and swimming, however, are a different matter. Dancing is closely associated with sex in the minds of most of the population, and no form of sexual rivalry is to be tolerated. In particular, it seems that European men feel they should protect their women from sexual temptation in case the latter are irresolute on the matter themselves. The laws on cross-racial sexual contact in Southern Rhodesia in no way challenge this hypothesis. "Caste will be lost" and the status of the Europeans endangered if conditions are permitted that may lead to sexual familiarity with Africans.

The objections to mixed bathing also contains a sexual element, but the most explicit arguments are on grounds of hygiene. Swimming facilities are viewed as potential pools of infection, and the proposition that Africans should be allowed into them receives no real support. It is preferred that they have their own swimming pools in their own areas.

To sum up, the philosophy of separation runs strongly through the responses to the category. While exceptions are sometimes made for educated, culturally acceptable Africans, the dominant theme is for the separation of social and recreational facilities. In this way Europeans can protect themselves from contagion, sexual temptation, and a psychologically tense atmosphere.

# 17

## SEXUAL RELATIONS

Sexual relations are, needless to say, an intimate and personal variety of social relations. Since they take place in private, and often in darkness, it is somewhat difficult to apply social sanctions to them. In this sense, they differ from other social contacts which tend to be more open and public.

Sexual relations between Europeans and Africans appear to have been relatively infrequent during Southern Rhodesia's history, judging by the available statistics. The 1901 census reported (see Table 1) that 0.1% of the total population was "Colored," and included in this category were immigrants from the Union of South Africa. At no time have Coloreds totaled more than 0.3% of the population. Their rate of growth has been variable (see Table 2), but not substantially different from other segments of the population. The available evidence suggests that, in the majority of cases, the parents of first-generation Colored offspring are European men and African women.

Census statistics about Coloreds are unreliable, however, just as the labeling of any person with mixed characteristics is problematic. The Native Affairs Department undertook a survey in 1914 to discover how many European men were living with African women in the

Reserves, and found only sixteen such cases. The belief persists that the number has always been greater, even in 1959 when only "about twenty-seven such cases are known," but no reliable data exist to eliminate speculation and myth. There are no known cases of African men married to European women residing in Southern Rhodesia.* One writer stated in 1954 [1] that the "evidence" suggested that as many as 6,000 Coloreds were living with their African mothers in the Reserves.† Welfare workers tell of the rather frequent practice by which newly-born Colored children are "dumped" on the doorsteps of Colored families in the larger towns of Southern Rhodesia. Some school teachers also speak knowingly about the number of children in their schools who "pass for White," although their neighbors are not always unaware of their ancestry.

Statistics are not available on the frequency of European-African sexual contacts, however. Liaisons between European men and African women seem to have been more frequent prior to 1900 than in later years. Father Hale, when minister at the Wankie Mission, commented on disease and heavy drinking among Europeans working on the construction of the railway line, and their sexual activities with African women.[2] Several observers (e.g., Jollie, 1924), especially ministers, commented on what appeared to them to be the shocking sexual laxness of European men, and the psychological satisfaction they obtained in getting African women to submit to them.

Sociologically, it is important to note that there were almost three European men to every European woman until the turn of the century (see Table 5). In situations with an imbalance between the sexes— as in Brazil and Canada during early settlement, and Germany and Japan when occupied by their military conquerors—men have often taken indigenous women as wives or concubines. This imbalance of European men and women was rectified relatively quickly in Southern Rhodesia, and the small Colored population may be attributed in measure to this demographic factor. Illicit unions were often motivated not only by biological drives, but also by cultural factors. European immigrants often assumed that Africans were "oversexed," that the custom of *lobola* was merely an institution by which African women were bought and sold, and that any group who practiced polygamy—an unacceptable deviation by Victorian standards—surely had no moral standards or system by which sexual relations were regulated and sanctioned. In some degree, then, sexual relations between European men and African women in the early years were similar

* One such couple, mentioned in Ch. 12, has returned to Holland. Another African who has married a European girl is presently residing in England.

† In such cases, the relationship of the child with its father and mother results primarily from the values of the Europeans, i.e., it could not be reared acceptably in a European family.

to those between masters and slaves, feudal lords and serfs, and conquerors and conquered in other countries.

With the increasing immigration of European women, there was
probably less sexual contact between African women and European
men. The arriving women were prevented from having sexual contacts
with African men by new ordinances and regulations. In addition,
many women's clubs and ministers pressed for a law that would
proscribe all interracial sexual contacts. The B. S. A. Administration
took a more lenient view, however, and the ordinance eventually
passed only proscribed sexual relations between African men and
European women. The highly emotional reactions of Europeans to
cases in which an African raped a European woman have been discussed in an earlier chapter. In at least two cases, there was European
mob action and near lynching of the defendants.[3]

Another factor that limited the growth of a large Colored population was the overwhelming percentage of males among the African
domestic servants, a situation quite unlike, say, the United States
during the first two centuries of European settlement. We mentioned
earlier the economic motives that prompted the greater mobility of
African men, but the biological functions of women—child-bearing
and child-rearing responsibilities that hindered their migration—
should not be ignored. Even so, the virtual absence of sexual relations
between African men and European women is quite remarkable when
the sheer number of opportunities for intimacy to develop are realized.

The basic reasons for the relative infrequency of interracial sexual
relations and marriages are not as obscure as generally believed.
According to most Europeans, such relations threaten to shake the very
foundation of the social system of Southern Rhodesia. The structure
of the European family can be maintained only if European women
are "untouchable," only if intimate and permanent relations with
African males are discouraged or prevented. If European households
are to function as they traditionally have, African domestic servants
must accept both a lower status and the rights, duties, and privileges
defined for them by Europeans. Europeans and Africans within one
household, that is, must share complementary role expectations: Africans must not try to impinge too closely upon the intimate relations
of the European household (Richmond, 1957:122). African servants,
for example, may be allowed to handle and care for European infants
and to wash dishes, towels, and diapers; they generally will not be
permitted, on the other hand, to use these dishes and towels or the lava-
tory and bathing facilities.

Most intimate relations—recreational, sexual, and marital—are
confined within the boundaries of one's social class. Illicit relations,
on the other hand, are frequently cross-class or interracial phenomena.

A European woman who married or was known to have sexual relations with an African would be certain to lose status, and be subjected to the sanctions of European public opinion and law. Should she marry an African, there would be a real possibility that she would have to forfeit all the traditional protection and support that surrounds her as a member of the dominant cultural group.

An interracial marriage in Southern Rhodesia would bring into conflict the systems of kinship relations which, on the whole, are still quite different. An African married to a European would have to learn new patterns of kinship behavior and terminology. Since Europeans trace their descent through both males and females, the African spouse would be participating in a system that maximizes the number of potential kin with whom reciprocal obligations need to be established. Since Europeans generally would disapprove or refuse to extend these obligations to the couple, the newly-weds would be left with only a restricted range of kin with whom they could enter into intimate and personalized relations.[4]

Among Africans, the interracial couple would have other difficulties. Africans in Southern Rhodesia have unilineal kinship systems, tracing their descent either through males or through females. But the kinship system is much more complex than this, and there are various rights and obligations that extend through both sides of an African's family. Such a system is foreign to the European, and he or she would be required to learn new patterns of expected behavior and terminology, property rights, and inheritance and succession customs. Furthermore, if the couple were rejected by the African's parents and other relations, they would find themselves participating in a kinship system under severe restrictions. If the relatives on both sides repudiated the marriage, the couple would have to seek compensatory relations among nonkinsmen, that is, among friends. In this case, kinship would cease to operate as a criterion for organizing social relations, indeed a rare and atypical situation anywhere in the world.

These difficulties do not preclude the possibility of success for an interracial couple, but they impose social and psychological impediments on their search for happiness and adjustment. As long as wide cultural differences persist in Southern Rhodesia, and as long as traditional European attitudes toward interracial marriages remain, it may be predicted that African-European marriages will be rare. On the other hand, cross-racial sexual relations, especially between European men and African women, will be more frequent as long as wide cultural differences persist and men interpret the conquest of African women as a symbol of status superiority.

CONTEMPORARY ATTITUDES

Having sensed the traditional opposition of Europeans to cross-racial sexual contacts,* the next step was to measure current attitudes. In practice this turned out to be more difficult than anticipated. A number of items were selected that seemed to embody a principal sexual component, but then proved not to. For example, the crime of cross-racial rape primarily involves the principle of equality in law, and so does the ordinance proscribing cross-racial sexual relations for European women but not for men. Another item that encompasses a sexual element is interpreted equivocally and has remained unclassified. On the other hand, our subsequent evidence illustrates that dancing can be included with the items on sex.

When the various criteria were taken into account there remained but three items for the category. It is appreciated that the stability of the category could have been increased by the inclusion of further suitable items, but inasmuch as we do no have them, this limitation will have to be accepted. The three statements, with their means and probable error limits, are given in Table 77.

TABLE 77. *Statements Relating to Sexual Relations*

| No. | Statement | −1 P.E. | +1 P.E. | Mean |
|-----|-----------|---------|---------|------|
| 62 | A European man who is suspected of having sex relations with an African woman is likely to be ostracized socially. | −.12 | 2.24 | 1.06 |
| 64 | A friendship between an African man and a European woman is generally viewed with suspicion. | −.13 | 2.21 | 1.04 |
| 22 | If a European woman becomes 'familiar' with an African man, she is almost certain to be ostracized socially. | −.25 | 1.95 | .85 |
|    |  | −.17 | 2.13 | .98 |

Of all the categories, that concerned with sexual relations receives the lowest rank; it is the one on which the population as a whole is most strongly against any alteration in current practices. Most of the individual scores are either 0 or 2, both on the maintain side of the continuum. From this it can be seen that the distributions are decidedly

* In Ch. 10, we discussed some of the traditional feelings of Europeans toward the justice of penal sanctions imposed upon Europeans and Africans found guilty of illicit sexual relations. In Ch. 12, we noted the difficulties, under the provisions of the Land Apportionment Act, that face an African-European married couple in finding a legal residence.

abnormal, i.e. skewed. The reasons for the skewing become clear as the interview material is analyzed.

*Statement 62* (M = 1.06) describes the social sanctions that come into effect if a European man has sexual relations with an African woman. The general feeling is that such a man should at least be ostracized, if not punished more heavily. "Quite right. This [act] has a very bad effect on both Europeans and Africans." "God meant us to be separate or he wouldn't have made us white and them black." "The higher the penalty, the greater the deterrent." "I do not agree with Europeans and Kaffirs fraternizing. A death penalty should be imposed on Black and White who have sex relations."

A few persons, while deploring cross-racial sexual relations, draw a careful distinction between a sin and a crime: "This may be a moral sin but ought not to be subject to legislation." Others base their argument on religious doctrine: "As this presumably refers to relationships out of wedlock, he is therefore sinning in the eyes of most churches and should be ostracized."

It was mentioned earlier that a belief persists that sexual relations have always been greater than can be detected from the statistics. This belief emerges in the interview material, as one reply illustrates: "The statement may be accurate in so far as the cities are concerned, but is certainly not true of 'bundu' [bush] society. 'Old so and so, . . . Oh he's alright, but colour blind, but then lots of the old-timers were like that old boy,' is heard around the campfire on many a chilly night in the veld." There is no way of checking on the validity of this belief, but it dies hard. At any rate, it is clear that the moral sanction of ostracism is not regarded as too severe for a violation of the European sexual code.

*Statement 64* (M = 1.04) reads, "A friendship between an African man and a European woman is generally viewed with suspicion." As the statement stands, there is no explicit reason why it should be translated into sexual terms, but in the great majority of cases it is. "Good sense, and pride in the purity of one's own race, should make such behavior rare." "While social integration in some form is inevitable, miscegenation is *not* to be encouraged." "Friendships between adult men and women rarely remain as such." "Quite so. There is at present no reason, except an immoral one, for such a friendship." "Few women can carry on a Platonic friendship with any man, and few males want women for friends." "There is almost never any reason for doing so other than sexual intent."

These are responses that lie with the typical scores of the population. Only a few are prepared to concede that a genuine Platonic friendship between an African man and a European woman is possible. To most persons, such a friendship is immediately suspect. The evidence seems to interlock with our previous hypothesis that Europeans believe their women require more protection from sexual temptation than do men.

*Statement 22* (M = .85) contains a definite sexual implication. Whereas statement 64 refers to the friendship of an African man and a European woman, here the relation is described as "familiar." The scores and verbal responses were predictable. "No self-respecting European woman would wish to get 'familiar' with an African man." The reactions to the statement are vigorous. The respondents as a whole can see no merit in such a relation. It is a violation of religious principles, the accepted moral codes, and the law of the land. "This is a sin in the eyes of the church." "I do not approve of mixed marriages or mixed sex relations." "It is most undesirable to create a society of 'God's step-children' who will never be wholly accepted by either race."

Others stress their opposition rather differently and bring into focus differences in cultural background: "I feel that until such time as the African male can show the same love, devotion and respect for his own women as the European does, he should only get 'familiar' with his own kind." "A European woman who is 'familiar' with an African man has become one of them." Still others believe that capital punishment would be a useful deterrent.

It does not matter much whether the general attitude of the individual is in favor of change or the status quo; the practice, if it does occur, is to be deplored and prohibited. Such attitudes, as we have noted, render the law prohibiting sexual relations between an African man and a European woman acceptable to the majority of the European population.

### THE SAMPLE CHARACTERISTICS

The breakdown of data by sample characteristics reveals without exception that every mean score is on the maintain side of the distribution. In no case does a majority of any subgrouping advocate the liquidation of social sanctions on cross-racial sexual behavior. Thus, because of the skewed pattern of the distributions, the analyses are restricted to a comparison of resistances to change in the status quo. The mean scores on which the comparisons are based are shown in Table 78.

#### COUNTRY OF BIRTH

The small number of non-Commonwealth respondents in our sample —Danes, Greeks, Americans, Italians, Portuguese, etc.—support the status quo least strongly. Their mean score of 1.74 is substantially

TABLE 78. *Scores Relating to Sexual Relations* (*M* = .98)

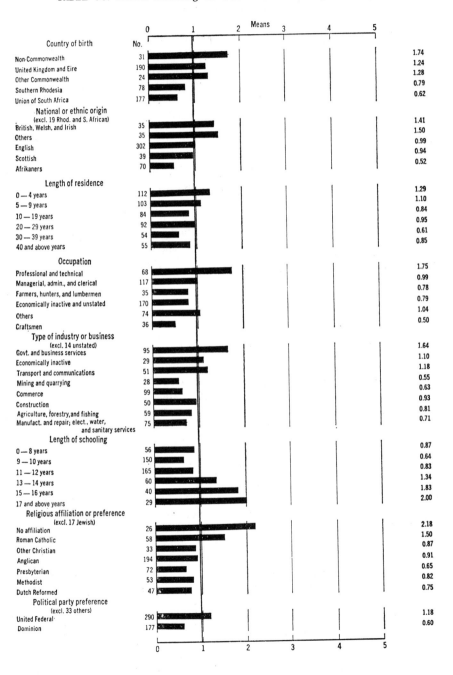

| | No. | | Mean |
|---|---|---|---|
| **Country of birth** | | | |
| Non-Commonwealth | 31 | | 1.74 |
| United Kingdom and Eire | 190 | | 1.24 |
| Other Commonwealth | 24 | | 1.28 |
| Southern Rhodesia | 78 | | 0.79 |
| Union of South Africa | 177 | | 0.62 |
| **National or ethnic origin** (excl. 19 Rhod. and S. African) | | | |
| British, Welsh, and Irish | 35 | | 1.41 |
| Others | 35 | | 1.50 |
| English | 302 | | 0.99 |
| Scottish | 39 | | 0.94 |
| Afrikaners | 70 | | 0.52 |
| **Length of residence** | | | |
| 0 — 4 years | 112 | | 1.29 |
| 5 — 9 years | 103 | | 1.10 |
| 10 — 19 years | 84 | | 0.84 |
| 20 — 29 years | 92 | | 0.95 |
| 30 — 39 years | 54 | | 0.61 |
| 40 and above years | 55 | | 0.85 |
| **Occupation** | | | |
| Professional and technical | 68 | | 1.75 |
| Managerial, admin., and clerical | 117 | | 0.99 |
| Farmers, hunters, and lumbermen | 35 | | 0.78 |
| Economically inactive and unstated | 170 | | 0.79 |
| Others | 74 | | 1.04 |
| Craftsmen | 36 | | 0.50 |
| **Type of industry or business** (excl. 14 unstated) | | | |
| Govt. and business services | 95 | | 1.64 |
| Economically inactive | 29 | | 1.10 |
| Transport and communications | 51 | | 1.18 |
| Mining and quarrying | 28 | | 0.55 |
| Commerce | 99 | | 0.63 |
| Construction | 50 | | 0.93 |
| Agriculture, forestry, and fishing | 59 | | 0.81 |
| Manufact. and repair; elect., water, and sanitary services | 75 | | 0.71 |
| **Length of schooling** | | | |
| 0 — 8 years | 56 | | 0.87 |
| 9 — 10 years | 150 | | 0.64 |
| 11 — 12 years | 165 | | 0.83 |
| 13 — 14 years | 60 | | 1.34 |
| 15 — 16 years | 40 | | 1.83 |
| 17 and above years | 29 | | 2.00 |
| **Religious affiliation or preference** (excl. 17 Jewish) | | | |
| No affiliation | 26 | | 2.18 |
| Roman Catholic | 58 | | 1.50 |
| Other Christian | 33 | | 0.87 |
| Anglican | 194 | | 0.91 |
| Presbyterian | 72 | | 0.65 |
| Methodist | 53 | | 0.82 |
| Dutch Reformed | 47 | | 0.75 |
| **Political party preference** (excl. 33 others) | | | |
| United Federal | 290 | | 1.18 |
| Dominion | 177 | | 0.60 |

higher than that of any of the Commonwealth groups. Of the three groups selected for further study, the South African-born display the most conservative attitudes (M = .62) in support of the sanctions, and persons from the United Kingdom the least conservative (M = 1.24). The Southern Rhodesian-born (M = .79) fall within this range, but somewhat closer to those who have immigrated from the Union of South Africa. On the ground that the environmental molding forces in Southern Rhodesia are more akin to those of the Union than of Britain, this finding is what we would predict.

NATIONAL OR ETHNIC GROUP

Of the different ethnic groupings, the Afrikaners support the social sanctions more strongly than any other. The English and the Scottish have much the same attitude toward cross-racial sexual behavior, and take a stand about midway between the Afrikaners and the composite British-Welsh-Irish grouping. Only a few atypical individuals are in favor of discontinuing present sanctions against sexual relations with Africans.

LENGTH OF RESIDENCE

The expected trend in attitudes does not emerge as definitively when the data are analyzed by length of residence. Whereas in some of the other categories, scores became progressively more conservative with the passing of years, this is less true where attitudes about cross-racial sexual behavior are concerned. There are some bumps in the distribution that we have not attempted to explain. Even so, if length of residence is divided into two broad bands, those who have lived in the Colony under twenty years, and those over, the former take a slightly more permissive attitude than the latter.

OCCUPATION

The two most contrasting occupational groupings are the professional-technical individuals and the craftsmen, with the former taking a profoundly different—although still conservative—line on all three items of the category. Whereas the lowest item score of the professional-technical people is 1.62, the highest for the craftsmen is .89. There seems to be a qualitative difference in responses as well as a quantitative difference in scores between these two groupings. The professional and technical persons in the sample insist more generally that an individual's sexual life is his private affair, but if the accepted codes are known to be infringed, they feel that others are then justified in expressing disapprobation. The craftsmen, on the other hand, argue more strongly in favor of legal as well as social sanctions to prohibit cross-racial sexual relations.

## TYPE OF INDUSTRY OR BUSINESS

Few further insights emerge from the breakdown of responses by type of industry or business. Persons in government and business services, a category that embraces the bulk of the professional and technical people, show the least conservative scores, while those in the mining industry show the most. The agricultural class, which occupies the most conservative position on the full scale, does not rank lowest in its attitude toward sexual relations with Africans.

## EDUCATION

There is an observable trend in the figures on schooling that seems to bear some significance. The mean scores for individuals with less than thirteen years of schooling are all of much the same magnitude. Thereafter there is a decided swing to a less conservative position until, at seventeen and above years, the mean attitude lies at 2.00.

One of the most interesting shifts is in attitudes about friendships between European women and African men. At the nine- and ten-year level, the mean score is .67; at the seventeen and above level, it is 2.34. Among persons with little education, it is considered that a Platonic friendship is impossible; at the higher levels, this is denied by a small but substantial number.

## RELIGIOUS AFFILIATION OR PREFERENCE

Of the larger religious groupings in the study, the Roman Catholics come out least strongly for the status quo. At the other end of the continuum, it is noteworthy that the Presbyterians adopt a more conservative attitude than do members of the Dutch Reformed church. This transposition may be entirely fortuitous; our data do not allow us to speculate. Whether or not this is so, individual members or adherents of both churches take a very solid stand against cross-racial friendships and sexual relations. The least conservative attitudes of all are found among those who have no religious affiliation, but these individuals are too heterogeneous to allow further generalization.

## POLITICAL PARTY PREFERENCE

As in every other category except that involving legal justice, differences emerge between the supporters of the two major political parties. Federal party supporters have a more permissive attitude about cross-

racial sexual relations. Although they also disapprove of such behavior, they are not as prone as supporters of the Dominion party to
introduce sanctions against individuals who violate the codes regulating sexual relations.

## THE PRINCIPAL THEMES

It is perhaps fitting that attitudes on sexual relations should be ex
amined last. They are more intense and, it seems to us, more pervasive
than attitudes associated with any other area of human behavior.
These attitudes are not greatly different from those generated in plural
societies elsewhere, except that the numerical inferiority of the Europeans may have sharpened their beliefs and feelings. In countries
like New Zealand and Canada, cross-racial sex relations are more
tolerated, perhaps because the status of the dominant group is little
threatened. But in Southern Rhodesia, the Europeans feel that the
ultimate result of cross-racial sexual relations might be the loss of
their identity and "racial purity." This fear is often expressed openly
and strongly, and Europeans therefore approve the continuance of
moral, social, and legal sanctions against cross-racial sexual relations.

The attitudes of Southern Rhodesians seem to differ in at least one
important respect from those described by Myrdal (1944) in the
Deep South of the United States. There, while protecting their women
from sexual contacts with Negroes, White males have not regarded
it as vital to proscribe their own activities. Sexual relations between a
White man and a Negro woman have generally been viewed with
some tolerance. In Southern Rhodesia, on the contrary, the general
attitude of Europeans is that both men and women should be discouraged or prevented from having sexual relations with Africans.

In the context of Southern Rhodesia, this attitude seems consistent
with those regarding other areas of interracial contact. If Europeans
are to retain their way of life and to protect themselves from contagion and undue competition, then Africans and Europeans must be
separated. Most important of all, they must be separated sexually.
Somewhat surprising is the belief held by a number of males that European women *need* protection from cross-racial sexual temptation
because they are more likely to be open to proposals from Africans.
The data do not suggest that this view is warranted. The mean attitude
score for all men is 1.06, as compared with .90 for the women, showing that the latter are equally or even more opposed to sexual relations
with Africans than are European men.

The dominant themes in the reasons given by Europeans seem to
be unified around the central idea of sexual separation. It is held that
material and moral standards will be lowered if the frequency of cross-
racial sexual contact increases. Biologically "mixed" offspring will

depreciate the status of the European population; and the separation in education, employment, land, public facilities, and so on, which is considered necessary, will become null and void. But the arguments are not devoid of idealistic motives. If Africans are to be led "out of darkness" into a new society with higher standards of living, better health, and greater employment opportunities, then Europeans must not lose pride in their own cultural and racial heritage. Radical changes might come from a removal of barriers on sexual relations. Whether or not these things are true, Europeans believe them to be so. In this respect they have many of the ideas, values, and positions of prestige and status of "other men in other valleys."

# 18

## SOCIAL STRUCTURE AND RACE ATTITUDES

To discover the contemporary racial attitudes of Europeans in Southern Rhodesia, we have administered a questionnaire and interviewed a sample of 500 people twenty years of age and over. By using two major principles—randomization and stratification—and 108 minor controls, we feel that the data from the sample are a microcosm of the total adult population. The questionnaire has also proved to be highly reliable and valid. That some of the practices or laws cited in it have changed since the study began should in no way vitiate our conclusions. On the contrary, they raise the more important question of the relevance of data about individual attitudes for understanding the dynamic character of relations between Africans and Europeans in Southern Rhodesia. We shall return to the matter of change in the concluding chapter.

### ATTITUDES AND SOCIAL CHARACTERISTICS

We have been interested not only in the attitudes of the entire European community, but also in discovering the relation between race attitudes and twelve selected personal and social characteristics. Our purpose, in fact, has not been to establish a general theory of race relations; different sociological settings and inadequate research techniques make such an attempt still premature. Rather, we have preferred to gather data that will permit lower-level generalizations, "statements of observed uniformities between two isolated and easily identified variables" [1] or "variates."

From the twelve "variates" or characteristics according to which we fragmented the European sample, we have sought to discover which Europeans feel most strongly about maintaining or changing the status quo of Southern Rhodesia's system of race relations. There are other criteria, of course, that would possibly have returned significant results; these include marital status, size of family, length of residence in Africa (not only in Southern Rhodesia), social class, membership in various groups and associations, frequency of church attendance, and intelligence. Obviously, some selection had to be made for our analyses; our choices were guided by considerations not only of the general literature on race relations, but also of the importance of what Lewin (1951) has called the "field." Race attitudes are learned in the setting of particular cultures and through participation in specific groups. Similarly, varying situations and the distinct roles that individuals fill affect the expression of attitudes both verbally and in action.[2]

However, it is worthwhile to provide a wider context for understanding the importance of particular variables in culturally and racially plural societies aside from Southern Rhodesia. Space does not allow an unlimited review of analogous societies elsewhere; nor can all of the important findings about the relation of personal and social characteristics to race attitudes be reviewed. Rather, it is necessary to impose some restrictions, and we shall comment only upon two matters. First, we shall examine the relation of race attitudes to only twelve personal and social characteristics. Secondly, the Southern Rhodesian findings will be juxtaposed with those of only three other societies—the Union of South Africa, the United States of America, and Great Britain.

Despite differing histories and variations in culture, many of the features of these societies are quite similar. This is especially true of Southern Rhodesia, South Africa, and the southern states of the United States. All have had constituent groups varying widely in culture and social organization, in the past if not now. Except in Great Britain, Africans or Negroes have been numerically preponderant in the whole or parts of the different nations. South Africa, the southern states, and, later, Southern Rhodesia were settled by culturally similar peoples from the northwestern corner of Europe. All are experiencing the social and cultural changes of rapid industrialization, urbanization, and public education. All are segments of an international economic system imposing some restrictions on their political sovereignty, and all are inheritors of a common religion. Their histories have been the product not only of these factors, however, but also of different lengths of European settlement, variable natural resources, particular geographical locations, disparate proportions of racial groups, and other features.

INSIGNIFICANT CHARACTERISTICS IN SOUTHERN RHODESIA

Table 79 shows the contrasting subpopulations within each of the twelve analyses of personal and social characteristics. These subpopulations are ranked by the size of their $t$ values, with the insignificant contrasts being entered last. It will prove useful to refer to this table as we proceed to discuss each of the characteristics used in our study. From three of the twelve characteristics analyzed in relation to European race attitudes in Southern Rhodesia—sex, age, and census district (region)—small and consistent differences in scores emerge between the subpopulations, but they are too small to be termed statistically significant by means of a $t$ test. However, the fact that there are consistencies in the scoring of individual items (e.g. the residents of Salisbury obtain higher mean scores on fifty-six of the sixty-six items) must be borne in mind. This implies that there may be differences that are masked by the size of the sample; with a larger N the gap might turn out to be significant. Another possibility is that the $t$ test is not sufficiently sensitive to pick up small differences of this type.

*Sex.* In Southern Rhodesia, sex is not related to race attitudes in any statistically significant degree. This suggests that males and females tend to have common experiences, or else these are shared across sexual lines in family settings and other peer groups. However, it may be noted that on fifty-four of the sixty-six items in the questionnaire, males obtain higher scores than do females. The men also are more consistently oriented toward the discontinuance of the laws and customs that differentiate Africans and Europeans on all twelve of the categories of items. The table shows that the maximum difference of males over females on any particular item is .57, whereas in category scores men exceed women at most by .22.

Outside Southern Rhodesia, no clear picture emerges between sex and race attitudes. In a recent study of university students in South Africa, Pettigrew (1960) found that females prefer a greater "social distance" between themselves and non-Whites than do males. Earlier, MacCrone (1937) reported that sex is insignificant in measures of social distance. In the United States, the evidence is variable, but females often show more conservative attitudes about Negroes.[3] Two studies in the United Kingdom returned contradictory findings about the relation of sex to race attitudes.[4]

TABLE 79. *Variation and Consistency in Attitudes among Contrasting Subpopulations*

| Characteristic | Contrasting subpopulations | t value | Mean difference | Maximum difference | | Consistency of higher scoring | |
|---|---|---|---|---|---|---|---|
| | | | | Items N = 66 | Categories N = 12 | Items N = 66 | Categories N = 12 |
| *Significant* | | | | | | | |
| 1. Political party preference | U. Federal : Dominion | 11.81 | 1.10 | 2.11 | 1.59 | 65 | 12 |
| 2. National or ethnic origin | English : Afrikaner | 7.84 | 1.09 | 3.52 | 2.29 | 65 | 12 |
| 3. Religious affiliation | R. Catholic : Dutch Ref. | 7.84 | 1.52 | 2.98 | 2.25 | 64 | 12 |
| 4. Length of schooling | 15–16 yrs. : 0–8 yrs. | 7.19 | 1.51 | 2.81 | 2.52 | 65 | 12 |
| 5. Country of birth | U.K. and Eire : S. Africa | 7.08 | .75 | 1.83 | 1.25 | 62 | 12 |
| 6. Occupation | Prof. and tech. : Craftsmen | 5.78 | 1.26 | 2.32 | 1.85 | 65 | 12 |
| 7. Type of industry | Govt. and bus. : Agriculture | 5.28 | .95 | 1.78 | 1.27 | 65 | 12 |
| 8. Length of residence | 0–4 yrs. : 30–39 yrs. | 3.62 | .71 | 1.59 | 1.01 | 66 | 12 |
| *Insignificant* | | | | | | | |
| 9. Income | £600–899 : Nil | 4.40 * | .73 * | 1.50 | 1.02 | 65 | 12 |
| 10. Census district | Salisbury : Bulawayo | 1.75 | .24 | 1.13 | .60 | 56 | 11 |
| 11. Age | 20–29 yrs. : 60 and above ** | 1.28 ** | .26 ** | 1.01 | .59 | 48 | 11 |
| 12. Sex | Male : Female | 1.21 | .12 | .57 | .22 | 54 | 12 |

* These values are significant, but the correlation between income and attitude is not.
** Collapsing three oldest age classes in Table 40.

*Age.* Individuals in Southern Rhodesia between the ages of 20 and 29 have more change-tolerant scores than do persons aged sixty and above on forty-eight items—the smallest number shown in Table 79. The low correlation of —.07 between age and attitude seems to result from the irregular pattern of European immigration. As the proportion of persons born in the Colony becomes greater in the future, a more significant correlation between these two variables can be anticipated.

In the other countries, Banton (1959) found no relation in Great Britain between age and attitudes about colored immigrants, but the reason for this is not clear. One other study in England, however, reported that older people tend to be more conservative.[5] This variable has not been tested in South Africa, as far as we know. In the United States, most studies indicate that conservatism toward Negroes increases with age, as is clear from the summary articles by Kerr (1944) and Harding et al (1954).

*Census District or Region.* The large proportion of recent immigrants in Southern Rhodesia also seems to have influenced the absence of any relationship between race attitude and census district of residence. Yet Bulawayo residents, according to our data, are slightly but consistently more conservative than those in Salisbury and elsewhere. This is also suggested by the greater support given by Bulawayo than Salisbury residents to the more conservative Dominion party in the 1958 elections. The former also has the greater concentration of industrial workers, whereas Salisbury district contains a higher proportion of professional people in the government services. Those districts in Southern Rhodesia that have the highest proportion of Afrikaner and Dutch Reformed residents return the most conservative scores, although the merging of census districts in our classification (because of small numbers in the rural areas) has obscured this finding.

In the United States, less favorable attitudes about Negroes have traditionally characterized the Southerners, as compared with Northerners.[6] In Great Britain, no reliable data are known about the importance of region although, as in the United States, the inhabitants of residential areas experiencing Negro immigration may have the more conservative scores.[7] MacCrone (1937) found that differences in race attitudes of European students in South Africa are related to geographical concentrations of Afrikaner and English ethnic groups.

*Income.* Income is the fourth variable that is unrelated to race attitudes in Southern Rhodesia (Table 79), a finding not always suggested by research in the other countries. The low frequency of poorly paid European workers in the Colony is complementary to the widespread employment of Africans in unskilled and skilled jobs. In the new and vigorous industrial society, there appears to be no stabilization thus far of wage differentials. The relatively large number of young new immigrants in the lower income brackets, the inclusion of part-time workers in the £1–599 class, and the concentration of skilled workers among persons earning £900–1199 helps to complicate the situation.

The relation of income to race attitude has not been investigated in South Africa, while Banton (1959) reported no correlation in his study in Britain. In the United States, the findings have often been inconclusive.[8] The variables that seem to be more valuable, therefore, are occupation and socioeconomic status.

THE SIGNIFICANT CHARACTERISTICS IN SOUTHERN RHODESIA

The remaining eight personal and social characteristics all show significant relations to European attitudes about Africans in Southern Rhodesia. Because of their importance, we will illustrate (Figures 4 through 11) not only the differences in the mean scores of the subpopulations on the *whole questionnaire,* but also their means on *each of the categories.* The five unclassified items are omitted; data on Type B public facilities are also excluded because of the virtual identity of scores and distributions between this category and the category of social and recreational facilities.

*Length of Residence.* As Table 79 shows, length of residence in Southern Rhodesia is the only characteristic upon which one contrasting subpopulation has less conservative scores on every item and on every category. The new arrivals are significantly more willing to discontinue laws and customs that differentiate Africans and Europeans than are persons who have lived longer in the Colony. More important, perhaps, is the sharp drop in change-tolerance from the first to the second five-year period of residence. Later, we will examine this relatively sudden increase in conservatism in more detail. Figure 4 displays the nature of the distribution according to the length of residence of the sample. It may be recalled that a correlation of —.17 obtains between race attitude and length of residence in Southern Rhodesia.

In South Africa, a similar relation is suggested by Pettigrew (1958), if it can be assumed that European students at Natal University born outside the African continent have lived in the Union for a shorter period than those born in Africa. We know of no studies in the United Kingdom that analyze European attitudes in relation to length of residence. In the United States, however, individuals consistently tend to have more unfavorable attitudes about Negroes the longer they live in the South (Killian and Haer, 1958, and Sims and Patrick, 1936).

But the same is not always true among Whites who reside in racially mixed housing projects or other residential areas in the North.[9] The American data suggest that length of residence is an important variable, but so are the nature of social relations between Negroes and Whites, the degree of free choice exercised in establishing a residence, and other factors.

*Type of Industry or Business.* Personnel in government and business services score significantly higher than persons in other industrial groupings in Southern Rhodesia, as Figure 5 clearly illustrates. Between all the other groupings, the range of mean scores is only from 2.20 to 2.39, hence it is insignificant. As mentioned earlier, the services subpopulation has a higher standard deviation of scores than other classes of industrial workers. Thus, except for services personnel, the type of industry in which a person works has virtually no value in predicting race attitude. An interesting point to note is that Government officials are responsible for the administration of many differentiating laws which they believe should be discontinued. This anomaly derives, in part, from the fact that about half of Southern Rhodesia's civil servants are recruited in the United Kingdom (Dvorin, 1958:73). The contrast between their attitudes—their "tendencies to act"—and what is required of them in their official roles illustrates the difficulty in predicting overt behavior solely from a knowledge of beliefs, feelings, and policy orientations.

We have found no studies in the literature that report on an examination of the relation between race attitudes and type of industry or business in either South Africa or Great Britain. This characteristic is likewise seldom considered by scholars in the United States. Hughes (1946, 1949), Remmers (1954), and others pointed to differences in race attitudes in American industry, but their classifications cannot be equated readily with those of Southern Rhodesia. Furthermore, Bullock (1951) found that occupational levels are more significantly associated with race attitudes than is the organization of industry. A similar deduction can be made from the Rhodesian data.

*Occupation.* A clearer and more significant relation emerges between occupation and attitude about Africans in Southern Rhodesia. Professional and technical persons, on the average, score considerably higher than craftsmen, as shown in Figure 6. People in managerial, administrative, and clerical positions also stand out clearly. Between farmers, nonworking adults, and individuals in sales work and skilled occupations, however, no very important differences emerge. Race attitudes are more conservative as the type of occupation becomes more "industrial," i.e., a factory setting or a venue in which manual labor is typical, in contrast to open farms, professional offices, or commercial

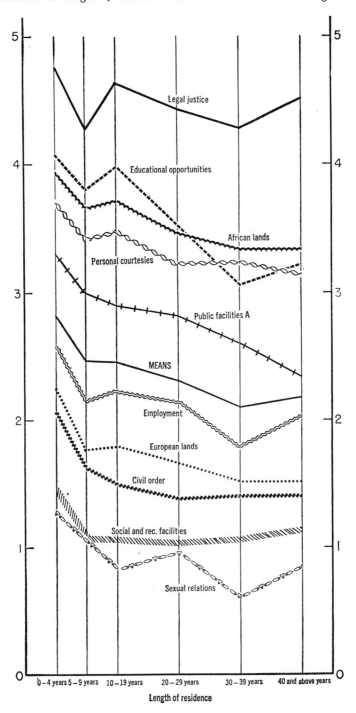

FIGURE 4. *Length of Residence and Attitude Scores on Categories*

Legal justice

Educational opportunities

African lands

Personal courtesies

Public facilities A

MEANS

Employment

European lands

Civil order

Social and rec. facilities

Sexual relations

0–4 years 5–9 years   10–19 years      20–29 years        30–39 years   40 and above years

Length of residence

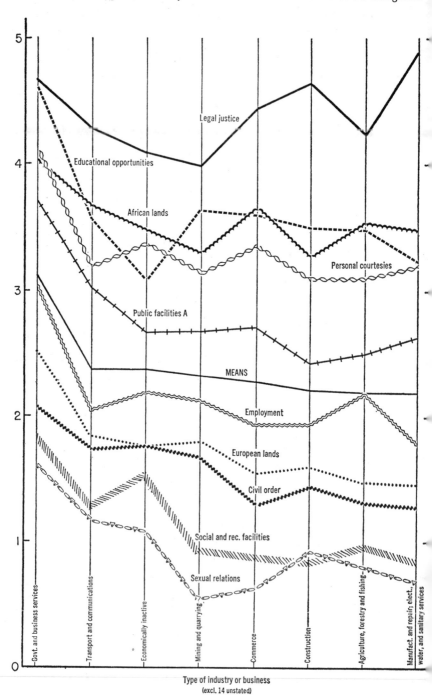

FIGURE 5. *Type of Industry or Business and Attitude Scores on Categories*

5

Legal justice

4

Educational opportunities

African lands

Personal courtesies

3

Public facilities A

MEANS

2

Employment

European lands

Civil order

Social and rec. facilities

1

Sexual relations

0

Govt. and business services
Transport and communications
Economically inactive
Mining and quarrying
Commerce
Construction
Agriculture, forestry and fishing
Manufact. and repair; elect., water, and sanitary services

Type of industry or business
(excl. 14 unstated)

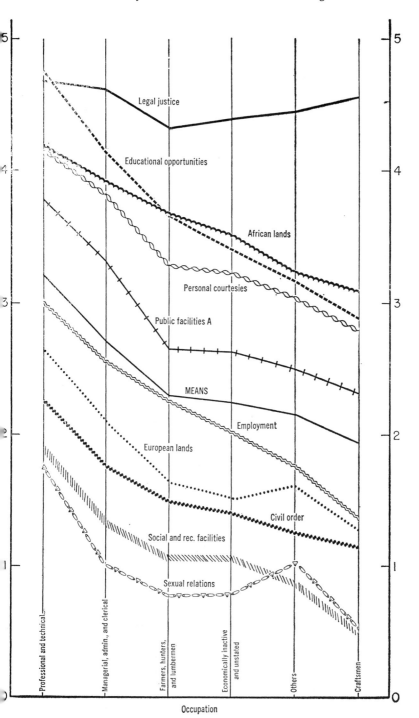

FIGURE 6. *Occupation and Attitude Scores on Categories*

enterprises. The heterogeneity of the subpopulations is an artifact of the Census classification. It seems possible that if an index of social status or social class were constructed, an even higher relation with attitude would emerge. Distinctions would need to be made, for example, between administrators and typists, plantation owners and hired farm hands, and lawyers, draftsmen, and missionaries.

Studies elsewhere are reasonably consistent with our findings and do not need to be cited at length. In the United States, White professional and managerial persons almost always show more tolerance of Negroes than do manual workers and laborers.[10] The findings also suggest that the character of interracial contacts in the work situation is equally if not more important than occupation per se. Scattered and unsystematic data about European attitudes in South Africa and Great Britain also show the same trend of relation to occupational status.[11]

*Country of Birth.* In Southern Rhodesia, this characteristic is related to attitudes about Africans even more clearly than occupation. Figure 7 indicates the relation between country of birth and attitudes on the categories of behavior. Persons born in Southern Rhodesia are consistently more conservative than immigrants from the United Kingdom and Eire. On the other hand, they are somewhat less conservative than the South African-born on all of the categories of differentiating practices except legal justice. It has been demonstrated in Chapter 9 that the United Kingdom-born do not differ from other subpopulations, according to country of birth, in becoming less tolerant of change the longer they live in Southern Rhodesia. Yet even after twenty or more years of residence, they are seldom as conservative as South Africans who have just arrived in the Colony.

Pettigrew's (1958) analyses, mentioned above, confirm the importance of the relation between birth in Africa and less favorable attitudes about Africans. From our data, this is what we would expect to find, since South Africa's social structure and European culture are similar to those of Southern Rhodesia. Unfortunately, almost no research has been carried out in Britain or the United States to examine the relation between country of birth and attitude about Negroes. In the latter country, some consideration of birthplace has been given in relation to attitudes about Jews, but these studies are neither conclusive nor directly applicable to our concern.[12] It should be recognized, however, that the proportion of nonnative-born Whites in the United Kingdom and the United States is considerably smaller than it is in Southern Rhodesia and South Africa. Consequently, country of birth has greater relevance to Southern Rhodesia than would be true in the northern societies.

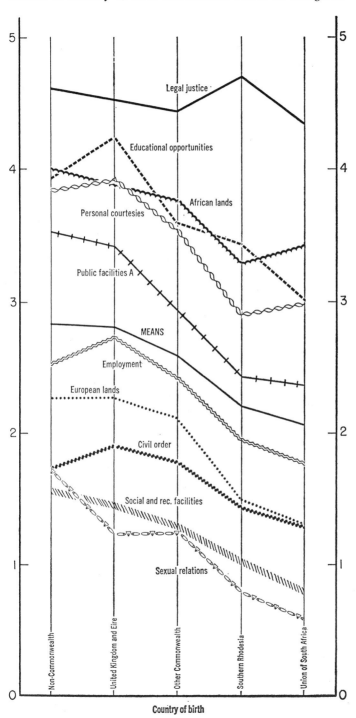

FIGURE 7. *Country of Birth and Attitude Scores on Categories*

Legal justice

Educational opportunities

African lands

Personal courtesies

Public facilities A

MEANS

Employment

European lands

Civil order

Social and rec. facilities

Sexual relations

Non-Commonwealth

United Kingdom and Eire

Other Commonwealth

Southern Rhodesia

Union of South Africa

Country of birth

*National or Ethnic Origin.* More significant sociological and statistical differences derive from the Southern Rhodesian data when they are analyzed by the national or ethnic groups with which persons identify themselves. The two highest ranking subpopulations are too heterogeneous to allow a discussion of their collective race attitudes. Of the remaining, the Scottish are virtually a replica of the English. Thus, the most significant difference among the clearly demarcated groups lies with the English and the Afrikaners, as Table 79 and Figure 8 indicate. A subanalysis has been made, but is not shown, of the South African-born to see whether their race attitudes vary depending on whether they identify themselves as ethnically English or Afrikaner. The same contrast emerges, but less significantly. From the data, we conclude that ethnic affiliation is of greater value than country of birth in predicting European attitudes about Africans in Southern Rhodesia, although the two criteria used jointly are more valuable than either one taken singly.

Over twenty years ago, MacCrone (1937) obtained similar significant differences in attitudes about Africans among European university students in South Africa. Recently, Pettigrew (1958, 1960) has added further support to the hypothesis of English-Afrikaner differences. South African Jewish students are also reported by Mac-Crone to have more tolerant attitudes than the ethnically English students. British studies on race attitudes have given little attention to the variable of ethnic identification. Hartley (1946) and Allport (1954) are among the many whose researches indicate that Jews in the United States tend to be more favorable than others in their attitudes about Negroes.[13]

*Religious Affiliation or Preference.* In Southern Rhodesia, religious affiliation or preference is as valuable as national or ethnic origin for understanding the nature of attitudes about Africans. Individuals who have no affiliation or preference return the highest mean score for the whole scale. Between them and Roman Catholics, the second-ranking group, half of the difference in mean score results from responses to items in the category of sexual relations. Anglicans and Presbyterians score close to the mean (2.45) for the entire sample; collectively, they may be termed conventional or middle of the road in Southern Rhodesia. Figure 9 shows the relation between religious affiliation and attitude about racially differentiating laws and customs. The widest contrast is between Roman Catholics and Dutch Reformed, an average difference of 1.52 (see Table 79). But the maximum variation on at least one item is 2.98, while a difference of 2.25 obtains on one category. The least variation in the attitudes of these two groups occurs on the category of sexual relations.

That the Dutch Reformed in South Africa are also more con-

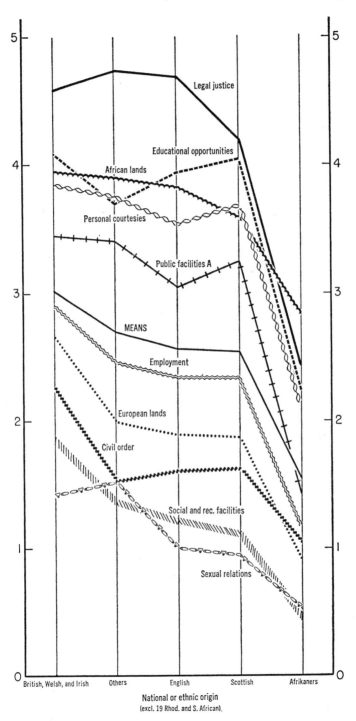

FIGURE 8. *National or Ethnic Origin and Attitude Scores on Categories*

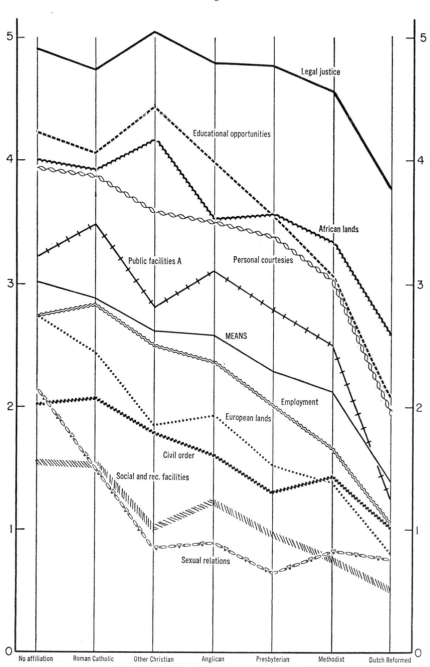

FIGURE 9. *Religious Affiliation or Preference and Attitude Scores on Categories*

Legal justice

Educational opportunities

Public facilities A

Personal courtesies

African lands

MEANS

Employment

European lands

Civil order

Social and rec. facilities

Sexual relations

No affiliation    Roman Catholic    Other Christian    Anglican    Presbyterian    Methodist    Dutch Reformed

Religious affiliation or preference
(excl. 17 Jewish)

servative in their race attitudes may be inferred from MacCrone's (1937) and Pettigrew's (1960) studies. Our data also indicate that individuals in the Dutch Reformed church who were born in South Africa have lower scores than do members of other religious organizations. On the other hand, our sample encompasses too few Jews (N = 17) to allow safe conclusions to be made about them. The skimpy data suggest that Jews in Southern Rhodesia, in contrast to South Africa and the United States, are not as tolerant of discontinuing racially differentiating laws and practices. Allport (1954) summarizes a considerable number of investigations and concludes that Jews in the United States generally tend to be less conservative than Protestants or Catholics. The last group, in contrast to the situation in Southern Rhodesia, are the most conservative of the three major religious divisions in that country, though the findings are not completely uniform.[14] "Fundamentalist" Protestants are frequently the least tolerant of Negroes;[15] they are reminiscent theologically and otherwise of the Dutch Reformed in southern Africa. No systematic findings have been published in Britain on the relation of religious affiliation or preference to race attitudes.

In addition to affiliation, other aspects of religious activity have been shown to be related to race attitudes, especially in the United States.[16] These aspects include sincerity of belief, frequency of church attendance, the nature of beliefs, and the social organization of religious groups. No examination of these variates has been made in Southern Rhodesia, but our interview material suggests that such an investigation might be very rewarding.

*Education.* Of all the continuous variables employed in our study, length of schooling is most closely related to race attitudes. A correlation of .41 indicates that an increase in schooling is positively related to a desire to change the social structure of the Colony. Figure 10 outlines the clear relation that derives from the analysis. Not illustrated, but of importance, is the fact that standard deviations of scores also increase with extension of schooling. This suggests that individuals with less education are both more conservative and more homogeneous in their race attitudes. The highly educated persons collectively are much more change-oriented, but they also show less consensus in their feelings about the differentiating laws and customs in Southern Rhodesia.

The importance of education is amply confirmed by studies in the United States, but less attention has been given to this variable in Great Britain and South Africa. Education, in fact, is the most consistent factor associated with attitudes about Negroes in the United States.[17] Samelson (1945) contended, however, that the length of education does not automatically alter the fundamental attitudes held by a com-

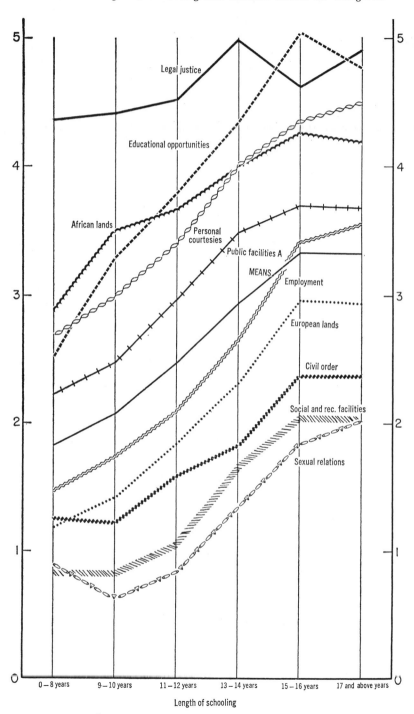

FIGURE 10. *Length of Schooling and Attitude Scores on Categories*

Legal justice

Educational opportunities

African lands

Personal courtesies

Public facilities A

MEANS

Employment

European lands

Civil order

Social and rec. facilities

Sexual relations

0 — 8 years    9 — 10 years    11 — 12 years    13 — 14 years    15 — 16 years    17 and above years

Length of schooling

munity. The nature and quality of education, and its association with other modes of social action, are also of importance.

*Political Party Preference.* Finally, the most significant of the twelve personal and social characteristics analyzed in relation to race attitudes in Southern Rhodesia proves to be political party preference (at the time of the 1958 Federal election). Only 6.6% of the sample have preferences for other than the two major parties. Supporters of the United Federal party obtain a mean score 1.10 higher on the full questionnaire than adherents of the Dominion party. As shown in Table 79, the maximum difference on a category is 1.59 (public facilities Type A). The greatest divergence on a single item is 2.11. The relation of attitudes on each of the categories to political party preference is portrayed in Figure 11.

This finding is not surprising, as we have indicated in Chapter 9. But it reveals the importance of the conative component of attitudes—beliefs about what should be done—or what has been termed a policy orientation. Policy about the future, of course, is the crucial interest that helps to structure the organization of political parties everywhere. Supporters of both parties are on the conservative side of the theoretical mean of 3.00; but the majority endorse the United Federalists, hence their center of gravity is nearer to that of the total population. Thus, party preference serves best as a negative indicator, since it differentiates supporters of the smaller group more clearly. The data suggest that, in so far as future political issues in Southern Rhodesia concern the maintenance or change of its differentiating laws and customs, it seems unlikely that the Dominion party will receive a majority of the votes from the European electorate. This inference *assumes,* of course, that the policies of the respective parties remain close to what they were in the 1958 Federal election or, alternatively, that the United Federal party's policies will remain equally attuned to the wishes of the voters who supported it at that time.

The value of this characteristic in cross-cultural comparisons is limited. Pettigrew (1958) showed that South African university students who prefer the Nationalist party are significantly less tolerant of Africans than are the supporters of other political parties. The Confederate party in Southern Rhodesia, whose stated policy seems to be closest to the Nationalist party in South Africa (Rogers, 1959), received virtually no support in the last Federal election in Southern Rhodesia. Comparisons between Rhodesian political parties and those in Great Britain or the United States are even less useful and more tenuous.

In the three countries other than Southern Rhodesia that we have considered, certain common attitudinal patterns can be observed de-

FIGURE 11. *Political Party Preference and Attitude Scores on Categories*

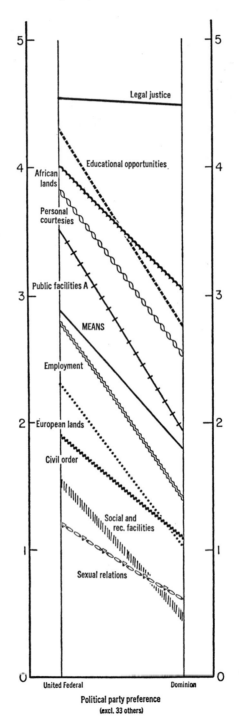

Legal justice

Educational opportunities

African lands

Personal courtesies

Public facilities A

MEANS

Employment

European lands

Civil order

Social and rec. facilities

Sexual relations

United Federal

Dominion

Political party preference
(excl. 33 others)

spite differences in history, social structure, and ethnic composition. Occupational status and length of schooling seem consistently to be related to race attitudes. At the higher socioeconomic and educational levels, attitudes about Africans and Negroes are generally more tolerant, less conservative, and more in favor of removing legal and nonlegal differentiations.

In Southern Rhodesia and the Union of South Africa, length of residence, country of birth, religious affiliation or preference, national or ethnic origin, and political party preference appear as important correlates of race attitudes. Comparisons with the United States and Great Britain are less valid because the data on income, age, sex, region, and industrial classification are inconsistent cross-culturally. These findings point to the importance of such factors as the ratio of Africans to Europeans, the length of European settlement, the cultural and social history of the country, the ethnic and religious identifications of the immigrants, and the proportion of newcomers in the population in examining the context or milieu that may influence the importance of the other correlates upon race attitudes.

The best predictor of race attitude among the continuous variables used in our study is length of schooling. But if, in addition, an individual's political party preference, religious affiliation, national or ethnic identification, and occupation are also considered, the probability of success in predicting race attitude may be enhanced.

### INTERRELATIONS OF SOCIAL CHARACTERISTICS

What generalizations can be made from the data on the total European population in Southern Rhodesia? We hypothesized that certain social characteristics are related to attitudes about Africans. Upon analysis, however, the subpopulations show considerable variation on each category of differentiating practice. This suggests the futility of assuming the existence of a "typical" European in Southern Rhodesia. Whatever uniformity in European opinion may have existed in the past—and it is facile to expect that it was highly constricted—present race attitudes are far from homogeneous on many laws and customs. Yet the data suggest that, since World War II, the European population has become more heterogeneous than before: the proportion of people born in Great Britain has increased; more professional, technical, managerial, and administrative positions have been created and filled as a result of the shift from the primacy of agriculture and mining to secondary industry; government and business services subsequently have expanded; the proportion of recent immigrants has risen; and many aliens detained in Southern Rhodesia during the Second World War have remained as new residents.

CONSENSUS AMONG SUBPOPULATIONS

A ranking of subpopulations by their standard deviations, as shown in Chapter 9, demonstrates that the extent of agreement within a subpopulation varies with the degree of conservatism in race attitude. Of the ten subpopulations with the *least* consensus, seven also obtain the highest scores in relation to certain characteristics, e.g., persons with no religious affiliation, an annual income of £ 600–899, or seventeen or more years of schooling. Of the ten groupings with the *greatest* consensus in race attitudes, four are at the most conservative end of the scale (according to different criteria) and four others are the next lowest in score, e.g., members of the Dutch Reformed church, craftsmen, Afrikaners, and supporters of the Dominion party. We may conclude, then, that race attitudes held by the conservative subpopulations tend to be less diversified than attitudes among the more change-oriented groupings. Homogeneity is related to conservatism in Southern Rhodesia.

Table 80 illustrates that the personal and social characteristics of Europeans are not randomly associated with attitudes about Africans. To construct this table, sixty-two of the subpopulations * identified in the study were ranked by the size of their mean attitude scores. Only those subpopulations containing at least twenty-five cases were included in the ranking. Then, for purposes of comparison, the highest and lowest quartiles were split from the ranking of means and placed in Table 80. The significance of these findings should be obvious to those acquainted with the past and present scene in Southern Rhodesia. These valuable data indicate, albeit in a limited fashion, the types of real groups in which a person is likely to participate, the kinds of cultural influences that pervaded the environment in which he was raised, and the likelihood of changing attitudes with an increasing period of residence in the Colony. Throughout our study, we have asserted the value of appreciating the influences that lie behind the contemporary attitudinal data. It should be noted that of the twelve characteristics used in analyzing the sample, three of them —age, sex, and census district—do not appear in Table 80.

The results presented in Table 80 should be interpreted with caution. Even though a religious grouping and an occupational class may have the same quantitative score on their race attitudes, this does not imply that all of the individuals in the one are members of the other. Neither do differences between the English and Afrikaner ethnic groups, for example, prove that the latter are necessarily more rigid or intolerant individuals. It is always essential to consider the social

* These are the subpopulations identified in Tables 39, 40 (collapsing "60–69," "70–79," and "80 and above"), 41, 42, 44, 45, 46, 47, 48 (collapsing "£1–299" and "£300–599"), 49, 50, and 51.

and cultural factors existing in the environment in which individuals were born and raised. Differences in attitude about Africans may primarily reflect dissimilar cultural backgrounds which, for the individual, are significant by virtue of his biological descent and membership in various social groups. These groups, like others elsewhere, vary in the degree of pressure they exert upon members for conformity in thinking, feeling, policy orientation, and acting in relation to Africans. Personality variables, such as temperament and intelligence, may have less effect upon behavior in such situations than they do in less rigidly structured societies.

TABLE 80. *Rank Order of Subpopulations \* within the Highest and Lowest Quartiles of Scores*

| Rank | Characteristic | No. | Subpopulation | Mean |
|------|----------------|-----|---------------|------|
| 1 | Education | 40 | 15–16 years | 3.34 |
| 2 | Education | 29 | 17 and above years | 3.33 |
| 3 | Occupation | 68 | Professional and technical | 3.21 |
| 4 | Type of industry | 95 | Government and business services | 3.15 |
| 5 | Religious affiliation | 26 | No affiliation | 3.03 |
| 6 | National or ethnic origin | 35 | British, Welsh, and Irish | 3.00 |
| 7 | Education | 60 | 13–14 years | 2.94 |
| 8 | Income | 74 | £600–899 | 2.92 |
| 9 | Religious affiliation | 58 | Roman Catholic | 2.90 |
| 10 | Political party preference | 290 | United Federal | 2.88 |
| 11 | Country of birth | 31 | Non-Commonwealth | 2.84 |
| 12 { | Country of birth | 190 | United Kingdom and Eire | } 2.82 |
| | Length of residence | 112 | 0–4 years | |
| 14 | Income | 44 | £1800 and above | 2.71 |
| 15 { | National or ethnic origin | 35 | Others (exc. Rhod. and S. Afr.) | } 2.70 |
| | Occupation | 117 | Managerial, admin., and clerical | |
| | | | **MEAN** | **2.45** |
| 48 { | Type of industry | 50 | Construction | } 2.22 |
| | Country of birth | 78 | Southern Rhodesia | |
| 50 { | Type of industry | 75 | Manuf. & repair; e., w., & s. serv. | } 2.20 |
| | Type of industry | 59 | Agriculture, forestry, and fishing | |
| 52 | Income | 148 | Nil | 2.19 |
| 53 | Length of residence | 55 | 40 and above years | 2.18 |
| 54 | Occupation | 74 | Others [skilled, sales, etc.] | 2.16 |
| 55 | Religious affiliation | 53 | Methodist | 2.14 |
| 56 | Length of residence | 54 | 30–39 years | 2.11 |
| 57 { | Education | 150 | 9–10 years | } 2.07 |
| | Country of birth | 177 | Union of South Africa | |
| 59 | Occupation | 36 | Craftsmen | 1.95 |
| 60 | Education | 56 | 0–8 years | 1.83 |
| 61 | Political party preference | 177 | Dominion | 1.78 |
| 62 | National or ethnic origin | 70 | Afrikaner | 1.48 |
| 63 | Religious affiliation | 47 | Dutch Reformed | 1.38 |

\* Wherein N = 25 or more cases.

The roles that mature individuals fill may sometimes offset the importance of the earlier cultural milieu. For example, the social status of craftsmen in Southern Rhodesia, as in many industrial countries, is comparatively low. Whether they are ethnically English or Afrikaner seems to have little relation to their race attitudes, particularly when the length of residence in the Colony is held constant. Again, there appears to be some occupational selection related to ethnic affiliation. If certain people are reluctant to serve Africans in shops and businesses, they may choose vocations in which their race attitudes bring no economic disadvantage. Such a proclivity for a "closed" commercial enterprise, for example, may be associated with the fact that there are relatively few Afrikaner businessmen in Southern Rhodesia.

REFERENCE GROUPS

Individual race attitudes may be better understood if the "reference groups" to which individuals refer in evaluating themselves are considered. Israeli immigrants assess their status and self-conception more by reference to Israel than to Southern Rhodesia, as do the United Kingdom- or South African-born with their country of birth or ethnic group. Or again, foreign missionaries tend to refer to the countries from which they have come or, either alternatively or jointly, to an "international brotherhood" that ideally has no national or ethnic boundaries. These various identifications help to explain the persistent influence of the values and norms learned in other societies on immigrants to Southern Rhodesia even after a lengthy period of residence (see Table 43). No complete shift occurs in race attitudes even though a large measure of racial and cultural differentiation obtains in the new society.

Race attitudes in Southern Rhodesia, therefore, seem to be only slightly related to such individual factors as age, sex, and constitution. Personal and social characteristics are relevant as *indicators* of the kinds of groups an individual participates in and the roles he plays; they also suggest possible groups that have both African and European members. Individuals need to be viewed in the context of the "field" in which they act, or may act: How do various subpopulations or groups interact with Africans in residential areas, Parliament, conferences, "sundowners," theaters, and on the street? Do craftsmen and professional people behave similarly toward Africans? What religious groups have different or similar practices in respect to the avoidance or acceptance of Africans? What kinds of Acts were legislated when the South African- or the United Kingdom-born were the largest proportion of the population? We have tried to answer some of these questions, but our attitudinal scale allows only a partial approximation to a definitive picture of all race relations during Southern Rhodesia's history.

We consider it extremely important that the most significant characteristics related to race attitudes (Table 79) in Southern Rhodesia point to real rather than artificial groups. Few existing social groups include all people of a given age, all males or females, all inhabitants of a populous district, or all persons who earn between £900 and £1199 annually. In contrast, religious affiliation, political party preference, ethnic affiliation, country of birth, length of schooling (by generating common interests), and occupation are common criteria for the formation and persistence of groups within Southern Rhodesian society. It is encouraging to find, therefore, that these six characteristics are the ones most related to race attitudes held by individuals of European descent. But even more, our findings show a considerable measure of consistency with some of the significant correlates of race attitudes elsewhere. In this sense, our study will allow for a fuller and more theoretical understanding of intergroup relations across national boundaries.

# 19

## THE ORGANIZATION OF RACE ATTITUDES

### CATEGORIES OF DIFFERENTIATING PRACTICES

Eleven categories of laws and customs that differentiate Africans and Europeans seem to flow from an analysis of the data on race attitudes, although five of the sixty-six items are not amenable to classification. In Chapter 7, the scores of the total sample on each of these categories were first introduced. Then we proceeded to analyze the relation between attitudes about each category and the eight significant personal and social characteristics. It is necessary now to pull together our discrete findings, and to discuss the significance of the variation in race attitudes in relation to the different categories of laws and practices.

### THE ANALYSIS OF FACTORS

The eleven categories established to facilitate more detailed analyses received confirmation from the factor analysis reported in Chapter 8. One general factor, "conservatism," had significant loadings on every item analyzed. From this, we concluded that race attitudes of Europeans in Southern Rhodesia vary on a continuum that ranges from "conservative" to "change-oriented." In addition, seven group factors emerged that indicated the presence of distinctive or essential features common to a number of items. These factors were generally equivalent to the eleven categories presented in Chapter 7. The principal difference was that one group factor, "physical separation," encompassed six of the distinctive categories: opportunities on European lands, social and recreational facilities, employment, opportunities on African lands, and two types of public facilities.

However, sixteen of the sixty-six items on the questionnaire were excluded from the factor analysis for statistical and other reasons. The five items excluded because of changes in law or practice clearly bear some relation to the established factor plan. Similarly, if the variability had been greater on the eleven items omitted for statistical considerations, it is reasonable to assume their loadings would have fallen on the same factors.* Ten of these were among the thirteen items in the entire scale on which the *most conservative* scores were obtained; the mean score of the ten items, in fact, was only .82. The only other statistically inappropriate item (no. 51, $M = 4.64$) received the *second highest* score among all statements in the questionnaire.†

THE BASIC CONTINUA

In focusing upon the eleven categories into which the sixty-one items (excluding the five "unclassifiable" ones) have been arranged, we are interested not only in the general attitudes of Europeans in Southern Rhodesia, but also in the extent of their consensus or disagreement.

A review of Table 28 indicates that Europeans want most to change those practices relating to inequalities in legal justice ($M = 4.52$). It may be noted that two of the three items in the category concern *principles* more than they do situations of on-going *interaction* between Africans and Europeans. The majority of the sample wishes to remove any practices that result in partial legal justice, but they also prefer to *tighten* the penalties given to both Europeans and Africans who violate the law. The conservative responses to the item on the ex-

* The following factors would probably have significant loadings on the items cited: Factor I: all sixteen omitted items; Factor II: 3 (?) and 18 (?); Factor III: 35, 3, 37, 40, 49, 32, 44, 39, 59, 43, 18, and 10 (?); Factor V: 51; Factor VI: 10 (?), 21, and 12; Factors VII and VIII: 35, 49, 32, 44, 39, 59, 43, 18, and 22. Our reasoning here is based upon the classification discussed in Ch. 7 and upon the rationalizations expressed by the sample for the responses they have made on the items.

† Looked at in another way, two of the sixteen items omitted for *any* reason received the *highest* scores within their categories. Also, thirteen of the fourteen remaining items were those with the *most conservative* scores in their categories.

clusion of Africans from jury duty (no. 15, $M = 2.26$) likewise suggest a general unwillingness to allow Africans to *participate* in one of the processes by which legal justice is determined. Equal legal justice, it is thought, can best be served through separate judicial procedures and groups.

Of all the. categories, legal justice receives the most irregular responses of the sample. This is manifested particularly in relation to type of industry, occupation, and country of birth (see Figures 5, 6, 7). When the three statements in the category are examined, even greater variability in attitude emerges. As on the category of legal justice, an anomalous response pattern occurs: the high scores indicate the wish of Europeans to rectify any partial justice in Southern Rhodesia, but the nature of the desired change is actually to toughen the penalties for violators of the law irrespective of their race or culture.

The other categories that receive scores above the theoretical midpoint of 3.00 are educational and training opportunities ($M = 3.71$), opportunities on African lands ($M = 3.63$), and personal courtesies and etiquette ($M = 3.42$). Of these three, only the last involves no support for the physical separation of Africans or the provision of "equal but separate" opportunities. Deference behavior, as we have said, is a mechanism by which status differences may be accommodated in necessary situations of interaction. That the sample wishes to discontinue some of these practices but to maintain others indicates a recognition of the evolutionary changes in the status system of Southern Rhodesia. But again, the principle of showing equal deference may be endorsed more readily than it is practiced. The same inference seems valid when considering opportunities for enlarging the size of African farms, the extension of municipal amenities, and the provision of better educational and training facilities. None of these immediately threaten to upset the customary segregation that pervades much of Southern Rhodesian life. The conservative score on item 34 ($M = 1.28$), the attendance of Europeans and Africans in the same schools, denotes the strength of feeling about maintaining segregation in education.

All the remaining categories include situations that involve progressively greater social contact with Africans. As the potentiality of close, intimate, and prolonged contact increases, European attitudes become more conservative. More than half of the sample agree that "the rate for the job" should be paid to all persons irrespective of race or culture (no. 8, $M = 3.36$); but the majority are unwilling to alter existing practices in employment ($M = 2.21$) whereby Africans are excluded from European trade unions, are not employed in some businesses or hired as counter attendants, and are rarely placed in supervisory positions over European workmen.

The contrast in the mean scores of the two types of public facilities (M = 2.89 and 1.20) has been noted before. It may also be observed that all the subpopulations give almost identical support to the maintenance of segregated social and recreational facilities (M = 1.17) and Type B facilities (M = 1.20). Since the distribution of subpopulation scores on these two categories is virtually identical, a more appropriate category, "Private facilities," may be suggested to include both sets of practices. The responses for maintaining the current customs relating to cross-racial sexual relations (M = .98) are close to those dealing with private facilities; but the scores and their distribution patterns among the subpopulations are sufficiently different to justify a separate identity for the category. Still, there is a high correlation, for example, between attitudes about cross-racial sexual relations and the desire to preserve segregated housing and residential areas.[1]

In the category of civil order and political control (M = 1.57), the highest score is obtained on the extension of the franchise to Africans in urban areas (no. 27, M = 2.49). But on the whole category of differentiating measures, Europeans have little desire to alter the status quo. Once more, the contrast between ideals and actual situations is illustrated by the divergent item scores. Europeans generally feel it important to change the practice of excluding Africans from political meetings open to the general public (no. 28, M = 3.80). On the other hand, the mean scores on items dealing with the present franchise arrangements (nos. 24, 23, 26) stand conservatively at 1.58, 1.44, and 1.18, respectively. The sample feels even more strongly about maintaining the practice of greater police surveillance at African meetings (no. 21, M = 1.03). It may be recalled that no discernible bias in the responses to our questionnaire resulted from the State of Emergency that was proclaimed in Southern Rhodesia in 1959.*

It was expected that responses to particular items and categories would differ. Indeed, on a six-point scale the range in item scores is from 4.83 to .41, while the category scores vary from 4.52 to .98. Thus, to report that Europeans in Southern Rhodesia collectively have

---

* The difference in test scores between persons living in the districts of Salisbury (fieldwork during the Emergency) and Bulawayo (prior to the Emergency) is .24. The difference in scores on the category of civil order and political control is .12; while smaller, it is not the least of the differences in category scores. On the items dealing with police surveillance at African meetings (no. 21) and the ownership of firearms (no. 12), the differences are .12 and .00, respectively. None of these differences are statistically significant.

a mean score of 2.45, and that it is significantly below the theoretical mean score of 3.00, has only limited utility. Firstly, the sample may have given more conservative responses to our questionnaire than they would have done either to unstructured or "free-response" items [2] or to a scale with more than four alternative response choices. Secondly, the mean score does not indicate feelings about particular differentiating laws or customs, or whether individuals are lukewarm in their support of the social system but favor changing some parts of it. Thus, in addition to the *item* score, it is important to know *how many people* feel strongly about maintaining or discontinuing (a) most or (b) some of the practices. Such findings will enable the researcher to discern subcultural and social class differences, viz. the English in contrast to the Afrikaners, or the professional persons in contrast to the craftsmen.

Despite variations in both item and individual scores, however, Europeans as a whole react consistently along two basic continua about the system of racial differentiation in Southern Rhodesia. First, if a differentiating law or custom involves an ideal *principle* rather than an evaluation of the advisability of *personal association* with Africans, then there is a correspondingly greater desire to implement the principle forthwith. But secondly, and on the other hand, it is the wish of most Europeans to maintain segregation or separation in *situations of cross-racial contact*. The more personal such relations might be, the greater is the conservatism in attitude. Thus, item scores correlate neatly with the transition from impersonal, transitory, and public settings to situations of privacy, intimacy, and less fleeting contact. The contrast in the mean scores for Type A (M = 2.89) and Type B (M = 1.20) categories of public facilities reinforces this observation. These data will be of value in supporting the themes discussed in the final chapter.

CONSENSUS ABOUT CATEGORIES

In Table 28, the mean scores and standard deviations of the categories of items were presented in ranked order. These same data are now given in Table 81 in the order of consensus, as indicated by the standard deviations. The rank order of categories by (a) standard deviations shows an interesting parallel with that of the previous ranking by (b) mean attitude scores. However, differences in standard deviations between some ranks are very small. Between the seven categories on which there is greatest consensus, the range in standard deviations is only .19. The range in the four categories with the least consensus (excluding unclassified) is but .15. But between the *nearest* categories in these two groupings (ranks 7 and 8), there is a difference of .16, the largest gap of all.

The ranking in Table 81, therefore, indicates that as Europeans feel more strongly about maintaining differentiating practices, they also are more homogeneous in their attitudes. Thus, the analysis of attitudes about the categories of differentiating measures suggests the same conclusion reached when attitudes were analyzed by subpopulations: the greater the conservatism of Europeans in Southern Rhodesia, the greater the homogeneity in attitudes.

TABLE 81. *Rank Order of Categories, by Standard Deviations*

| *Mean scores* | | | | *S.D. scores* | |
|---|---|---|---|---|---|
| *Mean* | *Rank* | *Category* | *Rank* | *Mean* | *Range* |
| 2.89 | 5 | Public facilities, Type A | 1 | 2.09 | |
| 4.52 | 1 | Legal justice | 2 | 2.07 | |
| 3.71 | 2 | Educational and training opportunities | 3 | 2.02 | |
| 3.42 | 4 | Personal courtesies and etiquette | 4 | 1.95 | .19 |
| 2.21 | 6 | Employment | 5 | 1.95 | |
| 1.80 | 7 | Opportunities on European lands | 6 | 1.93 | |
| 3.63 | 3 | Opportunities on African lands | 7 | 1.90 | |
| 1.57 | 8 | Civil order and political control | 8 | 1.74 | |
| .98 | 11 | Sexual relations | 9 | 1.70 | |
| 1.17 | 10 | Social and recreational facilities | 10 | 1.63 | .15 |
| 1.20 | 9 | Public facilities, Type B | 11 | 1.59 | |
| 3.24 | — | Unclassified | — | 2.03 | |
| 2.45 | Mean | | Mean | 1.87 | |

The greatest variations in the rankings by (a) and (b) occur in the categories of Type A public facilities and opportunities on African lands. These are explicable when the items in the categories are examined. In the Type A public facilities, four of the legal restrictions upon Africans were either discontinued by the Government or practices were changed during the course of fieldwork: elevators, lottery tickets and horse racing, entrances to banks and post offices, and railway booking offices. The responses to the item about sporting events were probably affected by the fact that Southern Rhodesia's first major interracial athletic meeting was held during the period of our fieldwork; in the three-mile race, a famous British runner was bested by an African from Northern Rhodesia. The question of interracial church services, which involves a moral principle more clearly than does the use of other public facilities, received the third least agreement ($\sigma = 2.29$) of all the items in the questionnaire. In the category of employment practices, the item concerning the costs to Africans of traveling to work had a significant loading on the factor of legal justice reported in Chapter 8. But since a standard deviation score .06 higher would rank this category in its "proper" place, the small difference may simply be anomalous.

The "White Man's Rank Order of Discrimination"

Neither space nor the existing research material permits an accurate assessment of cross-cultural attitudes about various types of racially differentiating laws and customs. Of the three countries we have discussed in this chapter, the attitudes of Europeans in South Africa seem to parallel most closely those in Southern Rhodesia. The limited information on European race attitudes in Great Britain suggests that any comparisons with Southern Rhodesia might reveal wide variations. The United States is intermediate in its similarity to Southern Rhodesia, in terms of the general nature of race relations.

The intercultural and interracial milieu of Southern Rhodesia and the United States (especially the Deep South) are not completely identical, of course. There are different legal sanctions in the two countries for practices concerning segregated rural reserves and urban locations, the franchise, marriage, freedom of movement, and the consumption of alcoholic spirits. But generally speaking, the culture and social organization of Europeans in Southern Rhodesia and whites in the southern United States are sufficiently analogous to invite a brief discussion. The wealth of American material invites many comparisons with the land of Rhodes. But we must be selective, and will choose only one apposite theory to discuss.

MYRDAL'S STUDY

In an extensive study of Negro-white relations in the United States, Myrdal (1944) perceived a pattern of behavior that he designated the "White Man's Rank Order of Discrimination." Assessing his own observations and the results of innumerable scientific studies, he argued that a "strategic constellation of forces in race relations," especially in the Deep South, was the anti-amalgamation doctrine of the whites. The degree of racial segregation or "discrimination" against Negroes varied with evaluations of particular situations (cf. our "categories" of behavior) that were made by whites. The following passage is worthy of quotation:

It is desirable that scientifically controlled, quantitative knowledge be substituted for impressionistic judgments as soon as possible. [A footnote to this sentence reads: Such studies should not only break the rank order into finer distinctions, but also develop a measure of the distance between the ranks in the order. It would, further, be desirable to ascertain individual differences in the apprehension of this rank order, and to relate these differences to age, sex, social class, educational level, and region.] It should be noted that the rank order is very apparently determined by the factors of sex and social status, so that the closer the association of a type of interracial behavior is to sexual and social intercourse on an equalitarian basis, the higher it ranks among the forbidden things.[3]

In this section, we will briefly compare the Southern Rhodesian data, by ranked categories, with the rank order theory proposed by Myrdal and studied later by other social scientists. To make the comparison, it is necessary to eliminate three of our categories (and the five unclassified items), since they are not directly comparable with those specified by Myrdal.[4] Another three of our categories also have been combined into one to facilitate the comparison. Table 82 presents

TABLE 82. *The "White Man's Rank Order of Discrimination" in Southern Rhodesia Compared with the Deep South of the United States*

|  | Deep South | Southern Rhodesia | | |
|---|---|---|---|---|
|  | Rank | Rank | | Categories |
| Myrdal's categories | order | order | Mean | (Table 28) |
| Legal justice | 2 | 1 | 4.52 | 1 |
| Personal courtesies and etiquette | 5 | 2 | 3.42 | 4 |
| Breadwinning and relief | 1 | 3 | 2.21 | 6 |
| Public services and facilities | 4 | 4 | 1.81 | 5, 9, 10 |
| Political participation | 3 | 5 | 1.57 | 8 |
| Sexual relations | 6 | 6 | .98 | 11 |

the result of this exercise. In reading the table, the practices that Europeans in Southern Rhodesia most desire to discontinue are ranked first. This necessitates a rephrasing of Myrdal's terminology, since the most "discriminatory" rank will be number 6.

Europeans in Southern Rhodesia closely agree with whites in the Deep South (in 1944) about the importance of removing inequalities in obtaining legal justice. In practice, however, fewer restrictions are placed upon Africans' receiving justice in Southern Rhodesia than was true of southern Negroes. Ranking second in Southern Rhodesia is the category of personal courtesies and etiquette, whereas in the U.S. this category ranked next to the bottom. The obverse ranking suggests, for whatever it is worth, that the "British concern for justice and respect for the individual" is stronger in Rhodesia than the whites' concern was in the southern states. Again, because more political power resides in the hands of white Rhodesians than in those of white Southerners, the former may feel it less necessary to insist on wide gaps in etiquette to maintain their status vis-à-vis Africans.

The category of breadwinning and relief receives the third most support for introducing changes in Southern Rhodesia. The desire to discontinue racially differentiating practices, however, is qualified by a preference to establish "separate but equal" opportunities. In the Deep South, the category ranked at the top, indicating the least desire to maintain discrimination in this area. But if questions of status differentials and supervision in employment are examined, much of the apparent diversity of attitude in the two countries virtually disappears.

Ranking fourth in both countries are the opportunities for Africans and Negroes to use various public services and facilities. On the other hand, Europeans in Southern Rhodesia differ substantially from southern whites about the franchise and other political activities. There has never been a universal adult franchise in the Colony, and Europeans generally believe that it is extremely important to maintain the present qualifications for an undefined number of years. In the Deep South, Negroes have had a *de jure* right to vote since 1869 (longer in some states), but *de facto* barriers have been imposed, especially in the states with the largest Negro populations. In Southern Rhodesia, the ratio of Africans to Europeans is many times greater than the racial proportions in the American South. There is also less similarity among cultural groups in Southern Rhodesia than in the United States. The social situations in the two countries are perhaps most divergent in these two ways.

Finally, in both countries the whites believe that cross-racial sexual relations, or marriages that involve white women, are the most important category of practices to be prohibited. Myrdal characterized the beliefs behind these differentiations as an "anti-amalgamation doctrine," and viewed the other types of behavior between Africans (or Negroes) and Europeans (or whites) as meaningful within the pervasiveness of the doctrine. Interracial marriages are illegal in the Deep South and legal in Southern Rhodesia; yet they rarely occur in Rhodesia, and they do not escape the moral censure of the European population. Extra-marital sexual relations have also been considerably less frequent between European masters and African servants in Southern Rhodesia than between masters and slaves (or servants) in the United States. As suggested in Chapter 2, this is probably due to the traditionally almost exclusive employment of males as domestic servants in Southern Rhodesia, in sharp contrast to the pattern in the United States. But the data indicate that both legal and moral sanctions operate to lend legitimate support to the anti-amalgamation doctrine in Southern Rhodesia.

OTHER STUDIES

If Myrdal's rank order is fully valid in other countries, it has not been empirically established, nor indeed has it even in the Deep South, as far as we know. Two social scientists have tested the rank order in less segregated areas of the United States.[5] In a New England town, Lee (1954) found that the pattern of race relations diverged somewhat from what Myrdal suggested as most characteristic of the Deep South. The amount of white discrimination against Negroes was smallest in education. Then, in descending order, were greater discrimination (cf. our "conservatism") in politics, the use of public facilities, religious and social activities, the more desirable jobs, and, finally, housing. It should be noted that this was a study of actual behavior rather than of attitudes.

The second study (Edmunds, 1954) was made in the southwestern states of Oklahoma and Texas, a "Mid-South" environment in terms of race relations. A sample of adults and college students were asked to rank the six categories of discrimination as described in Myrdal's own words. Edmunds' data showed that whites are least conservative about practices relating to jobs for Negroes. Then the rank order goes as follows: politics, public services, and courts. The most conservative ranks, by substantial margins, are categories involving social relations and, lastly, intermarriage.

Lee's categories are not closely comparable with those of Myrdal; hence direct comparisons are tenuous. Edmunds' data show greater support for Myrdal's hypothesis than do the findings from Southern Rhodesia. This is not unexpected, of course. But on many points, in both attitudes and overt behavior, there is much similarity between the Deep South and Southern Rhodesia. The differences may be better understood, however, by reference not only to the common features of culture and social structure developed in the two countries, but by paying attention as well to variations in values, legal and moral sanctions, social structure, population characteristics, and the spatial distribution of different racial and cultural groups. These data amply confirm the value of examining attitudes and overt behavior in the context of their sociocultural "fields."

# 20

## CONTINUITY AND CHANGE

### FROM PAST TO PRESENT

Southern Rhodesia is the end product of an era of expansion propelled by the desire of Europeans for adventure, the acquisition of new land, the drive to extend particular varieties of Christianity and civilization, and the search for raw materials and markets. Although one of the last areas in Africa to come into the known world, its development has been comparatively rapid and extensive.

The immigrants had come from societies that were late recipients of the impulses of civilization emanating principally from the eastern Mediterranean region (Linton, 1955). The indigenous people of southern Africa had been even farther removed from the cross-currents of cultural fertilization during the previous millennia. But they had made peculiar accomplishments of their own, now being reconstructed by the research of archaeologists and historians.

The indigenous and immigrant populations in Southern Rhodesia differed widely in religion, military and political power, knowledge, skills, and technology. Because so many types of differences coincided, they were often thought erroneously to be due to inherent racial superiority or inferiority. It was seldom understood that the *real* differences that structured social relations were nonbiological:

dissimilar systems of morality, medical knowledge, property owner-ship, belief about causation, work motivation, and the like.

Given the nature of these cultural and social differences, and given the assumption that the newcomers intended to make their home in a land that promised rich material rewards, Southern Rhodesia's sys-tem of segregation was in some ways inevitable. It was too late in history for the better equipped warriors to slaughter their opponents ruthlessly. Such irresponsibility and wild ambition had—for many Western European peoples—virtually extinguished itself in previous eras. The control of overt hostilities against native peoples was a corollary to the British tradition of respect for law and order.

Thus from the beginning, some kind of accommodation or modus vivendi was essential to permit the continued existence of plural cultures and societies. It was patent that an increasing interdependence would develop in time; and this was fostered by the Orders-in-Council of 1894 and 1898. It was relatively easy, however, to avoid intimate contacts during the early years.

Africans and Europeans complemented each other primarily in economic activities: Europeans provided the technical and organiza-tional skills and the capital funds, while Africans contributed their labor in a regimented system structured by an unfamiliar sense of time and regularity.

Residential and social segregation were casual at first, but as they developed during the first two decades, they came to be supported by legal as well as moral sanctions. Dual administrations were also sired, land reservation was implemented, virtually all Africans were excluded from the franchise, and separate educational and medical facilities appeared. In the Colony's early years, most of the expenses of African development came from the hut taxes and the contribu-tions of missionary organizations. Following the attainment of Self-Government in 1923, a more definite program for African develop-ment was formulated. After rather ad hoc beginnings, the Govern-ment broadened its policy in the 1930's. "Parallel development" be-came the object of widespread and conscious planning. The bifurcated administrative and educational systems helped to minimize contact between rural Africans and Europeans; its legacy still hinders African and European teachers and headmasters from making easy contacts and from undertaking joint discussions and planning.

Social relations between members of the two groups were generally informal on the farms and mines, although specific obligations were legally sanctioned by labor contracts and the Masters and Servants Act. But with increasing urbanization and industrialization, social relations became more impersonal and formal. The direct dependence of African laborers upon their employers gave way in the face of the demand for semi-skilled workers, an hourly pay scale, increased consumer purchases, and the growth of public welfare services. Europeans and Africans tended to associate as economic men, or automatons, rather than as whole persons. Even today, no social integration has occurred outside the work scene except for a few altruistic or politically "progressive" professional Europeans who associate with Africans. But increasing occupational competition between Africans and Europeans has brought a challenge to the traditional dominance of Europeans. That this has happened first in the economic realm should occasion no surprise; caste-like relations are usually less appealing to the administrators and managers than to the ordinary workmen in "rational" industries.

Because of their wealth, different tastes, and social status, upper-class Europeans had little occasion to come into direct social contact with Africans. Exceptions to this rule included Government officials responsible for administering African affairs, and their analogues among teachers, physicians, missionaries, and traders. On the other hand, farmers could avoid contact with Africans less frequently, partly due to the need for a laboring force, but also because of the greater ratio of Africans to Europeans in the rural population.

Europeans displayed hostility toward Africans in the early days, but aggressive actions declined with the introduction of systematic government, law, and order. In later years, aggression was displayed in strikes, restrictive legislation, verbal attacks, boycotting of African-grown crops, letters to the editor, housing covenants, humor, and personal assaults upon "cheeky" Africans. Segregation in residential and business areas, and in public facilities and services, was viewed as necessary to control or reduce friction and conflict. It was recognized that insufficient finances and self-interest led to disparities between facilities and services established for Africans and Europeans. Also, as most of these services and facilities were unknown to Africans before the immigrants came, the indigenous population did not demand them at first.

Only in the last decade has there emerged broad questioning of the assumption that urban areas are not designed to be the permanent home of an African proletariat. Yet the principle embodied in the Land Apportionment and other Acts is the keystone for many of the social relations between Europeans and Africans. The value of a stabilized and efficient labor force has been more fully recognized, and, in recent years, there has been greater realization of plans that will broaden the opportunities for African participation both in Southern Rhodesia's economy and in local political affairs. Programs for improving the quality and output of African farms have extended the degree to which Africans are accepted by Europeans. These include conservation schemes, the marketing of grain and livestock, campaigns against diseases and drought, and the increased participation of African consumers that has accompanied an enlarged per capita income.

As Africans have become acculturated, they have acquired many of the values and norms of Western culture. Few of them deny the merits of education, the satisfaction of owning land, the attractions of the city, and the paradoxical freedoms of "individualism." Common experiences, and the learning of a common set of ideas and aspirations, are fostering cooperation between the diverse cultural groups which met less than a century ago. The strongest forces working to conserve the status quo have only slowed, not prohibited, this process of change. The relative isolation of Rhodesia is now an historical cliché—modern communication networks and other social and political changes have thrown it fully into the contemporary world.

Thus, the trend of intergroup relations clearly seems to be a gradual but increased acceptance of Africans by Europeans. Having established their ascendancy over the indigenous peoples, the Europeans were able almost unilaterally to determine policy and the rate of African participation in the new social system. Although Southern Rhodesia's economic and political development have not been the product of joint planning, those days apparently are gone forever. The plural society is not free from conflicts and tensions, yet Europeans are increasingly aware that cohesion and consensus among all sections of the population are the foundations of the future. As the vortex of African nationalism sweeps southward from the Sahara, a growing number of Europeans realize that the viability of Southern Rhodesia lies more in the loyalty of its inhabitants than in the sanction of force which traditionally has been under the control of Europeans.

## RACIAL THEMES IN SOUTHERN RHODESIA

Throughout Southern Rhodesia's history, continuity as well as change has characterized the social relations of Europeans and Africans. Consistent patterns of European attitudes and overt behavior are observable vis-à-vis the indigenous population. Opler's concept of "themes" in culture may be useful in understanding intergroup behavior in Southern Rhodesia. For Opler (1948:120) a theme is "a postulate or position, declared or implied, and usually controlling behavior or stimulating activity, which is tacitly approved or openly promoted in a society."

For our purposes, themes may be inferred from historical documents, contemporary interview data, and personal observation and reflection. Themes are analogous to motivations and, as much research has shown, the latter also are seldom verbalized or explicitly stated. We also believe that the factor analysis reported in Chapter 8 is helpful in ascertaining themes that lie embedded in the culture of

Europeans in Southern Rhodesia. Thus, the interview data, historical documents, observation, and the factors extracted from the matrix of inter-item correlations jointly contribute to an appreciation of the reasons, motivations, and postulates that control or stimulate European race attitudes and behavior toward Africans in Southern Rhodesia.

Although we cannot speak quantitatively in describing themes, both the historical and contemporary data in Southern Rhodesia seem to lend a considerable measure of support to our analysis. Yet it is necessary to emphasize the tentative or hypothetical nature of these formulations. With proper research instruments and greater attention to the problem, themes may be verified or rejected with a higher degree of certainty that we can offer here. Similarly, it is essential to state that we are speaking in this section of the total European population, and not attempting to delineate subcultural variations.

MATERIALISM

A number of European ideas and values have centered on technological advancement, and on the manipulation and control of the physical environment. This theme was, and still is, combined with more than a tinge of idealistic optimism, however. It was generally believed that Southern Rhodesia's natural resources should be discovered, exploited, used, and traded. Numerous efforts were made by Europeans to gain and control the use of land, and also to redistribute the indigenous population, which possessed less knowledge and skill for developing the resources of the Colony. In time, this approach was extended to the lands reserved for Africans, being manifested in such legislation as the Natural Resources Act and the Land Husbandry Act.

Europeans in Southern Rhodesia, like Americans or Russians, point with pride to their success in modifying and controlling the physical environment. An early but extensive railway system, good roads that penetrate the country, growth in population, a rising per capita income, the Kariba Dam, the successful attraction of outside capital, and the new buildings and skyscrapers are all cited with enthusiasm. It is stated proudly that Southern Rhodesia's Prime Minister is the "second highest in the Commonwealth." This claim refers to the elevation above sea level of the Prime Minister's office; it is acknowledged, however, that the "highest" Prime Minister resides in Pretoria. Again, numerous official statements about Rhodesia's future have asserted the primacy of economic development. It is conceived that Africans will benefit from this and, at a later time, will be allowed to participate more fully in the municipal and territorial political systems.

MORAL IDEALISM

From their first appearance in what is now Southern Rhodesia, the Europeans thought of their activities as integral to the spread of "civilization." They were imbued with the idea of "progress," and viewed man and society as perfectable entities. Africans potentially could become "civilized" in the best British tradition through both religious and secular institutions. It was "good" that the indigenous population forsook its rustic and "pagan" habits and began to learn the "white man's ways."

The theme of moral idealism was frequently interpreted in terms of "the white man's burden." Much of this "burden," however, consisted of the benefits of materialism—profits from gold, copper, tobacco, and so on.[1] The altruistic motives probably were often rationalizations of the Europeans' superior power and technology. Not all immigrants explicitly stated their power motives as clearly as did Cecil Rhodes. Even though Rhodes failed to put the land from the Cape to Cairo under the Imperial Crown, speeches are still heard almost daily which assert that the destiny of Southern Rhodesia and the Federation is to provide an "answer" for Africa: by "successfully solving race relations," it will become the "center" of the rapidly changing continent.

From the beginning, there was uncertainty about how long it would take to transform Africans into "civilized" people. The dual administrative structure was conceived by many to be only temporary. In this undefined interim period, elaborate measures of control and the burden of developing services and facilities for Africans were imperative. But material expansion and moral idealism have not always complemented one another, and there has been persistent conflict about the Africans' proper "place" in the new society. As pointed out earlier, morality tended to be defined differently in Great Britain and Southern Rhodesia. The Colonists tended to think in terms of local circumstances. They possessed something of a "situational morality" that was difficult to reconcile with the "universal" or "absolute" moral principles of Christianity, socialism, or the more "humanitarian" ideology of Britain and the West. Consensus between these two philosophies has developed formally, if at all, in the doctrine of "parallel development." Much of the current controversy both within and outside Southern Rhodesia fundamentally revolves around these contrasting ideologies.

The cultural and situational heterogeneity of Southern Rhodesia gave rise to a host of separate and parallel institutions and practices. Much encouragement was given to maintaining African society and culture. An "administrative" conception of race [2] resulted in a dual division of government, partly to preserve the separate cultural communities and partly to minimize the possibility of competition and conflict. While it was thought desirable that Africans should learn European *culture,* it was not anticipated that they should become assimilated into European *society.* There was, in essence, an anti-assimilation and anti-amalgamation doctrine shared by most Europeans, and spatial segregation and social separation soon became institutionalized. British conceptions of "proper" social class relations found a "natural" home, and were reinforced in a setting that embraced peoples who also differed in language and race. "Separate but equal" facilities became the new conception of "paternalism" after Self-Government was attained in 1923. Few Europeans in Southern Rhodesia have questioned the validity of this policy, although in recent years a degree of doubt has become more noticeable. On the other hand, several schemes, such as the one for metropolitan transport, have been advanced that will enable a continuation of residential segregation as the cities keep spreading into the veld.

CONTAMINATION

Associated with the theme of separatism was the idea of preventing "contagion" or "contamination." Physical and social segregation were, and still are, justified by reference to Western medical knowledge and by fears of racial admixture. Both legal and moral sanctions have been applied by Europeans to prevent contamination through association with Africans. Considerations of health and racial "purity" led to the establishment of separate swimming pools, hotels, restaurants, clubs, theaters, schools, residential areas, train compartments, lavatories, hospitals, laws on the consumption of alcoholic spirits, and so on. The white woman was perhaps the major symbolic manifestation of this theme.[3] In many ways, she stood for all that was believed to be "good" in "civilization," including certain moral standards and the "superiority" of the "white race." Special laws were enacted to prohibit her from voluntary sexual contact with African men, in contrast to the absence of legal prohibitions on the same relationship between European men and African women.

In this connection, Africans have served as a "contrast conception."[4] Europeans and Africans have been imagined to have obverse personal and social characteristics. Some of this probably derives from the widespread association of black skin color with disease, darkness, terror, sorcery, lack of control, evil, and similar ideas and affairs.[5] In the Anglo-Saxon and Afrikaner cultures, there seems to be a traditional, deep-rooted reserve toward black people. In addition, the British particularly seem to have a dislike of "foreigners," since they are said to fail to understand or share the "unspoken language" of consensus in norms (Banton, 1959). The dislike of black people appears to be most typical of Rhodesian immigrants who have come from South Africa; but it also appears true of other immigrants, especially those of British descent who have lived in India. This distaste has extended not only to Africans as black individuals, but also to an array of African ideas and customs in marriage, law, religion, land ownership, and political organization.

PROTECTIONISM

The fifth main theme in European culture is closely allied to the two previous ones. Europeans set about informally—and after Self-Government, formally—to protect themselves from competition from Africans, and to prevent the loss of Western standards in the face of an overwhelming majority of indigenous people. This was rationalized, as indicated earlier, by a belief in their own inherent superiority, and the view that material rewards were justly due to people who possessed superior skills, broader knowledge, and greater military power.

The rationale was phrased as an unwillingness to lower "standards," even when the "standards" were "higher" than those existing in Great Britain. Protectionism was achieved through the various differentiating laws and customs mentioned above. The principal legislation in support of this theme included the Industrial Conciliation, Land Apportionment, Public Services, and various Electoral Acts. Protection was also extended to industry, as economically inefficient firms and practices were supported and maintained by Government subsidies (Leys, 1959). Artificially high wages were often paid to Europeans in relation to output, whereas Africans found, and still find, it impossible to earn a legitimate wage that puts them above "the poverty line" (Batson, 1945; Bettison, 1958). In agriculture, Europeans received larger subsidies for their crops, better marketing opportunities, technical facilities, fertilizers, and so on. Greater funds, more highly qualified personnel, and superior facilities reinforced the superior position of Europeans in education and health. Deference mechanisms were encouraged to symbolize the status of the dominant group. Africans were excluded from jury duty partly because it was considered essential to protect Europeans from partial legal justice.

Finally, in the political realm, high franchise qualifications protected the Europeans from any significant or sudden loss of political control. It was thought imperative to keep the Government in "civilized" hands, to confine African political activity primarily to the local councils in segregated Reserves, and to forbid the circulation of "communist" ideas and literature. In short, it was asserted that the only way to "assure democracy" was to protect the European community from political control by Africans in the foreseeable future. But in addition to the franchise, Africans were restricted in their freedom of movement and association, and in the possession of alcoholic spirits, arms, and ammunition. Belief in the morality of protecting themselves politically also led many Europeans in Southern Rhodesia to develop negative attitudes toward the British Government and the groups, organizations, and individuals outside the Colony who were critical of their way of life.

That these major themes persist among most Europeans today is not an anachronism. They are, like ideologies and myths, useful as a "social charter" to justify the existing order of things. The two themes of separatism and protectionism seem to pervade the reasons why individuals wish to maintain the current differentiating laws and customs in Southern Rhodesia. The fear of contagion is also strongly expressed, although with less certainty in the areas of employment, civil order, and legal justice. The theme of moral idealism seems common to the majority of Europeans in regard to land use, educational and training opportunities, public facilities, and civil order and political control. This theme, however, is combined with the desire for separate or parallel services, facilities, and opportunities for Africans and Europeans. Finally, the theme of materialism, while it has important psychological correlates of individual and group satisfaction and security, is related primarily to the economy and to the necessity of maximizing the development of Southern Rhodesia.

## CHANGES IN INDIVIDUAL ATTITUDES

In view of the continuity and change in Southern Rhodesia over time, what can our study contribute toward an understanding of changes in the race attitudes of individuals? Our data permit us to approach the question of attitudinal change only in an oblique way. We have discussed the importance of the context in which individuals acquire their race attitudes, and do or do not translate them into overt behavior. The effects of the cultural milieu and social situation upon attitudes may also be examined through the dimension of time. Since ours is not precisely a longitudinal study, we are unable to say how the race attitudes of discrete and named individuals have changed from one year to the next. Rather, we can seek to examine the change in attitudes by comparing classes of people according to some variable of time.

## ATTITUDE CHANGE AND SOCIAL CHARACTERISTICS

Of those characteristics analyzed in this study, age and length of residence are variables based upon the time dimension. We have found, however, that no significant relation exists between age and race attitude—the older Europeans are not significantly more conservative than the younger. On the other hand, length of residence is significantly related to race attitude, and this finding supports the argument presented earlier about the importance of the "field" upon individuals' attitudes.

TABLE 83. *Length of Residence and Attitudes among Contrasting Subpopulations*

| Characteristic | Contrasting subpopulations | No. | % more conservative, "Oldtimers" compared to "Newcomers" * (Mean difference = 20%) |
|---|---|---|---|
| Political party | United Federal | 290 | 24 |
| preference | Dominion | 177 | 23 |
| National or ethnic | English | 302 | 22 |
| origin | Afrikaners | 70 | 13 |
| Religious affiliation | Anglican | 194 | 13 |
| or preference | Dutch Reformed | 47 | —8 |
| Length of schooling | 15 and above years | 69 | 19 |
| | 0–8 years | 56 | 15 |
| Country of birth | U.K. and Eire | 190 | 21 |
| | Union of South Africa | 177 | 11 |
| Occupation | Craftsmen | 36 | 33 |
| | Prof. and technical | 68 | 16 |

* "Oldtimers" have lived in Southern Rhodesia for twenty or more years, and "Newcomers" have resided 0–4 years in the Colony.

If attitudes about Africans and length of residence are analyzed in relation to a third characteristic, some interesting observations emerge. But if a grouping based upon, say, occupation is subdivided in terms of length of residence, the resultant number of cases in each "cell" may be too small to permit any conclusive generalization. When the number of cases is small, perhaps under fifty or a hundred, the data must be interpreted with much caution. Table 83 shows the differences in race attitudes between "oldtimers" and "newcomers" in Southern Rhodesia when analyzed by a third characteristic. No analysis of attitudes in relation to type of industry and length of residence has been made, since the industrial groupings are generally quite similar in their atittudinal scores, except for persons in the government and business services.

The data in Table 83 indicate that the subpopulations whose attitudes are least affected by length of residence in Southern Rhodesia are the Dutch Reformed, the South African-born, the Afrikaners, and the Anglicans (especially those born in South Africa). Except for the Anglicans, these groupings also are among those having the more conservative attitudes *irrespective of length of residence.* This suggests that persons who have lived in South Africa, and who identify with the principal ethnic and religious groups among the Europeans in the Union, are least likely to alter their attitudes about Africans the longer they live in Southern Rhodesia. Given the similarities in the social and cultural milieu of the two countries, this finding is as expected.

On the other hand, the "oldtimer" and "newcomer" craftsmen show a greater difference in scores than do the professional and technical persons, even though the latter have significantly more tolerant race attitudes than the former. This anomalous finding is explained when the very small "cells" are examined. Of the thirty-six craftsmen, five fall in the newcomer class, whereas eleven are oldtimers. Among the latter, four are Southern Rhodesian-born and have a low mean score of 1.30. In contrast, no craftsmen appear elsewhere in our sample who were born in Southern Rhodesia. Thus, the unexpected finding is either due to random fluctuations within the small subpopulation, or it results from a selectiveness according to birthplace among the newer craftsmen. In sum, these differences in scores according to length of residence do not automatically indicate an increasing conservatism in the race attitudes of particular individuals. They may, on the contrary, partly reflect the operation of selective immigration at different periods in Southern Rhodesia's history (see Table 4).

ATTITUDE CHANGE AND CATEGORIES OF ITEMS

All but the Dutch Reformed among the subpopulations based upon the eight significant characteristics display the greatest conservatism among those who have lived in Southern Rhodesia for the longest period of time. Differences in attitudes can be analyzed not only by subpopulations, but also in relation to the categories of differentiating practices; that is, social characteristics other than length of residence can be held constant, while categories of items become variables.

It was observed earlier that the sharpest drop in attitude scores

TABLE 84. Length of Residence and Attitudes about Categories of Items

| Rank | Category (and no. items) | Years of residence | | | % more conservative compared to 0–4 yrs. | |
|---|---|---|---|---|---|---|
| | | 0–4 (N = 112) | 5–9 (N = 103) | 40 and above (N = 55) | 5–9 yrs. | 40 and above |
| 1 | Legal justice (3) | 4.78 | 4.29 | 4.52 | 10 | 5 |
| 2 | Educational and training opportunities (4) | 4.09 | 3.81 | 3.22 | 7 | 21 |
| 3 | Opportunities on African lands (4) | 3.97 | 3.64 | 3.32 | 8 ⎫ 9 | 16 ⎫ 18 |
| 4 | Personal courtesies and etiquette (9) | 3.73 | 3.43 | 3.17 | 8 ⎭ | 15 ⎭ |
| 5 | Public facilities, Type A (7) | 3.32 | 2.98 | 2.34 | 10 | 30 |
| 6 | Employment (4) | 2.59 | 2.16 | 2.03 | 17 | 22 |
| 7 | Opportunities on European lands (6) | 2.27 | 1.76 | 1.49 | 22 | 34 |
| 8 | Civil order and political control (9) | 2.09 | 1.63 | 1.39 | 22 | 33 |
| 9 | Public facilities, Type B (7) | 1.47 | 1.23 | 1.07 | 16 ⎫ 21 | 27 ⎫ 31 |
| 10 | Social and recreational facilities (5) | 1.47 | 1.07 | 1.15 | 27 ⎭ | 22 ⎭ |
| 11 | Sexual relations (3) | 1.29 | 1.10 | .85 | 15 | 34 |
| — | Unclassified (5) | 3.54 | 3.31 | 2.88 | 6 | 19 |
| | Means (66) | 2.82 | 2.46 | 2.18 | 13 | 22 |

339

may occur relatively early in the experience of European immigrants. Table 84 presents a further analysis of this finding. Persons who have lived in Southern Rhodesia 5–9 years display attitudes that are 13% more conservative than individuals with less than five years of residence.

When the difference in attitudes of these two groupings is examined by *categories* of items rather than on the entire questionnaire, however, some interesting findings become clear. In contrast to the 13% decline in scores for the whole scale, the largest variation is a 27% more conservative score about maintaining segregated social and recreational facilities. If the conservatism is analyzed in relation to the five highest and five lowest categories, Europeans in the 5–9 year period of residence show more willingness to preserve the status quo in the order of 9% and 21% respectively. This clearly suggests that the more personal and intimate the situations are in which interaction between Europeans and Africans might occur, the quicker the change in attitude in a conservative direction—in the direction, it may be noted, characteristic of Europeans born in Southern Rhodesia and South Africa who have had longer contacts with Africans.

If we move on to compare groupings based upon 0–4 and forty and above years (rather than 0–4 and 5–9 years) of residence, the total effect of the cultural milieu may be gauged. The oldtimers' attitudes are 22% more conservative than the newcomers'. In regard to particular categories, the oldtimers have scores about 33% lower on the opportunities (for Africans) on European lands, sexual relations, and civil order and political control. Finally, if the scores on the five top and five bottom categories are examined, they receive 18% and 31% less change-tolerant scores, respectively, among the older residents. Thus, the same inference as above can be made: the longer the residence in Southern Rhodesia, the greater the conservatism in race attitudes. But this is especially true about areas of behavior in which social contact with Africans is likely to occur, rather than in attitudes about segregated opportunities and facilities on reserved lands, personal courtesies and etiquette, and the morality of legal justice.

THE INDIVIDUAL AND THE SYSTEM

These considerations suggest that the more important influences upon attitudes are primarily nonindividual. Society and culture are supraindividual, and they exist largely outside the direct or conscious experiences and interests of individuals. As discussed in our study, these include various systems of socialization, education, communication, and propaganda; common geographical and climatic environment; the judicial system; particular methods by which elections are held; land apportionment; a dual administration for many African and European affairs; and segregated services and facilities.

Let us illustrate this point by looking briefly at some aspects of the socialization and status systems in Southern Rhodesia. The presence of cultural differences between Europeans and Africans, combined with the ready availability of a large and relatively inexpensive labor supply, encourage the persistence of the larger social system. In contrast to most societies, the European during infancy, childhood, and adolescence generally has one or more African servants whom he can command to fetch and carry. As a consequence, thousands of European children have had little experience in washing dishes, cleaning their own shoes, mowing the lawns, or carrying heavy articles (cf. Gibbs, 1947:55). The system of boarding schools for European pupils complements this socialization process: school vacations are too short for many to undertake regular jobs, especially for boys reared on farms who ordinarily might be expected to do two or three months of hard work alongside their fathers. Thus, between the early indulgence patterns of childhood and the responsibilities usually required in adulthood, there can be considerable discontinuity.

Yet again, European adults are generally able to continue directing numerous African workers rather than undertaking hard manual labor themselves. The Census statistics (Leys, 1959) show the rarity of Europeans in unskilled or semi-skilled occupations, and several observers have commented on this feature of the social system (e.g., Bray, 1958). This is the kind of situation, then, that greets many new immigrants and usually differs radically from the customary distribution of roles and prestige in the home country.

The young adult European worker in Southern Rhodesia is introduced to a system in which his status largely depends upon his income, and this is assured and protected by law and the traditionally high evaluation placed on color rather than on skill and output alone. Although this is now undergoing modification, the prospects of obtaining a higher social status and higher pay in Southern Rhodesia than elsewhere have been important stimuli for European immigration. The system thus seems to encourage a growth in the desire to preserve the status quo or else, it is feared, all that is gained will be lost. One of the stereotypes about colonists in general is that they are "manly, rough, and tough." That the contemporary social system of Southern Rhodesia discourages such behavior for most Europeans suggests a source of insecurity that many believe threatens their status and positions. For these reasons, it seems clear that attitudes about Africans should be, as they are, related to length of experience in Southern Rhodesia ("social age") rather than to chronological age.

There are, in brief, what may be called "imperatives" or "requirements" in the present system of race relations in Southern Rhodesia that do not depend primarily upon the attitudes of individual Europeans. The organization of society and many of the values in European culture contribute in large measure to the patterning of individual behavior. As Kluckhohn (1954:959) has said, behavior is never random because there are cultural pressures for conformity that pervade a society's beliefs, feelings, and values. Thus, to predict how a European will act in intergroup situations, more information is needed than his verbally expressed attitudes. Data should also be at hand regarding his self-conception, values, roles, cultural background, and the situation itself in which interaction is to occur. All of these are, as has been said, aspects of the "principle of limited possibilities." [6]

## ATTITUDES AND PUBLIC POLICY

One of the outstanding features of the Southern Rhodesian setting is the importance of the Government, and the values that lend support to it for making decisions affecting relations between Africans and Europeans. Under its Constitution, the Government assumes responsibility to find a compromise between the urgency for social change and the general desire of the European population to preserve the status quo.

Southern Rhodesia embraces a cultural heritage that is predominantly British. Its laws and customs, however, have reflected an adaptation of British traditions to local circumstances. In the period when the South African-born were the largest proportion of the European population, the Government's decisions tended to reflect their attitudes and values. In addition, the proximity of the Union of South Africa and its "native policy" have been among the strongest and most persistent influences upon Southern Rhodesia. Yet the direction of social change appears to be toward a more British and less South African emphasis. Throughout the whole period since European settlement began in Southern Rhodesia, the Government has been relatively stable and adaptable, an institution stimulating and protecting economic and social development. Although the British model of government has been traditional in the past, the political system of the future in Southern Rhodesia may still have to be worked out, and it could differ from that of an established constitutional democracy.

British traditions permit a tolerance of differing cultures and institutions, but they do not necessarily imply the loss of political control. From institutional tolerance—as seen clearest in "indirect rule"— it is but a "short step to cultural segregation" (Evans, 1950:11). Endogamous marriages in Britain, for example, have generally been within social classes. In Southern Rhodesia, endogamy has been ap plied easily in a culturally and racially mixed society: A "cultural segregation" has been combined with a tolerance of polygamous marriages, as the latter have not been legally proscribed as "repugnant to natural justice and morality." As in all societies, preferred patterns of marriage exist; and since they are never random, marriages have served as devices for cultural segregation.[7] Social clubs, other facilities and services, and residential restrictions have helped to structure social relations in the same way.

## THE LEGITIMACY OF GOVERNMENT

The British respect for authority and law rests largely on a belief in their sacredness. A reliance on faith and tradition allows the Government, as long as it is elected constitutionally, to make decisions and to take action with considerable freedom. Although the British Parliament now is less patrician than formerly, the hierarchical natures of both Parliament and society in the United Kingdom are distinctively illustrated in the distribution of deference, and in the symbolism of the monarchy and aristocratic society (Shils, 1956:48ff). The Southern Rhodesian Government also has power and legitimacy derived from the authority granted to it by the electorate.

In the colonies, as well as in Britain, "The concept of 'The Crown' expresses the subordination and responsibility of each person filling a political role to that symbolic role." [8] Political roles or offices are symbolically the "property" of Her Majesty's Government; thus, the legitimacy of government action is based upon office rather than upon the intellect, technical skill, experience, or race of the particular persons who assume positions of responsibility. In this sense, it may be noted, the moral and legal basis for the British type of government is not radically different from that in many other societies, including the indigenous African political systems in Southern Rhodesia.

## AFRICAN "POPULISM"

The British model of government meets with difficulties in Southern Rhodesia, however. The tendency to make decisions in closed party caucus, and to reveal few of the decisions made by the Government, for example, results in relatively little communication with "the common man." For Europeans in Southern Rhodesia, this poses little difficulty since most of them share the "silent" norms and procedures that give authority to the Government.[9] But for the total population, the distance of the Government "above" the people brings "built-in" or "structured difficulties" in obtaining the support and participation of Africans. What is a separation based upon social class in Britain becomes a racial separation as well in Southern Rhodesia. British traditions have made it difficult for the Government to consult with Africans. The system has given little encouragement to Europeans and Africans to discuss, formulate, approve, and implement common goals cooperatively.

Although they are reluctant to admit it, Europeans are in a hierarchical relationship vis-à-vis Africans in Southern Rhodesia. Since the aims of the "Responsible Government Association" were realized in 1923, there has been no significant "populist" or quasi-anarchist movement among the Europeans. On the whole, their political, economic, and social interests have been well protected. By the same token, the Africans are new to the British-derived system of government, and their divergences in class, culture, and race limit their acceptance and participation in the Government. The European system of government has functionally autonomous parts—Parliament, the Civil Service, commissions, industrial councils, and so on—that are absent in African society, where all institutions and associations are more tightly interrelated and less differentiated. Compared to the British and some others, the Africans in Southern Rhodesia traditionally have made less use of informers or secrecy. Chiefs, headmen, and elders in the community, clan, or tribe have collectively participated in making such decisions as those concerned with warfare, changing residences, and settling disputes. Their "jury" procedures have involved a larger number of interested persons who act cooperatively in an informal manner (Holleman, 1952).

Thus, in the evolving social system of Southern Rhodesia, virtually all of the populists are Africans. In so far as their nontraditional political parties and pressure groups will become better organized, the demands for more consultation and representation, and for less secrecy and authority based upon history, may be expected to increase. The Government—and perhaps the majority of the European population—wishes to have only "Left, Center, and Right" political parties in Southern Rhodesia, and it has consistently refused to recognize any African political movement as a legitimate contender for power. But it is difficult to see how parties can be nonracial, as long as the social system is generally structured on grounds of biological descent. The Administration, educational system, census statistics, residential areas, medical services, social clubs, and so on, are all predicated on differences in color and culture.

## ATTITUDES AND SOCIAL CHANGE

Finally, we need to consider the importance of changes in the race *attitudes of individuals* in relation to changes in the *social system*. We have shown that the social characteristics of the European population in Southern Rhodesia have varied through time, and may be expected to fluctuate in the future as well. We have also argued that the Government, supported by British values about "The Crown" and legitimate action that may be taken, can play a critical role in determining the future of relations between Europeans and Africans.

## IMMIGRATION AND THE FUTURE

The Government can partly build the kind of interracial or intercultural society it wishes, in terms of selected moral values, through a policy of selective European immigration. We have seen (cf. Table 80) that differences in race attitude are significantly related to various social characteristics. Several of these are relevant to any scheme for selecting immigrants: country of birth, national or ethnic origin, length of schooling, religious affiliation or preference, and occupation.

The data on differences in attitude have only limited practical utility, however. A selective immigration policy has as its corollary a large demand among outsiders to emigrate to the Colony. Countries such as Canada, Australia, and South Africa are in competition for many of the same Europeans in whom the Southern Rhodesian Government might be interested. Another factor, the relative prosperity of the mother country, also affects the number who seek economic or other satisfactions through emigration. And finally, the Southern Rhodesian Government realizes the difficulties of an open immigration policy for Europeans. Economic growth and differentiation produce "a need for continually higher levels of occupational performance in an increasing proportion of the population" (Parsons, 1959:29), yet the social system can absorb only a limited number of persons with unneeded talents. Whereas the least conservative scores on the whole questionnaire are made by technical and professional individuals with a long period of schooling, it is obviously impossible to fit more than a limited percentage of these persons into occupations that are psychologically and financially rewarding to them. These and other practical considerations obviously influence the decisions that can be and are made by policy-makers, and they need not concern us further. They simply indicate the multiple nature of the factors that bear upon immigration policy, as well as upon the nature and distribution of race attitudes.

Aside from these differences in the race attitudes of various subpopulations, they all show a progressive increase in conservatism the longer they live in Southern Rhodesia. Those who seem to alter their attitudes most are the least conservative groupings; whereas persons reared in southern Africa, who therefore have had more experience in the milieu of African and European relations, show a smaller increase in conservatism over the years (Table 83). These findings suggest the importance of what we have called *social age* rather than chronological age.

The European population generally wishes to alter little in the present pattern of race relations in Southern Rhodesia. The general factor of "conservatism" reported in Chapter 8 theoretically provides the most secure basis for predicting the possible behavior of individuals. But if a change in relations between Europeans and Africans is held to be desirable, whether in a more or less conservative direction, then the question may be asked as to the importance of changes in individual attitudes in relation to changes in Southern Rhodesian society.

AGREEMENT AND CHANGE

Many social scientists prefer to think of a particular attitude, trait, or factor as a variable continuously distributed in a "normal" fashion from one extreme to the other. Yet these characteristics "do not depend altogether on chance-biological determination. They depend also upon cultural determination, and here an entirely opposed principle is at work . . . [Cultures] tend to destroy the 'natural' variation in behavior through their demand for conformity" (Allport, 1937:333). Thus, in order to predict individual behavior, there must be an awareness of the degree of both the expected and the actual conformity and consensus in society. The data in Table 81 have indicated the degree of consensus among Europeans in Southern Rhodesia about maintaining or discontinuing the differentiating laws and customs. Where there are large standard deviations, the possibility of social change is theoretically greater than where the population is more homogeneous in its attitudes.

The possibility of social change when there is a wide lack of agreement in individual attitudes was well illustrated in the year after the fieldwork was undertaken for this study. Following the Proclamation of a State of Emergency in February, 1959, several racially differentiating laws or practices were changed: elevators ($M = 3.13$); betting in lotteries and on horse races ($M = 3.02$); entrances to some shops, banks, and post offices ($M = 2.56$); and railway booking offices ($M = 2.18$). All these changes were implemented with little overt friction and with no organized groups protesting and refusing to cooperate.

Since March 1959, laws or customs concerning fourteen other items cited in our questionnaire have either changed or else modifications (not necessarily a complete discontinuance) are imminent.* The attitude scores on these practices range from 3.91, on providing avenues to allow African grievances to be made known, to .41 on the item concerned with racially segregated lavatories. In all of the prac-

* These fourteen items are, in the rank order of their scores, numbers 41, 28, 9, 2, 3, 50, 8, 61, 10, 27, 11, 46, 48, and 44. "Imminent" means, in this connection, during the years 1960 and 1961.

tices discontinued or expected to change, only the one on lavatories has a standard deviation *below* the mean standard deviation (1.87) for all sixty-six items.

## THE ROLE OF ORGANIZED GROUPS

These events indicate that when the initiative is taken by the Government of Southern Rhodesia, it can successfully modify or eliminate the racial differentiations for which it has responsibility provided that (a) there is more than an average lack of consensus among the European population, (b) it acts rapidly and unequivocally, and (c) it faces no widespread opposition from organized interest groups. The last is illustrated by the early and recent opposition from European labor unions, and from the Dominion party and its predecessors, especially to making changes in the technical and apprenticeship training of Africans, the "rate for the job," and an "integrated" trade union structure. Other groups, based upon property ownership and residential neighborhoods, have also successfully organized opposition to the planned siting of recreational centers for Africans within existing European residential areas, and the location of African townships at a distance thought to be too close to European homes.

Just as conservative resistance comes from organized groups that wish to preserve the traditional structure of segregation—rather than from individuals acting singly and without organization—so does it appear that changes in relations between Europeans and Africans are the result of organized groups and associations. These include not only the Government of Southern Rhodesia, but also other groups among Africans and Europeans—to say nothing of Asians, Americans, and others—both inside and outside the country. We do not intend to exercise the reader with a review and analysis of these multiple groups and the pressures they exert. Rather, they are important to our study as they are mediated, in particular, by the Government; when, as Easton (1957) says, the in-puts of the political system are translated into out-puts or decisions.

The future of race relations in Southern Rhodesia, while related to the receptivity of individuals to the idea and fact of change, depends more upon the initiative of groups and associations. In particular, the British custom of delegating wide authority and initiative to the Government, including a permissiveness to make decisions and negotiations in secrecy, leaves it especially free to initiate whatever social changes are deemed to be desirable or necessary. Once the Southern Rhodesian Government has deliberated and acted, the European population—except for some of the Afrikaners, who in many ways resemble the "populist" Americans in the Midwest—generally accepts the decision even though it may be rather unpalatable. The symbol of "The Crown" not only allows administrators, judges, and police-men to execute their duties with considerable authority, but also produces wide respect for them among the European population.

Given the acceptance of the electorate, under the British system of government, the ruling party may follow a "middle strategy" between adhering to public opinion and introducing changes it thinks are desirable.[10] If the Government were required to wait for all individuals to alter their attitudes, the likelihood of substantially changing the present social system would be small. The direction of change, on the contrary, would be toward an increasing amount of segregation and differentiation. Thus, the Government, as with the law and the courts in Southern Rhodesia, Great Britain, and elsewhere, may be a creative agent and speed the rate of social change if this is believed to be worthwhile or necessary. The traditional and symbolic sanctions for making decisions and implementing policy, "in partial remove" from the electorate, constitute one of the peculiarities of the British system of government and the rule of law.

The course to be chartered in the future involves the Government's relations not only with Europeans, however, but increasingly with Africans as well. Here, differences in attitudes about authority and legitimacy pose a most crucial factor in intercultural and interracial relations among three million people in Southern Rhodesia. "Popu-lism" and "hierarchicalism" will need to be accommodated if the country's political system is to remain viable.


Our study has attempted to show the interrelation of the individual and society, of person and culture, and the effect of this interrelation on attitudes. Various groups provide the situations in which an individual acquires and expresses his attitudes in action. But more than race attitudes are learned by individuals during the period in which they acquire the set of values and ways of behaving patterned by a particular culture. They also learn and develop a set of attitudes about themselves and others, and about the role of collective versus individual behavior. Few Europeans in Southern Rhodesia, as we have pointed out before, have sought to take the law into their own hands.

Yet the motivation for social change is comparatively weak among Europeans. Their conservatism seems often to reflect an automatic membership in the dominant cultural group rather than a well-thought-out set of principles (neither is exclusive of the other, of course). Few Europeans or Africans know much about the others' systems of belief, value, ritual, social organization, and so on. Our interview data clearly indicate that relatively few individuals have subjected the social system of their country to a rational examination. As in other societies, the majority of the population pursue their daily round on the bases of faith and habit more than intellectual conviction; and they tend to rely extensively on beliefs about their racial and/or cultural superiority.[11]

Europeans do not always realize that there are imperatives or pressures for change that are independent of their individual attitudes, e.g., the need for efficiency in modern industry, the need for political representation of the total population, and the requirement of an adequate land base for all inhabitants. Yet evolutionary changes are continuing in Southern Rhodesia, as elsewhere in the world, and the *direction of change* is clearly one-way: toward increasing education, urbanization, industrialization, diversification, economic and political integration, and fewer nonrational practices such as differentiations based upon mythical suppositions about race.[12]

The direction of social change in Southern Rhodesia may be expected to parallel that in many countries. The requirements of an urbanized and industrialized "modern" society are matters of more than individual attitudes. They may, in fact, be considered as integral aspects of a social system whose future is based on an increasing degree of participation in the economic and political world beyond its boundaries. Given the conservative nature of race attitudes in the European population in Southern Rhodesia, any future goals would seem more probable of attainment if attempts were made to modify the system of race relations—that is, the social system—rather than to manipulate individual attitudes.

Yet the future complexion of race relations in Southern Rhodesia seems unclear. On the one hand, there are influences for social change embedded in the "rational" economic systems and "humanitarian" traditions in various sacred and secular ideologies of the Western world. These have been transmitted to both Africans and Europeans through schools, churches, books, radio, travel, and industry. The increasing tempo with which these factors are impinging upon Southern Rhodesia has brought some measure of awareness of the seemingly inevitable direction of change. Again, the lack of consensus in European attitudes about the racially differentiating laws and customs has enabled small modifications to be made. These decisions have been taken, it will be recalled, by an institutionalized group—the Government—charged with responsibility for more of Rhodesian life than is true of any other institution or group in the country. The attribution of a large measure of authority to the Government permits rather than necessitates the creation and implementation of a given policy.

On the other hand, social and cultural differences between Europeans and Africans in Southern Rhodesia have traditionally been supported by the values placed upon aristocracy, hierarchy, and preserving of "standards." The British tolerate—if they do not encourage—differences in institutions, beliefs, and practices. But as a corollary, they fail to endorse the assimilation of culturally and racially different populations as, say, the French have tried to do in their colonies.[13] Primarily because of the anti-assimilation and anti-amalgamation "doctrine" of Europeans in Southern Rhodesia, it can be anticipated that the elimination of racial segregation and differentiation will come more easily in economic and other secular activities. There, intercultural relations tend to be more casual and impersonal. Joint participation by Europeans and Africans will occur, if at all, more slowly in the sacred institutions of family and church, in which social relations are more intimate and frequent.[14] The most conservative attitudes among Europeans are about maintaining racially endogamous marriages in order to prevent a "leveling" of differences between Europeans and Africans.[15]

There seem to be three clear alternatives in the future of intergroup relations in Southern Rhodesia. Their efficacy undoubtedly varies, and no scientific evaluation can be made as to which is "best." The first, biracialism, seems to be preferred by the majority of the European population, according to our data. Their views are similar to what Myrdal (1944) termed the "anti-amalgamation" doctrine of southern whites in the United States. The second option, uniracialism or nonracialism, is supported by virtually no Europeans in Southern Rhodesia. The Government, on the other hand, seeks to have nonracial political parties despite the pervasive dualism in the social structure and life of the Colony. The third course is multiracialism, a concept open to as many interpretations as there are interpreters. The Southern Rhodesian Government, especially since its federation with Northern Rhodesia and Nyasaland, seems to be increasingly committed to a planned implementation of a measure of partnership between Africans and Europeans.

More accurately, since the biological fact of race is perhaps not the most important variable, these alternatives should be termed *biculturalism, uniculturalism, and multiculturalism.* Awkward terms they are, but they raise the significant factors in Southern Rhodesian "race relations" into proper perspective. As long as European and African values, interests, and behavior remain widely divergent, and especially when this divergence is reinforced by legal as well as by moral and religious sanctions, then it is unlikely that a uniracial or unicultural society will develop.

The future social system will therefore reflect an accommodation between the conservative attitudes of Europeans and the more vaguely formulated attitudes and values of most Africans. The Government is in the peculiar but valuable position of being able to exercise a large measure of culturally patterned leadership and authority. But at the same time, it cannot become fully alienated from an electorate which at present is predominantly conservative in race attitude.

# APPENDIXES

# A MEASURE OF SOCIAL BEHAVIOUR ABOUT THE AFRICAN
# AN EXPERIMENTAL STUDY

*A note to persons answering the Questionnaire*

The *purpose* of this study is to secure a valid cross-section of European attitudes towards the different treatment of Africans, and the use of public and private facilities in Southern Rhodesia. There has never previously been a serious, scientific attempt to discover what these attitudes are. The results should be of value to all Rhodesians; to help us to understand our country better, the social attitudes that we hold, and the reasons for them. Also, many visitors to this country carry back to their home countries a selective and biased assessment of Rhodesian opinion, and this study will contribute to removing such errors in the future.

The study is conceived, sponsored and supported in Southern Rhodesia. It is part of a research programme directed by Dr. C. A. Rogers of the University College of Rhodesia and Nyasaland, and carried on independently by him within the traditional freedom of the University. Naturally, it is non-political. Considerable time has been taken to check the accuracy of the 66 statements upon which opinion is solicited. Research scholars, advocates, teachers, workmen, farmers, and others have helped us to verify the statements. As they are designed to be true for Southern Rhodesia as a whole, you may find local variations in certain practices. Also, some legal regulations are in the process of being changed. For example, since this questionnaire was formulated, Africans may now participate in the state lottery.

Care has been taken to see that no personal opinions influenced the questionnaire, and no judgements are made as to whether the practices are morally just or unjust. Your task is to express your own personal opinions or attitudes, and the categories provided for your choice are designed to elicit these. Beyond marking 'x's', however, you are most welcome to indicate the reasons for your feelings or beliefs, and to indicate what proposals, modifications, or qualifications you would like to make to certain laws or customs. Just write them alongside the statements or on the back of the answer sheet. Such comments will be most useful to the study, and equally as important as the boxes that you cross out.

The *sample* will include at least 500 Europeans. It is carefully designed to obtain the correct percentages of people according to age, sex, country of birth, income, and so on—as indicated on the final page of the questionnaire. We know, for example, that we need exactly 52.5% males in our sample, that 14.0% must be between 25 and 29 years of age, that 5.0% must come from Umtali district, that 37.8% must have voted for or preferred the Dominion Party in the last Federal election, and so on. All this information is available in the 1956 census and in other official sources.

Some of the information requested on the final page, especially income, religious affiliation, and voting behaviour, are recognized as personal data. We hope that you will supply the information, however, and we guarantee that it will be held in the strictest confidence. Because of its personal nature, you are given the choice of whether you sign your name or not. We will never identify an individual or his opinions. As in all scientific research, we are interested in the population as a whole, and in sub-groups or categories of people classified by age, sex, district, occupation, and so on.

Good reasons are often given for the different treatment that Europeans and Africans receive. We have not listed them in the questionnaire as this would lengthen it unduly, and perhaps inhibit you from giving your own personal reasons. It may appear to you that some of the statements are 'half-truths', at least until the reasons behind these various practices (as stated) are provided. For example, Statement No. 2 reads: 'Meetings held by African leaders are attended more often by the Police (C.I.D.) than similar meetings held by Europeans.' The reasons for this include the need for security in the country as a whole, the safety of individuals attending, and so on. Statements Nos. 18 and 21 have to do with separate swimming baths and lavatories. Behind these practices lie important considerations of health. Statement No. 27 is concerned with the size of African land holdings, and one of the important reasons behind this legislation was the scarcity of land. There was also the desire to distribute land equitably among Africans. Statement No. 45 deals with representation in the Federal Parliament, and the reasons for the low number of African M.P.s clearly involve different levels of education and income. Finally, Statement No. 53, concerned with the requirement that Africans have to carry identity papers of some kind, is supported in order to restrict an influx into the urban areas where housing is short. It is also meant to reduce the difficulty of identifying Africans who use different names and aliases.

These examples illustrate that behind each of the practices of differential treatment there undoubtedly are substantial reasons. In a time of political tension, more reasons are supplied.

Your assistance in completing this questionnaire will be greatly appreciated. We intend to make public a report of the results of this study as quickly as possible. It will be equally accessible to all individuals, the press, the government, labour unions, churches, and all other interested groups. There is no secrecy to the project. Individuals are assured that their opinions will be held in complete confidence, as has been said above, but collectively we want the results to be known. This study, the first ever made in Southern Rhodesia as a whole, should help to dispel inaccurate assessments of opinion which Rhodesians and foreign visitors have made. It will provide statistically reliable information, where none has existed before. This in itself, it seems to me, is sufficient reason for conducting the study now.

Thanks again for your co-operation. Your contribution will enable all of us in the future to know more accurately what Rhodesians think about an important aspect of our society.

*C. A. Rogers*
*Senior Lecturer in Psychology*

## *General Directions*

After each statement in the Questionnaire, you are requested to record how *important* you consider the practice to be, and whether you think it should be maintained or discontinued (by changing the law or social custom). Endorse the statements with an X in the following manner on the answer sheet:

If you believe that the practice is VERY (VM)    ⊠ IM ID VD
IMPORTANT and should be MAIN-
TAINED:

If you believe that the practice is IM- (IM)    VM ⊠ ID VD
PORTANT and *probably* should be
MAINTAINED:

If you believe that the practice is IM- (ID)    VM IM ⊠ VD
PORTANT and *probably* should be
DISCONTINUED:

If you believe that the practice is VERY      (VD)    VM IM ID ⊠
IMPORTANT and should be DISCON-
TINUED:

Please answer frankly. Remember that this is not a test; there are no
'right' or 'wrong' answers. The answer required is your own personal
opinion. Be sure not to omit any questions, and do not consult another
person while you are giving your answers.

When you have finished, please supply the information requested on the
answer sheet. To repeat, your responses will be treated as completely
confidential.

CODE
NO.

(11)   1. In the main, Africans are prohibited        1. VM IM ID VD
          from buying beer and wines from
          shops in European areas, but must buy
          beer at the African beer halls or bottle
          stores.

(21)   2. Meetings held by African leaders are         2. VM IM ID VD
          attended more often by the Police
          (C.I.D.) than similar meetings held by
          Europeans.

( 1)   3. Africans are not accepted for appren-        3. VM IM ID VD
          ticeship training for the skilled trades.

(41)   4. It is more difficult for the Africans in     4. VM IM ID VD
          urban areas to find effective and sim-
          ple means of lodging protests than for
          Europeans to do so.

(59)   5. Africans are refused admission to Eu-        5. VM IM ID VD
          ropean dance halls.

(22)   6. If a European woman becomes 'fa-             6. VM IM ID VD
          miliar' with an African man she is al-
          most certain to be ostracized socially.

(12)   7. Africans are permitted to own or carry       7. VM IM ID VD
          firearms only in very exceptional cir-
          cumstances, while Europeans may do
          so with relatively fewer restrictions.

(13)   8. African organizations cannot rent of-        8. VM IM ID VD
          fices legally in European commercial
          areas.

( 2)   9. In general, Africans are not admitted        9. VM IM ID VD
          to the technical classes which are an

CODE
NO.

essential part of the apprentice training for a trade.

(42) 10. In some shops and cafes there is a little    10. VM IM ID VD
window through which Africans are
served.

(29) 11. In some parks there are separate    11. VM IM ID VD
benches for Europeans and Africans.

(51) 12. European children generally do not    12. VM IM ID VD
treat African adults with respect.

(14) 13. Africans are liable to be assaulted by a    13. VM IM ID VD
European employer, whereas Euro-
pean employees are less liable to receive this treatment.

(23) 14. The qualifications for the franchise are    14. VM IM ID VD
such that few Africans have a vote,
whereas practically all Europeans are
eligible.

(30) 15. African children do not receive the    15. VM IM ID VD
same educational opportunities as Eu-
ropean children.

(31) 16. Except on specified routes, Africans    16. VM IM ID VD
and Europeans may not ride in the
same buses.

( 3) 17. Africans may not lawfully buy lottery    17. VM IM ID VD
tickets or bet on horse racing in South-
ern Rhodesia.

(43) 18. Africans and Europeans are not per-    18. VM IM ID VD
mitted to use the same public swim-
ming baths.

( 4) 19. In some businesses and industries only    19. VM IM ID VD
Europeans are employed.

(15) 20. No provision is made for Africans to    20. VM IM ID VD
serve on juries in Southern Rhodesia.

(44) 21. Europeans and Africans generally are    21. VM IM ID VD
not permitted to use the same lava-
tories.

(60) 22. European men and women have on    22. VM IM ID VD
occasion dropped friends when they
have discovered them to have non-
European ancestors.

(32) 23. There are different compartments for    23. VM IM ID VD
Europeans and Africans on trains.

(45)   24. European sporting and social clubs are       24. VM IM ID VD
       not open to Africans.

(33)   25. Generally there are separate ceme-           25. VM IM ID VD
       teries for Africans and Europeans.

(16)   26. Africans and Europeans are sometimes         26. VM IM ID VD
       not punished equally by the court for
       the same crimes of violence.

( 5)   27. No matter how good an African                27. VM IM ID VD
       farmer is, under the Land Husbandry
       Act he cannot obtain more than three
       standard-sized holdings of land (total-
       ling 18 acres in high rainfall areas).

(52)   28. Africans normally are expected to            28. VM IM ID VD
       stand back and allow Europeans to go
       first through doorways, into lifts, and
       so on.

(34)   29. Europeans and Africans are required          29. VM IM ID VD
       by law to attend different schools.

(61)   30. Europeans who rape African women             30. VM IM ID VD
       sometimes are given lighter sentences
       than Africans who rape European
       women.

(46)   31. Many European restaurants and hotels         31. VM IM ID VD
       will not accept African clients.

(53)   32. Europeans generally do not shake             32. VM IM ID VD
       hands with Africans.

(62)   33. A European man who is suspected of           33. VM IM ID VD
       having sex relations with an African
       woman is likely to be ostracized so-
       cially.

(24)   34. In Southern Rhodesia, Europeans con-         34. VM IM ID VD
       trol the election of Africans to the
       Federal Government, whereas Afri-
       cans have virtually no control over the
       election of Europeans.

(35)   35. In many public buildings Africans are        35. VM IM ID VD
       not allowed to use lifts.

(54)   36. Africans nearly always are expected to       36. VM IM ID VD
       address Europeans as 'Sir', 'Boss',
       'Master', or 'Madam', whereas Eu-
       ropeans usually address Africans as
       'Boy', or 'Nanny.'

CODE
NO.

(36)  37. Most churches do not hold services       37. VM IM ID VD
      for multi-racial congregations.

(37)  38. Different entrances are provided for      38. VM IM ID VD
      Africans and Europeans in certain
      shops and banks and in many post of-
      fices.

( 6)  39. The Land Apportionment Act prevents       39. VM IM ID VD
      Africans from occupying land for busi-
      ness purposes within the recognized
      European commercial areas.

( 7)  40. Many Africans are required to pay         40. VM IM ID VD
      relatively higher costs in travelling to
      work than are Europeans, as they
      often must live at some distance from
      their places of employment.

( 8)  41. In many instances, Europeans and          41. VM IM ID VD
      Africans are not paid the same rates
      for similar jobs.

(25)  42. Pro-African 'nationalism' is viewed       42. VM IM ID VD
      with more suspicion by much of the
      European community than is pro-
      European 'nationalism.'

(47)  43. Africans are not hired often as counter   43. VM IM ID VD
      attendants in European shops or busi-
      nesses.

(55)  44. Europeans generally are served before     44. VM IM ID VD
      Africans at shop counters and places
      of business.

(26)  45. In the Federal Parliament there are       45. VM IM ID VD
      roughly four times as many European
      as African members, although the Eu-
      ropean population is about $\frac{1}{28}$ the
      size of the African population.

(63)  46. The legal regulations of Southern Rho-    46. VM IM ID VD
      desia make it extremely difficult for an
      African man to live with a European
      woman to whom he is married legally.

(64)  47. A friendship between an African man       47. VM IM ID VD
      and a European woman is generally
      viewed with suspicion.

(56)  48. Generally, Europeans do not treat         48. VM IM ID VD
      Africans with as much respect as they
      do members of their own race.

(27)  49. African householders living in urban      49. VM IM ID VD
          areas have no vote in municipal elec-
          tions.

(48)  50. Africans generally are not allowed into   50. VM IM ID VD
          European theatres.

(57)  51. In general, Africans are not placed in    51. VM IM ID VD
          charge of Europeans even when
          equally qualified.

(65)  52. European men may have sex relations       52. VM IM ID VD
          with African women without legal
          penalty, but African men are prohib-
          ited by law from having sex relations
          with European women.

(17)  53. African men are obliged by law to         53. VM IM ID VD
          carry identity papers, whereas Euro-
          peans are not.

(38)  54. African locations are equipped less fre-   54. VM IM ID VD
          quently than European townships with
          amenities such as tarred roads and
          electricity.

(39)  55. There are different hospitals and other    55. VM IM ID VD
          medical services for Africans and Eu-
          ropeans.

(18)  56. Under the Land Apportionment Act,          56. VM IM ID VD
          Africans are not allowed to own
          houses in the same areas as Europeans.

(40)  57. At railway stations there are generally    57. VM IM ID VD
          separate booking offices for Europeans
          and Africans.

(66)  58. African men have to take more care         58. VM IM ID VD
          not to become 'familiar' with Euro-
          pean women than do European men
          with African women.

(49)  59. Africans may not try on clothes in         59. VM IM ID VD
          most European shops.

(58)  60. Africans who question the authority        60. VM IM ID VD
          of Europeans often are accused of be-
          ing 'cheeky' and may be assaulted for
          such behaviour.

(19)  61. Africans in urban areas are not per-       61. VM IM ID VD
          mitted to own land outright, but have
          up to a 99 year lease, and this only in
          certain areas.

CODE
NO.

(50)  62. There are few opportunities for Africans to participate with or against Europeans in sporting events.  62. VM IM ID VD

( 9)  63. Facilities for the training of Africans in the skilled trades and professions are very limited.  63. VM IM ID VD

(28)  64. From time to time, African voters are refused admission to political meetings open to the general public.  64. VM IM ID VD

(20)  65. In general, Africans but not Europeans are forbidden by law to buy alcoholic spirits.  65. VM IM ID VD

(10)  66. Most European trade unions do not accept African members.  66. VM IM ID VD

# A MEASURE OF SOCIAL BEHAVIOUR
## ABOUT THE AFRICAN

*Answer Sheet*

*Please supply the following information:*

1. Name (if you wish) ..........................
2. Male or female ...............................
3. Age .........................................
4. Residence: Community ......................
5.            District ....................
6. Number of years lived in S. Rhodesia .............
7. Country where born (e.g. S. Rhodesia, Union of S. Africa, England, etc.,) ......................
8. National origin (e.g. Afrikaner, English, Irish, etc.) ............................................
9. Your approximate income in 1958:
   - ☐ Nil
   - ☐ £ 1–299
   - ☐ £ 300–599
   - ☐ £ 600–899
   - ☐ £ 900–1199
   - ☐ £ 1200–1499
   - ☐ £ 1500–1799
   - ☐ £ 1800 or more
10. Occupation or profession .....................
11. In what type of industry or business are you working ............................................
12. Father's occupation .........................
13. Number of years Primary .....................
    spent at school: Secondary ..................
                      College ..................
                      Total ..................
14. Religious affiliation or preference:
    - ☐ Dutch Reformed
    - ☐ Roman Catholic
    - ☐ Greek Orthodox
    - ☐ Presbyterian
    - ☐ Other (specify) ...............
    - ☐ Anglican
    - ☐ Methodist
    - ☐ Jewish
    - ☐ None
15. If you were a voter, for which political party did you vote in the 1958 *Federal* election? (If you did not vote, for which one did you have a preference?)
    - ☐ Dominion
    - ☐ United Federal
    - ☐ Constitution
    - ☐ Confederate

362

16. On the scale below, check the position with an "X" that you frankly consider represents your *general* attitude toward Africans. Let your experience be your guide.

····☐·······☐········☐·······☐······☐···
  Very Un-   Unfavour-   Neutral   Favour-   Very Fa-
favourable     able                able    vourable

## B.

### LEGAL BASIS OF THIRTY-SIX STATEMENTS IN THE QUESTIONNAIRE

As discussed in Chapter 4, at least thirty-six of the sixty-six statements relating to differentiating practices in Southern Rhodesia had legal sanctions behind them. Cited below are the relevant Chapters (Cap.) or Acts of the Statute Law of Southern Rhodesia alongside the item numbers (see Table 27 for complete statements). Where laws of the Federation of Rhodesia and Nyasaland are relevant, they also are given. Amendment Acts, Government Notices, or municipal by-laws are not included. A number of these legal sanctions have been removed since the fieldwork for the study was done; the new Acts or Amendments are not cited.

Some distinction can be made between these laws. In some, for example those on land apportionment (Act 11/1941) and liquor (Act 53/1953), the differentiation between Africans and Europeans was specifically cited. In others, such as those on the franchise (Act 27/1951, Fed. Act 6/1958), the *effect* of the laws has been to differentiate. In still others, powers were conferred on local authorities (Act 34/1952, Act 31/1953) which permitted them to differentiate through by-laws.

### LAWS

ITEM
NO.

1. Cap. 231, Act 21/1945, and Act 6/1949.
2. Cap. 75, Act 21/1945, and Act 6/1949.
3. Cap. 67 and Cap. 284.
4. Affected by Cap. 58, Cap. 75, Act 21/1945, Act 36/1946, Act 6/1949, and Federal Act 15/1956.
5. Act 52/1951.
6. Act 11/1941.
8. Act 21/1945 and Act 6/1949.
9. Cap. 58, Cap. 75, Cap. 231, Act 21/1945, Act 36/1946, and Federal Act 15/1956.
10. Act 21/1945, Act 26/1947, Act 6/1949, and Act 20/1951.
11. Act 53/1953.
12. Act 17/1956.
13. Act 11/1941.

ITEM
NO.

15. Ordinance 10/1908.
17. Act 9/1948, Act 20/1951, and Act 27/1957.
18. Cap. 84 and Act 11/1941.
19. Cap. 84 and Act 11/1941.
20. Act 53/1953.
23. Act 27/1951 and Federal Act 6/1958.
24. Act 27/1951 and Federal Act 6/1958.
26. Federal Act 6/1958.
27. Act 20/1951, Act 34/1952, and Act 31/1953.
29. Act 34/1952.
30. Cap. 58, Cap. 75, and Federal Act 15/1956.
31. Act 34/1952 and Act 31/1953.
32. Cap. 261 and Act 6/1949.
33. Cap. 101.
34. Cap. 58 and Federal Act 15/1956.
39. Cap. 140 and Federal Act 18/1957.
43. Act 34/1952 and Act 31/1953.
44. Act 20/1948, Act 34/1952, and Act 31/1953.
45. Act 20/1948, Act 34/1952, and Act 31/1953.
46. Cap. 91, Act 11/1941, and Act 31/1953.
48. Act 34/1952 and Act 31/1953.
59. Act 34/1952 and Act 31/1953.
63. Cap. 84, Act 11/1941, and Act 20/1951.
65. Ordinance 1/1916, Cap. 36, and Federal Act 36/1954.

# C.

## SOME PRESS COMMENTS ON THE FIELDWORK

*The Chronicle* (Bulawayo) and *The Rhodesia Herald* (Salisbury) have kindly given permission to reprint these comments.

### CHRONICLE: FEB. 6, 1959.

U.S. PROFESSOR CONDUCTS RACE SURVEY

One of the most forthright and provocative surveys ever carried out in the Federation is being conducted in Bulawayo this week in an effort to establish the reaction of people towards many forms of racial behaviour between Africans and Europeans.

An American professor from Chicago, who is at present attached to the University College in Salisbury under a Ford Foundation grant, is touring every suburb in the city and selecting 15 houses in each area.

The survey, which is entitled "A measure of social behaviour about the African," consists of 66 statements about the behaviour and custom existing between the races.

The people selected in the survey are asked to indicate whether they consider such practices should be maintained or discontinued by changing the law or custom.

*Statements.* These are some of the statements on which opinion is sought: Europeans and Africans generally are not permitted to use the same lavatories; European men and women have on occasion dropped friends when they have discovered them to have non-European ancestors; there are different compartments for Africans and Europeans on trains; generally there are separate cemeteries for Africans and Euopeans; if a Euopean woman becomes "familiar" with an African man she is almost certain to be ostracised socially; European children generally do not treat Africans with respect; Africans and Europeans are not permitted to use the same public swimming baths.

*Other subjects.* Other subjects dealt with in the survey include the divergence of sentences for the rape of African women by Europeans on the one hand, and the rape of European women by African men on the other, the bar on the apprenticeship of Africans, and the attendance by CID officers at political meetings.

Another part of the three-page survey form asks details about the person's income, religion and how they voted in the recent election.

CHRONICLE: FEB. 7, 1959.

SURVEY MAY SHOW MANY HIDDEN RACIAL ATTITUDES

Conclusions on one of the most provocative surveys ever carried out in the Federation about racial behaviour between Europeans and Africans will probably be made known at the end of the year by two experts from the University College.

The survey is likely to show many hidden facets of everyday life in the Federation.

The survey is being carried out by Dr. Cyril Rogers, educational psychologist, with the assistance of Prof. Charles Frantz, of Chicago, attached to the university on a Ford Foundation scholarship.

Dr. Rogers is now in England, finding out the attitudes of various representative groups. This will provide some basis of comparison for the Rhodesian survey.

He will return at the end of the month. Prof. Frantz is making a survey in Bulawayo, touring each suburb and selecting 15 houses in each area.

Prof. H. J. Rousseau, head of the Department of Education at the University College, said in an interview: "The attitudes of various local racial groups is a very important problem all over the world, even in Britain," and mentioned the Notting Hill riots.

*Key to future.* "In our own country," he said, "the problem is extremely important because our whole future depends on the attitude of one group to another.

"One of the practical applications of this investigation might be . . . that two groups have mistaken ideas about each other's attitudes.

"It has been found in the United States that the things which worry Negroes most are not the things that worry the Whites.

"Things that worry the Negroes most are the things which concern their day-to-day existence, like employment, wages and housing.

"Whites, on the other hand, are worried about social contacts which hardly ever enter into the thinking of the Negroes. The same may be found in the Federation.

"There are certain things which may worry the Europeans which are not worth worrying about, because the Africans give no thought to them.

"But there are many things in which the Africans and the Europeans think alike. For instance, all Africans and Europeans would agree that economic development and advancement are really very important."

## RHODESIA HERALD: FEB. 10, 1959.

RACE BEHAVIOUR SURVEY SHARPLY CRITICISED BY TERRITORIAL M.P.

The race behaviour survey which was conducted in Bulawayo last week by an American professor attached to the University College in Salisbury was sharply criticised today by Mr. Ian McLean, Bulawayo Territorial M.P.

"I am extremely dubious about the value of such social research, the object of which appears to be to confirm existing dogmas," said Mr. McLean.

The survey, which was conducted in 15 houses in each of the city's suburbs, listed 66 statements on racial behaviour and customs and asked people to say whether they considered such practices should be maintained or discontinued.

The subjects dealt with range from the use of separate lavatories by Europeans and Africans to the friendship between African men and European women.

*"Fallacious."* Mr. McLean, who said he was speaking in a personal capacity and not on behalf of the Dominion Party, said he believed that the findings of the survey would be "as fallacious as those of the Kinsey Report."

"Even the mechanics of the survey seem to be unscientific," he said. "The researcher will encounter all kinds of social and political prejudices which will not give an unbiased result.

"For example, it is difficult to imagine in this country, with its multi-racial structure, a member of one community being able to comment upon the activities of another community without any taint of social or economic bias.

"Furthermore, an inquiry of this nature offends the inherent sense of good manners, a result of which will be a reluctance to comment unfavourably on other persons."

Mr. McLean said it would be regrettable if American opinion of the Federation was based upon the findings of the survey.

"I feel the funds devoted to this sort of research would be better disbursed in more practical directions," he said.

## CHRONICLE: FEB. 10, 1959. (LETTER TO EDITOR)

THE BEAM IN THEIR OWN EYE

Sir—Your report on the American professor who is making a survey in Bulawayo makes interesting reading. For sheer audacity these people surely take the whole biscuit factory.

One has only to read early American history and the way in which they managed their own affairs in the middle and late 19th century to appreciate their colossal effrontery.

During this period the U.S. Army considered the mass murder of Red Indian women and children quite the thing.

Who are these people who dare set themselves up as leaders of world opinion where colour is concerned when their own house needs such a drastic spring cleaning?

We should bar them from this country until they have settled their own problems.

One gets sick and tired of their "We can do no wrong" attitude. Why don't they mind their own business?

SUFFERER, Bulawayo

RHODESIA HERALD: FEB, 12, 1959. (LETTER TO EDITOR)

SURVEY OF RACE BEHAVIOUR

Sir—We wish to protest in the strongest possible terms against the Race Behaviour Survey now being carried out in various towns in the Federation.

Apart from the abysmal ignorance of conditions pertaining in this country contained in the questions themselves, and the fact that any results obtained will not only be misleading, but likely to be used for propaganda purposes against us, we resent this interference in our internal affairs by an outsider belonging to a country already well-known to be antagonistic to the Europeans in Africa.

We do not want Dr. C. Frantz or his surveys here. He would be better employed on sorting out his own country's racial problems, or, for instance, explaining why armed riot squads are necessary in United States integrated schools.

Moreover, we do not want our University financed by Foundations whose philanthropies are almost solely devoted to the furtherance of race-mixing causes throughout the world.

D. W. W. BLACKMAN,
European National Congress, Salisbury.

CHRONICLE: FEB. 13, 1959. (LETTER TO EDITOR)

STUDENTS OR MEDDLERS?

Sir—I heartily agree with "Sufferer," about the race survey conducted in Bulawayo by an American Professor.

Just what is the big idea? Are these people here to learn something, or just to meddle?

The United States quite recently has been trying to force integration on her own people at gun point. Just imagine it—a "love your neighbour" policy by threat of force.

Britain is suffering from a frightful integration harvest, thanks to American Negro and Coloured air base personnel, apart from the Jamaican flood of immigrants.

A visit to Britain will convince any doubter.

NUFF SAID, Hillside.

RHODESIA HERALD: FEB. 14, 1959. (LETTER TO EDITOR)

U.S. PROFESSOR'S SURVEY: ADDING FUEL TO FIRES OF OVERSEAS CRITICS

Sir—The American professors have started something with their questionnaire. Some of the answers are going to seem shocking to our overseas critics and will be fuel for their fires.

One must have lived in Rhodesia for a few years to know why people think and behave as they do. Leaving aside the small nucleus of educated Africans who are indistinguishable by appearance from their fellows, one is left with millions of the ordinary type.

When one answers the questions one would refer to the majority of Africans as they are at present.

The answer therefore to the question of sharing lots of things would be "no." Simply because of the ordinary African's ideas of hygiene. How many babies die of dysentery each year? How often does one fumigate one's servants' quarters?

The second reason for saying "no" would be local knowledge. For instance, an employee of mine has just returned from Nyasaland. He spent four nights in the train without sleeping simply because he did not trust his fellow passengers not to get out at the next station with his luggage. I understand this is normal practice.

People living outside Africa will not try to understand that the question of racial integration to the ordinary person is a matter of commonsense and different customs and habits and not black and white skins.

COMMONSENSE, Greendale.

CHRONICLE: FEB. 26, 1959.

RACE SURVEY GIVEN FINANCIAL HELP BY UNIVERSITY

The Rhodesia University College gave financial assistance towards the expenses of the race survey carried out by a lecturer, whose findings are to be published as a book.

The survey team, headed by Dr. Cyril Rogers, senior lecturer in Psychology at the University's Department of Education, recently put out a 66-page questionnaire to houses in Bulawayo.

In an interview in Salisbury today, Dr. Rogers said he was directing the survey as part of his individual research programme, in consultation with the Social Science Research Committee of the University.

*Judgements*

The team's aim, he said, was to make an analysis of the structure of the Rhodesian community.

The problems of race which concerned Rhodesia were met in other countries, and one of science's tasks was to discover whether or not human behaviour was consistent in its reaction to those problems.

"What the solutions may be fall more within the province of the ordinary citizen, the representatives they elect, and the philosophers in our midst," said Dr. Rogers.

"Certainly, our study makes no judgments on whether the attitudes held by Europeans or Africans are right or wrong."

## CHRONICLE: FEB. 28, 1959. (EDITORIAL)

NONSENSICAL SURVEY?

Popular criticisms of an American survey into our way of life are reinforced by the disclosure that good money was contributed to it by our university. Most of us could soon think of better uses for money the public subscribed.

Many of the individual questions put to Bulawayo householders, relating to social contacts between the races, may have been thought objectionable and the answers, as a result, unrepresentative and misleading.

Other faults inevitably built into the analysis will arise from the eagerness of some people to give responses which will encourage an interviewer to continue the interview. It is a widespread human weakness to feel flattered when asked to speak for a whole group of people.

Equally inimical to the truth is the answer from one who seeks deliberately to load the result in accordance with a pre-misconceived mental picture of the whole survey's probable findings.

When these and many other destructive influences affect a sample survey their distortion of general attitudes completely invalidate it, especially when only a comparatively small number of people are used to interpret the innermost feelings of many thousands.

It would be disastrous if this sort of academic byplay contributed substantially to the formation of official American policy on Africa. We must hope that more conventional sources of information are given greater weight in the councils of State.

A more immediate issue is the vague approbation with which most liberal Rhodesians will have contemplated the project for a Chair of Race

Relations in Salisbury. Much can be done for the common weal by dispassionate examination of this multi-racial society of ours.

But if the university countenances unscientific methods, *parti pris* interrogation and positively disturbing examinations of the body politic and social, we should prefer the empirical rule of thumb; and the popular regard for higher education will change to Chestertonian contempt for what he called The Higher Bosh.

## CHRONICLE: MAR. 5, 1959. (LETTER TO EDITOR)

### Let's Be Charitable about the Questionnaire

Sir—I refer to the second leader appearing in the issue of February 28th. I feel you have shown an apparent inability to see the import behind the actual questionnaire on race attitudes now being distributed to certain sections of the community in the city by an American social-research worker.

It is surely a misrepresentation of the facts to say that this survey is being conducted by unscientific methods and as such is countenanced by the university. Perhaps this was unintentional but it reads as though this were "inter se."

You say that such surveys are "positively disturbing." But of course they are, if they are taken seriously, as they should be. Could it not also be that the criticism voiced by the "victims" has been rationalised (in the psychologist's meaning of the word)?

Could it not be that they have never before tried to ask themselves the questions with which they have been confronted, and at which they profess themselves to have been so shocked and affronted by the perhaps unwelcome directness of the questions?

### Allowance Made?

Granted there are dangers which you have illustrated, in any such system leading to misrepresentation (unrepresentative) and misleading results. It is hardly charitable, however, to assume that due allowance will not be made by the present research-worker and not to credit him with sufficient perception to see from the answers when these factors are operative.

Also it is not charitable to assume that he is such an inexperienced person, that this is the first such survey he has conducted; that he is not bringing earlier experience into his interpretation of the completed questionnaires he has had returned to him.

You suggest that more conventional sources of information have not been consulted. The United States Information Service in Salisbury could not exist as a unilateral organisation.

*Not Only Here*

Ironically "Optatus" column alongside was headed, "I forgot where I was!" Perhaps it would be healthier for the findings of the questionnaire if more of us in this city and country could forget where we are and realise that these problems of race attitudes are not confined to Southern Rhodesia or the Federation. Realise, perhaps, that other more forthright groups are trying to get down to basic assessments from the people at large, whether in their own or another's country.

As biological health demands adequate ventilation, so, too, does mental health demand ventilation of the problems of race attitudes to as large a section as possible of the healthfully minded community of fellow human beings.

SURVEYED, Bulawayo.

CENTRAL AFRICAN EXAMINER: JULY 18, 1959.

TEACH PARTNERSHIP IN SCHOOLS

In the past few months both the Federal and Southern Rhodesian Governments have taken bold steps towards the implementation of "partnership." Observers from abroad might choose to regard them as faint, surface scratchings, but in the context of Southern Africa—and that is the only realistic one to view them in—they appear almost spectacular. Some indication of the speed of recent changes can be grasped by a glance at a document produced this year by our local University. "A Measure of Social Behaviour about the African", the brain child of Dr. Cyril Rogers of the Department of Psychology, promises, on its completion, to be a fund of invaluable information about European race attitudes. What we know about this subject already is often imprecise, impressionistic, and selective. The aim of Dr. Rogers' researches is to correct this.

A cross-section of Europeans have been invited to comment on sixty-seven statements, each of which enumerates an example of the differential treatment of Africans in this country. In the hands of a British "liberal", the list—which is comprehensive—would read like a burning indictment of our Governments, on the usual charge of failure to carry out their professed aims. Not surprisingly the effect is precisely the opposite on anyone who lives here. What he will notice is that many of the examples are "conventional" and not matters immediately susceptible to alteration from above; that many others have now to be hedged around with saving qualifications (e.g., "Europeans *generally* are served before Africans in shops" or "In *some* shops separate serving hatches exist"). Finally he will remark that in the short space of time since the document appeared, five of the sixty-seven statements (i.e., nearly 8 per cent.) have become completely untrue. Outsiders will get a better grasp of the rate of change in this country by measuring it against a yardstick of this sort, rather than against fuzzy and amorphous ones of their own creation. . . .

# NOTES

## ABBREVIATIONS

C.A.A.  Central African Archives
G.N.    Government Notice
R.H.    *Rhodesia Herald* (Salisbury)
S.R.    Southern Rhodesia

## PREFACE

1. Hughes and Hughes (1952:19), Morris (1957), Rex (1959), and others have argued the utility of this conceptual approach.
2. Hyman (1955:334-48).
3. See discussions of this concept by Francis (1951) and Harris (1959).
4. Hughes and Hughes (1952:151). See also Morris (1957).
5. Myrdal (1958:51) and several others have emphasized this point.

## CHAPTER 1. A WORLD OF PLURAL SOCIETIES

1. For world coverages, see Coon (1954), Howells (1954), and Linton (1955).
2. See Redfield (1955), Herskovits (1955), Wolf (1956), Gluckman (1958), and Blumer (1958) for discussions of contextual frameworks in social science.
3. Studies of culturally and racially mixed societies have been appearing in increasing number, and area bibliographies are keeping pace. For a sampling of some of the principal countries and a representation of the variety of situations, the following may be consulted:
*Great Britain:* Little (1948), Richmond (1954, 1958), Banton (1955, 1959), and Collins (1957). *U.S.S.R.:* Kolarz (1953). *United States:* Thomas and Znaniecki (1927), Dollard (1937), Herskovits (1941), Davis, Gardner, and Gardner (1941), Klineberg (ed. 1944), Myrdal (1944), Steward (1945), Collier (1947), Frazier (1949), Underhill (1953), Pearce (1953), Handlin (1957), Blumer (1958), and Simpson and Yinger (1958). *Canada:* Miner (1939), Hughes (1943), Hawthorn, Belshaw, and Jamieson (1958), and Frantz (1958). *Guatemala:* Gillin (1948), Tax (1953), and Nash (1958). *Jamaica:* Henriques (1953). *British Guiana:* Smith (1956). *Puerto Rico:* Steward et al (1956). *Brazil:* Pierson (1942), Wagley (ed. 1952; 1953), and

Bastide (1957). *New Zealand:* Beaglehole (1946). *Indonesia:* Boeke (1942, 1948), Furnivall (1956), and Wertheim (1956). *India:* Hutton (1946), Marriott (ed. 1955), and Ghurye (1957).

For *Africa* generally: Haines (ed. 1955), Hailey (1957), Herskovits (1957), Brown and Lewis (1958), and Bascom and Herskovits (ed. 1959). *British Central Africa:* Wilson and Wilson (1945), Mitchell (1951, 1954, 1956, 1957), Jonas (1953), Barnes (1954), and Smith (ed. 1958). *Union of South Africa:* MacCrone (1937), Hellmann (ed. 1949), Jonas (1953), Patterson (1953, 1957), Gluckman (1955, 1958), and Smith (ed. 1958). *Bechuanaland:* Schapera (1934). *Swaziland:* Kuper (1947). *British East Africa:* Morris (1957) and Ward (1958). *Sierra Leone:* Banton (1957). *French Africa:* Delavignette (1950) and Balandier (1955, 1955a).

4. See Hinden (1949) and Burns (1957).

5. Perham (1941) gives a simplified brief account of British rule in Africa prior to World War II.

6. See Davidson (1959) for a recent popular account of African prehistory. See Linton (1955) and especially Murdock (1959) for more systematic analyses.

7. Axelson (1940) and Tabler (1955:Ch. 7).

8. Bullock (1950:9–13), Tabler (1955:104–07, 191–93), Bulpin (1956: 51–54 and Ch. 8), and Walker (1957).

9. For discussions of the indigenous African societies and cultures in Southern Rhodesia, see Posselt (1927, 1935), Bullock (1950), Holleman (1951, 1952), and Kuper, Hughes, and van Velsen (1955).

10. Thomas (1873) and Carnegie (1893).

11. See Hole (1926), Gross (1956), and Walker (1957), among others.

12. Great Britain, British South Africa Company's Territories (1897).

13. For recent analyses of "nativistic" movements, see Voget (1956), Wallace (1956), and Worsley (1957).

14. Rolin (1913), Hole (1926), DeKiewiet (1941), Kane (1954), Walker (1957), Gale (1958), Mason (1958), Gann (1958), and Leys (1959).


CHAPTER 2. THE PLURAL SOCIETY OF SOUTHERN RHODESIA

1. Simpson and Yinger (1958) and Blumer (1958).

2. These studies are reviewed in Harding et al (1954), Blumer (1958), and Simpson and Yinger (1958). See also Merton, West, and Jahoda (1949), DuBois (1950), Collins (1951), and Wilner, Walkley, and Cook (1952).

3. S.R., Legislative Assembly (1959:Col. 2228).

4. Long (1949), Simpson and Yinger (1958), and Blumer (1958) for discussions of empirical studies. On Great Britain, see Little (1948), Richmond (1954, 1958), Banton (1955, 1959), and Collins (1957).

5. Central African Statistical Office (1959:9).

6. Central African Statistical Office (1959:12).

7. *R.H.* (Oct. 21, 1959) and S.R. (1955).

8. For discussions of the ecological processes that affect the distribution of population in southern Africa, see Ibbotson (1946), Comhaire (1950), Gussman (1952–53), Kuper, Watts, and Davies (1958), and Irving (1958).

9. Mannoni (1956). See also Jollie (1924) in regard to Southern Rhodesia.

10. Firth has been responsible for drawing the furthest distinction between

these two terms. "Social structure," he says (1954:5), "is a conceptual, not an operational or descriptive tool."

11. Hughes and Hughes (1952) mention these aspects of social structure as related to ecological variables, but they would seem to be broader than this.

12. Alport (1952:132).

13. Alport (1952:134–35) and Leys (1959).

14. Wallis (1950:62 ff). See also Smith (1928:122–23).

15. Evans (1934:107).

16. See Hinden (1949) and Mason (1954:87) for examples of the vast literature which attempts to assess 19th-century British ideas about imperialism and civilization. See also Philipps (1956).

17. Simpson and Yinger (1958:175).

18. Redfield (1955, 1956) and Frazier (1957:46).

## CHAPTER 3. INFLUENCES ON ATTITUDES AND BEHAVIOR

1. Green (1954:335).

2. Quoted by Eysenck (1954).

3. Jahoda (1953) also gives examples of stereotypes held by Africans.

4. Burt (1945, 1948, 1949, 1951).

5. Frazier (1953). See also Frazier (1949), Wirth (1950), Lohman and Reitzes (1952, 1954), Long (1953), Deighton (1957), Freedman (1957), Blumer (1958), and Simpson and Yinger (1959). Blumer has a particularly trenchant critique of studies in the "field" of racial and cultural relations.

6. Von Wiese (1950–51). See also the references in the preceding note.

7. The influence of the family upon race attitudes is illustrated by Allport and Kramer (1946), Radke, Trager, and Davis (1949), Harris (1950), DuBois (1950), Goodman (1952), Trager and Radke-Yarrow (1952), Radke-Yarrow, Trager, and Miller (1952), MacCrone (1954), and Parsons and Bales (1955).

8. Supplementary material on the role of organized interest groups may be found in Hughes (1949), Saenger and Gordon (1950), Bullock (1951), Rose (1951), Lohman and Reitzes (1952, 1954), and Blumer (1958).

9. Hayes (1949), Montagu (1949), Levinson (1949), Ellis and Beechley (1950), Anastasi (1953), Vosk (1953), Hammer (1953), Goodstein (1953), and MacCrone (1955).

10. See Frazier (1947, 1949, 1953), Harding et al (1954), Blumer (1958), and Simpson and Yinger (1958, 1959).

11. Blackburn et al (1946), Long and Johnson (1947), Saenger and Shulman (1948), Long (1949), Walker (1950), Mussen (1950), Deutsch and Collins (1950, 1951), Wilner, Walkley, and Cook (1952), Irish (1952), Deutsch (1952), Lohman and Reitzes (1952, 1954), Bird, Monachesi, and Burdick (1952), Rose, Atelsek, and McDonald (1953), and Bird and Monachesi (1954).

## CHAPTER 4. THE MEASUREMENT OF ATTITUDES

1. Reichard (1948), Saenger and Proshansky (1950), and Korchin, Mitchell, and Meltzoff (1950).

2. Evaluations of questionnaires and interviews have been made by Vernon (1938, 1953), Merton (1940), McNemar (1946), Remmers (1954), Hyman (1955), and others.

3. Cronbach (1950), Gordon (1951), Baier (1951), Travers (1951), and Vernon (1953).

4. McNemar (1946), Guttman and Suchman (1947), Edwards and Kilpatrick (1948), Eysenck and Crown (1949), Hovland and Sherif (1952), and Hand (1953).

5. Hyman (1945), Holland (1951–52), and Paul (1953).

6. Campbell (1950), Weschler (1950), and Richmond (1953).

## CHAPTER 5. THE SAMPLING MODEL

1. Central African Statistical Office (1959a, 1960) and Federation of Rhodesia and Nyasaland (1959).

2. Data supplied by the Central African Statistical Office, July 15, 1959.

3. Federation of Rhodesia and Nyasaland (1957, 1958, 1959a).

## CHAPTER 6. THE SAMPLING TASK

1. Central African Statistical Office (1956).

## CHAPTER 8. A FACTORIAL ANALYSIS OF RACE ATTITUDES

1. Kelley (1928), Thurstone (1935), Burt (1940), Wolfle (1940), Thomson (1948), Cattell (1952), and Remmers (1954).

2. Thurstone (1947) and Thomson (1948).

3. Coombs (1941), McNemar (1942), Burt and Banks (1946–47), Guilford and Lacey (1947), and Burt (1951).

4. It should be pointed out that we are not unfamiliar with other rotational procedures such as Alexander's (1935) method of maximizing a reference item, Cattell's (1944, 1946, 1952) principle of proportional profiles, and Eysenck's (1950) criterion analysis; but for reasons it hardly seems necessary to list here, we have not considered them germane to the study.

## CHAPTER 10. LEGAL JUSTICE

1. These were *de facto* institutions until legally recognized in 1937 by the Native Law and Courts Act. See S.R. (1952).

2. Immorality Suppression Ordinance, No. 9 of 1903.

3. Ordinance No. 1 of 1916.

4. *R.H.* (Dec. 2, 1896).

5. Bryce (1898:287) and Huxley (1931).

6. Ordinance No. 10 of 1908. Section 2 of this Ordinance amended Ordinance No. 4 of 1899. See the discussion of this issue in Howman (1949).

7. Act No. 18 of 1927.
8. Lewin (1947:97).
9. Act No. 5 of 1948. See also G.N. 290 of 1949.
10. Order 36 of High Court Rules.
11. Rex v. Mloyi, S. R. Law Reports (1935:108).
12. Rex v. Kafakarotwe, S. R. Law Reports (1951:162–63).
13. Desai and Co. v. Bindura Town Management Board, S. R. Law Reports (1952:136–39).

CHAPTER 11. OPPORTUNITIES FOR EDUCATION, TRAINING,
AND EMPLOYMENT

1. S.R., Native Education Enquiry Commission (1951:par. 33).
2. Some writers, such as Jollie (1924:263), erroneously state that no agricultural or industrial training was provided for Africans in the early years.
3. S.R., Native Affairs Commission of Enquiry (1911:12).
4. R.H. (May 31, 1912).
5. R.H. (Mar. 18, 1910). See also Buell (1928), Browne (1933), and S.R. (1952a).
6. R.H. (Mar. 4, 1910).
7. R.H. (Feb. 8, 1907).
8. R.H. (Feb. 22, 1902 and Mar. 22, 1902).
9. De Briey (1951:490–91).
10. Saenger (1953:97), in discussing trade union discrimination in the United States, suggests that the bargaining strength of the union depends upon its monopoly of a certain skill or trade rather than upon an industry-wide organization of workers.
11. Hughes and Hughes (1952:63).
12. See Becker (1957:128) for a theoretical discussion of this phenomenon.
13. See Lohman and Reitzes (1952, 1954) and our discussion in Ch. 3.
14. S.R., Urban African Affairs Commission (1958).
15. Browne (1933), Gussman (1953), Haviland (1954), Hudson (1955, 1958), and International Labour Office (1958).
16. Bettison (1958).

CHAPTER 12. THE OCCUPATION AND USE OF LAND

1. Mason (1958:258, 260) uncritically accepts an incorrect statement of the 1914 Native Reserves Commission.
2. Fox (1910:22–29) and Gann (1958:147).
3. Fox (1912) and R.H. (Nov. 6, 1914).
4. Great Britain, Southern Rhodesia Native Reserves Commission (1915).
5. In Central African Archives.
6. S.R., Urban African Affairs Commission (1958:20).
7. S.R., Land Commission (1926) and Duignan (1961).
8. Mason (1958:268–69) erroneously states this was the policy both of Europeans in 1914 and the Land Commission of 1914.

9. *R.H.* (Oct. 21, 1959).
10. See discussion in Ch. 2.
11. *R.H.* (Mar. 3, 1911).
12. *R.H.* (Oct. 21, 1959).
13. See McGregor's (1940) discussion of this issue. He had attended the Chamber's discussion of the proposed Bill.
14. Central African Statistical Office (1957:23–24).
15. Hughes and Hughes (1952). Cf. Thompson (1939).
16. *R.H.* (Oct. 21, 1959).
17. *R.H.* (Oct. 21, 1959).
18. S.R., Native Affairs Department (1958:33).
19. *R.H.* (Oct. 21, 1959). See also S.R. (1955:14).
20. Barber (1957:329–30; 1959).
21. Lohman and Reitzes (1952:242).
22. Huggins (1941:3). See also S.R. (1952, 1952a, 1952b) and Todd (1957).

## CHAPTER 13. PERSONAL COURTESIES AND ETIQUETTE

1. This statement, based upon sociological analysis, is similar to the psychological reasoning of Mannoni (1956).
2. See Chs. 1 and 2, Mason (1954:87), and Philipps (1956).
3. It was greater than Mason (1958) seems to think. See, for example, documents N 3/7/2 in C.A.A.
4. *R.H.* (Dec. 20, 1898).
5. *R.H.* (Oct. 5, 1901).
6. Myrdal (1944), Wolf (1956), Frazier (1957), and Simpson and Yinger (1958).

## CHAPTER 14. PUBLIC FACILITIES

1. Gelfand (1953:73, 110).
2. *R.H.* (Mar. 27, 1908).
3. Gelfand (1953:147).
4. *R.H.* (July 14, 1911).
5. Letter to Secretary, Division of Administration, Sept., 1916 (C.A.A., a 3/18/42).
6. Frazier (1949:8). See Warner (1959).

## CHAPTER 15. CIVIL ORDER AND POLITICAL CONTROL

1. Spiro (1959) argues that these are necessary requirements for sound democratic government irrespective of place. See also Easton (1953) and Macridis (1955).
2. C.A.A., D 3/6/3.
3. *R.H.* (Feb. 2, 1901).
4. See the Native Councils Act (No. 19 of 1957) and Native Councils

General Regulations (G.N. 529 of 1957). See also Howman (1951–53:I, 13) and S.R. (1952).

5. Information provided by the Native Affairs Department, Dec. 29, 1959.

6. Farquhar (1946).

7. Act 6 of 1946 permitted the establishment of Native Advisory Councils in urban areas, with the Governor given power to define the mode of election or selection. But regulations were not gazetted until G.N. 415 of 1951. These were cancelled by new regulations in G.N. 524 of 1952, and further modifications were introduced. For discussions of Africans in urban centers, see Ibbotson (1942, 1945), Comhaire (1950), and Gussman (1952–53, 1953).

8. Howman (1951–53:VII, 11).

9. *Evening Standard* (Mar. 10, 1959).

10. *African Daily News* (July 14 and 17, and Aug. 17, 1959).

11. *African Daily News* (June 13 and 15, 1959).

12. *R.H.* (Aug. 5, 1950).

13. The different qualifications are specified in the Electoral Amendment Act, No. 38 of 1957. See also the discussion in Leys (1959).

14. Figures for 1958 provided by the Central Registering Office, Dec. 23, 1959.

15. Khama (1956:14).

16. Hailey (1958:3).

17. Coleman (1955:226–27) distinguishes a pressure group, which is interested in *influencing* political affairs, from a political party, which seeks to *control* government.

18. Neumann (1956:410).

19. These changes include new acts or amendments to the following Acts after 1945: Native Passes, Native Affairs, Prevention of Trespass (Native Reserves), Public Order, Natives (Registration and Identification), Police, Subversive Activities, Liquor, Native Beer, Natives (Urban Areas) Accommodation and Registration, Native Councils, Firearms, Sedition, Inter-Territorial Movement of Persons (Control), and Police Offences.

20. Statement on the State of Emergency by the Prime Minister. *R.H.* (Feb. 27, 1959).

21. *The Chronicle,* special edition (Feb. 26, 1959).

22. Acts 38 and 39 of 1959.

23. *R.H.* (Oct.' 14, 1959).

24. Qualifications for the Federal election, as amended, are given in the (Federal) Electoral Act, No. 6 of 1958. See also Leys (1959).

25. Information supplied by the Ministry of Home Affairs, Dec. 23, 1959.

26. See Leys (1959:41–48, 239).

27. See Junod (1959:160).

28. Dvorin (1954:372).

## CHAPTER 16. SOCIAL AND RECREATIONAL FACILITIES

1. Ibbotson (1942, 1944).

CHAPTER 17. SEXUAL RELATIONS

1. "Vates" (1954).
2. C.A.A., h/a 4–1.
3. See Wallis (1950:67–68, 112–14). See also Mason (1958).
4. See Alport (1952:83).


CHAPTER 18. SOCIAL STRUCTURE AND RACE ATTITUDES

1. Easton (1953:55).
2. Simpson and Yinger (1959:379).
3. Pettigrew (1960). See also Bogardus (1925, 1928, 1933, 1947).
4. Richmond (1954) and Banton (1959).
5. Richmond (1958).
6. Myrdal (1944), Frazier (1957), and Simpson and Yinger (1958), among hundreds of sources.
7. For the United States, see discussions in Harding et al (1954) and Blumer (1958). For Britain, see Little (1948), Richmond (1950, 1954, 1957), Collins (1951, 1957), and Banton (1955, 1959).
8. Allport and Kramer (1946), Harding et al (1954), and Simpson and Yinger (1959).
9. Harding et al (1954) and Blumer (1958).
10. Saenger and Gordon (1950), Remmers (1954), Harding et al (1954), Allport (1954), and Killian and Haer (1958).
11. Richmond (1954, 1957), Banton (1955, 1959), Stephens (1956), Reid (1956), Collins (1957), and Pettigrew (1958, 1960).
12. See, for example, Bettelheim and Janowitz (1950).
13. See also Harlan (1942), Allport and Kramer (1946), and *Fortune* (1946, 1947).
14. Parry (1949), Lindzey (1950), Harte (1951), Rose, Atelsek, and McDonald (1953), and the studies cited in Harding et al (1954).
15. Levinson and Huffman (1955).
16. See Harding et al (1954).
17. Rose (1948), Saenger and Gordon (1950), Kahn (1951), Rose, Atelsek, and McDonald (1953), Harding et al (1954), and Killian and Haer (1958).


CHAPTER 19. THE ORGANIZATION OF RACE ATTITUDES

1. See Bettelheim and Janowitz (1950:30n).
2. Brookover and Holland (1952:197).
3. Myrdal (1944:61, 1187).
4. Myrdal (1944:60–61). Elsewhere (pp. 587–88), Myrdal suggests a rank order that embraces nine categories. This number is obtained by a subdivision of "public facilities and services" into four separate categories. We prefer his simpler scheme because it reduces the amount of "impressionistic judgment" that needs to be accepted

5. At least one other study (Valdes, 1951) has been made, but it remains unpublished.

## CHAPTER 20. CONTINUITY AND CHANGE

1. See Simpson and Yinger (1958:137–40).
2. Simpson and Yinger (1958:38–39).
3. See Warner (1959).
4. Copeland (1939).
5. See Warner (1959) for an illuminating study of color and other symbols in the life of an American community.
6. Brookover and Holland (1952).
7. Harris (1959).
8. Apter and Lystad (1958:42). See also Philipps (1956:27–28).
9. Russell (1949), Landes (1952), Easton (1953), Shils (1956), and Banton (1959).
10. Simpson and Yinger (1959:390).
11. We have been stimulated in thinking about these relations by Berelson, Lazarsfeld, and McPhee (1954:305–23).
12. Hogbin (1958).
13. See Kennedy (1945), Maunier (1949), Delavignette (1950), and Padmore (1956:210).
14. See Frazier (1949:8).
15. Harris (1959:251).

# BIBLIOGRAPHY

Adorno, T. W. et al (1950), *The Authoritarian Personality*. New York: Harper.

Alexander, W. P. (1935), Intelligence, concrete and abstract. *British Journal of Psychology, Monograph Supplement, 19.*

Allport, G. W. (1935), Attitudes. In *A Handbook of Social Psychology* (Murchison, C., ed.). Worcester, Mass.: Clark University Press.

—— (1937), *Personality: A Psychological Interpretation*. New York: Henry Holt.

—— (1954), *The Nature of Prejudice*. Reading, Mass.: Addison-Wesley.

—— and Kramer, B. M. (1946), Some roots of prejudice. *Journal of Psychology, 22,* 9–39.

Alport, C. J. M. (1952), *Hope in Africa*. London: Herbert Jenkins.

Anastasi, A. (1953), Psychological traits and group relations. In *Group Relations at the Cross-roads* (Sherif, M. and Wilson, M. O., eds.). New York: Harper. Pp. 74–98.

Apter, D. E. and Lystad, R. A. (1958), Bureaucracy, party, and constitutional democracy: an examination of political role systems in Ghana. In *Transition in Africa: Studies in Political Adaptation* (Carter, G. M. and Brown, W. O., eds.). Boston: Boston University Press. Pp. 16–43.

Ash, P. and Abramson, E. (1952), The effect of anonymity of attitude-questionnaire response. *Journal of Abnormal and Social Psychology, 47,* 722–23.

Axelson, E. (1940), *South-East Africa 1488–1530*. London: Longmans, Green.

Baier, D. E. (1951), "Reply to Travers." A critical review of the validity and rationale of the forced-choice technique. *Psychological Bulletin, 48,* 421–34.

Balandier, G. (1955), Social changes and social problems in Negro Africa. In *Africa and the Modern World* (Stillman, C. W., ed.). Chicago: University of Chicago Press. Pp. 55–69.

—— (1955a), *Sociologie des Brazzavilles Noires*. Paris: Librairie Armand Colin.

Banks, W. S. M., II (1950), The rank order of sensitivity to discriminations of Negroes in Columbus, Ohio. *American Sociological Review, 15,* 529–34.

Banton, M. (1955), *The Coloured Quarter: Negro Immigrants in an English City*. London: Jonathan Cape.

—— (1957), *West African City: A Study of Tribal Life in Freetown*. London: Oxford University Press.

—— (1959), *White and Coloured: The Behaviour of British People towards Coloured Immigrants*. London: Jonathan Cape.

Barber, W. J. (1957), The Economy of Rhodesia and Nyasaland, 1930–1955: A Study in the Problems of Economic Development. D. Phil. thesis, Oxford University.

——— (1959), The political economy of Central Africa's experiment with inter-racial partnership. *Canadian Journal of Economics and Political Science, 25,* 324–35.

Barnes, J. A. (1954), *Politics in a Changing Society: A Political History of the Fort Jameson Ngoni.* Cape Town: Oxford University Press.

Bascom, W. R. and Herskovits, M. J., eds. (1959), *Continuity and Change in African Cultures.* Chicago: University of Chicago Press.

Bastide, R. (1957), Race relations in Brazil. *International Social Science Bulletin, 9,* 495–512.

Batson, E. (1945), *The Poverty Line in Salisbury.* Cape Town: University of Cape Town.

Beaglehole, E. (1946), *Some Modern Maoris.* Wellington, N.Z.: Whitcombe and Tombs.

Becker, G. S. (1957), *The Economics of Discrimination.* Chicago: University of Chicago Press.

Berelson, B. R., Lazarsfeld, P. F., and McPhee, W. N. (1954), *Voting: A Study of Opinion Formation in a Presidential Campaign.* Chicago: University of Chicago Press.

Bettelheim, B. and Janowitz, M. (1950), *Dynamics of Prejudice.* New York: Harper.

Bettison, D. G. (1958), The socio-economic circumstances of a sample of Africans in Salisbury, July 1957. In *Report* (Southern Rhodesia, Urban African Affairs Commission). Salisbury: Government Printer. Pp. 180–94.

Bird, C. and Monachesi, E. D. (1954), Prejudice and discontent. *Journal of Abnormal and Social Psychology, 49,* 29–35.

——— Monachesi, E. D., and Burdick, H. (1952), Infiltration and the attitudes of white and Negro parents and children. *Journal of Abnormal and Social Psychology, 47,* 688–99.

Blackburn, C. W. et al (1946), *A Study of 454 Negro Households in the Redevelopment Area, Indianapolis, Indiana.* Indianapolis: Flanner House.

Blumer, H. (1958), United States of America. *International Social Science Bulletin, 10,* 403–47.

Boeke, J. H. (1942), *The Structure of the Netherlands Indian Economy.* New York: Institute of Pacific Relations.

——— (1948), *The Interests of the Voiceless Far East.* Leiden: Universitaire Pers Leiden.

Bogardus, E. S. (1925), Measuring social distance. *Journal of Applied Sociology, 9,* 299–308.

——— (1928), *Immigration and Race Attitudes.* Boston: D. C. Heath.

——— (1933), A social distance scale. *Sociology and Social Research, 17,* 265–71.

——— (1947), Changes in racial distances. *International Journal of Opinion and Attitude Research, 1*(4), 55–62.

Bray, F. (1958), *Report of Survey of Facilities for Technical Education in the Federation.* Salisbury: Government Printer.

Brookover, W. B. and Holland, J. B. (1952), An inquiry into the meaning of minority group attitude expression. *American Sociological Review, 17,* 196–202.

Broomfield, G. W. (1944), *Colour Conflict: Race Relations in Africa.* London: Edinburgh House Press.

Brown, W. O. (1955), Commentary. In *Africa Today* (Haines, C. G., ed.). Baltimore: The Johns Hopkins Press. Pp. 197–202.

—— and Lewis, H. (1958), Racial situations and issues in Africa. In *The United States and Africa* (Goldschmidt, W., ed.). New York: The American Assembly, Columbia University. Pp. 141–63.

Browne, G. St. J. Orde (1933), *The African Labourer.* London: Oxford University Press.

Bryce, J. (1898), *Impressions of South Africa.* London: Macmillan.

Buell, R. L. (1928), *The Native Problem in Africa.* 2 vols. New York: Macmillan.

Bullock, C. (1950), *The Mashona and the Matabele.* 2nd ed. Cape Town: Juta.

Bullock, H. A. (1951), Racial attitudes and the employment of Negroes. *American Journal of Sociology, 56,* 448–57.

Bulpin, T. V. (1956), *Lost Trails of the Transvaal.* Cape Town: Howard B. Timmins.

Burns, A. C. (1957), *In Defence of Colonies: British Colonial Territories in International Affairs.* London: Allen and Unwin.

Burt, C. (1940), *The Factors of the Mind.* London: University of London Press.

—— (1945), Symposium on personality. I—The assessment of personality. *British Journal of Educational Psychology, 15,* 107–21.

—— (1948), The factorial study of temperament traits. *British Journal of Psychology: Statistical Section, 1,* 178–203.

—— (1949), Elementary Factor Analysis: I—Principles of Classification. MS. Psychology Department, University College, London. Pp. 1–16.

—— (1951), Factor Analysis. MS. Psychology Department, University College, London.

—— and Banks, C. (1946–47), A factor analysis of body measurements for British adult males. *Annals of Eugenics, 13,* 238–56.

Campbell, D. T. (1950), The indirect assessment of social attitudes. *Psychological Bulletin, 47,* 15–38.

Cantril, H. et al (1944), *Gauging Public Opinion.* Princeton, N.J.: Princeton University Press.

Carnegie, D. (1893), *Among the Matabele.* New York: Fleming H. Revell.

Cattell, R. B. (1944), "Parallel proportional profiles" and other principles for determining the choice of factors by rotation. *Psychometrika, 9,* 267–83.

—— (1946), *Description and Measurement of Personality.* New York: World.

—— (1950), *Personality: A Systematic Theoretical and Factual Study.* New York: McGraw-Hill.

—— (1950a), The discovery of ergic structure in man in terms of common attitudes. *Journal of Abnormal and Social Psychology, 45,* 598–618.

—— (1952), *Factor Analysis.* New York: Harper.

—— (1956), Validation and intensification of the sixteen personality factor questionnaire. *Journal of Clinical Psychology, 12,* 205–14.

———— and Miller, A. (1952), A confirmation of the ergic and self-sentiment patterns among dynamic traits (attitude variables) by R-technique. *British Journal of Psychology, 43,* 280–94.

———— et al (1949), The objective measurement of attitudes. *British Journal of Psychology, 40,* 81–90.

Central African Statistical Office (1956), *Census Coding, 1956 Census.* Salisbury: C.A.S.O. Duplicated.

———— (1957), *Report on the Census of Africans in Employment taken on 8th May, 1956.* Salisbury: C.A.S.O.

———— (1959), *Second Report of the Salisbury African Demographic Survey, August/September, 1958.* Salisbury: C.A.S.O.

———— (1959a), *Monthly Digest of Statistics, 6*(9), 4–5.

———— (1960), *Monthly Digest of Statistics, 6*(10), 2–3.

Chesire, L., Saffir, M., and Thurstone, L. L. (1933), *Computing Diagrams for the Tetrachoric Correlation Coefficient.* Chicago: University of Chicago Bookstore.

Clausen, J. A. and Ford, R. N. (1947), Controlling bias in mail questionnaires. *Journal of the American Statistical Association, 42,* 497–512.

Clegg, E. M. (1957), *The Franchise in Rhodesia and Nyasaland: A Summary of Recent Proposals.* London: Oxford University Press for the Royal Institute of International Affairs. Duplicated.

Cohen, A. (1959), *British Policy in Changing Africa.* London: Routledge and Kegan Paul.

Coleman, J. S. (1955), The emergence of African political parties. In *Africa Today* (Haines, C. G., ed.). Baltimore: The Johns Hopkins Press. Pp. 225–56.

———— (1958), The character and viability of African political systems. In *The United States and Africa* (Goldschmidt, W., ed.). New York: The American Assembly, Columbia University. Pp. 27–62.

Collier, J. (1947), *The Indians of the Americas.* New York: W. W. Norton.

Collins, S. F. (1951), The social position of white and "half-caste" women in colored groupings in Britain. *American Sociological Review, 16,* 796–802.

———— (1957), *Coloured Minorities in Britain.* London: Lutterworth Press.

Comhaire, J. L. L. (1950), Urban segregation and racial legislation in Africa. *American Sociological Review, 15,* 392–97.

Coombs, C. H. (1941), A criterion for significant common factor variance. *Psychometrika, 6,* 267–72.

Coon, C. (1954), *The Story of Man.* New York: Alfred A. Knopf.

Copeland, L. C. (1939), The Negro as a contrast conception. In *Race Relations and the Race Problem* (Thompson, E. T., ed.). Durham, N. C.: Duke University Press. Pp. 152–79.

Cornell, F. G. (1947), Sample plan for a survey of higher education enrollment. *Journal of Experimental Education, 15,* 312–18.

Cripps, A. S. (1927), *An Africa for Africans.* London: Longmans, Green.

Cronbach, L. J. (1947), Test "reliability": its meaning and determination. *Psychometrika, 12,* 1–16.

———— (1950), Further evidence on response sets and test design. *Educational and Psychological Measurement, 10,* 3–31.

Davidson, B. (1959), *Old Africa Rediscovered*. London: Victor Gollancz.

Davis, A., Gardner, B., and Gardner, M. (1941), *Deep South*. Chicago: University of Chicago Press.

de Briey, P. (1951), Industrialization and social problems in Central Africa. *International Labour Review*, 63, 475–605.

Deighton, H. S. (1957), History and the study of race relations. *Man*, 57, 123–24.

De Kiewiet, C. W. (1941), *A History of South Africa, Social and Economic*. Oxford: Oxford University Press.

Delavignette, R. (1950), *Freedom and Authority in French West Africa*. London: Oxford University Press.

Deming, W. E. (1945), On training in sampling. *Journal of the American Statistical Association*, 40, 307–16.

Deutsch, M. (1952), Social environment and attitudinal change: A study of the effects of different types of interracial housing. In *Problems in Social Psychology: An Interdisciplinary Inquiry* (Hulett, J. E. and Stagner, R., eds.). Urbana: University of Illinois Press. Pp. 85–95.

—— and Collins, M. E. (1950), Interracial housing. III—Influence of integrated, segregated occupancy on racial attitudes measured. *Journal of Housing*, 7, 127–29.

—— and Collins, M. E. (1951), *Interracial Housing: A Psychological Evaluation of a Social Experiment*. Minneapolis: University of Minnesota Press.

Dollard, J. (1937), *Caste and Class in a Southern Town*. New Haven: Yale University Press.

DuBois, R. D. (1950), *Neighbors in Action: A Manual for Local Leaders in Intergroup Relations*. New York: Harper.

Duignan, P. J. (1961), Native Policy in Southern Rhodesia, 1890–1923. Ph. D. thesis, Stanford University.

Duijker, H. C. J. (1955), Comparative research in social science with special reference to attitude research. *International Social Science Bulletin*, 7, 555–66.

Dvorin, E. P. (1954), Central Africa's first Federal election: background and issues. *Western Political Quarterly*, 7, 369–90.

—— (1958), Emergent federalism in Central Africa: problems and prospects. In *Transition in Africa: Studies in Political Adaptation* (Carter, G. M. and Brown, W. O., eds.). Boston: Boston University Press. Pp. 62–89.

Easton, D. (1953), *The Political System: An Inquiry into the State of Political Science*. New York: Alfred A. Knopf.

—— (1957), An approach to the analysis of political systems. *World Politics*, 9, 383–400.

Edmunds, E. R. (1954), The Myrdalian hypothesis: rank order of discrimination. *Phylon*, 15, 297–303.

Edwards, A. L. and Kilpatrick, F. P. (1948), Scale analysis and the measurement of social attitudes. *Psychometrika*, 13, 99–114.

Ellis, A. (1946), The validity of personality questionnaires. *Psychological Bulletin*, 43, 385–440.

—— and Beechley, R. (1950), Comparisons of Negro and white children seen at a child guidance clinic. *Psychiatric Quarterly Supplement*, 24, 93–101.

Epstein, A. L. (1958), Tribal elders to trade unions. In *Africa in Transition* (Smith, P., ed.). London: Max Reinhardt. Pp. 97–105.

Evans, E. W. (1950), Principles and methods of administration in the British colonial empire. In *Principles and Methods of Colonial Administration* (MacInnes, C. M., ed.). London: Butterworths Scientific Publications. Pp. 9–17.

Evans, I. L. (1934), *Native Policy in South Africa*. Cambridge: Cambridge University Press.

Eysenck, H. J. (1947), *Dimensions of Personality*. London: Routledge and Kegan Paul.

—— (1950), Criterion analysis: an application of the hypothetico-deductive method to factor analysis. *Psychological Review, 57*, 38–53.

—— (1954), *The Psychology of Politics*. London: Routledge and Kegan Paul.

—— and Crown, S. (1949), An experimental study in opinion-attitude methodology. *International Journal of Opinion and Attitude Research, 3*, 47–86.

Farquhar, J. H. (1946), Political representation of the African. *Native Affairs Department Annual* (Southern Rhodesia), *23*, 62–67.

Federation of Rhodesia and Nyasaland (1957), *Annual Report on Education for the Year 1956*. Salisbury: Government Printer.

—— (1958), *Annual Report on Education for the Year 1957*. Salisbury: Government Printer.

—— (1959), *Economic Report 1959*. Salisbury: Government Printer.

—— (1959a), *Annual Report on Education for the Year 1958*. Salisbury: Government Printer.

Firth, R. (1954), Social organization and social change. *Journal of the Royal Anthropological Institute, 84*, 1–20.

Fisher, R. A. (1950), *Statistical Methods for Research Workers*. Edinburgh: Oliver and Boyd.

—— and Yates, F. (1938), *Statistical Tables for Biological, Agricultural, and Medical Research*. Edinburgh: Oliver and Boyd.

Fletcher, B. A. (1958), *The Training of Teachers in Central Africa*. Salisbury: Edinburgh Press.

Fortes, M. (1945), An anthropologist's point of view. In *Fabian Colonial Essays* (Hinden, R., ed.). London: Allen and Unwin. Pp. 215–34.

*Fortune* (1946), Fortune survey. *Fortune, 33*(2), 257–60.

—— (1947), Fortune survey. *Fortune, 36*(4), 5–10.

Fox, H. W. (1910), *Memorandum by Mr. H. Wilson Fox on Problems of Development and Policy with Accompanying Papers, Maps and Plans*. London: British South Africa Company. Privately printed.

—— (1912), *Memorandum by Mr. H. Wilson Fox Containing Notes and Information Concerning Land Policy with Accompanying Papers and Maps*. London: British South Africa Company. Privately printed.

Francis, E. K. (1951), Minority groups—a revision of concepts. *British Journal of Sociology, 2*, 219–29, 254.

Franck, T. M. (1960), *Race and Nationalism: The Struggle for Power in Rhodesia-Nyasaland*. New York: Fordham University Press.

Frankel, S. H. (1953), *The Economic Impact on Under-developed Societies:*

*Essays on International Investment and Social Change.* Oxford: Blackwell.

Frantz, C. (1958), The Doukhobor Political System: Social Structure and Social Organization in a Sectarian Society. Ph. D. thesis, University of Chicago.

Frazier, E. F. (1947), Sociological theory and race relations. *American Sociological Review, 12,* 265–71.

—— (1949), Race contacts and social structure. *American Sociological Review, 14,* 1–11.

—— (1953), The theoretical structure of sociology and sociological research. *British Journal of Sociology, 4,* 293–311.

—— (1957), *Race and Culture Contacts in the Modern World.* New York: Alfred A. Knopf.

Freedman, M. (1957), The study of race relations. *Man, 57,* 120–21.

Furnivall, J. S. (1956), *Colonial Policy and Practice: A Comparative Study of Burma and Netherlands India.* New York: New York University Press.

Gale, W. D. (1958), *Zambesi Sunrise: How Civilization Came to Rhodesia and Nyasaland.* Cape Town: Howard B. Timmins.

Gann, L. H. (1958), *The Birth of a Plural Society: The Development of Northern Rhodesia under the British South Africa Company, 1894–1914.* Manchester: Manchester University Press.

Gardiner, F. G. and Lansdown, C. W. H. (1957), *South African Criminal Law and Procedure. Vol. I, General Principles and Procedure.* 6th ed. Cape Town: Juta.

Gelfand, M. (1953), *Tropical Victory: An Account of the Influence of Medicine on the History of Southern Rhodesia 1890–1923.* Cape Town: Juta.

Ghurye, G. S. (1957), *Caste. and Class in India.* 3rd ed. Bombay: Popular Book Depot.

Gibb, C. A. (1954), Leadership. In *Handbook of Social Psychology* (Lindzey, G., ed.). Cambridge, Mass.: Addison-Wesley. 2, 877–920.

Gibbs, P. (1947), *Land-Locked Island. A Commentary on Southern Rhodesia.* Bulawayo: Philpott and Collins.

Gillin, J. (1948), "Race" relations without conflict: a Guatemalan town. *American Journal of Sociology, 53,* 337–43.

Gluckman, M. (1955), *Custom and Conflict in Africa.* Oxford: Basil Blackwell.

—— (1958), Analysis of a social situation in modern Zululand. *Rhodes-Livingstone Papers,* 28. Manchester: Manchester University Press.

Golden, H. L. (1958), *Only in America.* Cleveland: World.

Goodman, M. E. (1952), *Race Awareness in Young Children.* Cambridge, Mass.: Addison-Wesley.

Goodstein, L. D. (1953), Intellectual rigidity and social attitudes. *Journal of Abnormal and Social Psychology, 48,* 345–53.

Gordon, L. V. (1951), Validities of the forced-choice and questionnaire methods of personality measurement. *Journal of Applied Psychology, 35,* 407–12.

Great Britain, British South Africa Company's Territories (1897), *Report by Sir R. E. R. Martin, K.C.M.G., on the Native Administration of the British South Africa Company, together with a Letter from the Company Commenting upon that Report.* London: H.M.S.O. (C.-8547).

Great Britain, Southern Rhodesia Native Reserves Commission (1915), *Papers relating to the Southern Rhodesia Native Reserves Commission.* London: H.M.S.O. (Cd. 8674).

Green, B. F. (1954), Attitude measurement. In *Handbook of Social Psychology* (Lindzey, G., ed.). Cambridge, Mass.: Addison-Wesley. *1,* 335–69.

Gross, F. (1956), *Rhodes of Africa.* London: Cassell.

Guilford, J. P. (1946), New standards for test evaluation. *Educational and Psychological Measurement, 6,* 427–38.

────── (1956), *Fundamental Statistics in Psychology and Education.* New York: McGraw-Hill.

────── and Lacey, J. I. (1947), *Printed Classification Tests.* (Army Air Forces Aviation Psychology Program, Research Report No. 5.) Washington, D.C.: Government Printing Office.

Gussman, B. W. (1952–53), *African Life in an Urban Area: A Study of the African Population of Bulawayo.* 2 vols. Bulawayo: Federation of African Welfare Societies in Southern Rhodesia. Duplicated.

────── (1953), Industrial efficiency and the urban African: a study of conditions in Southern Rhodesia. *Africa, 23,* 135–44.

Guttman, L. and Suchman, E. A. (1947), Intensity and zero point for attitude analysis. *American Sociological Review, 12,* 57–67.

Hailey, Lord (1951), *Native Administration in the British African Territories. Part IV: A General Survey of the System of Native Administration.* London: H.M.S.O.

────── (1957), *An African Survey Revised 1956: A Study of Problems Arising in Africa South of the Sahara.* London: Oxford University Press.

────── (1958), Introduction: government in a changing Africa. In *Africa in Transition* (Smith, P., ed.). London: Max Reinhardt.

Haines, C. G., ed. (1955), *Africa Today.* Baltimore: The Johns Hopkins Press.

Hammer, E. F. (1953), Negro and white children's personality adjustment as revealed by a comparison of their drawings. *Journal of Clinical Psychology, 9,* 9–10.

Hancock, W. K. (1942), *Survey of British Commonwealth Affairs. Vol. II, Part 2, Problems of Economic Policy 1918–1939.* London: Oxford University Press.

Hand, J. (1953), A method of weighting attitude scale items. *Journal of Clinical Psychology, 9,* 37–39.

Handlin, O. (1957), *Race and Nationality in American Life.* Boston: Little, Brown.

Hansen, M. H. and Deming, W. E. (1943), On some census aids to sampling. *Journal of the American Statistical Association, 38,* 353–57.

Harding, J., Kutner, B., Proshansky, H., and Chein, I. (1954), Prejudice and ethnic relations. In *Handbook of Social Psychology* (Lindzey, G., ed.). Cambridge, Mass.: Addison-Wesley. *2,* 1021–61.

Harlan, H. H. (1942), Some factors affecting attitude toward Jews. *American Sociological Review, 7,* 816–27.

Harris, D. B. (1950), How children learn interests, motives and attitudes. In *49th Yearbook, National Society for the Study of Education* (Henry, N. B., ed.). Chicago: University of Chicago Press. Pp. 129–55.

Harris, M. (1959), Caste, class, and minority. *Social Forces, 37,* 248–54.

Harte, T. J. (1951), Scalogram analysis of Catholic attitudes toward the Negro. *American Catholic Sociological Review, 12,* 66–74.

Hartley, E. L. (1946), *Problems in Prejudice.* New York: King's Crown Press.

Haviland, W. E. (1954), The use and efficiency of African labour in tobacco farming in Southern Rhodesia. *Canadian Journal of Economics and Political Science, 20,* 100–06.

Hawthorn, H. B., Belshaw, C. S., and Jamieson, S. M. (1958), *The Indians of British Columbia.* Berkeley: University of California Press.

Hayes, M. L. (1949), Personality and cultural factors in intergroup attitudes: I. *Journal of Educational Research, 43,* 122–28.

Hellmann, E., ed. (1949), *Handbook on Race Relations in South Africa.* London: Oxford University Press.

Henriques, F. (1953), *Family and Colour in Jamaica.* London: Eyre and Spottiswoode.

Herskovits, M. J. (1941), *The Myth of the Negro Past.* New York: Harper.

———— (1955), The African cultural background in the modern scene. In *Africa Today* (Haines, C. G., ed.). Baltimore: The Johns Hopkins Press. Pp. 30–49.

———— (1957), *Anthropology and Cultural Change in Africa.* Pretoria: University of South Africa.

Hilgard, E. R. and Payne, S. L. (1944), Those not at home: riddle for pollsters. *Public Opinion Quarterly, 8,* 254–61.

Hinden, R. (1949), *Empire and After: A Study of British Imperial Attitudes.* London: Essential Books.

Hodgkin, T. (1956), *Nationalism in Colonial Africa.* London: Frederick Muller.

Hogbin, H. I. (1958), *Social Change.* London: Watts.

Hole, H. M. (1926), *The Making of Rhodesia.* London: Macmillan.

Holland, J. B. (1951–52), The utility of social anthropology as an adjunct of a social survey. *International Journal of Opinion and Attitude Research, 5,* 455–64.

Holleman, J. F. (1951), Some "Shona" tribes of Southern Rhodesia. In *Seven Tribes of British Central Africa* (Colson, E. and Gluckman, M., eds.). London: Oxford University Press. Pp. 354–95.

———— (1952), *Shona Customary Law.* London: Oxford University Press.

Hovland, C. I. and Sherif, M. (1952), Judgmental phenomena and scales of attitude measurement: item displacement in Thurstone scales. *Journal of Abnormal and Social Psychology, 47,* 822–32.

Howells, W. W. (1954), *Back of History: The Story of our own Origins.* New York: Doubleday.

Howman, R. (1949), Trial by jury in Southern Rhodesia: an historical and sociological analysis of an institution. *Rhodes-Livingstone Journal, 7,* 41–66.

———— (1951–53), *Report on African Local Government for Southern Rhodesia* (7 parts). Salisbury: Native Affairs Department. Duplicated.

Hudson, W. (1955), Observations on African labour in East, Central and West Africa. *Journal of the National Institute of Personnel Research* (South Africa), *6,* 18–29.

———— (1958), Psychological research on the African worker. *Civilisations, 8,* 193–203.

Huggins, G. M. (1941), *Statement on Native Policy in Southern Rhodesia.* Salisbury: Government Printing Office.

———— (1954), The African's place in the Federation of Rhodesia and Nyasaland. *Optima, 4*(2), 1–5.

Hughes, E. C. (1943), *French Canada in Transition.* Chicago: University of Chicago Press.

———— (1946), Race relations in industry. In *Industry and Society* (Whyte, W. F., ed.). New York: McGraw-Hill. Pp. 107–22.

———— (1949), Queries concerning industry and society growing out of study of ethnic relations in industry. *American Sociological Review, 14,* 211–20.

———— and Hughes, H. M. (1952), *Where Peoples Meet: Racial and Ethnic Frontiers.* Glencoe, Ill.: The Free Press.

Hutchinson, B. (1949), Some problems of measuring the intensiveness of opinion and attitude. *International Journal of Opinion and Attitude Research, 3,* 123–31.

Hutton, J. H. (1946), *Caste in India: Its Nature, Function, and Origins.* Cambridge: Cambridge University Press.

Huxley, J. S. (1931), *Africa View.* London: Chatto and Windus.

Hyman, H. (1945), Community background in public opinion research. *Journal of Abnormal and Social Psychology, 40,* 411–13.

———— (1949), Inconsistencies as a problem in attitude measurement. *Journal of Social Issues, 5*(3), 38–42.

———— (1955), *Survey Design and Analysis: Principles, Cases and Procedures.* Glencoe, Ill.: The Free Press.

Ibbotson, P. (1942), Native welfare societies in Southern Rhodesia. *Race Relations, 9,* 71–74.

———— (1944), Federation of Native Welfare Societies in Southern Rhodesia. *Rhodes-Livingstone Journal, 2,* 35–39.

———— (1945), The urban native problem. *Native Affairs Department Annual* (Southern Rhodesia), *22,* 35–44.

———— (1946), Urbanization in southern Africa. *Africa, 16,* 73–82.

International Labour Office (1958), *African Labour Survey.* Geneva: I.L.O.

Irish, D. P. (1952), Reactions of Caucasian residents to Japanese-American neighbors. *Journal of Social Issues, 8*(1), 10–17.

Irving, J. (1958), Ecology of city growth in an urban context. In *Present Interrelations in Central African Rural and Urban Life* (Apthorpe, R. J., ed.). Lusaka, N. Rhodesia: The Rhodes-Livingstone Institute. Pp. 53–74. Duplicated.

Jahoda, G. (1953), Attitudes to Whites. MS. Sociology Department, University College of Ghana, Accra.

Jollie, E. T. (1924), *The Real Rhodesia.* London: Hutchinson.

Jonas, J. D. R. (1953), The effects of urbanization in South and Central Africa. *African Affairs, 52,* 37–44.

Junod, V. I. (1959), U.S. South and South Africa. *The Christian Century, 76,* 160–62.

Kahn, L. A. (1951), The organization of attitudes toward the Negro as a function of education. *Psychological Monographs, 65,* 1–39.

Kane, N. S. (1954), *The World's View: The Story of Southern Rhodesia.* London: Cassell.

Katz, D. (1942), Do interviewers bias poll results? *Public Opinion Quarterly,* *6,* 248–68.

Kelley, T. L. (1928), *Crossroads in the Mind of Man.* Stanford: Stanford University Press.

Kennedy, R. (1945), The colonial crisis and the future. In *The Science of Man in the World Crisis* (Linton, R., ed.). New York: Columbia University Press. Pp. 306–46.

Kerr, W. A. (1944), Correlates of politico-economic liberalism-conservatism. *Journal of Social Psychology, 20,* 61–77.

Kettner, N. W. (1952), Planning graphic rotations in factor analysis. *Technical Memo Number 1.* Department of Psychology, University of Southern California.

Khama, T. (1956), *Political Change in African Society: A Study of the Development of Representative Government.* London: The Africa Bureau.

Killian, L. M. and Haer, J. L. (1958), Variables related to attitudes regarding school desegregation among white southerners. *Sociometry, 21,* 159–64.

Klineberg, O., ed. (1944), *Characteristics of the American Negro.* New York: Harper.

Kluckhohn, C. (1954), Culture and behavior. In *Handbook of Social Psychology* (Lindzey, G., ed.). Cambridge, Mass.: Addison-Wesley. 2, 921–76.

Kolarz, W. (1953), *Russia and her Colonies.* 3rd ed. London: George Philip and Son.

Korchin, S. J., Mitchell, H. E., and Meltzoff, J. (1950), A critical evaluation of the Thompson Thematic Apperception Test. *Journal of Projective Techniques, 14,* 445–51.

Kuper, H. (1947), *The Uniform of Colour, A Study of White-Black Relationships in Swaziland.* Johannesburg: Witwatersrand University Press.

———— Hughes, A. J. B., and Van Velsen, J. (1955), *The Shona and Ndebele of Southern Rhodesia.* London: Oxford University Press.

Kuper, L., Watts, H., and Davies, R. (1958), *Durban: A Study in Racial Ecology.* London: Jonathan Cape.

Landes, R. (1952), A preliminary statement of a survey of Negro-White relationships in Britain. *Man, 52,* 133.

Lee, F. F. (1954), The race relations pattern by areas of behavior in a small New England town. *American Sociological Review, 19,* 138–43.

Levinson, D. J. (1949), An approach to the theory and measurement of ethnocentric ideology. *Journal of Psychology, 28,* 19–39.

———— and Huffman, P. E. (1955), Traditional family ideology and its relation to personality. *Journal of Personality, 23,* 251–73.

Lewin, J. (1947), *Studies in African Native Law.* Cape Town: The African Bookman.

Lewin, K. (1951), *Field Theory in Social Science: Selected Theoretical Papers* (Cartwright, D., ed.). New York: Harper.

Leys, C. (1959), *European Politics in Southern Rhodesia.* Oxford: Clarendon Press.

Likert, R. (1932), A technique for the measurement of attitudes. *Archives of Psychology, 22.* No. 140.

Lindzey, G. (1950), An experimental examination of the scapegoat theory of prejudice. *Journal of Abnormal and Social Psychology, 45,* 296–309.

Linton, R., ed. (1945), *The Science of Man in the World Crisis*. New York: Columbia University Press.

—— (1952), *Most of the World; The Peoples of Africa, Latin America, and the East Today*. New York: Columbia University Press.

—— (1955), *The Tree of Culture*. New York: Alfred A. Knopf.

Lippitt, R. and Radke, M. (1946), New trends in the investigation of prejudice. *Annals of the American Academy of Political and Social Science, 244*, 167–76.

Little, K. L. (1948), *Negroes in Britain: A Study of Racial Relations in English Society*. London: Kegan Paul, Trench, Trubner.

Lohman, J. D. and Reitzes, D. C. (1952), A note on race relations in mass society. *American Journal of Sociology, 58*, 240–46.

—— and Reitzes, D. C. (1954), Deliberately organized groups and racial behavior. *American Sociological Review, 19*, 342–44.

Long, H. H. (1949), Race restrictive housing covenants and social control. *Sociology and Social Research, 33*, 355–61.

—— (1953), Trends in race relations research. *Inventory of Research in Racial and Cultural Relations*, Bulletin #5, 45–54.

—— and Johnson, C. S. (1947), *People vs. Property: Race Restrictive Covenants in Housing*. Nashville: Fisk University Press.

Luyt, R. E. (1949), *Trade Unionism in African Colonies*. Johannesburg: South African Institute of Race Relations.

Maccoby, E. E. and Maccoby, N. (1954), The interview: a tool of social science. In *Handbook of Social Psychology* (Lindzey, G., ed.). Cambridge, Mass.: Addison-Wesley. *1*, 449–87.

MacCrone, I. D. (1937), *Race Attitudes in South Africa: Historical, Experimental and Psychological Studies*. London: Oxford University Press.

—— (1954), Parental origins and popular prejudices. *Proceedings of the South African Psychological Association, 5*, 10–12.

—— (1955), Factorial concomitants of ethnocentrism. *Proceedings of the South African Psychological Association, 6*, 8–10.

—— and Starfield, A. (1949), A comparative study in multiple-factor analysis of "neurotic" tendency. *Psychometrika, 14*, 1–20.

McGregor, R. (1940), Native Segregation in Southern Rhodesia: A Study of Social Policy. D.Phil. thesis, University of London.

McNemar, Q. (1942), On the number of factors. *Psychometrika, 7*, 9–18.

—— (1946), Opinion-attitude methodology. *Psychological Bulletin, 43*, 289–374.

Macridis, R. C. (1955), *The Study of Comparative Government*. Garden City, New York: Doubleday.

Mair, L. P. (1957), *Studies in Applied Anthropology*. London: University of London, The Athlone Press.

Mannoni, D. O. (1956), *Prospero and Caliban: The Psychology of Colonisation*. London: Methuen.

Marriot, McK., ed. (1955), *Village India: Studies in the Little Community*. Chicago: University of Chicago Press.

Mason, P. (1954), *An Essay on Racial Tension*. London: Royal Institute of International Affairs.

—— (1958), *The Birth of a Dilemma. The Conquest and Settlement of Rhodesia*. London: Oxford University Press.

Maunier, R. (1949), *The Sociology of Colonies: An Introduction to the Study of Race Contact.* 2 vols. London: Routledge and Kegan Paul.

Medland, F. F. (1947), An empirical comparison of methods of communality estimation. *Psychometrika, 12,* 101–09.

Merton, R. K. (1940), Fact and fictitiousness in ethnic questionnaires. *American Sociological Review, 5,* 13–28.

———, West, P. S., and Jahoda, M. (1949), *Social Fictions and Social Facts: The Dynamics of Race Relations in Hilltown.* New York: Bureau of Applied Social Research, Columbia University. Duplicated.

Miller, D. C. (1941), National morale of American college students in 1941. *American Sociological Review, 7,* 194–213.

Miner, H. M. (1939), *St. Denis: A French-Canadian Parish.* Chicago: University of Chicago Press.

Mitchell, J. C. (1951), A note on the urbanization of Africans on the Copperbelt. *Rhodes-Livingstone Journal, 12,* 20–27.

——— (1954), African urbanization in Ndola and Luanshya. *Communications from the Rhodes-Livingstone Institute, 6.*

——— (1956), *The Yao Village: A Study in the Social Structure of a Nyasaland Tribe.* Manchester: Manchester University Press.

——— (1957), Africans in industrial towns in Northern Rhodesia. In *His Royal Highness the Duke of Edinburgh's Study Conference on the Human Problems of Industrial Communities within the Commonwealth and Empire: Vol. 2: Background Papers Appendixes and Index.* London: Oxford University Press. Pp. 1–9.

Mitchell, P. (1955), Africa and the West in historical perspective. In *Africa Today* (Haines, C. G., ed.). Baltimore: The Johns Hopkins Press. Pp. 3–24.

Montagu, M. F. A. (1949), Some psychodynamic factors in race prejudice. *Journal of Social Psychology, 30,* 175–87.

Morris, H. S. (1957), The plural society. *Man, 57,* 124–25.

Moser, C. A. (1958), *Survey Methods in Social Investigation.* London: William Heinemann.

Munger, E. S. (1955), Geography of sub-Saharan race relations. In *Africa Today* (Haines, C. G., ed.). Baltimore: The Johns Hopkins Press. Pp. 175–96.

Murdock, G. P. (1959), *Africa: Its Peoples and their Culture History.* New York: McGraw-Hill.

Mussen, P. H. (1950), Some personality and social factors related to changes in children's attitudes toward Negroes. *Journal of Abnormal and Social Psychology, 45,* 423–41.

Myrdal, G. (1944), *An American Dilemma.* 2 vols. New York: Harper.

——— (1958), *Value in Social Theory: A Selection of Essays on Methodology by Gunnar Myrdal* (Streeten, P., ed.). London: Routledge and Kegan Paul.

Nash, M. (1958), *Machine Age Maya: The Industrialization of a Guatemalan Community.* Glencoe, Ill.: The Free Press.

Neumann, S. (1956), Toward a comparative study of political parties. In *Modern Political Parties* (Neumann, S., ed.). Chicago: University of Chicago Press. Pp. 395–421.

Neumark, S. D. (1958), The character and potential of African economies.

In *The United States and Africa* (Goldschmidt, W., ed.). New York: The American Assembly, Columbia University. Pp. 91–115.

Newcomb, T. M. (1952), *Social Psychology*. London: Tavistock Publications.

Opler, M. E. (1948), Some recently developed concepts relating to culture. *Southwestern Journal of Anthropology, 4,* 107–22.

Padmore, G. (1956), *Pan-Africanism or Communism? The Coming Struggle for Africa*. London: Dodson.

Park, R. E. (1950), *Race and Culture*. Glencoe, Ill.: The Free Press.

Parry, H. J. (1949), Protestants, Catholics, and prejudice. *International Journal of Opinion and Attitude Research, 3,* 205–13.

Parsons, T. (1959), General theory in sociology. In *Sociology Today: Problems and Prospects* (Merton, R. K., Broom, L., and Cottrell, L. S., Jr., eds.). New York: Basic Books. Pp. 3–38.

——— and Bales, R. F. (1955), *Family: Socialization and Interaction Process*. Glencoe, Ill.: The Free Press.

Patterson, S. (1953), *Colour and Culture in South Africa*. London: Routledge and Kegan Paul.

——— (1957), *The Last Trek: A Study of the Boer People and the Afrikaner Nation*. London: Routledge and Kegan Paul.

Paul, B. D. (1953), Interview techniques and field relationships. In *Anthropology Today* (Kroeber, A. L., ed.). Chicago: University of Chicago Press. Pp. 430–51.

Pearce, R. H. (1953), *The Savages of America: A Study of the Indian and the Idea of Civilization*. Baltimore: The Johns Hopkins Press.

Peatman, J. G. (1947), *Descriptive and Sampling Statistics*. New York: Harper.

Perham, M. (1941), *Africans and British Rule*. London: Oxford University Press.

Pettigrew, T. F. (1958), Personality and sociocultural factors in intergroup attitudes: a cross-national comparison. *Journal of Conflict Resolution, 2,* 29–42.

——— (1960), Social distance attitudes of South African students. *Social Forces, 38,* 246–53.

Philipps, T. (1956), British influence as a vehicle of European civilization in the Asian and African tropics. *Civilisations, 6,* 27–43.

Pierson, D. (1942), *Negroes in Brazil*. Chicago: University of Chicago Press.

Pledge, H. T. (1939), *Science Since 1500*. London: His Majesty's Stationery Office.

Plomer, W. (1933), *Cecil Rhodes*. London: Peter Davies.

Posselt, F. W. T. (1927), *A Survey of Native Tribes of Southern Rhodesia*. Salisbury: Government Printer.

——— (1935), *Fact and Fiction: A Short Account of the Natives of Southern Rhodesia*. Bulawayo: Rhodesian Printing and Publishing Co.

Radke, M., Trager, H., and Davis, H. (1949), Social perceptions and attitudes of children. *Genetic Psychology Monographs, 40,* 327–447.

Radke-Yarrow, M., Trager, H., and Miller, J. (1952), The role of parents in the development of children's ethnic attitudes. *Child Development, 23,* 13–53.

Redfield, R. (1955), *The Little Community: Viewpoints for the Study of a Human Whole*. Chicago: University of Chicago Press.

―――― (1956), *Peasant Society and Culture*. Chicago: University of Chicago Press.

Reichard, S. (1948), Rorschach study of prejudiced personality. *American Journal of Orthopsychiatry, 18*, 280–86.

Reid, J. (1956), The employment of Negroes in Manchester. *Sociological Review, 4*, 199–211.

Remmers, H. H. (1954), *Introduction to Opinion and Attitude Measurement*. New York: Harper.

Reuss, C. F. (1943), Differences between persons responding and not responding to a mailed questionnaire. *American Sociological Review, 8*, 433–38.

Rex, J. (1959), The plural society in sociological theory. *British Journal of Sociology, 10*, 114–24.

Richmond, A. H. (1950), Economic insecurity and stereotypes as factors in colour prejudice. *Sociological Review, 42*, 147–70.

―――― (1953), Social scientist in action. *Science News, 27*, 69–92.

―――― (1954), *Colour Prejudice in Britain: A Study of West Indian Workers in Liverpool, 1941–1951*. London: Routledge and Kegan Paul.

―――― (1957), Theoretical orientations in studies of ethnic group relations in Britain. *Man, 57*, 121–23.

―――― (1958), Britain. *International Social Science Bulletin, 10*, 344–72.

Rogers, C. A. (1953), The structure of verbal fluency. *British Journal of Psychology, 44*, 368–80.

―――― (1956), *Measuring Intelligence in New Zealand*. Auckland University College: Monograph series, No. 2.

―――― (1959), The organization of political attitudes in Southern Rhodesia. *Rhodes-Livingstone Journal, 25*, 1–19.

Rolin, H. (1913), *Les Lois et l'Administration de la Rhodésie*. Bruxelles: Etablissement Emil Bruylant.

Rose, A. M. (1948), *Studies in Reduction of Prejudice*. 2nd ed. Chicago: American Council on Race Relations.

―――― Atelsek, F. J., and McDonald, L. R. (1953), Neighborhood reactions to isolated Negro residents: an alternative to invasion and succession. *American Sociological Review, 18*, 497–507.

Rose, A. W. (1951), How Negro workers feel about their jobs. *Personnel Journal, 29*, 292–96.

Rudin, H. R. (1955), The history of European relations with Africa. In *Africa in the Modern World* (Stillman, C. W., ed.). Chicago: University of Chicago Press. Pp. 14–30.

Russell, B. (1949), *Authority and the Individual*. London: Allen and Unwin.

Saenger, G. (1953), *The Social Psychology of Prejudice*. New York: Harper.

―――― and Gordon, N. S. (1950), The influence of discrimination on minority group members in its relation to attempts to combat discrimination. *Journal of Social Psychology, 31*, 95–120.

―――― and Proshansky, H. (1950), Projective techniques in the service of attitude research. *Personality*, Symposium No. 2, 23–34.

―――― and Shulman, H. M. (1948), Some factors determining intercultural behaviour and attitudes of members of different ethnic groups in mixed neighbourhoods. *Journal of Psychology, 25*, 365–80.

Samelson, B. (1945), Does education diminish prejudice? *Journal of Social Issues, 1*(3), 11–13.

Schapera, I., ed. (1934), *Western Civilization and the Natives of South Africa.* London: George Routledge.

Segerstedt, T. T. (1951), Some assumptions in attitude research. *Theoria, 17,* 226–39.

Shils, E. A. (1956), *The Torment of Secrecy.* London: William Heinemann.

Shuttleworth, F. K. (1941), Sampling errors involved in incomplete returns to mail questionnaires. *Journal of Applied Psychology, 25,* 588–91.

Simons, H. J. (1949), The law and its administration. In *Handbook on Race Relations in South Africa* (Hellmann, E., ed.). London: Oxford University Press. Pp. 41–108.

——— (1958), The status of African women. In *Africa in Transition* (Smith, P., ed.). London: Max Reinhardt. Pp. 79–88.

Simpson, G. E. and Yinger, J. M. (1958), *Racial and Cultural Minorities: An Analysis of Prejudice and Discrimination.* Rev. ed. New York: Harper.

——— and Yinger, J. M. (1959), The sociology of race and ethnic relations. In *Sociology Today: Problems and Prospects* (Merton, R. K., Broom, L., and Cottrell, L. S., Jr., eds.). New York: Basic Books. Pp. 376–99.

Sims, V. M. and Patrick, J. R. (1936), Attitude toward the Negro of northern and southern college students. *Journal of Social Psychology, 7,* 192–204.

Smith, E. W. (1928), *The Way of the White Fields in Rhodesia: A Survey of Christian Enterprise in Northern and Southern Rhodesia.* London: World Dominion Press.

Smith, P., ed. (1958), *Africa in Transition: Some BBC Talks on Changing Conditions in the Union and the Rhodesias.* London: Max Reinhardt.

Smith, R. T. (1956), *The Negro Family in British Guiana.* London: Routledge and Kegan Paul.

Snedecor, G. W. (1946), *Statistical Methods.* Ames, Iowa: Iowa State College Press.

Southern Rhodesia (1952), *The African in Southern Rhodesia: Administration.* London: Office of the High Commissioner for Southern Rhodesia.

——— (1952a), *The African in Southern Rhodesia: Industry.* London: Office of the High Commissioner for Southern Rhodesia.

——— (1952b), *The African in Southern Rhodesia: Place in Community.* London: Office of the High Commissioner for Southern Rhodesia.

——— (1955), *What the Native Land Husbandry Act Means to the Rural African and Southern Rhodesia: A Five Year Plan that will Revolutionize African Agriculture.* Salisbury: Government Printer.

——— British South Africa Police (1959), *Annual Report, 1958.* Salisbury: Government Printer.

——— Land Commission (1926), *Report of the Land Commission, 1925.* Salisbury: Government Printer.

——— Legislative Assembly (1959), *Debates.* Salisbury: Government Printer.

——— Native Affairs Committee of Enquiry (1911), *Report.* Salisbury: Government Printer.

——— Native Affairs Department (1958), *Report of the Secretary for Native Affairs, Chief Native Commissioner and Director of Native Development for the Year 1957.* Salisbury: Government Printer.

—— Native Education Inquiry Commission (1951), *Report*. Salisbury: Government Printer.

—— Urban African Affairs Commission (1958), *Report*. Salisbury: Government Printer.

Spiro, H. J. (1959), *Government by Constitution: The Political Systems of Democracy*. New York: Random House.

Stanton, F. (1939), Notes on the validity of mail questionnaire returns. *Journal of Applied Psychology, 23,* 95–104.

Stephens, L. (1956), *Employment of Coloured Workers in the Birmingham Area*. London: Institute of Personnel Management.

Steven-Hubbard, N. (1955), Commentary. In *Africa Today* (Haines, C. G., ed.). Baltimore: The Johns Hopkins Press. Pp. 256–61.

Steward, J. H. (1945), The changing American Indian. In *The Science of Man in the World Crisis* (Linton, R., ed.). New York: Columbia University Press. Pp. 282–305.

—— et al (1956), *The People of Puerto Rico*. Urbana: University of Illinois Press.

Tabler, E. (1955), *The Far Interior: Chronicles of Pioneering in the Matabele and Mashona Countries, 1847–1879*. Cape Town: A. A. Balkema.

Tax, S. (1953), *Penny Capitalism: A Guatemalan Indian Economy*. Washington, D.C.: Institute of Social Anthropology, Smithsonian Institution.

Thomas, T. M. (1873), *Eleven Years in Central South Africa*. London: John Snow.

Thomas, W. I. and Znaniecki, F. (1927), *The Polish Peasant in Europe and America*. 2 vols. New York: Alfred A. Knopf.

Thompson, E. T. (1939), The plantation: the physical basis of traditional race relations. In *Race Relations and the Race Problem* (Thompson, E. T., ed.). Durham: Duke University Press. Pp. 181–218.

Thomson, G. H. (1948), *The Factorial Analysis of Human Ability*. London: University of London Press.

Thouless, R. H. (1936), Test unreliability and function fluctuation. *British Journal of Psychology, 26,* 325–43.

Thurstone, L. L. (1935), *The Vectors of Mind*. Chicago: University of Chicago Press.

—— (1938), Primary mental abilities. *Psychometric Monographs, 1.*

—— (1947), *Multiple-Factor Analysis*. Chicago: University of Chicago Press.

Todd, R. S. G. (1957), The meaning of partnership in the Rhodesian Federation. *Optima, 7*(4), 174–80.

Trager, H. G. and Radke-Yarrow, M. (1952), *They Learn What They Live: Prejudice in Young Children*. New York: Harper.

Travers, R. M. W. (1951), A critical review of the validity and rationale of the forced-choice technique. *Psychological Bulletin, 48,* 62–70.

Tredgold, R. C. (1960), The concept of justice in western civilization and its application in the Federation. In *The Multi-Racial State* (Maynard, E., ed.). Salisbury: Rhodesia National Affairs Association. Pp. 1–14.

Underhill, R. M. (1953), *Red Man's America*. Chicago: University of Chicago Press.

Valdes, D. M. (1958), The Rank Order of Discriminations toward Negroes by White Persons in Newark, Ohio. Ph. D. thesis, Ohio State University.

"Vates" (1954), The step-children. *The New Rhodesia, 23*(91), 9.

Vernon, P. E. (1933), The American v. the German methods of approach to the study of temperament and personality. *British Journal of Psychology, 24,* 156–77.

———— (1938), *The Assessment of Psychological Qualities by Verbal Methods.* London: His Majesty's Stationery Office.

———— (1945), Correlation Methods. MS. Institute of Education, London University.

———— (1946), Statistical methods in the selection of Navy and Army personnel. *Journal of the Royal Statistical Society,* Supplement 8, 139–53.

———— (1947), Psychological tests in the Royal Navy, Army, and A.T.S. *Occupational Psychology, 21,* 53–74.

———— (1949), How many factors? MS. Admiralty Report.

———— (1950), *The Structure of Human Abilities.* London: Methuen.

———— (1950a), Factor Analysis. MS. Institute of Education, London University.

———— (1953), *Personality Tests and Assessments.* London: Methuen.

———— and Parry, J. B. (1949), *Personnel Selection in the British Forces.* London: University of London Press.

Voget, F. W. (1956), The American Indian in transition: reformation and accommodation. *American Anthropologist, 58,* 249–63.

von Wiese, L. (1950–51), Studien über das vorurteil. *Kölner Zeitschrift für Soziologie und Sozialpsychologie, 3,* 214–21.

Vosk, M. (1953), Correlates of prejudice. *Review of Educational Research, 23,* 353–61.

Wagley, C. (1953), *Amazon Town: A Study of Man in the Tropics.* New York: Macmillan.

———— ed. (1952), *Race and Class in Rural Brazil.* Paris: U.N.E.S.C.O.

Walker, E. A. (1957), *A History of Southern Africa.* 3rd ed. London: Longmans, Green.

Walker, H. J. (1950), The nature and characteristics of the Negro community. *Journal of Negro Education, 19,* 219–31.

Wallace, A. F. C. (1956), Revitalization movements. *American Anthropologist, 58,* 264–81.

Wallis, J. P. R. (1950), *One Man's Hand: The Story of Sir Charles Coghlan and the Liberation of Southern Rhodesia.* London: Longmans, Green.

Walter, O. M. (1951), The improvement of attitude research. *Journal of Social Psychology, 33,* 143–46.

Ward, B. E. (1958), East Africa. *International Social Science Bulletin, 10,* 372–86.

Warner, W. L. (1959), *The Living and the Dead: A Study of the Symbolic Life of Americans.* New Haven: Yale University Press.

Wertheim, W. F. (1956), *Indonesian Society in Transition: A Study of Social Change.* New York: Institute of Pacific Relations.

Weschler, I. R. (1950), Indirect methods of attitude measurement. *International Journal of Opinion and Attitude Research, 4,* 209–28.

Westermann, D. (1949), *The African To-day and To-morrow.* 3rd ed. London: Oxford University Press.

White, L. (1949), *The Science of Culture.* New York: Farrar, Straus.

Wilner, D. M., Walkley, R. P., and Cook, S. W. (1952), Residential proximity and intergroup relations in public housing projects. *Journal of Social Issues*, 8(1), 45–69.

Wilson, G. and Wilson, M. (1945), *The Analysis of Social Change: Based on Observations in Central Africa*. Cambridge: Cambridge University Press.

Wirth, L. (1950), Problems and orientations of research in race relations in the United States. *British Journal of Sociology*, 1, 117–25.

Wolf, E. R. (1956), Aspects of group relations in a complex society: Mexico. *American Anthropologist*, 58, 1065–78.

Wolfle, D. (1940), Factor analysis to 1940. *Psychometric Monographs*, 3.

Worsley, P. (1957), *The Trumpet Shall Sound: A Study of "Cargo" Cults in Melanesia*. London: MacGibbon and Kee.

# INDEX

Abramson, E., 73

Acculturation, African, 21, 27, 138, 142, 143–45, 163, 165, 186, 222, 247–48, 250–52, 330–31. *See also* Change

Act Number 18 of *1927,* 379

Administration. *See* Government

Adorno, T. W., 38

Africa: colonial contacts and development, 4–6; studies of plural societies in, 375–76; cultures compared with Europe, 328–29; European dislike of cultures in, 335

African cultures and societies in Southern Rhodesia, 7–8, 9, 11, 187, 376. *See also* Acculturation; Population

African National Congress. *See* Civil order; Parliaments; Political participation; Political parties; State of Emergency

African Welfare Societies. *See* Native Welfare Societies

Afrikaners: early settlement, 8; values of, 29, 30–31, 316; as populists, 347. *See also* Dutch Reformed church; National or ethnic origin; Union of South Africa

Age: sample compared with population, 56–57, 69–70; race attitudes analyzed by, 117–19, 132, 133, 296–98, 313, 314, 316–17, 337. *See also* Population

Aggression, European against African, changes in display of, 330

Agricultural Union, 184

Agriculture: classified as type of industry or business, 126–29; historical development, 17–18, 182–84, 188–91, 245, 330, 331, 335; Land Development Officers, 189; associations, 18, 37, 162, 187; government subsidies, 335; methods used by Africans, 188–91, 330–31; training for Africans, 159–61, 164–66; recruitment of African workers for European farms, 186, 209–10, 329–30; political control by Europeans over African workers, 187, 245–46; number of Africans employed on European farms, 186. *See also* Industry; Labor: division of; Lands; Occupation; Schools

Alcohol. *See* Liquor

Algeria, 4

Allport, G. W., 38, 105, 306, 307, 346

Alvord, Emory, 161, 189

Amenities. *See* Lands

American Negroes: accommodation in Southern Rhodesian hotels, 274; athletes in Southern Rhodesia, 229. *See also* United States

Anglican church. *See* Religious affiliation

Anglo-American Corp. of South Africa, Ltd., 187

Anti-amalgamation doctrine in Southern Rhodesia and United States, 324–27, 334, 350. *See also* Ethno-

405